The Great IRS Hoax
Why We Don't Owe Income Tax
(VOLUME 7: Sections 6.1-8)

"Ye Shall Know the Truth and the Truth Shall Make You Free"

John 8:32

LIABILITY

IRS

IRC

February 14, 2014
Version 4.54
©2000 thru 2014
Family Guardian Fellowship

<u>Written by:</u>
Department of the Treasury
Tax Research Division

http://famguardian.org/ *(primary site)*

WHERE TO GET COPIES OF THIS BOOK: If you like this publication, then you can manufacture your own very nice book from the electronic version downloadable from our website at http://famguardian.org/Publications/GreatIRSHoax/GreatIRSHoax.htm. Simply call up any FedEx Office or other publishing store and give them the web address above or take a USB drive CD-R of the Acrobat file (or email it to them or have them download it off our website) and then have them print it out *on double-sided paper*. Then have them comb-bind (19 hole punch) it and use thick dark- blue vinyl covers. The total cost is about $120. You will end up with an attractive, durable document to add to your reference library which will prove *very useful* to you over the years as you organize and defend your case with the IRS. If you don't have a FedEx Office in your area, then we're sure you can find at least one in the country who will do this by phone using a credit card and drop the result in the mail for you overnight. If the document is too big to bind into a single volume, then we recommend splitting it into four volumes. Volume 1 will be chapters 1-3. Volume 2 will be chapters 4-5. Volume 3 will be chapters 6-9. If you are making a copy of the book for the IRS or your state tax authorities to include in your administrative record with your tax return, we recommend printing only Chapters 4 through 6, which will cost you about $60. **When you print the book, we recommend printing the book in modular fashion, so that each chapter is independent of the other and can be removed by itself.** That way, as chapters are updated, you replace them along with the preface at the beginning without reprinting the *whole* book. This makes keeping up to date simpler and more cost-effective. If you are making a copy of the book for the IRS or your state tax authorities to include in your administrative record with your tax return, we recommend printing only chapters 1-6. Line numbers are included on every page of this document to make it easier to refer to when people are talking about the content of a specific item in it. That makes it useful as a litigation tool as well, since you can make it an exhibit and refer to sections within it in your pleadings. If you want to reduce the size of the finished book, the best way we have found is to tell your printer to print two pages per page, so that if you print the book on double-sided paper, you will get four pages per page, cutting the size down to only about 650 physical pages.

Finally, if you are viewing this document with *Adobe Acrobat Reader*, we recommend clicking on the "Show/Hide Navigation Pane" button in the upper left-hand corner of your screen (in the Acrobat toolbar) to make it MUCH easier to navigate this rather large document. This button presents a hotlinked table of contents for the document to make it easy to locate the section you want to look at.

NOTE: As a nonprofit ministry, we do not make any money from FedEx Office in making the above recommendation and have *no financial relationship whatsoever* with FedEx Office or anyone else in connection with this book or our website.

DISCLAIMER, COPYRIGHT, AND LICENSE AGREEMENT:

The disclaimer, copyright, and license agreement protecting this document is found at:

http://famguardian.org/disclaimer.htm

6. *HISTORY OF GOVERNMENT INCOME TAX FRAUD, RACKETEERING AND EXTORTION IN THE U.S.A.*

Page

6. HISTORY OF GOVERNMENT INCOME TAX FRAUD, RACKETEERING AND EXTORTION IN THE U.S.A. 6-1
    6.1 Main purpose of law is to LIMIT government power to ensure freedom and sovereignty of the people 6-9
    6.2 How our system of government became corrupted: Downes v. Bidwell 6-11
    6.3 How Scoundrels Corrupted Our Republican Form of Government 6-17
        6.3.1 Original Design of our Republic 6-17
        6.3.2 Main Technique of Corruption: Introduce Franchises to replace UNALIENABLE PRIVATE Rights with REVOCABLE PUBLIC Statutory PRIVILEGES 6-25
        6.3.3 Graphical Depiction of the Corruption 6-31
        6.3.4 God's Remedy for the Corruption 6-39
        6.3.5 De Jure v. De Facto Government 6-42
    6.4 How De Jure Governments are Transformed into Corrupt De Facto Governments 6-44
    6.5 General Evolution 6-53
    6.6 The Laws of Tyranny 6-64
    6.7 Presidential Scandals Related to Income Taxes and Socialism 6-65
        6.7.1 1925: William H. Taft's Certiorari Act of 1925 6-65
        6.7.2 1933: FDR's Great American Gold Robbery 6-69
            6.7.2.1 Money Background 6-69
            6.7.2.2 Outlawing of Gold Coin 6-71
            6.7.2.3 The Trading With the Enemy Act: Day the President Declared War on His Own People and Confiscated all the Gold! 6-72
            6.7.2.4 FDR Defends the Federal Damn Reserve 6-75
        6.7.3 1935: FDR's Socialist (Social) Security Act of 1935 6-77
            6.7.3.1 FDR's Pep-Talk to Congress, January 17, 1935 6-77
            6.7.3.2 FDR and the Birth of Social Security: Destroying Rugged Individuality 6-80
        6.7.4 1937: FDR's Stacking of the Supreme Court 6-83
        6.7.5 1943: FDR's Executive Order 9397: Bye-Bye Privacy and Fourth Amendment! 6-84
    6.8 Congressional Cover-Ups, Scandals, and Tax Code Obfuscation 6-85
        6.8.1 No taxation without representation! 6-87
        6.8.2 The Corruption of Our Tax System by the Courts and the Congress: Downes v. Bidwell, 182 U.S. 244 (1901) 6-87
        6.8.3 The Anti-Injunction Act statute, 26 U.S.C. §7421 6-88
        6.8.4 Why the Lawyers in Congress Just Love the Tax Code 6-90
        6.8.5 Congressional Propaganda and Lies 6-94
        6.8.6 Whistleblower Retaliation, Indifference, and Censorship 6-94
            6.8.6.1 We The People Truth In Taxation Hearing, February 27-28, 2002 6-94
            6.8.6.2 We The People Efforts: April 5, 2001 Senate Finance Committee Hearing 6-100
            6.8.6.3 Cover-Up of Jan. 20, 2002: Congress/DOJ/IRS/ Renege on a Written Agreement to Hold a Truth in Taxation Hearing with We The People Under First Amendment 6-102
        6.8.7 Cover-Up of 2002: 40 U.S.C. §255 obfuscated 6-111

6.8.8	Cover-Up of 1988: Changed Title of Part I, Subchapter N to Make it Refer Only to Foreign Income	6-111
6.8.9	Cover-Up of 1986: Obfuscation of IRC Section 931	6-111
6.8.10	Cover-Up of 1982: Footnotes Removed from IRC Section 61 Pointing to Section 861	6-113
6.8.11	Cover-Up of 1978: Confused IRS Regulations on "Sources"	6-113
6.8.12	Cover-Up of 1954: Hiding of Constitutional Limitations in IRC On Congress' Right To Tax	6-114
6.8.13	1952: Office of Collector of Internal Revenue Eliminated	6-119
6.8.14	Cover-Up of 1939: Removed References to Nonresident Aliens from the Definition of "Gross Income"	6-120
6.8.15	1932: Revenue Act of 1932 imposes first excise income tax on federal judges and public officers	6-123
6.8.16	1923: Classification Act, 42 Stat. 1488	6-124
6.8.17	1918: "Gross income" first defined in the Revenue Act of 1918	6-125
6.8.18	1911: Judicial Code of 1911	6-125
6.8.19	1909: Corporate Excise Tax of 1909	6-126
6.8.20	1872: Office of the Assessor of Internal Revenue Eliminated	6-126
6.8.21	1862: First Tax on "Officers" of the U.S. Government	6-127
6.9	**Treasury/ IRS Cover-Ups, Obfuscation, and Scandals**	**6-128**
6.9.1	Elements of the IRS Cover-Up/Conspiracy to Watch For	6-129
6.9.2	26 C.F.R. 1.0-1: Publication of Internal Revenue Code WITHOUT Index	6-131
6.9.3	Official/Qualified Immunity and Anonymity	6-132
6.9.4	Church Censorship, Manipulation, and Castration by the IRS	6-133
6.9.5	Illegal Treasury Regulation 26 C.F.R. §301.6331-1	6-136
6.9.6	IRS Trickery on the 1040 Form to Get Us Inside the Federal Zone	6-137
6.9.7	IRS Form 1040: Irrational Conspiracy to Violate Rights	6-137
6.9.8	IRS Form W-4 Scandals	6-139
6.9.8.1	Fraud on the W-4 Form	6-139
6.9.8.2	Unconstitutional IRS/Treasury Regulations Relating to the W-4	6-141
6.9.8.3	Line 3a of W-4 modifies and obfuscates 26 U.S.C. §3402 (n)	6-144
6.9.9	Whistleblower Retaliation	6-144
6.9.9.1	1998: IRS Historian Quits-Then Gets Audited	6-144
6.9.9.2	1993: IRS Raided the Save-A-Patriot Fellowship	6-148
6.9.10	IRS has NO Delegated Authority to Impose Penalties or Levies or Seizures for Nonpayment of Subtitle A Personal Income Taxes!	6-151
6.9.10.1	What Particular Type of Tax is Part 301 of Treasury Regulations?	6-151
6.9.10.2	Parallel Table of Authorities 26 C.F.R. to 26 U.S.C	6-152
6.9.11	Service of Illegal Summons	6-153
6.9.12	IRS Publication 1: Taxpayer rights…Oh really?	6-154
6.9.13	Cover-Up of March 2004: IRS Removed List of Return Types Authorized for SFR from Internal Revenue Manual (I.R.M.), Section 5.1.11.6.8	6-154
6.9.14	Cover-Up of Jan. 2002: IRS Removed the Internal Revenue Manual (IRM) from their Website Search Engine	6-155
6.9.15	Cover-Up of 2002: W-8 Certificate of Foreign Status Form Removed from the IRS Website December 2000 and replaced with W-8BEN	6-156
6.9.16	Cover-Up of 1999: IRS CID Agent Joe Banister Terminated by IRS For Discovering The Truth About Voluntary Nature of Income Taxes!	6-157
6.9.17	Cover-Up of 1995: Modified Regulations to Remove Pointers to Form 2555 for IRC Section 1 Liability for Federal Income Tax	6-158
6.9.18	Cover-Up of 1993--HOT!!: IRS Removed References in IRS Publication 515 to Citizens Not Being Liable for Tax and Confused New Language	6-158

6.10 Department of State (DOS) Scandals Related to Income Taxes 6-162

6.11 Department of Justice (DOJ) Scandals Related to Income Taxes 6-164
    6.11.1   Prosecution of Dr. Phil Roberts: "Political Tax Prisoner" 6-164
    6.11.2   Fraud On The Court: Demjanuk v. Petrovsky, 10 F.3d. 338 6-169

6.12 Judicial Scandals Related to Income Tax 6-169
    6.12.1   Abuse of "Case Law" 6-170
    6.12.2   The Federal Mafia Courts Stole Your Seventh Amendment Right to Trial by Jury! .. 6-171
    6.12.3   You Cannot Obtain Declaratory Judgments in Federal Income Tax Trials Held in Federal Courts 6-173
    6.12.4   The Changing Definition of "Direct, Indirect, and Excise Taxes" 6-174
        6.12.4.1   Definition of terms and legal framework 6-176
        6.12.4.2   The Early Supreme Court View of Direct vs. Indirect/Excise Taxes Prior to Passage of the 16th Amendment 1913 6-179
        6.12.4.3   Common Manifestations of the Judicial Conspiracy 6-180
        6.12.4.4   Judicial Conspiracy Following Passage of 16th Amendment in 1913 6-181
        6.12.4.5   The Federal District/Circuit Court Conspiracy to Protect the Income Tax 6-183
        6.12.4.6   State Court Rulings 6-188
    6.12.5   2003: Federal Court Bans Irwin Schiff's Federal Mafia Tax Book 6-189
    6.12.6   2002: Definition for "Acts of Congress" removed from Federal Rules of Criminal Procedure 6-193
    6.12.7   1992: William Conklin v. United States 6-193
    6.12.8   1986: 16th Amendment: U.S. v. Stahl, 792 F.2d. 1438 (1986) 6-196
    6.12.9   1938: O'Malley v. Woodrough, 307 U.S. 277 6-196
    6.12.10   1924: Miles v. Graham, 268 U.S. 501 6-199
    6.12.11   1915: Brushaber v. Union Pacific Railroad, 240 U.S. 1 6-200
    6.12.12   Conclusions 6-201

6.13 Legal Profession Scandals 6-201
    6.13.1   Legal Dictionary Definitions for "United States" 6-201
    6.13.2   The Taxability of Wages and Income Derived from "Labor" Rather than "Profit" as Described in CLE Materials 6-203

6.14 Social Security Chronology 6-203

6.15 Conclusion: The Duck Test 6-209

Also in the table of contents above section 6.10:

    6.9.19   Obfuscation of 2004: IRS Publication 519 added deceptive reference to "United States" to deceive and confuse readers 6-159
    6.9.20   Cover-Up of 2012: IRS removed exemption for withholding and reporting for "U.S. persons" on the W-9 form even though it is still in the regulations 6-161

> *"The only thing new in the world is the history you do not know"*
> [Author unknown]

> *"A nation can survive its fools, and even the ambitious. But it cannot survive treason from within [our own government]. An enemy at the gates is less formidable, for he is known and carries his banners openly. But the traitor moves amongst those within the gate freely, his sly whispers rustling through all the alleys, heard in the very halls of government[and Congress] itself. For the traitor appears not a traitor; he speaks in accents familiar to his victims, and he wears their face and their garments, and he appeals to the baseness that lies deep in the hearts of all men. He rots the soul of a nation, he works secretly and unknown in the night to undermine the pillars of a city, he infects the body politic so that it can no longer resist. A murderer is less to be feared"*
> [Marcus Tullius Cicero 42 BC]

> *"Americans have the government officials they deserve. Our society openly castigates the Almighty, thus making tolerable judicial pronouncements like that of today (6-26-02, Ninth Circuit Court of Appeals declared the national pledge unconstitutional because it used the phrase "one nation under God") which banished God from our national pledge. The darkness of night follows the light of day, and similarly when any nation shakes its angry fist at the maker of the universe, it can expect the withdrawal of divine protection. Conditions are now riper for a strike by our national tormentors. Those who disdain our sacred pledge are no better than our enemies."*
> [Larry Becraft, Attorney]

> *"A nation which does not remember what it was yesterday, does not know what it is today, nor what it is trying to do. We are trying to do a futile thing if we do not know where we came from or what we have been about."*
> [Woodrow Wilson, President of the United States]

> *"I believe there are more instances of the abridgement of the freedom of the people by gradual and silent encroachments of those in power than by violent and sudden usurpations."*
> [James Madison (1751-1863), President of the United States]

> *"In politics, nothing happens by accident. If it happens, it was planned that way."*
> [Franklin D. Roosevelt, President of the United States]

> *"The strongest reason for the people to retain the right to keep and bear arms is, as a last resort, to protect themselves against tyranny in government."*
> [Thomas Jefferson (1743-1826), Founding father and President of the United States]

> *"There is no pillow so soft as a clear conscience."*
> [French Proverb]

After having diligently read Chapter 5 of this book, which documents extensively using current case law, statutes, and regulations why most Americans, and especially those who do not consent, are not liable to either file returns or pay income taxes under Internal Revenue Code, Subtitle A, you most likely are thinking something like the following:

> *"The conclusions you reached and thoroughly documented in Chapter 5 of this book are totally incredible! I am simply stunned and rendered speechless by them and still have trouble believing them because they sound too good to be true. Surely our federal government wouldn't lie to us on **that** large a scale and get away with it, would they? Wouldn't the courts have blown the whistle on this a long time ago? Why doesn't my lawyer know this and if he does, why won't he tell me? I would feel much more thoroughly convinced of your arguments if you could analyze the issues and assertions you are making from a historical perspective to show how our nation evolved to the allegedly lawless state it currently finds itself in with regard to federal income taxes. If what you are saying is true, and so far I have no reason to doubt that it isn't, then there is a historical explanation for all of this that is completely consistent with your conclusions. Being the perpetual skeptic that I am [GOOD!..KEEP IT UP!], I therefore demand to see historical evidence that is consistent with your conclusions to make the picture completely clear for me and remove all remaining doubt."*

Answering the above concerns is therefore the main focus of this chapter. We will show how corrupt lawyers and politicians over the years have conspired to deceive you into volunteering for a tax that didn't apply to you and which they had no jurisdiction to make you liable for paying. We will show how they cleverly weaved and perfected the deceptive spider web that snares you into their system and makes you into an unwilling slave of a federal government that has turned from the chief protector of your rights to the worst possible violator of your rights. Other additional but very valid reasons for documenting the history of this alleged conspiracy to defraud Americans of their income include the following:

1. There are two main statutory crimes involving federal income taxes that could possibly affect those who choose not to "volunteer" to pay federal income taxes:
   1.1. Tax Evasion, 26 U.S.C. §7201
   1.2. Willful Failure to File, 26 U.S.C. §7203

2. Both of the above statutory crimes are most often proved or demonstrated conclusively in court by the government by showing the jury that there was a *willful* attempt to conceal "taxable" income by the defendant. This requires the government to prove that:
    2.1. The defendant is completely familiar with the Internal Revenue Code and the implementing regulations found in 26 C.F.R..
    2.2. The defendant had income that was "taxable", which means that Internal Revenue Code (somewhere in the code) made you *liable* (you had a legal *duty*) for paying the tax.
    2.3. Because the defendant was liable to pay a tax, then he was also liable to file a return under the tax imposed in 26 U.S.C. §1.
    2.4. The defendant knew that that the law made him *liable* to pay the tax but he still refused to pay it and tried to circumvent it or the collection of it (Tax Evasion, 26 U.S.C. §7201)
    2.5. He violated a legal duty he knew he had by refusing to file the return showing his liability (26 U.S.C. §7203).
3. The motive for the act of concealment is extremely important in establishing the basis for the charge of "willfulness". If the motive for the concealment did *not* involve hiding taxable income or violating a known legal duty, but simply a desire to protect one's constitutional rights, one's property, obey the law, and guarantee that the government also obeys the law, then the act of concealment cannot be "willful".
4. There are more motives or reasons to conceal "income" from the government than simply just to evade taxes. One major additional reason might be because the government is quite frankly corrupt and lawless and simply can't be trusted to obey the laws on federal income taxes, which clearly show that there is no liability to either file a return or pay a tax. The act of concealing income under such circumstances is simply an exercise of liberty and pursuit of justice in conformance with laws designed to protect oneself from unlawful government abuse which essentially amounts to organized extortion and fraud.
5. The contents of this chapter will therefore trace the history of our country to convincingly and clearly show the basis for the conclusion and good faith belief that:
    5.1. We have a *criminal and abusive federal government* that tramples our Constitutional rights and which is downright dishonest in its dealings with most Americans with regard to federal income taxes. The main motive for that dishonesty is a love and lust for money and power, which the Bible says in 1 Tim. 6:10 is "the root of all evil".
    5.2. The criminal nature of our federal government and its widespread violation of our Constitutional rights and tax statutes found in the Internal Revenue Code and regulations undermines its credibility and violates the public trust and fiduciary relationship that it clearly has with Americans as document in Section 2.1 of this book.
    5.3. This tyrannical violation of law and public trust causes Americans to distrust their government, creates civil unrest, undermines our prosperity, and makes most people want to run and hide from the government to protect their privacy and liberty rather than risk being harmed by it. For instance, it makes people want to conceal private information from the federal government because of a fear that the information they provide will be misused to illegally single them out or prosecute them wrongfully using fabricated evidence and misquoted or falsified or misleading statements about their lawful tax responsibilities. This type of treatment is called blackmail and extortion when anyone other than the government does it, but the government seldom prosecutes or enforces such criminal laws when its own officers undertake such abuses.
    5.4. Running and hiding from our government because of our mistrust and its lawless behavior is a legitimate and honorable motivation for concealing income, and that this motivation has *nothing* to do with defying a known legal duty or with the notion of "willfulness". To the contrary, it is the *only* cost-effective way, in the absence of a government that obeys its own taxing statutes and the presence of a corrupt legal profession, to ensure that the outcome in our case is more consistent with the requirements of the law in the presence of a criminal government.

> "*When the wicked arise, men hide themselves;*
> But when they perish, the righteous increase."
> [Prov. 28:28, Bible, NKJV]
>
> "A prudent man foresees evil and hides himself [and his assets from plunder and harm],
> But the simple pass on and are punished."
> [Prov. 22:3, Bible, NKJV]
>
> "A **prudent** man foresees evil and hides himself; The simple pass on and are punished."
> [Prov. 27:12, Bible, NKJV]
>
> "The simple believes every word,
> But the prudent man considers well his steps.
> *A wise man fears and departs from evil*,
> But a fool rages and is self-confident."
> [Prov. 14:15, Bible, NKJV]

- 5.5. Because there is no such thing as taxable income under Subtitle A for Americans who refuse to volunteer for the tax, it constitutes a fraud for our government to claim or imply otherwise, whether it be in the IRS Publications, the Internal Revenue Code, or 26 Code of Federal Regulations. In spite of this fact, we will show how the government has committed a constructive fraud by obfuscating the tax code over the years to further violate the public trust and illegally and fraudulently broaden public perception of their otherwise very limited jurisdiction to tax incomes only within the federal United States.
- 5.6. Fear created in the reader by a knowledge and complete understanding of this chapter will hopefully provide a sufficient basis to forever avoid the charge of "willfulness" in the act of concealment because we can show a valid and honorable and lawful motive for concealment related to other than criminal intent or defiance of a known legal duty.

Before we begin our first section within the chapter, we'd like to give you the big picture, or 20,000 foot view, of why you should believe that history confirms what we said in Chapter 5. All you have to do is consider the scenario below to realize that there is something *seriously wrong* going on here with our federal government.

1. The Supreme Court in 1895, in the case of *Pollock v. Farmers' Loan & Trust Co., 157 U.S. 429*, 158 U.S. 601 (1895), declared that the first income tax imposed on Americans as **unconstitutional**.
2. The Sixteenth Amendment to the Constitution of the United States of America,, fraudulently ratified in 1913, is what most federal politicians and tax lawyers erroneously say *overcame* the Pollock decision in 1895 and authorized the imposition of direct income taxes on sovereign Americans.
3. The Supreme Court declared in 1916, *after* the passage of the Sixteenth Amendment, the following in a case that has *never been overruled*:

> "..by the previous ruling it was settled that **the provisions of the Sixteenth Amendment conferred no new power of taxation** but simply prohibited the previous complete and plenary power of income taxation possessed by Congress from the beginning from being taken out of the category of indirect taxation to which it inherently belonged and being placed in the category of direct taxation subject to apportionment by a consideration of the sources from which the income was derived, that is by testing the tax not by what it was -- a tax on income, but by a mistaken theory deduced from the origin or source of the income taxed."
> [*Stanton v. Baltic Mining Co., 240 U.S. 103 (1916)*]

4. No changes to the Constitution that would affect income taxation have been made that would authorize the ruling in *Pollock v. Farmers' Loan and Trust,* 158 U.S. 601 (1895) to be invalidated or superseded.
5. In spite of all of the above, to this day, the federal government, and especially our dishonest Congressmen and the IRS, *still* continues to commit fraud and deceive the public by insisting that:
  - 5.1. The Sixteenth Amendment authorized Subtitle A income taxes on natural persons.
  - 5.2. The Sixteenth Amendment was properly ratified and therefore valid.
  - 5.3. Income taxes are legal and lawful for natural persons.
  - 5.4. Income taxes do not violate our constitutional rights.
  - 5.5. All Americans are "taxpayers" (persons *liable* for the payment of income taxes under Subtitle A), even though there is not statute or regulation creating such a liability.
  - 5.6. All Americans are statutory "U.S. citizens" pursuant to 8 U.S.C. §1401, which means they are domiciled federal territory subject to the sovereignty of the U.S. government. This is a fraud, because they are in most cases "nationals" but not statutory "citizens" pursuant to 8 U.S.C. §1101(a)(21) who are effectively "nonresident aliens" as far as the Internal Revenue Code is concerned. "U.S. citizens" are defined in 26 C.F.R. §31.3121(e)-1 to mean

    "... a citizen of the Commonwealth of Puerto Rico or the Virgin Islands, and, effective January 1, 1961, a citizen of Guam or American Samoa."

  - 5.7. That being a statutory "U.S. citizen" is what makes a person liable for income taxes, and that it is a patriotic duty to "pay our fair share."
  - 5.8. That the "individual" described at the top of the income tax form means statutory "U.S. citizen", when in fact it really means "U.S. resident alien" or "nonresident alien" as per 26 C.F.R. §1.1441-1(c)(3).
  - 5.9. That the IRS publications are to be trusted to establish a good faith belief about our legal liabilities, even though the courts and even the IRS claim that they can't be relied upon for such purposes and that only the law is useful in establishing good faith belief.

Do you smell something **_REALLY FISHY_** going on here? We hope we have at least made you curious enough to finish reading this chapter and see for yourself that what we are saying is truthful and completely consistent with the law and with our country's history.

George Washington, in his Farewell Address to our country, said that religion and morality are indispensable aspects of our government. We believe this chapter painfully and forcefully confirms what happens when they cease to be priorities of our government and our courts:

> ***Of all the dispositions and habits which lead to political prosperity, religion and morality are indispensable supports. In vain would that man claim the tribute of patriotism who should labor to subvert these great pillars of human happiness—these firmest props of the duties of men and citizens. The mere politician, equally with the pious man, ought to respect and to cherish them.*** *A volume could not trace all their connections with private and public felicity. Let it simply be asked, "where is the security for property, for reputation, for life, if the sense of religious obligation desert the oaths which are the instruments of investigation in courts of justice?" And let us with caution indulge the supposition that morality can be maintained without religion. Whatever may be conceded to the influence of refined education on minds of peculiar structure, reason and experience both forbid us to expect that national morality can prevail in exclusion of religious principle.*
>
> *It is substantially true that virtue or morality is a necessary spring of popular government. The rule indeed extends with more or less force to every species of free government. Who that is a sincere friend to it can look with indifference upon attempts to shake the foundation of the fabric?*
>
> *Promote, then, as an object of primary importance, institutions for the general diffusion of knowledge. In proportion as the structure of a government gives force to public opinion, it is essential that public opinion should be enlightened.*

George Washington also confirmed the above assertions in the following quotes:

> *"Propitious smiles of heaven can never be expected on a nation that disregards the eternal rules of order and right which heaven itself has ordained."* - George Washington (1732-1799)
>
> *"One's **god** dictates the kind of **law** one implements and also controls the application and development of that law over time. Given enough time, **all** non-Christian systems of law **self-destruct** in a fit of tyranny."*

The history of our country is ripe with examples of noble statesmen like George Washington, who were wise statesmen of faith and character. Contemporary liberal media, liberal politicians, and a liberal education system have conspired to hide the deeds and beliefs of these noble men from the view of our young ones, and corrupted them to believe that there is no God, no absolute source of truth, and no right and wrong and everything is relative. The new god of the 21st century has become science and evolutionism, which together have robbed our children of religion and faith and mocked the Bible and God and our marvelous national birthright.

In the process of promoting their selfish agenda in our educational system, licentious and corrupt individuals in the legal, education, and media professions have made us into a carnal, licentious, and idolatrous society where the government robs us of our income using the ignorance it created in us as a weapon and thereby forces us to therefore depend on and trust it instead of God or our own initiative. In effect, they have outlawed personal responsibility by forcing us to participate in a Social Security Ponzi Scheme and income tax system. This violates the first commandment of the Bible.

> *"You shall have no other gods [including government] before Me."*
> *[Exodus 20:3, Bible, NKJV]*

Now we have a whole generation of conceited and idolatrous people (the "ME generation") who have known nothing but this selfish lie and deception and who do not know any other reality or even the way things used to be in our country because our public school history books have been censored to remove our spiritual heritage. See the following website created by David Barton for more information on this liberal censorship scam:

http://www.wallbuilders.com/

To make things even worse, public distaste for lawyers has caused few men of character to be attracted to public service or political office, thus leaving our government and our courts in the hands of selfish rogue lawyers and arrogant thieves. As our leaders, these losers set the standard for our society and are dragging it down with them:

> "Our government is the potent, the omnipresent teacher. For good or of for ill, it teaches the whole people by its example. Crime is contagious. If the government becomes a lawbreaker, it breeds contempt for the law; it invites every man to become a law unto himself; it invites anarchy. To declare that in the administration of the criminal law the end justifies the means...would bring terrible retribution. Against that pernicious doctrine this Court should resolutely set its face."
> [Justice Brandeis, Olmstead v. United States, 277 U.S. 438, 485 (1928)]

Is it therefore any surprise to see the extent of corruption in our government with these types of selfish and lawless individuals writing our laws and enforcing them? We think not.

The one thought we want you to finish this chapter with is the following, right from the Bible in Jeremiah 17:9-11:

> **_The heart is deceitful above all things,_**
> **_And desperately wicked_**;
> **_Who can know it?_**
> I, the Lord, search the heart,
> I test the mind,
> Even to give every man according to his ways,
> According to the fruit of his doings
> As a partridge that broods but does not hatch,
> **_So is he who gets riches, but not by right_**;
> It will leave him in the midst of his days,
> **_And at his end he will be a fool._**
> [Jeremiah 17:9-11, Bible, NKJV]

In the meantime while we are waiting for Divine Justice and doing justice ourselves at every turn as Micah 6:8 requires, the Bible warns us what to expect and how we should behave in Micah 7:2-10:

> The faithful man has perished from the earth,
> And there is no one upright among men,
> They all lie in wait for blood;
> Every man hunts his brother with a net.
>
> That they may successfully do evil with both hands—
> **_The prince asks for gifts,_**
> **_The judge seeks a bribe,_**
> And the great man utters his evil desire;
> **_So they scheme together._**
> The best of them is like a brier;
> The most upright is sharper than a thorn edge;
> The day of your watchman and your punishment comes;
> Now shall be their perplexity.
>
> Do not trust in a friend;
> Do not put your confidence in a companion;
> Guard the doors of your mouth
> From her who lies in your bosom.
> For son dishonors father,
> Daughter rises against her mother,
> Daughter-in-law against her mother-in-law;
> A man's enemies are the men of his own household.
> Therefore I will look to the Lord;
> I will wait for the God of my salvation;
> My God will hear me.
>
> Do not rejoice over me, my enemy;
> When I fall, I will arise;
> When I sit in darkness,
> The Lord will be a light to me.
> I will bear the indignation of the Lord,
> Because I have sinned against Him,
> Until He pleads my case
> And executes justice for me.
> He will bring me forth to the light;
> I will see His righteousness.
> Then she who is my enemy will see,
> And shame will cover her who said to me,
> "Where is the Lord your God?"

> *My eyes will see her;*
> *Now she will be trampled down*
> *Like mud in the streets."*
> *[Micah 7:2-10, Bible, NKJV]]*

Finally, if you find that the contents of the chapter leave questions unanswered about the history of the income tax fraud and the moral decay in this country and you would like a clearer or more complete picture, we refer you to another *excellent* book that is very thoroughly researched and authoritative by David Barton:

> *Original Intent: The Courts, the Constitution, and Religion*
> by David Barton, ISBN 0-925279-57-9
> Available from: Wallbuilders, http://www.wallbuilders.com/, Phone 800-873-2845.

If you also happen to be interested generally in the subject of freedom and would like a much broader and more complete view of the history of freedom in our country that focuses on *all* aspects of freedom, including taxation, then we refer you to the CD-ROM entitled *Highlights of American Legal and Political History: The Conquering of the American Republic by the U.S. Democracy*. This CD is jam-packed with 640 Mbytes of evidence from the government's own *original* publications and documents showing how our freedoms and liberties have been systematically, maliciously, and willfully destroyed and undermined in violation of the Constitution from the very foundation of this country. Over three years and 2,000 man-hours went into assembling the CD that will save you thousands of hours of research on your own. This resource will therefore greatly accelerate your learning on the subject of freedom and liberty. You can obtain this incredible resource at:

> http://sedmorg/ItemInfo/EBooks/HOALPH/HOALPH.htm

6.1 Main purpose of law is to LIMIT government power to ensure freedom and sovereignty of the people[1]

The main purpose of law is to limit government power in order to protect and preserve, freedom, choice, and the sovereignty of the people.

> *"When we consider the nature and theory of our institutions of government, the principles upon which they are supposed to rest, and review the history of their development, we are constrained to conclude that they do not mean to leave room for the play and action of purely personal and arbitrary power. Sovereignty itself is, of course, not subject to law, for it is the author and source of law; but in our system, while sovereign powers are delegated to the agencies of government, sovereignty itself remains with the people, by whom and for whom all government exists and acts. **And the law is the definition and limitation of power.***
> *[Downes v. Bidwell, 182 U.S. 244 (1901)]*

An important implication of the use of law to limit government power is the following inferences unavoidably arising from it:

1. The purpose of law is to define and thereby limit government power.
2. All law acts as a delegation of authority order upon those serving in the government.
3. You cannot limit government power without definitions that are limiting.
4. A definition that does not limit the thing or class of thing defined is no definition at all from a legal perspective and causes anything that depends on that definition to be political rather than legal in nature. By political, we mean a function exercised ONLY by the LEGISLATIVE or EXECUTIVE branch.
5. Where the definitions in the law are clear, judges have no discretion to expand the meaning of words. Therefore the main method of expanding government power and creating what the supreme court calls "arbitrary power" is to use terms in the law that are vague, undefined, "general expressions", or which don't define the context implied.
6. We define "general expressions" as those which:
   6.1. The speaker is either not accountable or REFUSES to be accountable for the accuracy or truthfulness or definition of the word or expression.
   6.2. Fail to recognize that there are multiple contexts in which the word could be used.
      6.2.1. CONSTITUTIONAL (States of the Union).
      6.2.2. STATUTORY (federal territory).

---

[1] *Legal Deception, Propaganda, and Fraud*, Form #05.014, Section 4; http://sedm.org/Forms/FormIndex.htm.

6.3. Are susceptible to two or more CONTEXTS or interpretations, one of which the government representative interpreting the context stands to benefit from handsomely. Thus, "equivocation" is undertaken, in which they TELL you they mean the CONSTITUTIONAL interpretation but after receiving your form or pleading, interpret it to mean the STATUTORY context.

> *equivocation*
>
> *EQUIVOCA'TION, n. Ambiguity of speech; the use of words or expressions that are susceptible of a double signification. Hypocrites are often guilty of equivocation, and by this means lose the confidence of their fellow men. Equivocation is incompatible with the Christian character and profession.*
>
> *[SOURCE: http://1828.mshaffer.com/d/search/word,equivocation]*

> *Equivocation ("to call by the same name") is an informal logical fallacy. It is the misleading use of a term with more than one meaning or sense (by glossing over which meaning is intended at a particular time). It generally occurs with polysemic words (words with multiple meanings).*
>
> *Albeit in common parlance it is used in a variety of contexts, when discussed as a fallacy, equivocation only occurs when the arguer makes a word or phrase employed in two (or more) different senses in an argument appear to have the same meaning throughout.*
>
> *It is therefore distinct from (semantic) ambiguity, which means that the context doesn't make the meaning of the word or phrase clear, and amphiboly (or syntactical ambiguity), which refers to ambiguous sentence structure due to punctuation or syntax.*
>
> *[Wikipedia: Equivocation, Downloaded 9/15/2015; SOURCE: https://en.wikipedia.org/wiki/Equivocation]*

6.4. PRESUME that all contexts are equivalent, meaning that CONSTITUTIONAL and STATUTORY are equivalent.
6.5. Fail to identify the specific context implied.
6.6. Fail to provide an actionable definition for the term that is useful as evidence in court.
6.7. Government representatives actively interfere with or even penalize efforts by the applicant to define the context of the terms so that they can protect their right to make injurious presumptions about their meaning.

7. Any attempt to assert any authority by anyone in government to add anything they want to the definition of a thing in the law unavoidably creates a government of UNLIMITED power.
8. Anyone who can add anything to the definition of a word in the law that does not expressly appear SOMEWHERE in the law is exercising a LEGISLATIVE and POLITICAL function of the LEGISLATIVE branch and is NOT acting as a judge or a jurist.
9. The only people in government who can act in a LEGISLATIVE capacity are the LEGISLATIVE branch under our system of three branches of government: LEGISLATIVE, EXECUTIVE, and JUDICIAL.
10. Any attempt to combine or consolidate any of the powers of each of the three branches into the other branch results in tyranny.

> "**When the legislative and executive powers are united in the same person, or in the same body of magistrates, there can be no liberty; because apprehensions may arise, lest the same monarch or senate should enact tyrannical laws, to execute them in a tyrannical manner.**
>
> **Again, there is no liberty, if the judiciary power be not separated from the legislative and executive.** Were it joined with the legislative, the life and liberty of the subject would be exposed to arbitrary control; for the judge would be then the legislator. **Were it joined to the executive power, the judge might behave with violence and oppression [sound familiar?].**
>
> **There would be an end of everything, were the same man or the same body, whether of the nobles or of the people, to exercise those three powers, that of enacting laws, that of executing the public resolutions, and of trying the causes of individuals.**"
>
> [. . .]
>
> **In what a situation must the poor subject be in those republics! The same body of magistrates are possessed, as executors of the laws, of the whole power they have given themselves in quality of legislators. They may plunder the state by their general determinations; and as they have likewise the judiciary power in their hands, every private citizen may be ruined by their particular decisions.**"

6.2 How our system of government became corrupted: Downes v. Bidwell[2]

The dissenting opinion of Justice Harlan in the monumentally important U.S. Supreme Court case of Downes v. Bidwell described how the word game mechanisms at the end of the previous section would be abused to corrupt our system of government with a stern warning to future generations:

> *In view of the adjudications of this court, I cannot assent to the proposition, whether it be announced in express words or by implication, that the National Government is a government of or by the States in union, and that the prohibitions and limitations of the Constitution are addressed only to the States. That is but another form of saying that like the government created by the Articles of Confederation, the present government is a mere league of States, held together by compact between themselves; whereas, as this court has often declared, it is a government created by the People of the United States, with enumerated powers, and supreme over States and individuals, with respect to certain objects, throughout the entire territory over which its jurisdiction extends. If the National Government is, in any sense, a compact, it is a compact between the People of the United States among themselves as constituting in the aggregate the political community by whom the National Government was established.* **The Constitution speaks not simply to the States in their organized capacities, but to all peoples, whether of States or territories, who are subject to the authority of the United States.** *Martin v. Hunter, 1 Wheat. 304, 327.*
>
> *In the opinion to which I am referring it is also said that the "practical interpretation put by Congress upon the Constitution has been long continued and uniform to the effect that the Constitution is applicable to territories acquired by purchase or conquest only when and so far as Congress shall so direct;" that while all power of government may be abused, the same may be said of the power of the Government "under the Constitution as well as outside of it;" that "if it once be conceded that we are at liberty to acquire foreign territory, a presumption arises that 379*379 our power with respect to such territories is the same power which other nations have been accustomed to exercise with respect to territories acquired by them;" that "the liberality of Congress in legislating the Constitution into all our contiguous territories has undoubtedly fostered the impression that it went there by its own force, but there is nothing in the Constitution itself, and little in the interpretation put upon it, to confirm that impression;" that as the States could only delegate to Congress such powers as they themselves possessed, and as they had no power to acquire new territory, and therefore none to delegate in that connection, the logical inference is that "if Congress had power to acquire new territory, which is conceded, that power was not hampered by the constitutional provisions;" that if "we assume that the territorial clause of the Constitution was not intended to be restricted to such territory as the United States then possessed, there is nothing in the Constitution to indicate that the power of Congress in dealing with them was intended to be restricted by any of the other provisions;" and that "the executive and legislative departments of the Government have for more than a century interpreted this silence as precluding the idea that the Constitution attached to these territories as soon as acquired."*
>
> *These are words of weighty import. They involve consequences of the most momentous character. I take leave to say that if the principles thus announced should ever receive the sanction of a majority of this court, a radical and mischievous change in our system of government will be the result. We will, in that event, pass from the era of constitutional liberty guarded and protected by a written constitution into an era of legislative absolutism.*
>
> *Although from the foundation of the Government this court has held steadily to the view that the Government of the United States was one of enumerated powers, and that no one of its branches, nor all of its branches combined, could constitutionally exercise powers not granted, or which were not necessarily implied from those expressly granted, Martin v. Hunter, 1 Wheat. 304, 326, 331,* **we are now informed that Congress possesses powers outside of the Constitution, and may deal with new territory, 380*380 acquired by treaty or conquest, in the same manner as other nations have been accustomed to act with respect to territories acquired by them. In my opinion, Congress has no existence and can exercise no authority outside of the Constitution. Still less is it true that Congress can deal with new territories just as other nations have done or may do with their new territories. This nation is under the control of a written constitution, the supreme law of the land and the only source of the powers which our Government, or any branch or officer of it, may exert at any time or at any place. Monarchical and despotic governments, unrestrained by written constitutions, may do with newly acquired territories what this Government may not do consistently with our fundamental law. To say otherwise is to concede that Congress may, by action taken outside of the Constitution, engraft upon our republican institutions a colonial system such as exists under monarchical governments. Surely such a result was never contemplated by the fathers of the Constitution. If that instrument had contained a word suggesting the possibility of a result of that character it would never have been adopted by the People of the United States. The idea that this country may acquire territories anywhere upon the earth, by conquest or treaty, and hold them as mere colonies or provinces — the people inhabiting them to enjoy only such rights as Congress chooses**

---

[2] Source: *Legal Deception, Propaganda, and Fraud*, Form #05.014, Section 5; http://sedm.org/Forms/FormIndex.htm.

to accord to them — is wholly inconsistent with the spirit and genius as well as with the words of the Constitution.

The idea prevails with some — indeed, it found expression in arguments at the bar — that we have in this country substantially or practically two national governments; one, to be maintained under the Constitution, with all its restrictions; the other to be maintained by Congress outside and independently of that instrument, by exercising such powers as other nations of the earth are accustomed to exercise. It is one thing to give such a latitudinarian construction to the Constitution as will bring the exercise of power by Congress, upon a particular occasion or upon a particular subject, within its provisions. It is quite a different thing to say that Congress may, if it so elects, proceed outside of the Constitution. The glory of our American system 381*381 of government is that it was created by a written constitution which protects the people against the exercise of arbitrary, unlimited power, and the limits of which instrument may not be passed by the government it created, or by any branch of it, or even by the people who ordained it, except by amendment or change of its provisions. "To what purpose," Chief Justice Marshall said in Marbury v. Madison, 1 Cranch, 137, 176,"are powers limited, and to what purpose is that limitation committed to writing, if these limits may, at any time, be passed by those intended to be restrained? The distinction between a government with limited and unlimited powers is abolished if those limits do not confine the persons on whom they are imposed, and if acts prohibited and acts allowed are of equal obligation."

The wise men who framed the Constitution, and the patriotic people who adopted it, were unwilling to depend for their safety upon what, in the opinion referred to, is described as "certain principles of natural justice inherent in Anglo-Saxon character which need no expression in constitutions or statutes to give them effect or to secure dependencies against legislation manifestly hostile to their real interests." They proceeded upon the theory — the wisdom of which experience has vindicated — that the only safe guaranty against governmental oppression was to withhold or restrict the power to oppress. They well remembered that Anglo-Saxons across the ocean had attempted, in defiance of law and justice, to trample upon the rights of Anglo-Saxons on this continent and had sought, by military force, to establish a government that could at will destroy the privileges that inhere in liberty. They believed that the establishment here of a government that could administer public affairs according to its will unrestrained by any fundamental law and without regard to the inherent rights of freemen, would be ruinous to the liberties of the people by exposing them to the oppressions of arbitrary power. Hence, the Constitution enumerates the powers which Congress and the other Departments may exercise — leaving unimpaired, to the States or the People, the powers not delegated to the National Government nor prohibited to the States. That instrument so expressly declares in 382*382 the Tenth Article of Amendment. It will be an evil day for American liberty if the theory of a government outside of the supreme law of the land finds lodgment in our constitutional jurisprudence. No higher duty rests upon this court than to exert its full authority to prevent all violation of the principles of the Constitution.

Again, it is said that Congress has assumed, in its past history, that the Constitution goes into territories acquired by purchase or conquest only when and as it shall so direct, and we are informed of the liberality of Congress in legislating the Constitution into all our contiguous territories. This is a view of the Constitution that may well cause surprise, if not alarm. Congress, as I have observed, has no existence except by virtue of the Constitution. It is the creature of the Constitution. It has no powers which that instrument has not granted, expressly or by necessary implication. I confess that I cannot grasp the thought that Congress which lives and moves and has its being in the Constitution and is consequently the mere creature of that instrument, can, at its pleasure, legislate or exclude its creator from territories which were acquired only by authority of the Constitution.

By the express words of the Constitution, every Senator and Representative is bound, by oath or affirmation, to regard it as the supreme law of the land. When the Constitutional Convention was in session there was much discussion as to the phraseology of the clause defining the supremacy of the Constitution, laws and treaties of the United States. At one stage of the proceedings the Convention adopted the following clause: "This Constitution, and the laws of the United States made in pursuance thereof, and all the treaties made under the authority of the United States, shall be the supreme law of the several States and of their citizens and inhabitants, and the judges of the several States shall be bound thereby in their decisions, anything in the constitutions or laws of the several States to the contrary notwithstanding." This clause was amended, on motion of Mr. Madison, by inserting after the words "all treaties made" the words "or which shall be made." If the clause, so amended, had been inserted in the Constitution as finally adopted, perhaps 383*383 there would have been some justification for saying that the Constitution, laws and treaties of the United States constituted the supreme law only in the States, and that outside of the States the will of Congress was supreme. But the framers of the Constitution saw the danger of such a provision, and put into that instrument in place of the above clause the following: "This Constitution, and the laws of the United States which shall be made in pursuance thereof, and all treaties made, or which shall be made, under the authority of the United States, shall be the supreme law of the land; and the judges in every State shall be bound thereby, anything in the constitution or laws of any State to the contrary notwithstanding." Meigs's Growth of the Constitution, 284, 287. That the Convention struck out the words "the supreme law of the several States" and inserted "the supreme law of the land," is a fact of no little significance. The "land" referred to manifestly embraced all the peoples and all the territory, whether within or without the States, over which the United States could exercise jurisdiction or authority.

Further, it is admitted that some of the provisions of the Constitution do apply to Porto Rico and may be invoked as limiting or restricting the authority of Congress, or for the protection of the people of that island. And it is said *that there is a clear distinction between such prohibitions "as go to the very root of the power of Congress to act at all, irrespective of time or place, and such as are operative only `throughout the United States' or among the several States." In the enforcement of this suggestion it is said in one of the opinions just delivered: "Thus, when the Constitution declares that `no bill of attainder or ex post facto law shall be passed,' and that `no title of nobility shall be granted by the United States,' it goes to the competency of Congress to pass a bill of that description." I cannot accept this reasoning as consistent with the Constitution or with sound rules of interpretation. The express prohibition upon the passage by Congress of bills of attainder, or of ex post facto laws, or the granting of titles of nobility, goes no more directly to the root of the power of Congress than does the express prohibition against the imposition by Congress of any 384*384 duty, impost or excise that is not uniform throughout the United States.* **The opposite theory, I take leave to say, is quite as extraordinary as that which assumes that Congress may exercise powers outside of the Constitution, and may, in its discretion, legislate that instrument into or out of a domestic territory of the United States.**

In the opinion to which I have referred it is suggested that conditions may arise when the annexation of distant possessions may be desirable. "If," says that opinion, "those possessions are inhabited by alien races, differing from us in religion, customs, laws, methods of taxation and modes of thought, the administration of government and justice, according to Anglo-Saxon principles, may for a time be impossible; and the question at once arises whether large concessions ought not to be made for a time, that ultimately our own theories may be carried out, and the blessings of a free government under the Constitution extended to them. We decline to hold that there is anything in the Constitution to forbid such action." In my judgment, the Constitution does not sustain any such theory of our governmental system. Whether a particular race will or will not assimilate with our people, and whether they can or cannot with safety to our institutions be brought within the operation of the Constitution, is a matter to be thought of when it is proposed to acquire their territory by treaty. A mistake in the acquisition of territory, although such acquisition seemed at the time to be necessary, cannot be made the ground for violating the Constitution or refusing to give full effect to its provisions. **The Constitution is not to be obeyed or disobeyed as the circumstances of a particular crisis in our history may suggest the one or the other course to be pursued. The People have decreed that it shall be the supreme law of the land at all times. When the acquisition of territory becomes complete, by cession, the Constitution necessarily becomes the supreme law of such new territory, and no power exists in any Department of the Government to make "concessions" that are inconsistent with its provisions. The authority to make such concessions implies the existence in Congress of power to declare that constitutional provisions may be ignored under special or 385*385 embarrassing circumstances. No such dispensing power exists in any branch of our Government. The Constitution is supreme over every foot of territory, wherever situated, under the jurisdiction of the United States, and its full operation cannot be stayed by any branch of the Government in order to meet what some may suppose to be extraordinary emergencies.** *If the Constitution is in force in any territory, it is in force there for every purpose embraced by the objects for which the Government was ordained. Its authority cannot be displaced by concessions, even if it be true, as asserted in argument in some of these cases, that if the tariff act took effect in the Philippines of its own force, the inhabitants of Mandanao, who live on imported rice, would starve, because the import duty is many fold more than the ordinary cost of the grain to them.* **The meaning of the Constitution cannot depend upon accidental circumstances arising out of the products of other countries or of this country. We cannot violate the Constitution in order to serve particular interests in our own or in foreign lands. Even this court, with its tremendous power, must heed the mandate of the Constitution.** *No one in official station, to whatever department of the Government he belongs, can disobey its commands without violating the obligation of the oath he has taken. By whomsoever and wherever power is exercised in the name and under the authority of the United States, or of any branch of its Government, the validity or invalidity of that which is done must be determined by the Constitution.*

In DeLima v. Bidwell, just decided, we have held that upon the ratification of the treaty with Spain, Porto Rico ceased to be a foreign country and became a domestic territory of the United States. We have said in that case that from 1803 to the present time there was not a shred of authority, except a dictum in one case, "for holding that a district ceded to and in possession of the United States remains for any purpose a foreign territory;" that territory so acquired cannot be "domestic for one purpose and foreign for another;" and that any judgment to the contrary would be "pure judicial legislation," for which there was no warrant in the Constitution or in the powers conferred upon this court. Although, as we have just decided, 386*386 Porto Rico ceased, after the ratification of the treaty with Spain, to be a foreign country within the meaning of the tariff act, and became a domestic country — "a territory of the United States" — it is said that if Congress so wills it may be controlled and governed outside of the Constitution and by the exertion of the powers which other nations have been accustomed to exercise with respect to territories acquired by them; in other words, we may solve the question of the power of Congress under the Constitution, by referring to the powers that may be exercised by other nations. I cannot assent to this view. **I reject altogether the theory that Congress, in its discretion, can exclude the Constitution from a domestic territory of the United States, acquired, and which could only have been acquired, in virtue of the Constitution.** *I cannot agree that it is a domestic territory of the United States for the purpose of preventing the application of the tariff act imposing duties upon imports from foreign countries, but not a part of the United States for the purpose of enforcing the constitutional requirement that all duties, imposts and excises imposed by Congress "shall be uniform throughout the United States."* **How Porto Rico can be a domestic territory of the United States, as distinctly held in DeLima v. Bidwell, and yet, as is now held, not embraced by the words "throughout the United States," is more than I can understand.**

We heard much in argument about the "expanding future of our country." It was said that the United States is to become what is called a "world power;" and that if this Government intends to keep abreast of the times and be equal to the great destiny that awaits the American people, it must be allowed to exert all the power that other

nations are accustomed to exercise. *My answer is, that the fathers never intended that the authority and influence of this nation should be exerted otherwise than in accordance with the Constitution. If our Government needs more power than is conferred upon it by the Constitution, that instrument provides the mode in which it may be amended and additional power thereby obtained. The People of the United States who ordained the Constitution never supposed that a change could be made in our system of government 387*387 by mere judicial interpretation. They never contemplated any such juggling with the words of the Constitution as would authorize the courts to hold that the words "throughout the United States," in the taxing clause of the Constitution, do not embrace a domestic "territory of the United States" having a civil government established by the authority of the United States. This is a distinction which I am unable to make, and which I do not think ought to be made when we are endeavoring to ascertain the meaning of a great instrument of government.*
[Downes v. Bidwell, 182 U.S. 244 (1901), Justice Harlan, Dissenting]

Could it possibly be doubted that if Congress has been handed by the U.S. Supreme Court ANY CIRCUMSTANCE in which it can exercise its discretion in a way that COMPLETELY disregards the entire constitution, that they would not succumb to the temptation to enact it, expand it, and make it apply through trickery to everyone, as they have done with the income tax and federal franchises in general? NOT!

> "In every government on earth is some trace of human weakness, some germ of corruption and degeneracy, which cunning will discover, and wickedness insensibly open, cultivate and improve."
> [Thomas Jefferson: Notes on Virginia Q.XIV, 1782. ME 2:207]

THIS in fact, is what Justice Harlan was talking about in the following excerpt in the above:

> *"These are words of weighty import. They involve consequences of the most momentous character.* **I take leave to say that if the principles thus announced should ever receive the sanction of a majority of this court, a radical and mischievous change in our system of government will be the result. We will, in that event, pass from the era of constitutional liberty guarded and protected by a written constitution into an era of legislative absolutism."**
>
> [...]
>
> *"This nation is under the control of a written constitution, the supreme law of the land and the only source of the powers which our Government, or any branch or officer of it, may exert at any time or at any place. Monarchical and despotic governments, unrestrained by written constitutions, may do with newly acquired territories what this Government may not do consistently with our fundamental law. To say otherwise is to concede that Congress may, by action taken outside of the Constitution, engraft upon our republican institutions a colonial system such as exists under monarchical governments. Surely such a result was never contemplated by the fathers of the Constitution. If that instrument had contained a word suggesting the possibility of a result of that character it would never have been adopted by the People of the United States.* **The idea that this country may acquire territories anywhere upon the earth, by conquest or treaty, and hold them as mere colonies or provinces — the people inhabiting them to enjoy only such rights as Congress chooses to accord to them — is wholly inconsistent with the spirit and genius as well as with the words of the Constitution."**
>
> *"The idea prevails with some — indeed, it found expression in arguments at the bar — that we have in this country substantially or practically two national governments; one, to be maintained under the Constitution, with all its restrictions; the other to be maintained by Congress outside and independently of that instrument, by exercising such powers as other nations of the earth are accustomed to exercise."* It is one thing to give such a latitudinarian construction to the Constitution as will bring the exercise of power by Congress, upon a particular occasion or upon a particular subject, within its provisions. It is quite a different thing to say that Congress may, if it so elects, proceed outside of the Constitution. *The glory of our American system 381*381 of government is that it was created by a written constitution which protects the people against the exercise of arbitrary, unlimited power, and the limits of which instrument may not be passed by the government it created, or by any branch of it, or even by the people who ordained it, except by amendment or change of its provisions. "To what purpose," Chief Justice Marshall said in Marbury v. Madison, 1 Cranch, 137, 176, "are powers limited, and to what purpose is that limitation committed to writing, if these limits may, at any time, be passed by those intended to be restrained? The distinction between a government with limited and unlimited powers is abolished if those limits do not confine the persons on whom they are imposed, and if acts prohibited and acts allowed are of equal obligation."*
> [Downes v. Bidwell, 182 U.S. 244 (1901), Justice Harlan, Dissenting]

Justice Harlan is saying that we now have a Dr. Jekyll and Mr. Hyde government. They did in fact do what he predicted: Graft a monarchical colonial system for federal territory onto an egalitarian free republican system. Starting with the Downes case, the U.S. Supreme Court declared and recognized essentially that:

1. NO PART of the Constitution limits what the national government can do in a territory, including the prohibition against Titles of Nobility and even ex post facto laws.
2. As long as Congress is legislating for territories, it can do whatever it wants, including an income tax, just like every other nation of the earth. In fact, this is the source of all the authority for enacting the income tax to begin with.
3. If Congress wants to invade the states commercially and tax them, all it has to do is:
    3.1. Write such legislation ONLY for the territories and implement it as a franchise. Since all franchises are based on contract, then they can be enforced extraterritorially, including in a state. This is the basis for the Social Security Act of 1935, in fact.

    > *Debt and contract [franchise agreement, in this case] are of no particular place.*
    >
    > *Locus contractus regit actum.*
    > *The place of the contract [franchise agreement, in this case] governs the act.*
    > *[Bouvier's Maxims of Law, 1856;*
    > *SOURCE: http://famguardian.org/Publications/BouvierMaximsOfLaw/BouviersMaxims.htm]*

    > *"It is generally conceded that a franchise is the subject of a contract between the grantor and the grantee, and that it does in fact constitute a contract when the requisite element of a consideration is present.[3] Conversely, a franchise granted without consideration is not a contract binding upon the state, franchisee, or pseudo-franchisee.[4] "*
    > *[36 American Jurisprudence 2d, Franchises, §6: As a Contract (1999)]*

    For further details on the Social Security FRAUD, see:
    > *Resignation of Compelled Social Security Trustee*, Form #06.002
    > http://sedm.org/Forms/FormIndex.htm

    3.2. Entice people in states of the Union with a bribe to sign up for the territorial franchise, and make it IMPOSSIBLE to quit the system. This uses capitalism to implement socialism.
    3.3. Through legal deception and fraud, make the franchise legislation LOOK like:
        3.3.1. It applies to CONSTITUTIONAL states rather than only STATUTORY "States" and territories.
        3.3.2. It ISN'T a franchise or excise.
        These things are done through "equivocation", in which TERRITORIAL STATUTORY "States" under 4 U.S.C. §110(d) and CONSTITUTIONAL States of the Union are made ot appear and act the same. This was also done in the Sixteenth Amendment, which granted no new powers to Congress, as held by the U.S. Supreme Court in Stanton v. Baltic Mining Co., 240 U.S. 103 (1916). See:
        > *Why You Aren't Eligible for Social Security*, Form #06.001
        > http://sedm.org/Forms/FormIndex.htm

    3.4. Establish a EXTRACONSTITUTIONAL revenue collection apparatus that is NOT part of the constitutional government. Namely the I.R.S. is not now and never has been part of the U.S. Government. Instead, it is a straw man for the Federal Reserve. The Federal Reserve, in fact, is not more governmental than Federal Express. See:
        > *Origins and Authority of the Internal Revenue Service*, Form #05.005
        > http://sedm.org/Forms/FormIndex.htm

    3.5. Use propaganda and abusive regulation of the banking system and employers to turn banks and private companies in states of the Union into federal employment recruiters, in which you can't open an account or pursue

---

[3] Larson v. South Dakota, 278 U.S. 429, 73 L.Ed. 441, 49 S.Ct. 196; Grand Trunk Western R. Co. v. South Bend, 227 U.S. 544, 57 L.Ed. 633, 33 S.Ct. 303; Blair v. Chicago, 201 U.S. 400, 50 L.Ed. 801, 26 S.Ct. 427; Arkansas-Missouri Power Co. v. Brown, 176 Ark. 774, 4 S.W.2d. 15, 58 A.L.R. 534; Chicago General R. Co. v. Chicago, 176 Ill. 253, 52 N.E. 880; Louisville v. Louisville Home Tel. Co., 149 Ky. 234, 148 S.W. 13; State ex rel. Kansas City v. East Fifth Street R. Co., 140 Mo. 539, 41 S.W. 955; Baker v. Montana Petroleum Co., 99 Mont. 465, 44 P.2d. 735; Re Board of Fire Comrs. 27 N.J. 192, 142 A.2d. 85; Chrysler Light & P. Co. v. Belfield, 58 N.D. 33, 224 N.W. 871, 63 A.L.R. 1337; Franklin County v. Public Utilities Com., 107 Ohio.St. 442, 140 N.E. 87, 30 A.L.R. 429; State ex rel. Daniel v. Broad River Power Co. 157 S.C. 1, 153 S.E. 537; Rutland Electric Light Co. v. Marble City Electric Light Co., 65 Vt. 377, 26 A. 635; Virginia-Western Power Co. v. Commonwealth, 125 Va. 469, 99 S.E. 723, 9 A.L.R. 1148, cert den 251 U.S. 557, 64 L.Ed. 413, 40 S.Ct. 179, disapproved on other grounds Victoria v. Victoria Ice, Light & Power Co. 134 Va. 134, 114 S.E. 92, 28 A.L.R. 562, and disapproved on other grounds Richmond v. Virginia Ry. & Power Co. 141 Va. 69, 126 S.E. 353.

[4] Pennsylvania R. Co. v. Bowers, 124 Pa 183, 16 A 836.

"employment" without becoming a privileged and enfranchised public officer representing an PUBLIC/GOVERNMENT office domiciled on federal territory and subject to the territorial law. See:

> *Federal and State Tax Withholding Options for Private Employers*, Form #09.001
> http://sedm.org/Forms/FormIndex.htm

3.6. Bribe CONSTITUTIONAL states with "commercial incentives" or subsidies if they in essence agree by compact or agreement to act as federal territories and allow the income tax to be enforced within their borders. This is done through DEBT and the Federal Reserve as well as the Agreements on Coordination of Tax Administration (A.C.T.A.) between the national government and the states. Now obviously, they can only do that within ENCLAVES within their external borders using the Public Salary Tax Act of 1939, but they will PRETEND for the sake of filthy lucre that it applies EVERYWHERE in the state by:

    3.6.1. Not defining the term "State" within their revenue codes.

    3.6.2. Calling those who insist on these limits "frivolous" in court.

3.7. Engage in an ongoing propaganda campaign to discredit and persecute all those who expose and try to remedy the above. This is done by making the government UNACCOUNTABLE for the truth or accuracy of ANYTHING it says or does administratively. We have been a target of that campaign. See:

> *Reasonable Belief About Income Tax Liability*, Form #05.007
> http://sedm.org/Forms/FormIndex.htm

3.8. Legislatively create a conflict of interest in the judges administering the territorial franchise so that they will be forced to apply it to the states of the Union.

3.9. Get the U.S. Supreme Court, through pressure on individual justices, to allow the financial conflict of interest to stand and expand.

3.10. Use the U.S. Supreme Court as a method to embargo challenges to the above illegalities by denying appeals. This was done using the Certiorari Act of 1925 proposed by former President and Chief Justice William Howard Taft. This was the same President who proposed the Sixteenth Amendment and FRAUDULENTLY got it passed by lame duck Secretary of State Philander Knox.[5]

That last step: creating a conflict of interest in judges was accomplished starting in 1918, right after Downes v. Bidwell and just after the Sixteenth Amendment and Federal Reserve Act were passed in 1913. In particular, here is how it was accomplished:

1. Making judges into "taxpayers" started in 1918. This allowed them to become the target of political persecution by the Bureau of Internal Revenue if they properly enforce and protect the civil status of parties.
   1.1. This began first with the Revenue Act of 1918, 40 Stat. 1065, Section 213(a) and was declared unconstitutional.
   1.2. The second attempt to make judges taxpayers occurred the Revenue Act of 1932, 47 Stat. 169 and this time it stuck.
   1.3. This conflict of interest is also documented in Evans v. Gore, 253 U.S. 245 (1920), Miles v. Graham, 268 U.S. 501 (1925), O'Malley v. Woodrough, 309 U.S. 277 (1939), and U.S. v. Hatter, 532 U.S. 557, 121 S.Ct. 1782, (2001).
2. Judges have been allowed, illegally, to serve as BOTH franchise judges under Article IV of the Constitution and CONSTITUTIONAL judges under Article III. When given a choice of the two, they will always pick the Article IV franchise judge status, because it financially rewards them and unduly elevates their own importance and jurisdiction.
3. The IRS is allowed to financially reward judges and prosecutors for convicting those who do not consent to the identity theft. See 26 U.S.C. §7623, I.R.M. 25.2.2.

The above process is EXACTLY what they have done. From the 10,000 foot or MACRO view, it essentially amounts to identity theft. That identity theft is exhaustively described in the following:

> *Government Identity Theft*, Form #05.046
> http://sedm.org/Forms/FormIndex.htm

The rest of this document essentially describes how that identity theft is accomplished by the abuse of conflict of interest, the rules of statutory interpretation, and equivocation from a general perspective. That language abuse is also particularized in the above document to specific other legal contexts, such as:

---

[5] See: *The Law that Never Was*, William Benson. It documents the fraudulent ratification of the Sixteenth Amendment. See also *Great IRS Hoax*, Form #11.302, Section 6.6.1; http://famguardian.org/Publications/GreatIRSHoax/GreatIRSHoax.htm.

1. Domicile identity theft.
2. Citizenship identity theft.
3. Franchise identity theft.

Ultimately, however, all of the identity theft they employ is accomplished by misrepresenting their authority and enforcing laws outside their territory. It really boils down to:

1. Replacing PRIVATE rights with PUBLIC privileges.
2. Turning "citizens" and "residents" into the equivalent of government public officers or employees.
3. Turning all civil law essentially into the employment agreement of virtually everyone who claims to be a STATUTORY "citizen" or "resident".
4. A commercial invasion of the states of the Union in violation of Article 4, Section 4.
5. The abuse of franchises and privileges within the states of the Union to create a caste system that emulates the British Monarchy we tried to escape by fighting a revolution.
6. Using the civil statutory law as a mechanism to limit and control PEOPLE rather than the GOVERNMENT.
7. Creating a government of UNLIMITED powers. There are no limits on what an EMPLOYER can order his EMPLOYEES or OFFICERS to do, and THAT is what you are if you claim to be a STATUTORY "citizen" under any act of Congress.
8. Using "selective enforcement" to discredit and destroy all those who attempt to QUIT their job as a government officer or employee called a STATUTORY "citizen" or "resident". THIS is how the fraudulent identity theft scheme and government mafia protects and expands itself.

6.3 How Scoundrels Corrupted Our Republican Form of Government

> "*All systems of government suppose they are to be administered by men of common sense and common honesty. In our country, as all ultimately depends on the voice of the people, they have it in their power, and it is to be presumed they generally will choose men of this description: but if they will not, the case, to be sure, is without remedy. If they choose fools, they will have foolish laws. If they choose knaves, they will have knavish ones.* But this can never be the case until they are generally fools or knaves themselves, which, thank God, is not likely ever to become the character of the American people." [Justice Iredell] (Fries's Case (CC) F Cas No 5126, supra.)
> [Ludecke v. Watkins, 335 U.S. 160, 92 L.Ed. 1881, 1890, 68 S.Ct. 1429 (1948)]

> "The chief enemies of republican freedom are mental sloth, conformity, bigotry, superstition, credulity, monopoly in the market of ideas, and utter, benighted ignorance."
> [Adderley v. State of Florida, 385 U.S. 39, 49 (1967)]

6.3.1 Original Design of our Republic

We very thoroughly covered the foundations of our republican form of government earlier in chapter 4. We showed you in section 4.1 the hierarchy of sovereignty and where you fit personally in that hierarchy. We showed you in section 4.4.1 that Article 4, Section 4 of the U.S. Constitution guarantees to all Americans a "republican form of government". Then in section 5.1.1 we showed you the order that our state and federal governments were created and the distinct sovereignties that comprise all the elements of our republican (not democratic) political system. Now we are going to tie the whole picture together and show you graphically the tools and techniques that specific covetous government servants have used over the years to corrupt and debase that system for their own personal financial and political benefit.

> "The king establishes the land by justice; but he who receives bribes overthrows it."
> [Prov. 29:4, Bible, NKJV]

After you have learned these techniques by which corruption was introduced, we will spend the rest of the chapter showing *exactly* how these techniques have been specifically applied over the years to corrupt and debase and destroy our political system and undermine our personal liberties, rights, and freedoms. This will train your perception to be on the lookout for any future attempts by our covetous politicians to further corrupt our system so that you can act swiftly at a political level to oppose and prevent it.

First of all, the foundation of our republican form of government is all the following as a group:

1. Sovereign power held by the People through their direct participation in the affairs of government as jurists and voters.

Chapter 6: History of Government Income Tax Fraud, Racketeering and Extortion in the U.S.A.

> "The sovereignty of a state does not reside in the persons who fill the different departments of its government, but in the People, from whom the government emanated; and they may change it at their discretion. Sovereignty, then in this country, abides with the constituency, and not with the agent; and this remark is true, both in reference to the federal and state government."
> [Spooner v. McConnell, 22 F. 939, 943]

> "There is no such thing as a power of inherent sovereignty in the government of the United States .... In this country sovereignty resides in the people, and Congress can exercise no power which they have not, by their Constitution entrusted to it: All else is withheld."
> [Julliard v. Greenman: 110 U.S. 421, (1884)]

2. All powers exercised by government are directly delegated to those serving in government by the people, both collectivly and individually.

   > "The question is not what power the federal government ought to have, *but what powers, in fact, have been given by the people*... The federal union is a government of delegated powers. It has only such as are expressly conferred upon it, and such as are reasonably to be implied from those granted. In this respect, we differ radically from nations where all legislative power, without restriction or limitation, is vested in a parliament or other legislative body subject to no restriction except the discretion of its members." (Congress)
   > [U.S. v. William M. Butler, 297 U.S. 1 (1936)]

   > "The Government of the United States is one of delegated powers alone. Its authority is defined and limited by the Constitution. All powers not granted to it by that instrument are reserved to the States or the people."
   > [United States v. Cruikshank, 92 U.S. 542 (1875)]

   > "It is again to antagonize Chief Justice Marshall, when he said: 'The government of the Union, then (whatever may be the influence of this fact on the case), is emphatically and truly a government of the people. In form and in substance it emanates from them. Its powers are granted by them, and are to be exercised directly on them and for their benefit. This government is acknowledged by all to be one of enumerated powers.' 4 Wheat. 404, 4 L.Ed. 601."
   > [Downes v. Bidwell, 182 U.S. 244 (1901)]

   The implication is that the people AS INDIVIDUALS are EQUAL to the government in the eyes of the law because you can't delegate what you don't have:

   > "Derativa potestas non potest esse major primitiva.
   > The power which is derived cannot be greater than that from which it is derived."
   >
   > Nemo dat qui non habet. No one can give who does not possess. Jenk. Cent. 250.
   >
   > Nemo plus juris ad alienum transfere potest, quam ispe habent. One cannot transfer to another a right which he has not. Dig. 50, 17, 54; 10 Pet. 161, 175.
   >
   > Nemo potest facere per alium quod per se non potest. No one can do that by another which he cannot do by himself.
   >
   > Qui per alium facit per seipsum facere videtur. He who does anything through another, is considered as doing it himself. Co. Litt. 258.
   >
   > Quicpuid acquiritur servo, acquiritur domino. Whatever is acquired by the servant, is acquired for the master. 15 Bin. Ab. 327.
   >
   > Quod per me non possum, nec per alium. What I cannot do in person, I cannot do by proxy. 4 Co. 24.
   >
   > What a man cannot transfer, he cannot bind by articles.
   > [Bouvier's Maxims of Law, 1856;
   > SOURCE: http://famguardian.org/Publications/BouvierMaximsOfLaw/BouviersMaxims.htm]

3. Separation of powers between three branches of government. That separation is described in:
   > *Government Conspiracy to Destroy the Separation of Powers*, Form #05.023
   > https://sedm.org/Forms/FormIndex.htm

4. Distinct separation of property rights between PUBLIC and PRIVATE. By "public" we mean GOVERNMENT property. That separation is described in:

The Great IRS Hoax: Why We Don't Owe Income Tax, version 4.54
TOP SECRET: *For Official Treasury/IRS Use Only (FOUO)*   Copyright Family Guardian Fellowship   http://famguardian.org/

> *Separation Between Public and Private Course*, Form #12.025
> https://sedm.org/Forms/FormIndex.htm

Without ALL of the above, every government becomes corrupt and turns into a de facto government as described in:

> *De Facto Government Scam*, Form #05.043
> https://sedm.org/Forms/FormIndex.htm

The concept separation of powers is called the "Separation of Powers Doctrine":

> **"Separation of powers.** *The governments of the states and the United States are divided into three departments or branches: the legislative, which is empowered to make laws, the executive which is required to carry out the laws, and the judicial which is charged with interpreting the laws and adjudicating disputes under the laws. Under this constitutional doctrine of "separation of powers," one branch is not permitted to encroach on the domain or exercise the powers of another branch. See U.S. Constitution, Articles I-III. See also Power (Constitutional Powers)."*
> [Black's Law Dictionary, Sixth Edition, p. 1365]

Here is how no less than the U.S. Supreme Court described the purpose of this separation of powers:

> *"We start with first principles. The Constitution creates a Federal Government of enumerated powers. See U.S. Const., Art. I, 8. As James Madison wrote, "[t]he powers delegated by the proposed Constitution to the federal government are few and defined. Those which are to remain in the State governments are numerous and indefinite." The Federalist No. 45, pp. 292-293 (C. Rossiter ed. 1961).* **This constitutionally mandated division of authority "was adopted by the Framers to ensure protection of our fundamental liberties."** *Gregory v. Ashcroft,* **501 U.S. 452, 458 (1991) (internal quotation marks omitted). "Just as the separation and independence of the coordinate branches of the Federal Government serves to prevent the accumulation of excessive power in any one branch, a healthy balance of power between the States and the Federal Government will reduce the risk of tyranny and abuse from either front."** *Ibid.*
> [U.S. v. Lopez, 514 U.S. 549 (1995)]

The founding fathers believed that men were inherently corrupt. They believed that absolute power corrupts absolutely so they avoided concentrating too much power into any single individual.

> *"When all government, domestic and foreign, in little as in great things, shall be drawn to Washington as the center of all power, it will render powerless the checks provided of one government on another and will become as venal and oppressive as the government from which we separated."*
> [Thomas Jefferson to Charles Hammond, 1821. ME 15:332]

> *"Our government is now taking so steady a course as to show by what road it will pass to destruction; to wit: by consolidation first and then corruption, its necessary consequence. The engine of consolidation will be the Federal judiciary; the two other branches the corrupting and corrupted instruments."*
> [Thomas Jefferson to Nathaniel Macon, 1821. ME 15:341]

> *"The [federal] judiciary branch is the instrument which, working like gravity, without intermission, is to press us at last into one consolidated mass."*
> [Thomas Jefferson to Archibald Thweat, 1821. ME 15:307]

> *"There is no danger I apprehend so much as the consolidation of our government by the noiseless and therefore unalarming instrumentality of the Supreme Court."*
> [Thomas Jefferson to William Johnson, 1823. ME 15:421]

> *"I wish... to see maintained that wholesome distribution of powers established by the Constitution for the limitation of both [the State and General governments], and never to see all offices transferred to Washington where, further withdrawn from the eyes of the people, they may more secretly be bought and sold as at market."*
> [Thomas Jefferson to William Johnson, 1823. ME 15:450]

> *"What an augmentation of the field for jobbing, speculating, plundering, office-building and office-hunting would be produced by an assumption of all the State powers into the hands of the General Government!"*
> [Thomas Jefferson to Gideon Granger, 1800. ME 10:168]

> "I see,... and with the deepest affliction, the rapid strides with which the federal branch of our government is advancing towards the usurpation of all the rights reserved to the States, and the consolidation in itself of all powers, foreign and domestic; and that, too, by constructions which, if legitimate, leave no limits to their power... It is but too evident that the three ruling branches of [the Federal government] are in combination to strip their colleagues, the State authorities, of the powers reserved by them, and to exercise themselves all functions foreign and domestic."
> [Thomas Jefferson to William Branch Giles, 1825. ME 16:146]
>
> "We already see the [judiciary] power, installed for life, responsible to no authority (for impeachment is not even a scare-crow), advancing with a noiseless and steady pace to the great object of consolidation. The foundations are already deeply laid by their decisions for the annihilation of constitutional State rights and the removal of every check, every counterpoise to the engulfing power of which themselves are to make a sovereign part."
> [Thomas Jefferson to William T. Barry, 1822. ME 15:388]

For further quotes supporting the above, see:

> *Thomas Jefferson on Politics and Government*
> http://famguardian.org/Subjects/Politics/ThomasJefferson/jeff1060.htm

They instead wanted an egalitarian and utopian society. They loathed the idea of a king because they had seen how corrupt the monarchies of Europe had become by reading the history books. They loathed it so much that they specifically prohibited titles of nobility in Article 1, Section 9, Clause 8:

> *U.S. Constitution; Article 1, Section 9, Clause 8*
>
> *No Title of Nobility shall be granted by the United States: And no Person holding any Office of Profit or Trust under them, shall, without the Consent of the Congress, accept of any present, Emolument, Office, or Title, of any kind whatever, from any King, Prince or foreign State.*

So the founders instead distributed and dispersed political power into several independent branches of government that have sovereign power over a finite sphere and prohibited the branches from assuming each other's duties. This, they believed, would prevent collusion against their rights and liberties. They therefore divided the government into the Executive, Legislative, and Judicial branches and made them independent of each other, and assigned very specific duties to each. In effect, these three branches became "foreign" to each other and in constant competition with each other for power and control.

The founders further dispersed political power by dividing power between the several states and the federal government and gave most of the power to the states. They gave each state their own seats in Congress, in the Senate. They made the states just like "foreign countries" and independent nations so that there would be the greatest separation of powers possible between the federal government and the states:

> "***The States between each other are sovereign and independent***. *They are distinct and separate sovereignties, except so far as they have parted with some of the attributes of sovereignty by the Constitution.* **They continue to be nations, with all their rights, and under all their national obligations, and with all the rights of nations in every particular**; *except in the surrender by each to the common purposes and objects of the Union, under the Constitution. The rights of each State, when not so yielded up, remain absolute.*"
> [Bank of Augusta v. Earle, 38 U.S. (13 Pet.) 519, 10 L.Ed. 274 (1839)]

Then the founders created multiple states so that the states would be in competition with each other for citizens and for commerce. When one state got too oppressive or taxed people too much, the people could then move to an economically more attractive state and climate. This kept the states from oppressing their citizens and it gave the people a means to keep their state and their government in check. Then they put the federal government in charge of regulating commerce among and between the states, and the intention of this was to *maximize*, not obstruct, commerce between the states so that we would act as a unified economic union and like a country. Even so, they didn't want our country to be a "nation" under the law of nations, because they didn't want a national government with unlimited powers. They wanted a "federation", so they called our central government the "federal government" instead of a "national government". To give us a "national government" would be a recipe for tyranny:

> ***"By that law the several States and Governments spread over our globe, are considered as forming a society, not a NATION.***
> *It has only been by a very few comprehensive minds, such as those of Elizabeth and the Fourth Henry, that this last great idea has been even contemplated. 3rdly. and chiefly, I shall examine the important question before us, by the Constitution of the United States, and the legitimate result of that valuable instrument. "*
> [Chisholm v. Georgia, 2 Dall. (U.S.) 419, 1 L.Ed. 440 (1793)]

The ingenious founders also made the people the sovereigns in charge of both the state and federal governments by giving them a Bill of Rights and mandating frequent elections. Frequent elections:

1. Ensured that rulers would not be in office long enough to learn enough to get sneaky with the people or abuse their power.
2. Kept the rulers accountable to the people and provided a prompt feedback mechanism to make sure politicians and rulers were incentivized to listen to the people.
3. Created a stable political system that would automatically converge onto the will of the majority so that the country would be at peace instead of at war within itself.

The founders even gave the people their own house in Congress called the House of Representatives, so that the power between the states, in the Senate, and the People, in the House, would be well-balanced. They also made sure that these sovereign electors and citizens were well armed with a good education, so they could keep their government in check and capably defend their freedom, property, and liberty by themselves. When things got rough and governments became corrupt, these rugged and self-sufficient citizens were also guaranteed the right to defend their property using arms that the U.S. Constitution said in the Second Amendment that they had a right to keep and use. This ensured that citizens wouldn't need to depend on the government for a handout or socialist benefits and wouldn't have to worry about having a government that would plunder their property or their liberty.

Finally, the founding fathers created the institution of trial by jury, so that if government got totally corrupt and passed unjust laws that violated God's laws, the people could put themselves back in control through jury nullification. This also effectively dealt with the problem of corrupt judges, because both the jury and the grand jury could override the judge as well when they detected a conflict of interest by judging both the facts *and* the law. Here is how Thomas Jefferson described the duty of the jury in such a circumstance:

> *"It is left... to the juries, if they think the permanent judges are under any bias whatever in any cause, to take on themselves to judge the law as well as the fact. They never exercise this power but when they suspect partiality in the judges; and by the exercise of this power they have been the firmest bulwarks of English liberty."*
> [Thomas Jefferson to Abbe Arnoux, 1789. ME 7:423, Papers 15:283]

Then the founders separated church and state and put the state and the church in competition with each other to protect and nurture the people. We talked about this church/state separation and dual sovereignty earlier in section 4.3.6.

The design that our founding fathers had for our political system was elegant, unique, unprecedented, ingenious, perfectly balanced, and inherently just. It was founded on the concept of Natural Order and Natural Law, which as we explained in section 4.1 are based on the sequence that things were created. This concept made sense, even to people who didn't believe in God, so it had wide support among a very diverse country of immigrants from all over the world and of many different religious faiths. Natural Law and Natural Order unified our country because it was just and fair and righteous. That is the basis for the phrase on our currency, which says:

> *"E Pluribus Unum"*

...which means: *"From many, one."* Our system of Natural Law and Natural Order also happened to be based on God's sovereign design for ***self*-government**, as we explained throughout chapter 4. The founders also recognized that liberty without God and morality are impossible:

> *"We have no government armed with the power capable of contending with human passions unbridled by morality and religion. Avarice [greed], ambition, revenge, or gallantry [debauchery], would break the strongest cords of our Constitution as a whale goes through a net. **Our Constitution was made only for a moral and religious people. It is wholly inadequate to the government of any other.**"*
> [John Adams, 2nd President.]

So the founders included the requirement for BOTH God and Liberty on all of our currency. They put the phrase "*In God We Trust*" and the phrase "Liberty" side by side, and they were probably thinking of the following scripture when they did that!:

> "Now the Lord is the Spirit; and where the Spirit of the Lord is, there is liberty."
> [2 Cor. 3:17, Bible, NKJV]

By creating such distinct separation of powers among all the forces of government, the founders ensured that the only way anything would get done within government was exclusively by informed consent and *not* by force or terror. The Declaration of Independence identifies the source of ALL "just" government power as "consent". Anything not consensual is therefore unjust and tyrannical. An informed and sovereign People will only do things voluntarily and consensually when it is in their absolute best interests. This would ensure that government would never engage in anything that wasn't in the best interests of everyone as a whole, because people, at least theoretically, would never consent to anything that would either hurt them or injure their Constitutional rights. The Supreme Court described this kind of government by consent as "government by compact":

> "In Europe, the executive is synonymous with the sovereign power of a state...where it is too commonly acquired by force or fraud, or both...In America, however the case is widely different. **Our government is founded upon compact [consent expressed in a written contract called a Constitution or in positive law]. Sovereignty was, and is, in the people.**"
> [The Betsy, 3 (U.S.) Dall 6]

Here is the legal definition of "compact" to prove our point that the Constitution and all federal law written in furtherance of it are indeed a "compact":

> "**Compact**, n. An agreement or contract between persons, nations, or states. Commonly applied to working agreements between and among states concerning matters of mutual concern. A contract between parties, which creates obligations and rights capable of being enforced and contemplated as such between the parties, in their distinct and independent characters. A mutual consent of parties concerned respecting some property or right that is the object of the stipulation, or something that is to be done or forborne. See also Compact clause; Confederacy; Interstate compact; Treaty."
> [Black's Law Dictionary, Sixth Edition, p. 281]

Enacting a mutual agreement into positive law then, becomes the vehicle for expressing the fact that the People collectively agreed and consented to the law and to accept any adverse impact that law might have on their liberty. Public servants then, are just the apparatus that the sovereign People use for governing themselves through the operation of positive law. As the definition above shows, the apparatus and machinery of government is simply the "rudder" that steers the ship, but the "Captain" of the ship is the People *both* individually and collectively. In a true Republican Form of Government, the REAL government is the people individually and collectively, and not their "public servants". That is the true meaning of the phrase "a government of the people, by the people, and for the people" used by Abraham Lincoln in the Gettysburg Address.

Our de jure Constitutional Republic started out as a perfectly balanced and just system indeed. But somewhere along the way, it was deliberately corrupted by evil men for personal gain. Just like Cain (in the Bible) destroyed the tranquility and peace of an idyllic world and divided the family of Adam by first introducing murder into the world, greedy politicians who wanted to line their pockets corrupted our wonderful system and brought evil into our government. How did it happen? They did it with a combination of force, fraud, and the corrupting influence of money. This process can be shown graphically and described in scientific terms over a period of years to show *precisely* how it was done. We will now attempt to do this so that the process is crystal clear in your mind. What we are trying to show are the following elements in our diagram:

1. The distinct sovereignties *between* governments:
    1.1. States
    1.2. The federal government
2. The sovereignties *within* governments:
    2.1. Executive branch
    2.2. Legislative branch
    2.3. Judicial branch
3. The hierarchy of sovereignty between all the sovereignties based on their sequence of creation.
4. The corrupting influence of force, fraud, and money, including the branch that initiated it, the date it was initiated, and the object it was initiated against.

To meet the above objectives, we will start off with the diagram found in section **Error! Reference source not found.** and expand it with some of the added elements found in the Natural Order diagram found earlier in section 4.1. To the bottom of the diagram, we add the Ten Commandments, which establishes the "Separation of Church v. State". The first four commandments in Exodus 20:2-11 establish the church and the last six commandments found in Exodus 20:12-17 define how we should relate to other people, who Jesus later called our "neighbor" in Matt. 22:39. The main and only purpose of government is to love and protect and serve its inhabitants and citizens, who collectively are "neighbors". What results is a schematic diagram of the initial political system that the founders gave us absent all corruption. This is called the "De jure U.S. Government". It is the only lawful government we have and its organization is defined by our Constitution. It's organization is also defined by the Bible, which we also call "Natural Law" throughout this document.

Figure 6-1: Natural Order Diagram of Republican Form of Government

Chapter 6: History of Government Income Tax Fraud, Racketeering and Extortion in the U.S.A. 6-24

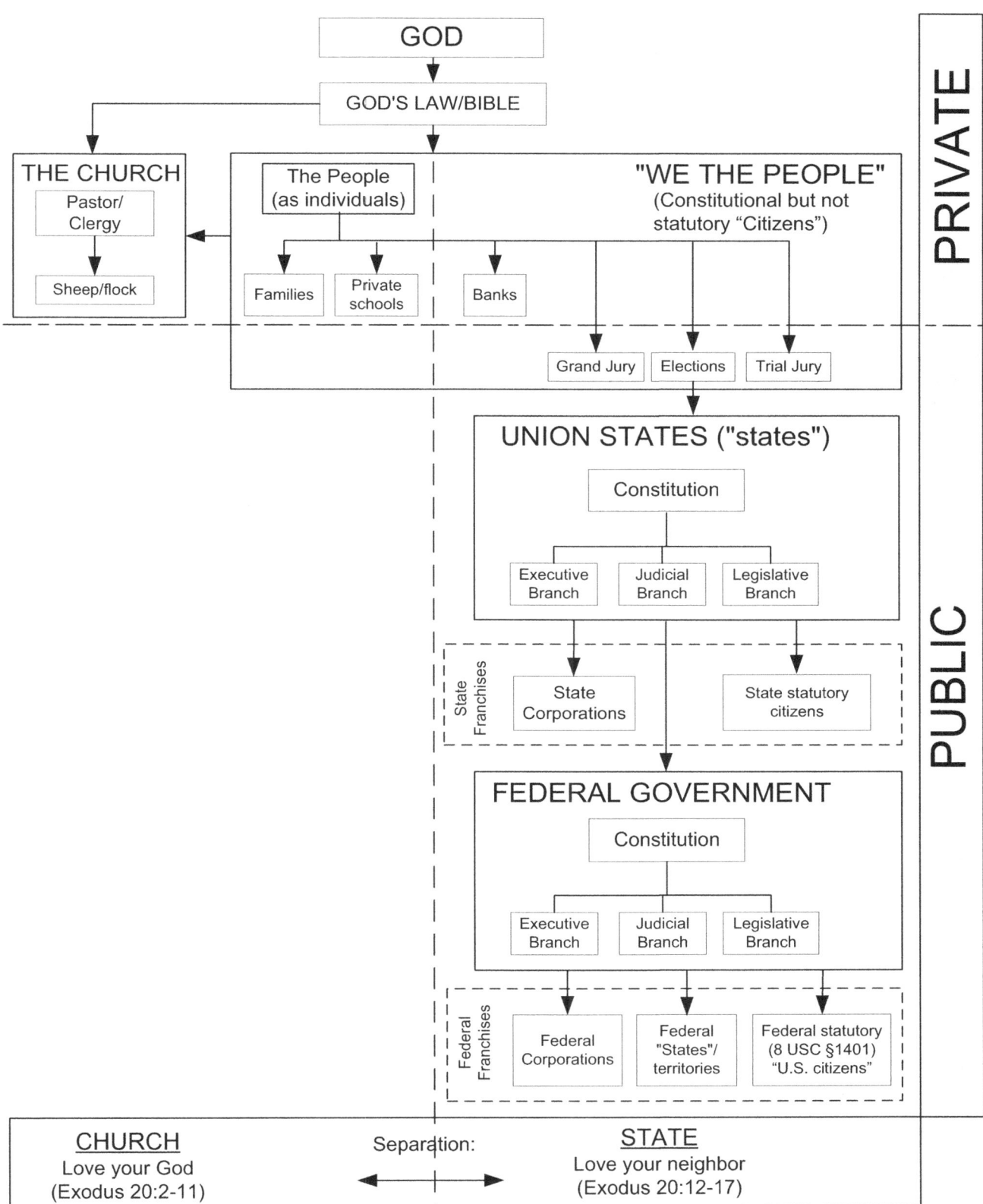

Each box in the above diagram represents a sovereignty or sovereign entity that helps distribute power throughout our system of government to prevent corruption or tyranny. The arrows with dark ends indicate an act of creation by the sovereign above. That act of creation carries with it an implied delegation of authority to do specific tasks and establishes a fiduciary relationship between the Creator, and his subordinate creation. The above system as shown functions properly and fully and provides the best defense for our liberties *only* when there is *complete* separation between each sovereignty, which is to say that *all actions* performed and *all choices* made by any one sovereign:

1. Are completely free of fraud, force, conflict of interest, or duress.
2. Are accomplished *completely voluntarily*, which is to say that they are done for the mutual benefit of *all* parties involved rather than any one single party exercising undue influence.
3. Involve *fully informed* consent made with a *full awareness* by all parties to the agreement of all rights which are being surrendered to procure any imputed benefits.
4. Are done mainly or exclusively for the benefit of the Sovereign above the agent who is the actor.
5. Are done for *righteous reasons* and noble intent, meaning that they are accomplished for the benefit of *someone else* rather than one's own personal or financial benefit. This requirement is the foundation of what a fiduciary relationship means and also the *only* way that conflicts of interest and the corruption they can cause can be eliminated.

6.3.2 Main Technique of Corruption: Introduce Franchises to replace UNALIENABLE PRIVATE Rights with REVOCABLE PUBLIC Statutory PRIVILEGES

> *"The rich ruleth over the poor, and the borrower [is] servant to the lender."*
> *[Prov. 22:7, Bible, NKJV]*

The secret to how scoundrels corrupt our republic based on inalienable rights and replace it with a democracy based on revocable statutory privileges is to offer to loan you government property with conditions or legal strings attached. That process is called a "franchise". The Bible and the U.S. Supreme Court both describe EXACTLY, from a legal perspective, WHEN AND HOW you personally facilitate this inversion of the de jure hierarchy in the previous section to make public servants into masters and make you the sovereign into a government employee or officer. It is done with loans of government property that have legal strings attached. This loan is what we call "government franchises" (Form #05.030) on our website. The word "privilege" in fact is synonymous with loans of absolutely owned GOVERNMENT property and the legal strings attached to the loan.

> *"The rich rules over the poor,*
> *And the borrower is servant to the lender."*
> *[Prov. 22:7, Bible, NKJV]*

> *"The State in such cases exercises no greater right than an individual may exercise over the use of his own property when leased or loaned to others. The conditions upon which the privilege shall be enjoyed being stated or implied in the legislation authorizing its grant, no right is, of course, impaired by their enforcement. The recipient of the privilege, in effect, stipulates to comply with the conditions. It matters not how limited the privilege conferred, its acceptance implies an assent to the regulation of its use and the compensation for it."*
> *[Munn v. Illinois, 94 U.S. 113 (1876)]*

Curses of Disobedience [to God's Laws]

> *"The alien [Washington, D.C. is legislatively "alien" in relation to states of the Union] who is among you shall rise higher and higher above you, and you shall come down lower and lower [malicious destruction of EQUAL PROTECTION and EQUAL TREATMENT by abusing FRANCHISES]. He shall lend to you [Federal Reserve counterfeiting franchise], but you shall not lend to him; he shall be the head, and you shall be the tail.*

> *"Moreover all these curses shall come upon you and pursue and overtake you, until you are destroyed, because you did not obey the voice of the Lord your God, to keep His commandments and His statutes which He commanded you. And they shall be upon you for a sign and a wonder, and on your descendants forever.*

> *"Because you did not serve [ONLY] the Lord your God with joy and gladness of heart, for the abundance of everything, therefore you shall serve your [covetous thieving lawyer] enemies, whom the Lord will send against you, in hunger, in thirst, in nakedness, and in need of everything; and He will put a yoke of iron [franchise codes] on your neck until He has destroyed you. The Lord will bring a nation against you from afar [the District of CRIMINALS], from the end of the earth, as swift as the eagle flies [the American Eagle], a nation whose language [LEGALESE] you will not understand, a nation of fierce [coercive and fascist] countenance, which does not respect the elderly [assassinates them by denying them healthcare through bureaucratic delays on an Obamacare waiting list] nor show favor to the young [destroying their ability to learn in the public FOOL system]. And they*

> *shall eat the increase of your livestock and the produce of your land [with "trade or business" franchise taxes], until you [and all your property] are destroyed [or STOLEN/CONFISCATED]; they shall not leave you grain or new wine or oil, or the increase of your cattle or the offspring of your flocks, until they have destroyed you.*
> *[Deut. 28:43-51, Bible, NKJV]*

The problem with all such loans is that the covetous de facto (Form #05.043) government offering them can theoretically attach ANY condition they want to the loan. If the property is something that is life threatening to do without, then they can destroy ALL of your constitutional rights and leave you with no judicial or legal remedy whatsoever for the loss of your fundamental or natural PRIVATE rights and otherwise PRIVATE property! This, in fact, is EXACTLY what Pharaoh did to the Israelites during the famine in Egypt, described in Genesis 47.

> *"But when Congress creates a statutory right [a "privilege" or "public right" in this case, such as a "trade or business"], it clearly has the discretion, in defining that right, to create presumptions, or assign burdens of proof, or prescribe remedies; it may also provide that persons seeking to vindicate that right must do so before particularized tribunals created to perform the specialized adjudicative tasks related to that right. FN35 Such provisions do, in a sense, affect the exercise of judicial power, but they are also incidental to Congress' power to define the right that it has created. No comparable justification exists, however, when the right being adjudicated is not of congressional creation. In such a situation, substantial inroads into functions that have traditionally been performed by the Judiciary cannot be characterized merely as incidental extensions of Congress' power to define rights that it has created. Rather, such inroads suggest unwarranted encroachments upon the judicial power of the United States, which our Constitution reserves for Art. III courts."*
> *[Northern Pipeline Const. Co. v. Marathon Pipe Line Co., 458 U.S. 50, 102 S.Ct. 2858 (1983)]*

> *The Court developed, for its own governance in the cases confessedly within its jurisdiction, a series of rules under which it has avoided passing upon a large part of all the constitutional questions pressed upon it for decision. They are:*
>
> *[. . .]*
>
> *6. **The Court will not pass upon the constitutionality of a statute at the instance of one who has availed himself of its benefits.** FN7 Great Falls Mfg. Co. v. Attorney General, 124 U.S. 581, 8 S.Ct. 631, 31 L.Ed. 527; Wall v. Parrot Silver & Copper Co., 244 U.S. 407, 411, 412, 37 S.Ct. 609, 61 L.Ed. 1229; St. Louis Malleable Casting Co. v. Prendergast Construction Co., 260 U.S. 469, 43 S.Ct. 178, 67 L.Ed. 351.*
>
> *FN7 Compare Electric Co. v. Dow, 166 U.S. 489, 17 S.Ct. 645, 41 L.Ed. 1088; Pierce v. Somerset Ry., 171 U.S. 641, 648, 19 S.Ct. 64, 43 L.Ed. 316; Leonard v. Vicksburg, etc., R. Co., 198 U.S. 416, 422, 25 S.Ct. 750, 49 L.Ed. 1108.*
> *[Ashwander v. Tennessee Valley Authority, 297 U.S. 288, 56 S.Ct. 466 (1936)]*

> *"The words "privileges" and "immunities," like the greater part of the legal phraseology of this country, have been carried over from the law of Great Britain, and recur constantly either as such or in equivalent expressions from the time of Magna Charta. For all practical purposes they are synonymous in meaning, and originally signified a peculiar right or private law conceded to particular persons or places **whereby a certain individual or class of individuals was exempted from the rigor of the common law**. Privilege or immunity is conferred upon any person when he is invested with a legal claim to the exercise of special or peculiar rights, authorizing him to enjoy some particular advantage or exemption."*
> *[The Privileges and Immunities of State Citizenship, Roger Howell, PhD, 1918, pp. 9-10;*
> *SOURCE:*
> *http://famguardian.org/Publications/ThePrivAndImmOfStateCit/The_privileges_and_immunities_of_state_c.pdf]*
>
> *See Magill v. Browne, Fed.Cas. No. 8952, 16 Fed.Cas. 408; 6 Words and Phrases, 5583, 5584; A J. Lien, "Privileges and Immunities of Citizens of the United States," in Columbia University Studies in History, Economics, and Public Law, vol. 54, p. 31.*

Whether you know it or not, by accepting such physical or intangible property you are, in effect, manifesting your implied consent (assent) under the Uniform Commercial Code (U.C.C.) to enter into a contract with the government that offered it in the process. Lawyers commonly call this type of interaction a "quid pro quo". That contract represents a constructive waiver of the sovereignty and sovereign immunity that comes from God Himself. Because the government is asking you to GIVE PRIVATE/CONSTITUTIONAL rights in relation to them as consideration that would otherwise be INALIENABLE (Form #12.038), they are acting in a private, non-governmental capacity as a de facto government (Form #05.043) with no real official, judicial, or sovereign immunity. That franchise contract (Form #12.012) will, almost inevitably, end up being an adhesion contract that will be extremely one-sided and will not only NOT "benefit" you (the "Buyer") in the aggregate, but will work an extreme injury, inequality, and injustice (Form #05.050) that God actually forbids:

> **Lending to the Poor**
>
> *If one of your brethren becomes poor [desperate], and falls into poverty among you, then you shall help him, like a stranger or a sojourner [transient foreigner and/or non-resident non-person, Form #05.020], that he may live with you. Take no usury or interest from him; but fear your God, that your brother may live with you. You shall not lend him your money for usury, nor lend him your food at a profit. I am the Lord your God, who brought you out of the land of Egypt, to give you the land of Canaan and to be your God.*
>
> **The Law Concerning Slavery**
>
> *And if one of your brethren who dwells by you becomes poor, and sells himself to you, you shall not compel him to serve as a slave. As a hired servant and a sojourner he shall be with you, and shall serve you until the Year of Jubilee. And then he shall depart from you—he and his children with him—and shall return to his own family. He shall return to the possession of his fathers. **For they are My servants [Form #13.007], whom I brought out of the land of Egypt; they shall not be sold as slaves.** You shall not rule over him with rigor, but you shall fear your God."*
> [Lev. 25:35-43, Bible, NKJV]

> *Adhesion Contract*
>
> *Also found in:* Dictionary, Thesaurus, Financial, Wikipedia.
>
> *Related to Adhesion Contract:* unilateral contract, exculpatory clause, personal contract, Unconscionable contract
>
> *Adhesion Contract*
>
> A type of contract, a legally binding agreement between two parties to do a certain thing, in which one side has all the bargaining power and uses it to write the contract primarily to his or her advantage.
>
> *An example of an adhesion contract is a standardized contract form that offers goods or services to consumers on essentially a "take it or leave it" basis without giving consumers realistic opportunities to negotiate terms that would benefit their interests. When this occurs, the consumer cannot obtain the desired product or service unless he or she acquiesces to the form contract.*
>
> *There is nothing unenforceable or even wrong about adhesion contracts. In fact, most businesses would never conclude their volume of transactions if it were necessary to negotiate all the terms of every Consumer Credit contract. Insurance contracts and residential leases are other kinds of adhesion contracts. This does not mean, however, that all adhesion contracts are valid. Many adhesion contracts are Unconscionable; they are so unfair to the weaker party that a court will refuse to enforce them. An example would be severe penalty provisions for failure to pay loan installments promptly that are physically hidden by small print located in the middle of an obscure paragraph of a lengthy loan agreement. In such a case a court can find that there is no meeting of the minds of the parties to the contract and that the weaker party has not accepted the terms of the contract.*
>
> *West's Encyclopedia of American Law, edition 2. Copyright 2008 The Gale Group, Inc. All rights reserved.*
>
> *adhesion contract (contract of adhesion)*
>
> *n. a contract (often a signed form) so imbalanced in favor of one party over the other that there is a strong implication it was not freely bargained. Example: a rich landlord dealing with a poor tenant who has no choice and must accept all terms of a lease, no matter how restrictive or burdensome, since the tenant cannot afford to move. An adhesion contract can give the little guy the opportunity to claim in court that the contract with the big shot is invalid. This doctrine should be used and applied more often, but the same big guy-little guy inequity may apply in the ability to afford a trial or find and pay a resourceful lawyer. (See:* contract*)*
>
> *Copyright © 1981-2005 by Gerald N. Hill and Kathleen T. Hill. All Right reserved.*
> *[The Free Dictionary by Farlex: Adhesion Contract; Downloaded 10/9/2019; SOURCE:* https://legal-dictionary.thefreedictionary.com/Adhesion+Contract*]*

The temptation of the offer of the government franchise as an adhesion contract is exhaustively described, personified, and even dramatized in the following:

1. The Temptation of Jesus by Satan on the Mountain in Matthew 4:1-11.
   https://www.biblegateway.com/passage/?search=Matthew+4&version=NKJV
2. *Devil's Advocate: Lawyers-What We are Up Against*, SEDM (OFFSITE LINK)
   https://sedm.org/what-we-are-up-against/
3. *Philosophical Implications of the Temptation of Jesus*, Stefan Molyneux
   https://sedm.org/philosophical-implications-of-the-temptation-of-jesus/
4. *Social Security: Mark of the Beast*, Form #11.407
   http://famguardian.org/Publications/SocialSecurity/TOC.htm

James Madison, whose notes were used to draft the Bill of Rights, predicted this perversion of the de jure Constitutional design, when he very insightfully said the following:

> *"With respect to the words general welfare, I have always regarded them as qualified by the detail of powers connected with them. To take them in a literal and unlimited sense would be a metamorphosis of the Constitution into a character which there is a host of proofs was not contemplated by its creator."*

> *"If Congress can employ money indefinitely to the general welfare, and are the sole and supreme judges of the general welfare, they may take the care of religion into their own hands; they may appoint teachers in every State, county and parish and pay them out of their public treasury; they may take into their own hands the education of children, establishing in like manner schools throughout the Union; they may assume the provision of the poor; they may undertake the regulation of all roads other than post-roads; in short, every thing, from the highest object of state legislation down to the most minute object of police, would be thrown under the power of Congress.... Were the power of Congress to be established in the latitude contended for, it would subvert the very foundations, and transmute the very nature of the limited Government established by the people of America."*

> *"If Congress can do whatever in their discretion can be done by money, and will promote the general welfare, the government is no longer a limited one possessing enumerated powers, but an indefinite one subject to particular exceptions."*
> [James Madison. House of Representatives, February 7, 1792, On the Cod Fishery Bill, granting Bounties]

The term "general welfare" is synonymous with "benefit" in franchise language. "general welfare" as used above is, in fact, the basis for the entire modern welfare state that will eventually lead to a massive financial collapse and crisis worldwide.[6]. Anyone who therefore supports such a system is ultimately an anarchist intent on destroying our present dysfunctional government and thereby committing the crime of Treason:[7]

> *Socialism: The New American Civil Religion*, Form #05.016
> https://sedm.org/Forms/05-MemLaw/SocialismCivilReligion.pdf

The Bible also describes how to REVERSE this inversion, how to restore our constitutional rights, and how to put public servants back in their role as servants rather than masters. Note that accepting custody or "benefit" or loans of government property in effect behaves as an act of contracting, because it accomplishes the same effect, which is to create implied "obligations" in a legal sense:

---

[6] For details on the devastating political effects of the modern welfare state, see:

> *Communism, Socialism, Collectivism Page*, Section 10: Welfare State, Family Guardian Fellowship,
> https://famguardian.org/Subjects/Communism/Communism.htm#Welfare_State

[7] In the landmark case of Steward Machine Co. v. Davis, 310 U.S. 548 (1937) legalizing social security, the U.S. Supreme Court had the following to say about the treason of inverting the relationship of the states to the federal government:

> *"If the time shall ever arrive when, for an object appealing, however strongly, to our sympathies, the dignity of the States shall bow to the dictation of Congress by conforming their legislation thereto, when the power and majesty and honor of those who created shall become subordinate to the thing of their creation, I but feebly utter my apprehensions when **I express my firm conviction that we shall see `the beginning of the end.'**"*
> [Steward Machine Co. v. Davis, 310 U.S. 548, 606 (1937)]

> *"For the Lord your God will bless you just as He promised you; **you shall lend to many nations, but you shall not borrow**; you shall reign over many nations, but they shall not reign over you."*
> *[Deut. 15:6, Bible, NKJV]*

> *"The Lord will open to you His good treasure, the heavens, to give the rain to your land in its season, and to bless all the work of your hand.* ***You shall lend to many nations, but you shall not borrow.***
> *[Deut. 28:12, Bible, NKJV]*

> ***"You shall** make no covenant [contract or franchise] with them **[foreigners, pagans], nor with their [pagan government] gods [laws or judges]**. They shall not dwell in your land [and you shall not dwell in theirs by becoming a "resident" or domiciliary in the process of contracting with them], lest they make you sin against Me [God]. For if you serve their [government] gods [under contract or agreement or franchise], it will surely be a snare to you."*
> *[Exodus 23:32-33, Bible, NKJV]*

> *"I [God] brought you up from Egypt [slavery] and brought you to the land of which I swore to your fathers; and I said, 'I will never break My covenant with you. And **you shall make no covenant [contract or franchise or agreement of ANY kind] with the inhabitants of this [corrupt pagan] land; you shall tear down their [man/government worshipping socialist] altars.**' But you have not obeyed Me. Why have you done this?*
>
> *"Therefore I also said, '**I will not drive them out before you; but they will become as thorns [terrorists and persecutors] in your side and their gods will be a snare [slavery!] to you.**'"*
>
> *So it was, when the Angel of the LORD spoke these words to all the children of Israel, that the people lifted up their voices and wept.*
> *[Judges 2:1-4, Bible, NKJV]*

Following the above commandments requires not signing up for and quitting any and all government benefits and services you may have consensually signed up for or retained eligibility for. All such applications and/or eligibility is called "special law" in the legal field.

> *"**special law.** One relating to particular persons or things; one made for individual cases or for particular places or districts; one operating upon a selected class, rather than upon the public generally. A private law. A law is "special" when it is different from others of the same general kind or designed for a particular purpose, or limited in range or confined to a prescribed field of action or operation. A "special law" relates to either particular persons, places, or things or to persons, places, or things which, though not particularized, are separated by any method of selection from the whole class to which the law might, but not such legislation, be applied. Utah Farm Bureau Ins. Co. v. Utah Ins. Guaranty Ass'n, Utah, 564 P.2d. 751, 754. A special law applies only to an individual or a number of individuals out of a single class similarly situated and affected, or to a special locality. Board of County Com'rs of Lemhi County v. Swensen, Idaho, 80 Idaho 198, 327 P.2d. 361, 362. See also Private bill; Private law. Compare General law; Public law."*
> *[Black's Law Dictionary, Sixth Edition, pp. 1397-1398]*

We also prove that all such "special law" is not "law" in a classical sense, but rather an act of contracting, because it does not apply equally to all. It is what the U.S. Supreme Court referred to as "class legislation" in Pollock v. Farmers Loan and Trust in which they declared the first income tax unconstitutional:

> *"**The income tax law under consideration is marked by discriminating features which affect the whole law. It discriminates between those who receive an income of four thousand dollars and those who do not. It thus vitiates, in my judgment, by this arbitrary discrimination, the whole legislation.** Hamilton says in one of his papers, (the Continentalist,) "the genius of liberty reprobates everything arbitrary or discretionary in taxation. It exacts that every man, by a definite and general rule, should know what proportion of his property the State demands; whatever liberty we may boast of in theory, it cannot exist in fact while [arbitrary] assessments continue." 1 Hamilton's Works, ed. 1885, 270. The legislation, in the discrimination it makes, is class legislation. **Whenever a distinction is made in the burdens a law imposes or in the benefits it confers on any citizens by reason of their birth, or wealth, or religion, it is class legislation, and leads inevitably to oppression and abuses, and to general unrest and disturbance in society [e.g. wars, political conflict, violence, anarchy].** It was hoped and believed that the great amendments to the Constitution which followed the late civil war had rendered such legislation impossible for all future time. But the objectionable legislation reappears in the act under consideration. It is the same in essential character as that of the English income statute of 1691, which taxed Protestants at a certain rate, Catholics, as a class, at double the rate of Protestants, and Jews at another and separate rate. Under wise and constitutional legislation every citizen should contribute his proportion, however small the sum, to the support of the government, and it is no kindness to urge any of our citizens to escape from*

> *that obligation. If he contributes the smallest mite of his earnings to that purpose he will have a greater regard for the government and more self-respect 597*597 for himself feeling that though he is poor in fact, he is not a pauper of his government. And it is to be hoped that, whatever woes and embarrassments may betide our people, they may never lose their manliness and self-respect. Those qualities preserved, they will ultimately triumph over all reverses of fortune."*
> [Pollock v. Farmers' Loan & Trust Co., 157 U.S. 429 (Supreme Court 1895)]

To realistically apply the above biblical prohibitions against contracting with any government so as to eliminate the reversal of roles and destroy the dulocracy, see:

Path to Freedom, Form #09.015
https://sedm.org/Forms/09-Procs/PathToFreedom.pdf

Section 5 of the above document in particular deals with how to eliminate the dulocracy. Section 5.6 also discusses the above mechanisms.

The idea of a present day dulocracy is entirely consistent with the theme of our website, which is the abuse of government franchises and privileges to destroy PRIVATE rights, STEAL private property, promote unhappiness, and inject malice and vitriol into the political process, as documented in:

Government Instituted Slavery Using Franchises, Form #05.030
FORMS PAGE: https://sedm.org/Forms/FormIndex.htm
DIRECT LINK: https://sedm.org/Forms/05-MemLaw/Franchises.pdf

The U.S. Supreme Court and the Bible both predicted these negative and unintended consequences of the abuse of government franchises, when they said:

> *"Here I close my opinion. I could not say less in view of questions of such gravity that they go down to the **very foundations of the government**. If the provisions of the Constitution can be set aside by an act of Congress, where is the course of usurpation to end?*
>
> *The present **assault upon capital** [THEFT! and WEALTH TRANSFER by unconstitutional CONVERSION of PRIVATE property to PUBLIC property] is but the beginning. **It will be but the stepping stone to others larger and more sweeping**, until our political contest will become war of the poor against the rich; a war of growing intensity and bitterness."*
> [Pollock v. Farmers' Loan & Trust Co., 157 U.S. 429, 158 U.S. 601 (1895), hearing the case against the first income tax passed by Congress that included people in states of the Union. They declared that first income tax UNCONSTITUTIONAL, by the way]

> *"Where do wars and fights come from among you? **Do they not come from your desires for pleasure [unearned money or "benefits", privileges, or franchises, from the government] that war in your members [and your democratic governments]**? You lust [after other people's money] and do not have. You murder [the unborn to increase your standard of living] and covet [the unearned] and cannot obtain [except by empowering your government to STEAL for you!]. You fight and war [against the rich and the nontaxpayers to subsidize your idleness]. Yet you do not have because you do not ask [the Lord, but instead ask the deceitful government]. You ask and do not receive, because you ask amiss, that you may spend it on your pleasures. **Adulterers and adulteresses! Do you not know that friendship [statutory "citizenship"] with the world [or the governments of the world] is enmity with God?** Whoever therefore wants to be a friend [STATUTORY "citizen", "resident", "inhabitant", "person" franchisee] of the world [or the governments of the world] makes himself an enemy of God."*
> [James 4:4, Bible, NKJV]

The "foundations of the government" spoken of above are PRIVATE property, separation between public and private, and equality of treatment and opportunity, which collectively are called "legal justice", as we point out on our opening page:

> *Our ministry accomplishes the above goals by emphasizing:*
>
> *12. The pursuit of legal "justice" (Form #05.050), which means absolutely owned private property (Form #10.002), and equality of TREATMENT and OPPORTUNITY (Form #05.033) under REAL LAW (Form #05.048). The following would be INJUSTICE, not JUSTICE:*

12.1 Outlawing or refusing to recognize or enforce absolutely owned private property (Form #12.025).

12.2 Imposing equality of OUTCOME by law, such as by abusing taxing powers to redistribute wealth. See Form #11.302.

12.3 Any attempt by government to use judicial process or administrative enforcement to enforce any civil obligation derived from any source OTHER than express written consent or to an injury against the equal rights of others demonstrated with court admissible evidence. See Form #09.073 and Form #12.040.

12.4 Offering, implementing, or enforcing any civil franchise (Form #05.030). This enforces superior powers on the part of the government as a form of inequality and results in religious idolatry. This includes making justice into a civil public privilege (Form #05.050, Section 13) or turning CONSTITUTIONAL PRIVATE citizens into STATUTORY PUBLIC citizens engaged in a public office and a franchise (Form #05.006).

Not only would the above be INJUSTICE, it would outlaw HAPPINESS, because the right to absolutely own private property is equated with "the pursuit of happiness" in the Declaration of Independence, according to the U.S. Supreme Court. See Form #05.050 for the definition of "justice". Click here to view a video on why all franchises produce selfishness, unhappiness, inequality, and ingratitude.
[SEDM Website Opening Page; SOURCE: http://sedm.org]

Too many public servants have assumed absolute authority over the people they are supposed to serve. This REVERSAL of roles and making the SERVANTS into the MASTERS was never the intent of the Founding Fathers who established the American governments as republics where the rights of the people are to be paramount and the sovereignty of the governments are limited by the rights of the people. Sovereignty in America is not based on the same premise as sovereignty in Europe. Sovereignty in Europe was based on the notion of the Divine Right of Kings where the king's sovereignty was absolute and the people were his subjects. Sovereignty in America is based on the notion that citizens are endowed by the Creator with unalienable rights and then lend their permission to the governments to carry out certain, limited responsibilities on their behalf. In a republican form of government, the government is never allowed to overstep its authority or trample on the rights of the citizen no matter how egalitarian the political arguments may be.

Jesus Himself also emphasized that public SERVANTS should never become RULERS or have superior authority to the people they are supposed to SERVE when He said the following.

*"You know that the rulers of the Gentiles [unbelievers] lord it over them [govern from ABOVE as pagan idols], and those who are great exercise authority over them [supernatural powers that are the object of idol worship]. **Yet it shall not be so among you; but whoever desires to become great among you, let him be your servant [serve the sovereign people from BELOW rather than rule from above]. And whoever desires to be first among you, let him be your slave—just as the Son of Man did not come to be served, but to serve, and to give His life a ransom for many."***
[Matt. 20:25-28, Bible, NKJV]

Notice the word "ransom for many" in the above. This is an admission that Jesus acknowledges that cunning public servant lawyers have KIDNAPPED our legal identity from the protection of God's law and that legal identity has been transported to a legislatively foreign jurisdiction, the District of Criminals. We exhaustively prove this with evidence in the following memorandum of law:

> *Government Identity Theft*, Form #05.046
> https://sedm.org/Forms/05-MemLaw/GovernmentIdentityTheft.pdf

Jesus also states in Matt. 20:25-28 that it is the DUTY and obligation of every Christian to fight this corruption of our political system. The Holy Bible is our Delegation of Authority to do precisely this, in fact, and to restore God to His proper role as the ruler of ALL nations and ALL politicians and the only rightful Lawgiver of all human law. That delegation of authority is described in:

> *Delegation of Authority Order from God to Christians*, Form #13.007
> https://sedm.org/Forms/13-SelfFamilyChurchGovnce/DelOfAuthority.pdf

6.3.3 Graphical Depiction of the Corruption

With the above in mind, we will now add all of the corrupting influences accomplished to our system of government over the years. These are shown with dashed lines representing the application of unlawful or immoral force or fraud. The hollow

Chapter 6: History of Government Income Tax Fraud, Racketeering and Extortion in the U.S.A.

end of each line indicates the sovereign against which the force or fraud is applied. The number above or next to the dotted line indicates the item in the table that follows the diagram which explains each incidence of force or fraud.

Figure 6-2: Process of Corrupting Republican Form of Government

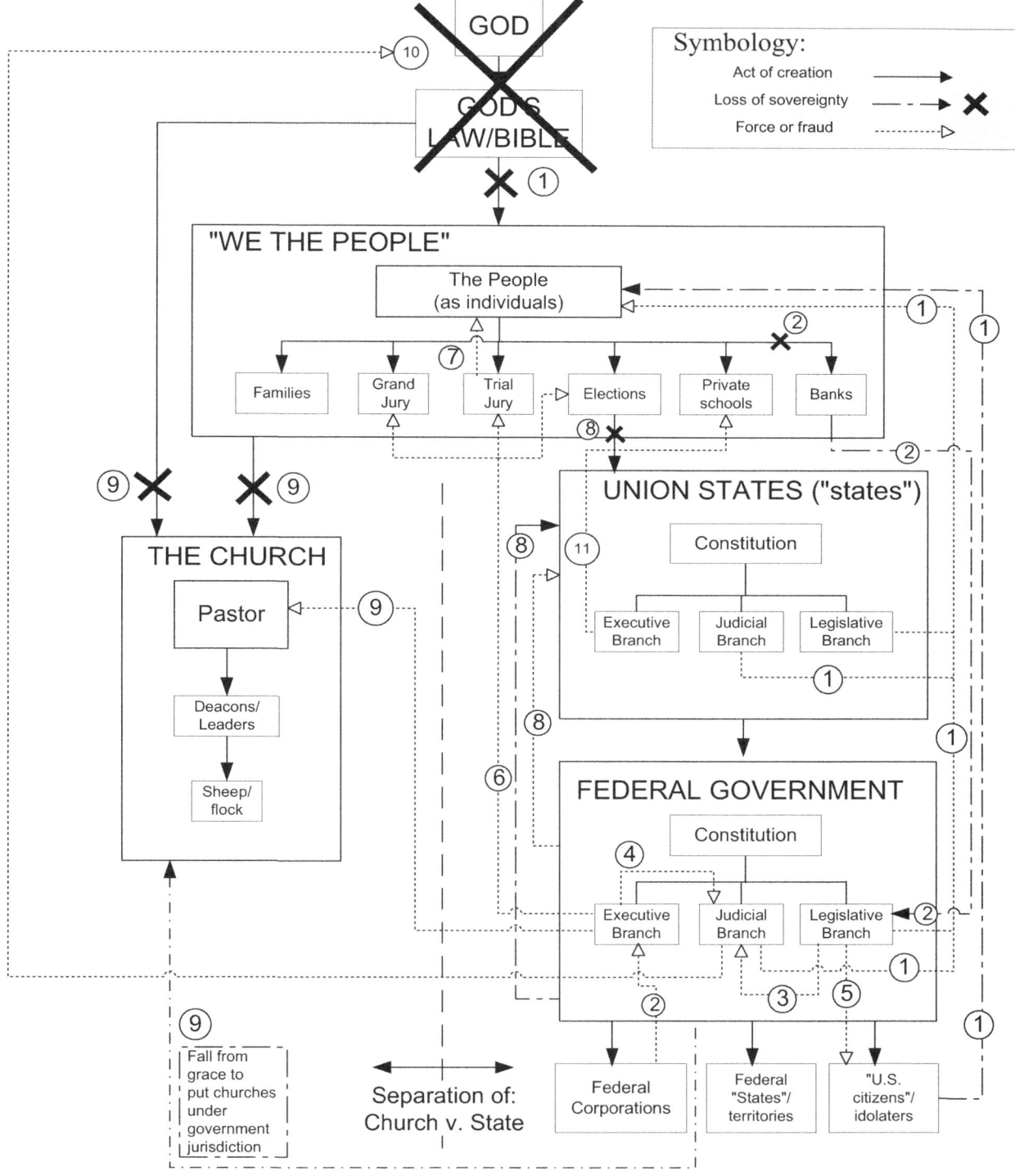

Below is a table explaining each incidence of force or fraud that corrupted the originally perfect system:

Table 6-1: Specific instances of force, fraud, and conflict of interest that corrupted our political system

# (on diagram above)	Year(s)	Acting Sovereignty/ agent	Law(s) violated	Explanation
1	1868	State legislatures State judges Federal legislature Federal judges	18 U.S.C. §241 (conspiracy against rights) Thirteenth Amendment (slavery and peonage) 42 U.S.C. §1994 (peonage) 18 U.S.C. §1581 (peonage/slavery) 18 U.S.C. §2381 (treason)	After the civil war, the 14th Amendment was passed in 1868. That amendment along with "words of art" were used as a means to deceive constitutional citizens to falsely believe that they were also privileged statutory "U.S. citizens" pursuant to 8 U.S.C. §1401, and thus to unconstitutionally extent federal jurisdiction and enforce federal franchises within states of the Union. The citizenship status described in that amendment was only supposed to apply to emancipated slaves but the federal government in concert with the states confused the law and the interpretation of the law enough that everyone thought they were statutory federal citizens rather than the "non-resident non-persons" immune from federal jurisdiction, which is foreign with respect to states of the Union. This put Americans in the states in a privileged federal status and put them under the jurisdiction of the federal government. At the point that Americans voluntarily and unknowingly accept privileged federal citizenship, they lose their sovereignty and go to the bottom of the sovereignty hierarchy. State courts and state legislatures cooperated in this conspiracy against rights by requiring electors and jurists to be presumed statutory "U.S. citizens" in order to serve. At the same time, they didn't define the term "U.S. citizen" in their election laws or voter registration, creating a "presumption" in favor of people believing that they are statutory "citizens of the United States", even though technically they are not.
2	1913	Corporations/ businesses/and special interests	18 U.S.C. §201 (bribery of public officials) Const. Art. 1, Sect. 2, Clause 3 (direct taxes) Const. Art. 1, Sect. 9, Clause 4 (direct taxes) 18 U.S.C. §219 (government employees acting as agents of foreign principals- Federal Reserve)	Around the turn of the century, the gilded age created a lot of very wealthy people and big corporations. The corrupting influence of the money they had lead them to dominate the U.S. senate and the Republican party., which was the majority party at the time The people became restless because they were paying most of the taxes indirectly via tariffs on imported goods while the big corporations were paying very little. This lead to a vote by Congress to send the new Sixteenth Amendment to the states for ratification. Corporations heavily influenced this legislation so that it would favor taxing individuals instead of corporations, which lead the Republicans in the Senate to word the Amendment ambiguously so that it could or would be misconstrued to apply to natural persons instead of the corporations it was really intended to apply to by the American people. This created much subsequent litigation and confusion on the part of the Average American about exactly what the taxing powers of Congress are, and gave Congressman a lot of wiggle room to misrepresent the purpose of the Sixteenth Amendment to their constituents. Today, Congressmen use the ambiguity of the Amendment to regularly lie to their Constituents by saying that the "Sixteenth Amendment" authorizes Congress to tax the income of every American. This is an absolute lie and is completely inconsistent with the rulings of the U.S. Supreme Court. Courts below the Supreme Court have also used the same ambiguity mechanism to expand the operation of the income tax beyond its clearly limited application to the federal zone. During the same year as the Sixteenth Amendment was ratified, in 1913, the Congress also passed the Federal Reserve Act immediately after the Sixteenth Amendment. By doing this, they surrendered their control over the money system to a consortium of private banks. The Sixteenth Amendment was passed first in February of 1913 because it was the lender-security for the Non-Federal Reserve that would be needed to create a "credit line" and collateral. The Federal Reserve Act was passed in December of that same year. At that point, the Congress had an unlimited private credit line from commercial banks and a means to print as much money as they wanted in order to fund socialist expansion of the government. But remember that the bible says: *"The rich ruleth over the poor, and the borrower [is] servant to the lender."* *[Prov. 22:7]*

# (on diagram above)	Year(s)	Acting Sovereignty/ agent	Law(s) violated	Explanation
3	1911-1939	Federal legislature	28 U.S.C. §144 (conflict of interest of federal judges) 28 U.S.C. §455 (conflict of interest of federal judges)	In 1911, the U.S. Congress passed the Judicial Code of 1911 and thereby made all District and Circuit courts into entirely administrative courts which had jurisdiction over only the federal zone. All the federal courts except the U.S. Supreme Court changed character from being Article III courts to Article IV territorial courts only. All the district courts were renamed from "District Court of the United States" to "United States District Court". The Supreme Court said in *Balzac v. Porto Rico*, 258 U.S. 298 (1922) that the "United States District Court" is an Article IV territorial court, not an Article III constitutional court. Consequently, all the federal courts excepting the Supreme Court became administrative courts that were part of the Executive rather than the Judicial Branch of the government and all the judges became Executive Branch employees. See our article "Authorities on Jurisdiction of Federal Courts" for further details. The Revenue Act of 1932 than tried to apply income taxes against federal judges. The purpose was to put them under complete control of the Executive Branch through terrorism and extortion by the IRS. This was litigated by the Supreme Court in 1932 in the case of *O'Malley v. Woodrough*, 309 U.S. 277 (1939) just before the war started. The court ruled that the Executive Branch couldn't unilaterally modify the terms of their employment contracts, so they rewrote the tax code to go around it subsequent to that by only taxing NEW federal judges and leaving the existing ones alone so as not to violate the Constitutional prohibition against reducing judges salaries. Since that time, federal judges have been beholden to the greed and malice of the Legislative branch because they are under IRS control. This occurred at a time when we had a very popular socialist President who threatened the Supreme Court if they didn't go along with his plan to replace capitalism with socialism, starting with Social Security. President Roosevelt tried to retire all the U.S. Supreme Court justices and then double the size of the court and pack the court with all of his own socialist cronies in a famous coup called "The Roosevelt Supreme Court Packing Plan".
4	1939-Present	Federal executive branch	28 U.S.C. §144 (conflict of interest of federal judges) 28 U.S.C. §455 (conflict of interest of federal judges) Separation of powers Doctrine	Right after the Supreme Court case of O'Malley v. Woodrough in 1939, the U.S. Congress wasted no time in passing a new Revenue Act that skirted the findings of the Supreme Court's that declared income taxes levied against them to be unconstitutional. In effect, they made the payment of income taxes by federal judges an implied part of their employment agreement as "appointed officers" of the United States government in receipt of federal privileges. Once the judges were under control of the IRS, they could be terrorized and plundered if they did not cooperate with the enforcement of federal income taxes. This also endowed all federal judges with an implied conflict of interest in violation of 28 U.S.C. §455 and 28 U.S.C. §144
5	1939-Present	Federal legislative branch	Const. Art. 1, Sect. 2, Clause 3 Const. Art. 1, Sect. 9, Clause 4 18 U.S.C. §1589(3) (forced labor)	The Revenue Act of 1939 passed by the U.S. Congress instituted a very oppressive income tax to fund the upcoming World War II effort. It was called the "Victory Tax" and it was a voluntary withholding effort, but after the war and after people on a large scale got used to sending their money to Washington, D.C. every month through payroll withholding, the politicians cleverly decided not to tell them the truth that it was voluntary. The politicians then began rewriting the tax code to further confuse and deceive people and hide the truth about the voluntary nature of the income tax. This included the Internal Revenue Codes of 1954 and 1986, which were major updates of the IRC that further hid the truth from the legal profession and added so much complexity to the tax code that no one even understands them anymore.

# (on diagram above)	Year(s)	Acting Sovereignty/ agent	Law(s) violated	Explanation
6	1950- Present	Federal executive branch	18 U.S.C. §597 (expenditures to influence voting) 18 U.S.C. §872 (extortion) 18 U.S.C. §880 (receiving the proceeds of extortion) 18 U.S.C. §1957 (Engaging in monetary transactions in property derived from specified unlawful activity)	Federal government uses income tax revenues after World War II to begin socialist subsidies, starting with Lyndon Johnson's "Great Society" plan. Instead of paying off the war debt and ending the income tax like we did after the Civil war in 1872, the government adopted socialism and borrowed itself into a deep hole, following the illustrious example of Franklin Roosevelt's "New Deal" program. This socialist expansion was facilitated by the enactment of the Federal Reserve Act of 1913, which gave the government unlimited borrowing power. The income tax, however, had to continue because it was the "lender security" for the PRIVATE Federal Reserve banking trust that was creating all this debt and fake money. The income tax had the effect of making all Americans into surety for government debts they never authorized. The Civil Rights movement of the 1960's accelerated the growth of the socialist cancer to cause voters to abuse their power to elect politicians who would subsidize and expand the welfare-state concept. "*Democracy has never been and never can be so desirable as aristocracy or monarchy, but while it lasts, is more bloody than either. Remember, democracy never lasts long. It soon wastes, exhausts, and murders itself. There never was a democracy that never did commit suicide.*" John Adams, 1815.
7	1939- Present	Trial jury	18 U.S.C. §2111 (robbery)	Trial juries filled with people receiving government socialist handouts (money STOLEN from hard-working Americans) vote against tax protesters to illegally enforce the Internal Revenue Code, and especially in the case of the wealthy. Trial by jury becomes MOB RULE and a means to mug and rob the producers of society. The jurists are also under duress by the judge, who does not allow evidence to be admitted that would be prejudicial to government (or his retirement check) and who makes cases unpublished where the government lost on income tax issues. Because these same jurists were also educated in public schools, they are easily lead like sheep to do the government's dirty work of plundering their fellow citizens by upholding a tax that is actually voluntary. The result is slavery of wage earners and the rich to the IRS. The war of the "have-nots" and the "haves" using the taxing authority of the government continues on and expands.
8	1960- Present	Federal government	18 U.S.C. §873 (blackmail) 18 U.S.C. §208 (acts affecting a personal financial interest 18 U.S.C. §872 (extortion)	The federal government begins using income tax revenues and socialist welfare programs to manipulate the states. For instance: 1. They made it mandatory for states to require people getting drivers licenses to provide a Socialist Security Number or their welfare subsidies would be cut off. 2. They encourage states to require voters and jurists to be "U.S. citizens" in order to serve these functions so that they would also be put under federal jurisdiction. 3. They mandate that all persons receiving welfare benefits or unemployment benefits that include federal subsidies to have Socialist Security Numbers.
9	1980's- Present	Federal executive branch	18 U.S.C. §208 (conflict of interest) 18 U.S.C. §872 (extortion) 18 U.S.C. §876 (mailing threatening communications)	IRS abuses its power to manipulate and silence churches that speak out about government abuses or are politically active. This has the effect of making the churches politically irrelevant forces in our society so that the government would have no competition for the affections and the allegiance of the people.
10	1960- Present	Federal judicial branch	God's laws (bible)	Federal judiciary eliminates God and prayer in the schools. This leaves kids in a spiritual vacuum. Drugs, sex, teenage pregnancy run rampant. Families begin breaking apart. God is blasphemed. Single parents raise an increasing number of kids and these children don't have the balance they need in the family to have proper sex roles. Gender identity crisis and psychology problems result, causing homosexuality to run rampant. This further accelerates the breakdown of the family because these dysfunctional kids have dysfunctional families of their own. Because God is not in the schools, eventually the people begin to reject God as well. This expands the power of government because when the people aren't governed by God, they are ruled by tyrants and become peasants and serfs eventually. That is how the Israelites ended up in bondage to the Egyptians: because they would not serve God or trust him for their security. They wanted a big powerful Egyptian government to take care of them and be comfortable and safe, which was idolatry toward government.

# (on diagram above)	Year(s)	Acting Sovereignty/ agent	Law(s) violated	Explanation
11	2000-Present	State executive branch	18 U.S.C. §208 (acts affecting a personal financial interest)	The state executive branches abuse their power to set very high licensing requirements for home schools and private schools, backed by teachers unions and contributions of these unions to their political campaigns. Licensing requirements become so high that only public schools have the capital to comply, virtually eliminating private and home schooling. Teachers and inferior environment in public schools further contributes to bad education and liberal socialist values, further eroding sovereignty of the people and making them easy prey for sly politicians who want to enslave them with more unjust laws and expand their fiefdom. Government continues to grow in power and rights and liberties simultaneously erode further.

After our corrupt politicians are finished socially re-engineering our system of government using the tax code and a corrupted federal judiciary, below is what happens to our original republican government system. This is what we refer to as the "*De facto* U.S. Government". It has replaced our "*De jure* U.S. Government" not through operation of law, but through fraud, force, and corruption. One or our readers calls this new architecture for social organization "The New Civil Religion of Socialism", where the collective will of the majority or whatever the judge says is sovereign, not God, and is the object of worship and servitude in courtrooms all over the country, who are run by devil-worshipping modern-day monarchs called "judges". These tyrants wear black-robes and chant in Latin and perform exorcism on hand-cuffed subjects to remove imaginary "demons" from the people that are defined by majority vote among a population of criminals (by God's law), homosexuals, drug abusers, adulterers, and atheists. The vilification of these demons are legislated into existence with "judge-made law", which is engineered to maximize litigation and profits to the legal industry. The legal industry, in turn, has been made into a part of the government because it is licensed and regulated by government. This profession "worships" the judge as an idol and is comprised of golf and law school buddies and fellow members of the American Bar Association (ABA), who hobnob with the judge and do whatever he says or risk having their attorney license pulled. In this totalitarian socialist democracy/oligarchy shown below, the people have *no inalienable or God-given individual rights*, but only statutory "privileges" and franchises granted by the will of the majority that are excise taxable. After all, when God and Truth are demoted to being a selfish creation of man and a politically correct vain fantasy, then the concept of "divine right" vanishes entirely from our political system.

Figure 6-3: Result of Corrupting Our Republican Form of Government

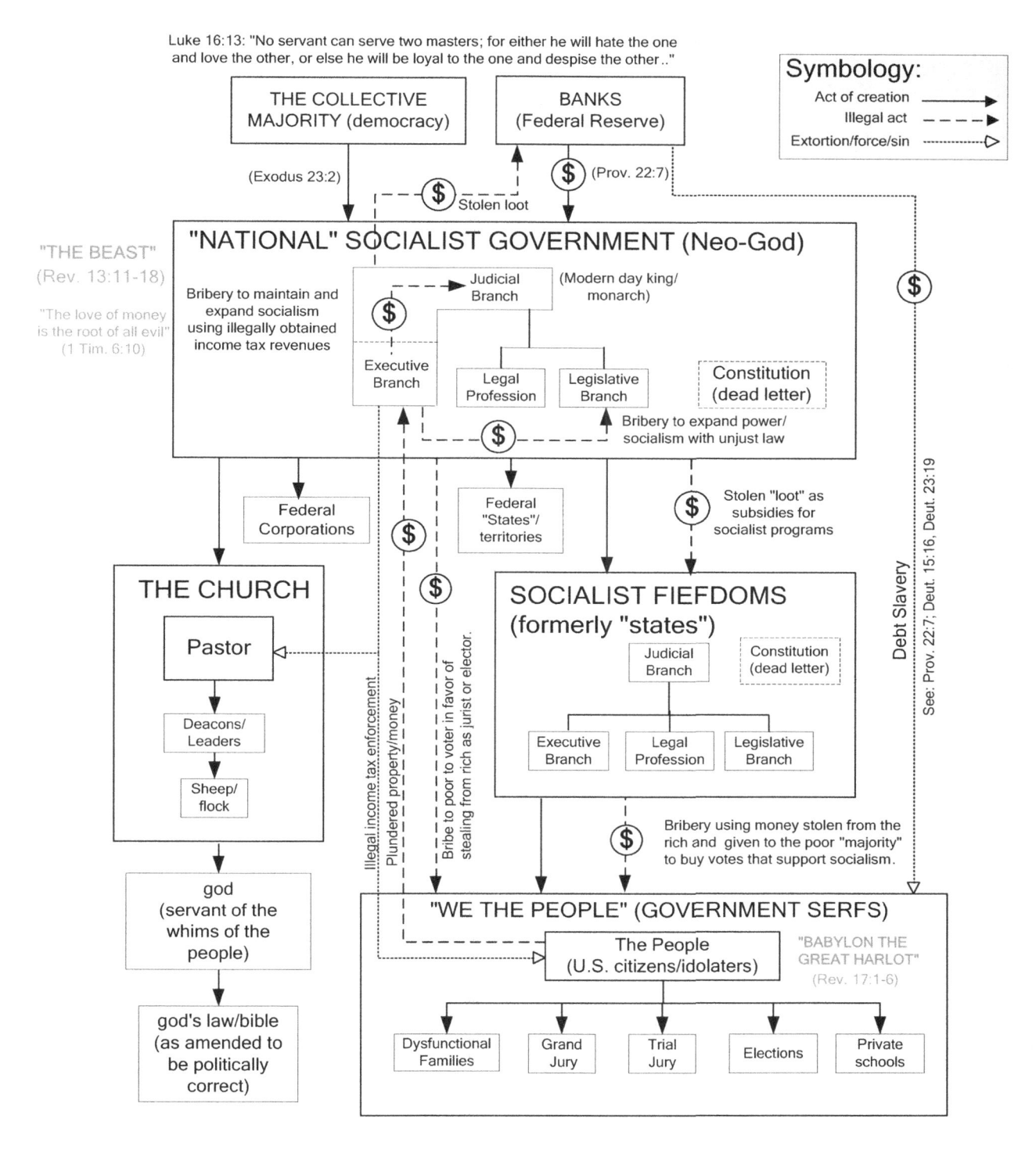

In the above diagram, all people in receipt of federal funds *stolen* through illegally collected or involuntarily paid federal income taxes effectively become federal "employees" or "public officers". They identified themselves as such when they filed their W-4 payroll withholding form, which is a contract that says on the top "***Employee*** Withholding Allowance Certificate". The Internal Revenue Code identifies "employee" to mean someone who works for the federal government in 26 U.S.C. §3401(c). These federal "employees" are moral and spiritual "whores" and "harlots". They are just like Judas or

Essau...they exchanged the Truth for a lie and liberty for slavery and they did it mainly for money and personal security. They are:

1. So concerned about avoiding being terrorized by their government or the IRS for "making waves".
2. So immobilized by their own fear and ignorance that they don't dare do anything.
3. So addicted to sin and other unhealthy distractions that they don't have the time to do justice.
4. So poor that they can't afford an expensive lawyer to be able to right the many wrongs imposed on them by a corrupted government. Justice is a luxury that only the rich can afford in our society.
5. So legally ignorant, thanks to our public "fool", I mean "school" system that they aren't able to right their wrongs on their own in court without a lawyer.
6. So afraid of corrupt judges and lawyers who are bought and paid for with money that they stole from hardworking Americans in illegally enforcing what is actually a voluntary Subtitle A income against those who in fact and indeed can only be described per the law as "nontaxpayers".
7. So unable to take care of their own needs because:
    7.1. Most of their money has been plundered by a government unable and unwilling to control its spending.
    7.2. They have allowed themselves to depend too much on government and allowed too much of their own hard-earned money to be stolen from them.
    7.3. They spent everything they had and went deep in debt to buy things they didn't need.
8. So covetous of that government welfare or socialist security or unemployment check or paycheck that comes in the mail every month.

...that they wouldn't dare upset the apple cart or try to right the many wrongs that maintain the status quo by doing justice as a voter or jurist. As long as they get their socialist handout and they live comfortably on the "loot" their "Parens Patriae", or "Big Brother" sends them, they don't care that massive injustice is occurring in courtrooms and at the IRS every day and that they are sanctioning, aiding, and abetting that injustice as voters and jurists with a financial conflict of interest in criminal violation of 18 U.S.C. §§201 and 208. In effect, they are bribed to look the other way while their own government loots and oppresses their neighbor and then uses that loot to buy votes and influence.

> *"Thou shalt not steal."*
> *[Exodus 20:15]*
>
> *For **all the law is fulfilled in one word**, even in this: "You shall love your neighbor as yourself."*
> *[Gal 5:14, Bible, NKJV]*

Would you rob your neighbor? No you say? Well then, would you look the other way while someone else robs him in your name? Government is **YOUR AGENT**. If government robs your neighbor, God will hold *you*, not the agent who did it for you, personally responsible, because government is your agent. God put you in charge of your government and you are the steward. Frederic Bastiat described the nature of this horrible corruption of the system in the following book on our website:

The Law, Frederic Bastiat
http://famguardian.org/Publications/TheLaw/TheLaw.htm

If you want to know what the above type of government is like spiritually, economically, and politically, read the first-hand accounts in the book of Judges found in the Bible. Corruption, sin, servitude, violence, and wars characterize this notable and most ignominious period and "social experiment" as documented in the Bible. Now do you understand why God's law mandates that we serve ONLY Him and *not* be slaves of man or government? When we don't, the above totalitarian socialist democracy/tyranny is the result, where politicians and judges in government become the *only* sovereign and the people are there to bow down to and "worship" and serve an evil and corrupt government as slaves.

6.3.4 God's Remedy for the Corruption

Below is the way God himself describes the corrupted dilemma we find ourselves in because we have abandoned the path laid by our founding fathers, as described in Isaiah 1:1-26:

> *Alas, sinful nation,*
> *A people laden with iniquity,*
> *A brood of evildoers,*
> *Children who are corrupters!*

They have forsaken the Lord

They have provoked to anger
The Holy One of Israel,
They have turned away backward.
Why should you be stricken again?
You will revolt more and more.
The whole head is sick [they are out of their minds!; insane or STUPID or both],
And the whole heart faints....

Wash yourselves, make yourselves clean;
Put away the evil of your doings from before My eyes.
Cease to do evil,
Learn to do good;
Seek justice,
Rebuke the oppressor [the IRS and the Federal Reserve and a corrupted judicial system];
Defend the fatherless,
Plead for the widow [and the "nontaxpayer"]....

How the faithful city has become a harlot!
It [the Constitutional Republic] was full of justice;
Righteousness lodged in it,
But now murderers [and abortionists, and socialists, and democrats, and liars and corrupted judges].
Your silver has become dross,
Your wine mixed with water.
Your princes [President, Congressmen, Judges] are rebellious,
Everyone loves bribes,
And follows after rewards.
They do not defend the fatherless,
nor does the cause of the widow [or the "nontaxpayer"] come before them.

Therefore the Lord says,
The Lord of hosts, the Mighty One of Israel,
"Ah, I will rid Myself of My adversaries,
And take vengeance on My enemies.
I will turn My hand against you,
And thoroughly purge away your dross,
And take away your alloy.
I will restore your judges [eliminate the BAD judges] **as at the first,**
And your counselors [eliminate the BAD lawyers] **as at the beginning.**
Afterward you shall be called the city of righteousness, the faithful city."
[Isaiah 1:1-26, Bible, NKJV]

So according to the Bible, the *real* problem is corrupted lawyers and judges and people who are after money and rewards, and God says the way to fix the corruption and graft is to ***eliminate the bad judges and lawyers***. Whose job is that? It is the even more corrupted Congress! (see 28 U.S.C. §134(a) and 28 U.S.C. §44(b))

> *"O My people! Those who lead you cause you to err,*
> *And destroy the way of your paths."*
> [Isaiah 3:12, Bible, NKJV]

> *"The king establishes the land by justice; but he who receives bribes overthrows it."*
> [Prov. 29:4, Bible, NKJV]

Can thieves and corrupted judges and lawyers and jurors, who are all bribed with unlawfully collected money they lust after in the pursuit of socialist benefits, reform themselves if left to their own devices?

> *"When you [the jury] saw a thief [the corrupted judges and lawyers paid with extorted and stolen tax money],*
> *you consented with him, And have been a partaker with adulterers."*
> [Psalm 50:18, Bible, NKJV]

> **"The people will be oppressed,**
> **Every one by another and every one by his [socialist] neighbor [sitting on a jury who**
> **was indoctrinated and brainwashed in a government school to trust government];**
> *The child will be insolent toward the elder,*
> *And the base toward the honorable."*
> [Isaiah 3:5, Bible, NKJV]

> "It must be conceded that there are rights [and property] in every free government beyond the control of the State [or any judge or jury]. A government which recognized no such rights, which held the lives, liberty and property of its citizens, subject at all times to the disposition and unlimited control of even the most democratic depository of power, is after all a despotism. It is true that it is a despotism of the many--of the majority, if you choose to call it so--but it is not the less a despotism."
> [Loan Ass'n v. Topeka, 87 U.S. (20 Wall.) 655, 665 (1874)]

The answer is an emphatic no. It is up to **_We The People_** as the sovereigns in charge of our lawless government to right this massive injustice because a corrupted legislature and judiciary and the passive socialist voters in charge of our government today simply cannot remedy their own addiction to the money that was stolen from their neighbor by the _criminals_ they elected into office. These elected representatives were supposed to be elected to _serve and protect_ the people, but they have become the worst abusers of the people because they only got into politics and government for selfish reasons. Notice we didn't say they got into "public service", because we would be lying to call it that. It would be more accurate to call what they do "self-service" instead of "public service". One of our readers has a name for these kinds of people. He calls them SLAT: Scum, Liars, and Thieves. If you add up all the drug money, all the stolen property, all the white collar crime together, it would all pale in comparison to the "extortion under the color of law" that our own de facto government and the totally corrupted people who work for it are instituting against its own people. If we solve no crime problem other than that one problem, then the government will have done the most important thing it can do to solve our crime problem and probably significantly reduce the prison population at the same time. There are lots of people in jail who were put there wrongfully for income tax crimes that aren't technically even crimes. These people were maliciously prosecuted by a corrupted Satan worshipping DOJ with the complicity of a corrupted judiciary and they MUST be freed because they have become slaves and political prisoners of a corrupted state for the sake of statutes that operate as the equivalent of a "civil religion" and which are not and cannot be law in their case. That's right: the corrupted state has erected a counterfeit church and religion that is a cheap imitation of God's design complete with churches, prayers, priests, deacons, tithes, and even its own "Bible" (franchise) and they have done so in violation of the First Amendment. The nature of that civil religion is exhaustively described below:

> _Socialism: The New American Civil Religion_, Form #05.016
> DIRECT LINK: http://sedm.org/Forms/05-MemLaw/SocialismCivilReligion.pdf (OFFSITE LINK)
> FORMS PAGE: http://sedm.org/Forms/FormIndex.htm (OFFSITE)

Why does God describe the source of the corruption as bad lawyers and judges instead of the people accepting the franchises as "Buyers", you might ask? The answer is that:

1. The Constitution and the Declaration of Independence recognize natural rights as INALIENABLE. See
   > _Unalienable Rights Course_, Form #12.038
   > https://sedm.org/LibertyU/UnalienableRights.pdf
2. An INALIENABLE right is one that YOU AREN'T ALLOWED BY LAW to consent (Form #05.003) to give away.
3. If you can't even lawfully consent (Form #05.003) to give away the right, then you can never lose it or contract it away by participating in a government franchise (Form #05.030) or accepting a loan of government property.
4. The fact that judges and lawyers ALLOW inalienable rights (Form #12.038) to be given away in a place where they aren't allowed to be given away is a sign that they love money and enhancing their own power more than they love freedom or the Constitution.
5. Because they love money and power more than they love freedom and obeying the constitution, they are committing treason punishable by death in violation of 18 U.S.C. §2381 and serving Satan himself.

Below is how we explain this conundrum in our Disclaimer:

> _Every attempt by anyone in government to alienate rights that the Declaration of Independence says are UNALIENABLE shall also be treated as "PRIVATE BUSINESS ACTIVITY" that cannot be protected by sovereign, official, or judicial immunity. So called "government" cannot make a profitable business or franchise out of alienating inalienable rights without ceasing to be a classical/de jure government and instead becoming in effect an economic terrorist and de facto government in violation of Article 4, Section 4._
>
> _"No servant [or government or biological person] can serve **two masters**; for either he will hate the one and love the other, or else he will be loyal to the one and despise the other._
> **_You cannot serve God and mammon [government]._**_"_
> _[Luke 16:13, Bible, NKJV]_
>
> [Disclaimer, Section 4: Meaning of Words: "Private"; SOURCE: https://famguardian.org/disclaimer.htm]

6.3.5 De Jure v. De Facto Government

We will now close this section with a tabular summary that compares our original "de jure" government to the "de facto" government that we presently suffer under. This corrupted "de facto" government only continues to exist because of our passive and tolerant approach towards the illegal activities of our government servants. We can fix this if we really want to, folks. Let's do it!

Table 6-2: Comparison of our "De jure" v. "De facto" government

#	Type of separation of powers	De jure government	De facto government
1	Separation of Church and State	Government has no power to control or regulate the political activities of churches	IRS 501(c) designation allows government to remove tax exemption from churches if they get politically involved
2	Separation of Money and State	Only lawful money is gold and the value of the dollar is tied to gold. Government can't manufacture more gold so they can't abuse their power to coin money to enrich themselves.	Fiat currency is Federal Reserve Notes (FRNs). Government can print any amount of these it wants and thereby enrich itself and steal from the those who hold dollars by lowering the value of the dollars in circulation (inflation)
3	Separation of Marriage and State	People getting married did not have marriage licenses from the state. Instead, the ceremony was exclusively ecclesiastical and it was recorded only in the family Bible and church records.	Pastor acts as an agent of both God and the state. He performs the ceremony and is also licensed by the state to sign the state marriage license. Churches force members getting married to obtain state marriage license by saying they won't marry them without a state-issued marriage license.
4	Separation of School and State	Schools were rural and remote and most were private or religious. There were very few public schools and a large percentage of the population was home-schooled.	Most student go to public schools. They are dumbed-down by the state to be good serfs/sheep by being told they are "taxpayers" and being shown in high school how to fill out a tax return without even being shown how to balance a check book. They are taught that government is the sovereign and not the people, and that people should obey the government.
5	Separation of State and Federal government	States control the Senate and all legislation and taxation internal to a state. Federal government controls only foreign commerce in the form of imposts, excises, and duties under Article 1, Section 8, Clause 3 of the Constitution.	Federal government receives lion's share of income taxes over both internal and external trade. It redistributes the proceeds from these taxes to the socialist states, who are coerced to modify their laws in compliance with federal dictates in order to get their fair share of this stolen "loot".
6	Separation between branches of government: Executive, Legislative, Judicial	Three branches of government are entirely independent and not controlled by other branches.	Judges are "employees" of the executive branch and have a conflict of interest because they are beholden to IRS extortion. Executive controls the illegal tax collection activities of the IRS and dictates to other branches it's tax policy through illegal IRS extortion. Using the IRS, Executive becomes the "Gestapo" that controls everything and everyone. Congress and the courts refuse to reform this extortion because they benefit most financially by it.
7	Separation of Commerce and State	Federal government regulates only foreign commerce of corporations. States regulate all internal commerce. Private individuals have complete privacy and are not regulated because they don't have Socialist Security Numbers and are not monitored by the IRS Gestapo. Banks are independent and do not have to participate in a national banking system so they don't coerce their depositors to bet government-issued numbers nor do they snoop/spy on their depositors as an agent of the IRS Gestapo. Private employers are not regulated or monitored by federal Gestapo and their contracts with their employees are private and sacred.	All credit issued by a central, private Federal Reserve consortium. Federal Reserve rules coerce private banks to illegally enforce federal laws in states of the Union that only apply in the federal zone. Namely, they force depositors to have Socialist Security Numbers and they report all currency transactions over $3,000 to the Dept of the Treasury (CTR's). "Spying" on financial affairs citizens by government makes citizens afraid of IRS and government and coerces them to illegally pay income taxes by government. Employers are coerced to enslave their employees to IRS through wage reporting and withholding, often against the will of employees.

#	Type of separation of powers	De jure government	De facto government
8	Separation of Media and State	Press was free to report as they saw fit under the First Amendment. Most newspapers were small-town newspapers and were private and independent.	Television, radio, the internet, and corporations have taken over the media and concentrated control of it to the hands of a very few huge and "privileged" corporations that are in bed with the federal and state governments. Media is no longer independent, and broadcasters don't dare cross the government for fear of either losing their FCC license, being subjected to an IRS audit, or having their government sponsorship revoked.
9	Separation of Family and State	Families were completely separate from the state. Private individuals were not subject to direct taxation or regulation by either state or federal government. No Socialist Security Numbers and no government surveillance of private commerce by individuals. Women stayed home and out of the workforce. Men dominated the political and commercial landscape and also defended their family from encroachments by government. Children were home-schooled and worked on the farm. They inherited the republican values of their parents. Morality was taught by the churches and there was an emphasis on personal responsibility, modesty, manners, respect, and humility.	Using income taxes, mom was removed from the home to enter the workforce so she could replace the income stolen from dad by the IRS through illegal enforcement of the Internal Revenue Code. Conflict over money breaks families down and divorce rate reaches epidemic proportions. Children are neglected by their parents because parents both have to work full-time and duke it out with each other in divorce court. Majority of children raised in single parent homes. Television and a liberal media dominates and distorts the thoughts and minds of the children. Public schools filled with homosexuals and liberals, many of whom have no children of their own, teach our children to be selfish, rebellious, sexually promiscuous, homosexual drug-abusers. Pornography invades the home through the internet, cable-TV, and video rentals, creating a negative fixation on sex. Television interferes with family communication so that children are alienated from their parents so that they do not inherit good morals or respect for authority from their parents.. Crime rate and prison population reaches unprecedented levels. Citizens therefore lose their ability to govern themselves and the legal field and government come in and take over their lives.
10	Separation of Charity and State	Churches and families were responsible for charity. When a person was old or became unemployed, members of the church or family would take them. Personal responsibility and morality within churches and families would encourage them to improve their lives.	Monolithic, huge, and terribly inefficient government bureaucracies replace families and churches as major source of charity. These bureaucracies have no idea what personal responsibility is and are not allowed to talk about morality because they are not allowed to talk about God. Generations of people grow up under this welfare umbrella without ever having to take responsibility for themselves, and these people abuse their voting power to perpetuate it. Supremacy of families and churches is eliminated and government becomes the new "god" for everyone to worship. See Jeremiah 2:26-28.
11	Separation of Public and Private Property	All property is presumed to be absolutely owned, private, and not subject to state or public or government control. This is the foundation of the Fifth Amendment protection for private property. See Separation Between Public and Private Course, Form #12.025.	Corrupt and covetous public servants implement socialism, where all property is presumed to be absolutely owned by the government, and everyone is a BORROWER of said property with conditions. Those conditions are called "franchises", and government can regulate and control ANYONE and ANYTHING it wants. See Government Instituted Slavery Using Franchises, Form #05.030.

If you would like to know more about how our system of government became de facto and corrupted, see:

1. *Government Corruption*, Form #11.401
   http://sedm.org/home/government-corruption/
2. *Government Corruption: Causes and Remedies*, Form #12.026
   http://sedm.org/Forms/FormIndex.htm
3. *De Facto Government Scam*, Form #05.043
   http://sedm.org/Forms/FormIndex.htm

6.4 How De Jure Governments are Transformed into Corrupt De Facto Governments[8]

> *"Governments never do anything by accident; if government does something you can bet it was carefully planned."*
> [Franklin D. Roosevelt, President of the United States]

Franchises and/or their abuse are the main method by which:

1. De jure governments are transformed into corrupted de facto governments.
2. The requirement for consent of the governed is systematically eliminated.
3. The equal protection that is the foundation of the Constitution is replaced with inequality, privilege, hypocrisy, and partiality in which the government is a parens patriae and possesses an unconstitutional "title of nobility" in relation to those it is supposed to be serving and protecting.
4. The separation of powers between the states and federal government are eliminated.
5. The separation between what is "public" and what is "private" is destroyed. Everything becomes PUBLIC and is owned by the "collective". There is no private property and what you think is ABSOLUTE ownership of PRIVATE property is really just equitable title and QUALIFIED ownership of PUBLIC property.
6. Constitutional rights attaching to the land you stand on are replaced with statutory privileges created through your right to contract and your "status" under a franchise agreement.

> *"You shall make no covenant [contract or franchise] with them [foreigners, pagans], nor with their [pagan government] gods [laws or judges]. They shall not dwell in your land [and you shall not dwell in theirs by becoming a "resident" or domiciliary in the process of contracting with them], lest they make you sin against Me [God]. For if you serve their [government] gods [under contract or agreement or franchise], it will surely be a snare to you."*
> [Exodus 23:32-33, Bible, NKJV]

7. Your legal identity is "laundered", and kidnapped or transported to a foreign jurisdiction, the District of Criminals, and which is not protected by the Constitution. This is usually done by compulsion or duress, as in the case of compelled licensing.

> *"For the upright will dwell in the land,*
> *And the blameless will remain in it;*
> ***But the wicked will be cut off from the earth,***
> ***And the unfaithful will be uprooted from it."***
> [Prov. 2:21-22, Bible, NKJV]

8. The protections of the Constitution for your rights are eliminated.
9. Rights are transformed into privileges.
10. Republics based on individual rights are transformed into socialist democracies based on collective rights and individual privileges.
11. The status of "citizen, resident, or inhabitant" is devolved into nothing but an "employee" or "officer" of a corporation.
12. Constitutional courts are transformed into franchise courts.
13. Conflicts of interest are introduced into the legal and court systems that perpetuate a further expansion of the de facto system.
14. Socialism is introduced into a republican form of government.
15. The sovereignty of people in the states of the Union are destroyed.

The gravely injurious effects of participating in government franchises include the following.

1. Those who participate become domiciliaries of the federal zone, "U.S. persons", and "resident aliens" in respect to the federal government.
2. Those who participate become "trustees" of the "public trust" and "public officers" of the federal government and suffer great legal disability as a consequence:

---

[8] Adapted from: *Government Instituted Slavery Using Franchises*, Form #05.030, Section 14; http://sedm.org/Forms/FormIndex.htm.

> "As expressed otherwise, the powers delegated to a public officer are held in trust for the people and are to be exercised in behalf of the government or of all citizens who may need the intervention of the officer. 9 **_Furthermore, the view has been expressed that all public officers, within whatever branch and whatever level of government, and whatever be their private vocations, are trustees of the people, and accordingly labor under every disability and prohibition imposed by law upon trustees relative to the making of personal financial gain from a discharge of their trusts. 10 That is, a public officer occupies a fiduciary relationship to the political entity on whose behalf he or she serves. 11 and owes a fiduciary duty to the public. 12 It has been said that the fiduciary responsibilities of a public officer cannot be less than those of a private individual. 13_** Furthermore, it has been stated that any enterprise undertaken by the public official which tends to weaken public confidence and undermine the sense of security for individual rights is against public policy.14"
> [63C American Jurisprudence 2d, Public Officers and Employees, §247 (1999)]

3. Those who participate are stripped of ALL of their constitutional rights and waive their Constitutional right not to be subjected to penalties and other "bills of attainder" administered by the Executive Branch without court trials. They then must function the degrading treatment of filling the role of a federal "public employee" subject to the supervision of their servants in the government.

> "**_The restrictions that the Constitution places upon the government in its capacity as lawmaker, i.e., as the regulator of private conduct, are not the same as the restrictions that it places upon the government in its capacity as employer._** We have recognized this in many contexts, with respect to many different constitutional guarantees. Private citizens perhaps cannot be prevented from wearing long hair, but policemen can. Kelley v. Johnson, 425 U.S. 238, 247 (1976). Private citizens cannot have their property searched without probable cause, but in many circumstances government employees can. O'Connor v. Ortega, 480 U.S. 709, 723 (1987) (plurality opinion); id., at 732 (SCALIA, J., concurring in judgment). Private citizens cannot be punished for refusing to provide the government information that may incriminate them, but government employees can be dismissed when the incriminating information that they refuse to provide relates to the performance of their job. Gardner v. Broderick, [497 U.S. 62, 95] 392 U.S. 273, 277 -278 (1968). With regard to freedom of speech in particular: Private citizens cannot be punished for speech of merely private concern, but government employees can be fired for that reason. Connick v. Myers, 461 U.S. 138, 147 (1983). Private citizens cannot be punished for partisan political activity, but federal and state employees can be dismissed and otherwise punished for that reason. Public Workers v. Mitchell, 330 U.S. 75, 101 (1947); Civil Service Comm'n v. Letter Carriers, 413 U.S. 548, 556 (1973); Broadrick v. Oklahoma, 413 U.S. 601, 616 -617 (1973)."
> [Rutan v. Republican Party of Illinois, 497 U.S. 62 (1990)]

4. Those who participate may lawfully be deprived of equal protection of the law, which is the foundation of the U.S. Constitution. This deprivation of equal protection can lawfully become a provision of the franchise agreement.
5. Those who participate can lawfully be deprived of remedy for abuses in federal courts.

> "**_These general rules are well settled: (1) That the United States, when it creates rights in individuals against itself [a "public right", which is a euphemism for a "franchise" to help the court disguise the nature of the transaction], is under no obligation to provide a remedy through the courts._** United States ex rel. Dunlap v. Black, 128 U.S. 40, 9 Sup.Ct. 12, 32 L.Ed. 354; Ex parte Atocha, 17 Wall. 439, 21 L.Ed. 696; Gordon v. United States, 7 Wall. 188, 195, 19 L.Ed. 35; De Groot v. United States, 5 Wall. 419, 431, 433, 18 L.Ed. 700; Comegys v. Vasse, 1 Pet. 193, 212, 7 L.Ed. 108. (2) That where a statute creates a right and provides a special remedy, that remedy is exclusive. Wilder Manufacturing Co. v. Corn Products Co., 236 U.S. 165, 174, 175, 35 Sup.Ct. 398, 59 L.Ed. 520, Ann. Cas. 1916A, 118; Arnson v. Murphy, 109 U.S. 238, 3 Sup.Ct. 184, 27 L.Ed. 920; Barnet v. National Bank, 98 U.S. 555, 558, 25 L.Ed. 212; Farmers' & Mechanics' National Bank v. Dearing, 91 U.S. 29, 35, 23 L.Ed. 196. Still the fact that the right and the remedy are thus intertwined might not, if the provision stood alone, require us to hold that the remedy expressly given excludes a right of review by the Court of Claims, where

---

[9] State ex rel. Nagle v. Sullivan, 98 Mont. 425, 40 P.2d. 995, 99 A.L.R. 321; Jersey City v. Hague, 18 N.J. 584, 115 A.2d. 8.

[10] Georgia Dep't of Human Resources v. Sistrunk, 249 Ga. 543, 291 S.E.2d. 524. A public official is held in public trust. Madlener v. Finley (1st Dist) 161 Ill.App.3d. 796, 113 Ill.Dec. 712, 515 N.E.2d. 697, app gr 117 Ill.Dec. 226, 520 N.E.2d. 387 and revd on other grounds 128 Ill.2d. 147, 131 Ill.Dec. 145, 538 N.E.2d. 520.

[11] Chicago Park Dist. v. Kenroy, Inc., 78 Ill.2d. 555, 37 Ill.Dec. 291, 402 N.E.2d. 181, appeal after remand (1st Dist) 107 Ill.App.3d. 222, 63 Ill.Dec. 134, 437 N.E.2d. 783.

[12] United States v. Holzer (CA7 Ill) 816 F.2d. 304 and vacated, remanded on other grounds 484 U.S. 807, 98 L.Ed.2d. 18, 108 S.Ct. 53, on remand (CA7 Ill) 840 F.2d. 1343, cert den 486 U.S. 1035, 100 L.Ed.2d. 608, 108 S.Ct. 2022 and (criticized on other grounds by United States v. Osser (CA3 Pa), 864 F.2d. 1056) and (superseded by statute on other grounds as stated in United States v. Little (CA5 Miss) 889 F.2d. 1367) and (among conflicting authorities on other grounds noted in United States v. Boylan (CA1 Mass) 898 F.2d. 230, 29 Fed.Rules.Evid.Serv. 1223).

[13] Chicago ex rel. Cohen v. Keane, 64 Ill.2d. 559, 2 Ill.Dec. 285, 357 N.E.2d. 452, later proceeding (1st Dist) 105 Ill.App.3d. 298, 61 Ill.Dec. 172, 434 N.E.2d. 325.

[14] Indiana State Ethics Comm'n v. Nelson (Ind App), 656 N.E.2d. 1172, reh gr (Ind App) 659 N.E.2d. 260, reh den (Jan 24, 1996) and transfer den (May 28, 1996).

> the decision of the special tribunal involved no disputed question of fact and the denial of compensation was rested wholly upon the construction of the act. See Medbury v. United States, 173 U.S. 492, 198, 19 Sup.Ct. 503, 43 L.Ed. 779; Parish v. MacVeagh, 214 U.S. 124, 29 Sup.Ct. 556, 53 L.Ed. 936; McLean v. United States, 226 U.S. 374, 33 Sup.Ct. 122, 57 L.Ed. 260; United States v. Laughlin (No. 200), 249 U.S. 440, 39 Sup.Ct. 340, 63 L.Ed. 696, decided April 14, 1919.
> [U.S. v. Babcock, 250 U.S. 328, 39 S.Ct. 464 (1919)]

6. Those who participate can be directed which federal courts they may litigate in and can lawfully be deprived of a Constitutional Article III judge or Article III court and forced to seek remedy ONLY in an Article I or Article IV legislative or administrative tribunal within the Legislative rather than Judicial branch of the government.

> *Although* Crowell *and* Raddatz *do not explicitly distinguish between rights created by Congress and other rights, such a distinction underlies in part* Crowell's *and* Raddatz' *recognition of a critical difference between rights created by federal statute and rights recognized by the Constitution. Moreover, such a distinction seems to us to be necessary in light of the delicate accommodations required by the principle of separation of powers reflected in Art. III. The constitutional system of checks and balances is designed to guard against "encroachment or aggrandizement" by Congress at the expense of the other branches of government.* Buckley v. Valeo, 424 U.S., at 122, 96 S.Ct., at 683. *But when Congress creates a statutory right [a "privilege" in this case, such as a "trade or business"], it clearly has the discretion, in defining that right, to create presumptions, or assign burdens of proof, or prescribe remedies; it may also provide that persons seeking to vindicate that right must do so before particularized tribunals created to perform the specialized adjudicative tasks related to that right.FN35 Such provisions do, in a sense, affect the exercise of judicial power, but they are also incidental to Congress' power to define the right that it has created. No comparable justification exists, however, when the right being adjudicated is not of congressional creation. In such a situation, substantial inroads into functions that have traditionally been performed by the Judiciary cannot be characterized merely as incidental extensions of Congress' power to define rights that it has created. Rather, such inroads suggest unwarranted encroachments upon the judicial power of the United States, which our Constitution reserves for Art. III courts.*
> [Northern Pipeline Const. Co. v. Marathon Pipe Line Co., 458 U.S. at 83-84, 102 S.Ct. 2858 (1983)]

Since the founding of our country, franchises have systematically been employed in every area of government to transform a government based on equal protection into a for-profit private corporation based on privilege, partiality, and favoritism. The effects of this form of corruption are exhaustively described in the following memorandum of law on our website:

> *Government Instituted Slavery Using Franchises*, Form #05.030
> http://sedm.org/Forms/FormIndex.htm

What are the mechanisms by which this corruption has been implemented by the Executive Branch? This section will detail the main mechanisms to sensitize you to how to fix the problem and will relate how it was implemented by exploiting the separation of powers doctrine.

The foundation of the separation of powers is the notion that the powers delegated to one branch of government by the Constitution cannot be re-delegated to another branch.

> *"...a power definitely assigned by the Constitution to one department can neither be surrendered nor delegated by that department, nor vested by statute in another department or agency. Compare Springer v. Philippine Islands, 277 U.S. 189, 201, 202, 48 S.Ct. 480, 72 L.Ed. 845."*
> [Williams v. U.S., 289 U.S. 553, 53 S.Ct. 751 (1933)]

Keenly aware of the above limitation, lawmakers over the years have used it to their advantage in creating a tax system that is exempt from any kind of judicial interference and which completely destroys all separation of powers. Below is a summary of the mechanism, in the exact sequence it was executed at the federal level:

1. Create a franchise based upon a "public office" in the Executive Branch. This:
    1.1. Allows statutes passed by Congress to be directly enforced against those who participate.
    1.2. Eliminates the need for publication in the Federal Register of enforcement implementing regulations for the statutes. See 5 U.S.C. §553(a) and 44 U.S.C. §1505(a)(1).
    1.3. Causes those engaged in the franchise to act in a representative capacity as "public officers" of the United States government pursuant to Federal Rule of Civil Procedure 17(b), which is defined in 28 U.S.C. §3002(15)(A) as a federal corporation.
    1.4. Causes all those engaged in the franchise to become "officers of a corporation", which is the "United States", pursuant to 26 U.S.C. §6671(b) and 26 U.S.C. §7343.
2. Give the franchise a deceptive "word of art" name that will deceive everyone into believing that they are engaged in it.

2.1. The franchise is called a "trade or business" and is defined in 26 U.S.C. §7701(a)(26) as "the functions of a public office". How many people know this and do they teach this in the public (government) schools or the IRS publications? NOT!

2.2. Earnings connected with the franchise are called "effectively connected with a trade or business in the United States". The term "United States" deceptively means the GOVERNMENT, and not the geographical United States.

3. In the franchise agreement, define the effective domicile or choice of law of all those who participate as being on federal territory within the exclusive jurisdiction of the United States. 26 U.S.C. §7408(d) and 26 U.S.C. §7701(a)(39) place the effective domicile of all "franchisees" called "taxpayers" within the District of Columbia. If the feds really had jurisdiction within states of the Union, do you think they would need this devious device to "kidnap your legal identity" or "res" and move it to a foreign jurisdiction where you don't physically live?

4. Place a excise tax upon the franchise proportional to the income earned from the franchise. In the case of the Internal Revenue Code, all such income is described as income which is "effectively connected with a trade or business within the United States".

> *"Excises are taxes laid upon the manufacture, sale or consumption of commodities within the country, upon licenses to pursue certain occupations and upon corporate privileges...the requirement to pay such taxes involves the exercise of [220 U.S. 107, 152] privileges, and the element of absolute and unavoidable demand is lacking...*
>
> *...It is therefore well settled by the decisions of this court that when the sovereign authority has exercised the right to tax a legitimate subject of taxation as an exercise of a franchise or privilege, it is no objection that the measure of taxation is found in the income produced in part from property which of itself considered is nontaxable...*
>
> *Conceding the power of Congress to tax the business activities of private corporations.. the tax must be measured by some standard..."*
> *[Flint v. Stone Tracy Co., 220 U.S. 107 (1911)]*

5. Mandate that those engaged in the franchise must have usually false evidence submitted by ignorant third parties that connects them to the franchise. IRS information returns, including IRS Forms W-2, 1042-S, 1098, and 1099, are the mechanism. 26 U.S.C. §6041 says that these information returns may ONLY be filed in connection with a "trade or business", which is a code word for the name of the franchise.

6. Write statutes prohibiting interference by the courts with the collection of "taxes" (kickbacks) associated with the franchise based on the idea that courts in the Judicial Branch may not interfere with the *internal* affairs of another branch such as the Executive Branch. Hence, the "INTERNAL Revenue Service". This will protect the franchise from interference by other branches of the government and ensure that it relentlessly expands.

    6.1. The Anti-Injunction Act, 26 U.S.C. §7421 is an example of an act that enjoins judicial interference with tax collection or assessment.

    6.2. The Declaratory Judgments Act, 28 U.S.C. §2201(a) prohibits federal courts from pronouncing the rights or status of persons in regard to federal "taxes". This has the effect of gagging the courts from telling the truth about the nature of the federal income tax.

    6.3. The word "internal" means INTERNAL to the Executive Branch and the United States government, not INTERNAL to the geographical United States of America.

7. Create administrative "franchise" courts in the Executive Branch which administer the program pursuant to Articles I and IV of the United States Constitution.

    7.1. The U.S. Supreme Court calls such courts "The Fourth Branch of Government", as indicated in:
    > *Government Instituted Slavery Using Franchises*, Form #05.030, Section 18
    > http://sedm.org/Forms/FormIndex.htm

    7.2. U.S. Tax Court. 26 U.S.C. §7441 identifies the U.S. Tax Court as an Article I court.

    7.3. U.S. District Courts. There is no statute establishing any United States District Court as an Article III court. Consequently, even if the judges are Article III judges, they are not filling an Article III office and instead are filling an Article IV office. Consequently, they are Article IV judges. All of these courts were turned into franchise courts in the Judicial Code of 1911 by being renamed from the "District Court of the United States" to the "United States District Court".

    For details on the above scam, see:
    > *What Happened to Justice?*, Form #06.012
    > http://sedm.org/Forms/FormIndex.htm

8. Create other attractive federal franchises that piggyback in their agreements a requirement to participate in the franchise. For instance:

8.1. The original Social Security Act of 1935 contains a provision that those who sign up for this program, also simultaneously become subject to the Internal Revenue Code.

> *Section 8 of the Social Security Act*
> *INCOME TAX ON EMPLOYEES*
>
> *SECTION 801. <u>In addition to other taxes, there shall be levied, collected, and paid upon the income of every individual a tax</u> equal to the following percentages of the wages (as defined in section 811) received by him after December 31, 1936, with respect to employment (as defined in section 811) after such date:*
>
> *(1) With respect to employment during the calendar years 1937, 1938, and 1939, the rate shall be 1 per centum.*
> *(2) With respect to employment during the calendar years 1940, 1941, and 1942, the rate shall 1 1/2 per centum.*
> *(3) With respect to employment during the calendar years 1943, 1944, and 1945, the rate shall be 2 per centum.*
> *(4) With respect to employment during the calendar years 1946, 1947, and 1948, the rate shall be 2 1/2 per centum.*
> *(5) With respect to employment after December 31, 1948, the rate shall be 3 per centum.*

8.2. Most state vehicle codes have "residence" in the state as a prerequisite to signing up for a driver's license and they also mandate supplying a Social Security Number to get a license. Hence, by signing up for a driver's license, you are signing up for the following THREE franchises:

8.2.1. The Vehicle code franchise.

8.2.2. The domicile "civil protection franchise" tied to those who are "residents". This is what makes the applicant a "taxpayer" in the state's income tax codes. See:

> *Why Domicile and Becoming a "Taxpayer" Require Your Consent*, Form #05.002
> http://sedm.org/Forms/FormIndex.htm

8.2.3. The Social Security Franchise. See:

> *Resignation of Compelled Social Security Trustee*, Form #06.002
> http://sedm.org/Forms/FormIndex.htm

9. Offer an opportunity for private citizens not domiciled within the jurisdiction of Congress to "volunteer" by license or private agreement to participate in the franchise and thereby become "public officers" within the Legislative Branch. The IRS Form W-4 and Social Security SS-5 form are an example of such a contract.

9.1. Call these volunteers "taxpayers".

9.2. Call EVERYONE "taxpayers" so everyone believes that the franchise is MANDATORY.

9.3. Do not even acknowledge the existence of those who do not participate in the franchise. These people are called "nontaxpayers" and they are not mentioned in any IRS publication, even though the following recognize their existence:

9.3.1. The U.S. Supreme Court in South Carolina v. Regan, 465 U.S. 367 (1984).

9.3.2. 26 U.S.C. §7426, which refers to them as "persons other than taxpayers".

9.4. Make the process of signing the agreement invisible by calling it a "Withholding Allowance Certificate" instead of what it really is, which is a "license" to become a "taxpayer" and call all of your earnings "wages" and "gross income".

> *26 C.F.R. §31.3401(a)-3 Amounts deemed wages under voluntary withholding agreements*
>
> *(a) In general.*
>
> ***Notwithstanding the exceptions to the definition of wages specified in section 3401(a) and the regulations thereunder, the term "wages" includes the amounts described in paragraph (b)(1) of this section with respect to which there is a voluntary withholding agreement in effect under section 3402(p).*** *References in this chapter to the definition of wages contained in section 3401(a) shall be deemed to refer also to this section (§31.3401(a)–3.*

> *Title 26: Internal Revenue*
> *PART 31—EMPLOYMENT TAXES AND COLLECTION OF INCOME TAX AT SOURCE*
> *Subpart E—Collection of Income Tax at Source*
> *§31.3402(p)-1 Voluntary withholding agreements.*
>
> *(a) In general.*
>
> *An employee and his employer may enter into an agreement under section 3402(b) to provide for the withholding of income tax upon payments of amounts described in paragraph (b)(1) of §31.3401(a)–3, made after December 31, 1970.* ***An agreement may be entered into under this section only with respect to amounts which are***

includible in the gross income of the employee under section 61, and must be applicable to all such amounts paid by the employer to the employee. The amount to be withheld pursuant to an agreement under section 3402(p) shall be determined under the rules contained in section 3402 and the regulations thereunder. See §31.3405(c)–1, Q&A–3 concerning agreements to have more than 20-percent Federal income tax withheld from eligible rollover distributions within the meaning of section 402.

10. Create a commissioner to service the franchise who:
    10.1. Becomes the "fall guy", who then establishes a "bureau" without the authority of any law and which is a private corporation that is not part of the U.S. government.

    > 53 Stat. 489
    > Revenue Act of 1939, 53 Stat. 489
    > Chapter 43: Internal Revenue Agents
    > Section 4000 Appointment
    >
    > *The Commissioner may, whenever in his judgment the necessities of the service so require, employ **competent agents**, who shall be known and designated as internal revenue agents, and, except as provided for in this title, **no general or special agent or inspector of the Treasury Department** in connection with internal revenue, by whatever designation he may be known, **shall be appointed, commissioned, or employed**.*

    10.2. Creates and manages a PRIVATE company that is not part of the government. The IRS, in fact, is NOT part of the U.S. government and has no legal authority to exist, and therefore can service only those INTERNAL to the government. All agencies that interact DIRECTLY with the PRIVATE public must be authorized by Congress. Hence, "INTERNAL Revenue Service". See:

    > *Origins and Authority of the Internal Revenue Service*, Form #05.005
    > http://sedm.org/Forms/FormIndex.htm

    The above means that everyone who works for the Internal Revenue Service is private contractor not appointed, commissioned, or employed by anyone in the government. They operation on commission and their pay derives from the amount of plunder they steal. See also:

    > *Department of Justice Admits under Penalty of Perjury that the IRS is Not an Agency of the Federal Government, Family Guardian Fellowship*
    > http://famguardian.org/Subjects/Taxes/Evidence/USGovDeniesIRS/USGovDeniesIRS.htm

11. Create an environment that encourages omission in enforcing justice, irresponsibility, lies, and dishonesty within the bureau that administers the franchise.
    11.1. Indemnify these private contractors from liability by giving them "pseudonames" so that they can disguise their identify and be indemnified from liability for their criminal acts. The IRS Restructuring and Reform Act, Pub.Law 105-206, Title III, Section 3706, 112 Stat. 778 and Internal Revenue Manual (I.R.M.), Section 1.2.4 both authorize these pseudonames.
    11.2. Place a disclaimer on the website of this private THIEF contractor indemnifying them from liability for the truthfulness or accuracy of any of their statements or publications. See Internal Revenue Manual (I.R.M.), Section 4.10.7.2.8.

    > *"IRS Publications, issued by the National Office, explain the law in plain language for taxpayers and their advisors... While a good source of general information, publications should not be cited to sustain a position."*
    > *[Internal Revenue Manual (I.R.M.), Section 4.10.7.2.8 (05-14-1999)]*

    11.3. Allow employees of the agency to operate without either identifying their full legal birthname but rather a pseudonym. IRS employees DO NOT use their real name so they can act essentially as anonymous, masked, international terrorists (the states are nations under the law of nations) sanctioned by law. See:

    > *Notice of Pseudonym Use and Unreliable Tax Records*, Form #04.206
    > http://sedm.org/Forms/FormIndex.htm

    11.4. Omit the most important key facts and information from publications of the franchise administrator that would expose the proper application of the "tax" and the proper audience. See the following, which is over 2000 pages of information that are conveniently "omitted" from the IRS website about the proper application of the franchise and its nature as a "franchise":

    > *Great IRS Hoax*, Form #11.302
    > http://sedm.org/Forms/FormIndex.htm

    11.5. Establish precedent in federal courts that you can't trust anything that anyone in the government tells you, and especially those who administer the franchise. See:
    http://famguardian.org/Subjects/Taxes/Articles/IRSNotResponsible.htm

12. Use the lies and deceptions created in the previous step to promote several false perceptions in the public at large that will expand the market for the franchise. These include:
    12.1. That the franchise is NOT a franchise, but a mandatory requirement that applies to ALL. In fact it can and does apply ONLY to statutory "taxpayers" and you have to VOLUNTEER to become a statutory "taxpayer" before it can have the "force of law" in your case.
    12.2. That participation is mandatory for ALL, instead of only for franchisees called "taxpayers".
    12.3. That the IRS is an "agency" of the United States government that has authority to interact directly with the public at large. In fact, it is a "bureau" that can ONLY lawfully service the needs of other federal agencies within the Executive Branch and which may NOT interface directly with the public at large.
    12.4. That the statutes implementing the franchise are "public law" that applies to everyone, instead of "private law" that only applies to those who individually consent to participate in the franchise.
13. Create a system to service those who prepare tax returns for others whereby those who accept being "licensed" and regulated get special favors. This system created by the IRS essentially punishes those who do not participate by deliberately giving them horrible service and making them suffer inconvenience and waiting long in line if they don't accept the "privilege" of being certified. Once they are certified, if they begin telling people the truth about what the law says and encourage following the law by refusing to volunteer, their credentials are pulled. This sort of censorship is accomplished through:
    13.1. IRS Enrolled Agent Program.
    13.2. Certified Public Accountant (CPA) licensing.
    13.3. Treasury Circular 230.
14. Engage in a pattern of "selective enforcement" and propaganda to broaden and expand the scam. For instance:
    14.1. Refuse to answer simple questions about the proper application of the franchise and the taxes associated with it. See:

    > *If the IRS Were Selling Used Cars*, Family Guardian Fellowship
    > http://famguardian.org/Subjects/Taxes/FalseRhetoric/IRSSellingCars.htm

    14.2. Prosecute those who submit false TAX returns, but not those who submit false INFORMATION returns. This causes the audience of "taxpayers" to expand because false reports are connecting innocent third parties to franchises that they are not in fact engaged in.
    14.3. Use confusion over the rules of statutory construction and the word "includes" to fool people into believing that those who are "included" in the franchise are not spelled out in the law in their entirety. This leaves undue discretion in the hands of IRS employees to compel ignorant "nontaxpayers" to become franchisees. See the following:

    > *Legal Deception, Propaganda, and Fraud*, Form #05.014
    > http://sedm.org/Forms/FormIndex.htm

    14.4. Refuse to define the words used on government forms, use terms that are not defined in the code such as "U.S. citizen", and try to confuse "words of art" found in the law with common terms in order to use the presumptuous behavior of the average American to expand the misperception that everyone has a legal DUTY to become a "franchisee" and a "taxpayer".
    14.5. Refuse to accept corrected information returns that might protect innocent "nontaxpayers" so that they are inducted involuntarily into the franchise as well.

The above process is WICKED in the most extreme way. It describes EXACTLY how our public servants have made themselves into our masters and systematically replaced every one of our rights with "privileges" and franchises. The Constitutional prohibition against this sort of corruption are described as follows by the courts:

> *"It would be a palpable incongruity to strike down an act of state legislation which, by words of express divestment, seeks to strip the citizen of rights guaranteed by the federal Constitution, but to uphold an act by which the same result is accomplished under the guise of a surrender of a right in exchange for a valuable privilege which the state threatens otherwise to withhold. It is not necessary to challenge the proposition that, as a general rule, the state, having power to deny a privilege altogether, may grant it upon such conditions as it sees fit to impose. But the power of the state in that respect is not unlimited, and one of the limitations is that it may not impose conditions which require the relinquishment of Constitutional rights. If the state may compel the surrender of one constitutional right as a condition of its favor, it may, in like manner, compel a surrender of all. It is inconceivable that guaranties embedded in the Constitution of the United States may thus be manipulated out of existence."*
> [Frost v. Railroad Commission, 271 U.S. 583, 46 S.Ct. 605 (1926)]

> *"A right common in every citizen such as the right to own property or to engage in business of a character not requiring regulation CANNOT, however, be taxed as a special franchise by first prohibiting its exercise and then permitting its enjoyment upon the payment of a certain sum of money."*

> *[Stevens v. State, 2 Ark. 291, 35 Am.Dec. 72; Spring Val. Water Works v. Barber, 99 Cal. 36, 33 Pac. 735, 21 L.R.A. 416. Note 57 L.R.A. 416]*
>
> *"The individual, unlike the corporation, cannot be taxed for the mere privilege of existing. The corporation is an artificial entity which owes its existence and charter power to the State, but the individual's right to live and own property are natural rights for the enjoyment of which an excise cannot be imposed."*
> *[Redfield v. Fisher, 292 Oregon 814, 817]*
>
> *"Legislature...cannot name something to be a taxable privilege unless it is first a privilege." [Taxation West Key 43]..."The Right to receive income or earnings is a right belonging to every person and realization and receipt of income is therefore not a 'privilege', that can be taxed."*
> *[Jack Cole Co. v. MacFarland, 337 S.W.2d. 453, Tenn.]*

Through the above process of corruption, the separation of powers is completely destroyed and nearly every American has essentially been "assimilated" into the Executive Branch of the government, leaving the Constitutional Republic bequeathed to us by our founding fathers vacant and abandoned. Nearly every service that we expect from government has been systematically converted over the years into a franchise using the techniques described above. The political and legal changes resulting from the above have been tabulated to show the "BEFORE" and the "AFTER" so their extremely harmful effects become crystal clear in your mind. This process of corruption, by the way, is not unique to the United States, but is found in every major industrialized country on Earth.

Table 6-3: Effect of turning government service into a franchise

#	Characteristic	DE JURE CONSTITUTIONAL GOVERNMENT	DE FACTO GOVERNMENT BASED ENTIRELY ON FRANCHISES
1	Purpose of government	Protection	Provide "social services" and "social insurance" to government "employees" and officers
2	Nature of government	Public trust Charitable trust	For-profit private corporation (see 28 U.S.C. §3002(15)(A))
3	Citizens	The Sovereigns "nationals" but not "citizens" pursuant to 8 U.S.C. §1101(a)(21) and 1452	1. "Employees" or "officers" of the government 2. "Trustees" of the "public trust" 3. "customers" of the corporation 4. Statutory "U.S. citizens" pursuant to 8 U.S.C. §1401
4	Effective domicile of citizens	Sovereign state of the Union	Federal territory and the District of Columbia
5	Ownership of real property is	Legal	Equitable. The government owns the land, and you rent it from them using property taxes.
6	Type of property ownership	Absolute and allodial	Qualified (shared with government). Owned by the public office and managed by the person volunteering into the office.
7	Meaning of word "rights"	Constitutional rights	Statutory privileges under a civil franchise. Constitutional rights don't exist and are irrelevant.
8	Purpose of tax system	Fund "protection"	1. Socialism. 2. Political favors. 3. Wealth redistribution 4. Consolidation of power and control (corporate fascism) 5. Bribe PRIVATE people to join the franchise and become public officers collecting "benefits"
9	Equal protection	Mandatory	Optional
10	Nature of courts	Constitutional Article III courts in the Judicial Branch	Administrative or "franchise" courts within the Executive Branch
11	Branches within the government	Executive Legislative Judicial	Executive Legislative (Judiciary merged with Executive. See Judicial Code of 1911)
12	Purpose of legal profession	Protect individual rights	1. Protect collective (government) rights. 2. Protect and expand the government monopoly. 3. Discourage reforms by making litigation so expensive that it is beyond the reach of the average citizen. 4. Persecute dissent.
13	Lawyers are	Unlicensed	Privileged and licensed and therefore subject to control and censorship by the government.

#	Characteristic	DE JURE CONSTITUTIONAL GOVERNMENT	DE FACTO GOVERNMENT BASED ENTIRELY ON FRANCHISES
14	Votes in elections cast by	"Electors"	"Franchisees" called "registered voters" who are surety for bond measures on the ballot. That means they are subject to a "poll tax".
15	Driving is	A common right	A licensed "privilege"
16	Marriage is	A common right	A licensed "privilege"
17	Purpose of the military	Protect the sovereign citizens. No draft within states of the Union is lawful. See Federalist Paper #15	1. Expand the corporate monopoly internationally 2. Protect public servants from the angry populace who want to end the tyranny.
18	Money is	1. Based on gold and silver. 2. Issued pursuant to Article 1, Section 8. Clause 5.	1. A corporate bond or obligation borrowed from the Federal Reserve at interest. 2. Issued pursuant to Article 1, Section 8. Clause 2.
19	Purpose of sex	Procreation	Recreation
20	Responsibility	The individual sovereign is responsible for all his actions and choices.	The collective "social insurance company" is responsible. Personal responsibility is outlawed.
21	Meaning of "State", "this State"	"Body politic" and NOT "body corporate"	"Body corporate" and NOT "body politic". There is no body politic and everyone is presumed to be part of the body corporate as a public officer.
22	Meaning of "in this State" or "in the State" in statutes	PHYSICALLY PRESENT within the geographic limits of the territory composing the state.	LEGALLY and NOT PHYSICALLY present within the corporation as a "person" and therefore "public officer" of the corporation.
23	Real party in interest in criminal actions filed by the state	Specific human being injured who is within the body politic	Private CORPORATION called "State of". Most actions are "penal" or "quasi criminal" rather than "criminal" in a classical sense. Such penal actions can only be associated with franchisees under a civil franchise.

If you would like to know more about the subjects discussed in this section, please refer to the following free memorandums of law on our website focused exclusively on this subject:

1. *De Facto Government Scam*, Form #05.043
   http://sedm.org/Forms/FormIndex.htm
2. *Corporatization and Privatization of the Government*, Form #05.024
   http://sedm.org/Forms/FormIndex.htm
3. *Government Instituted Slavery Using Franchises*, Form #05.030
   http://sedm.org/Forms/FormIndex.htm

6.5 General Evolution

If the average American is not legally liable to pay taxes on his earned income, then how did we evolve to the point where we have to pay income taxes in violation of our constitutional rights? We've scoured every tax book and government publication we could find totaling thousands of pages to compile a chronological sequence for how the fraud was perpetrated over the last century. Because this process involves essentially criminal activity, there has been a concerted effort by the government to cover it up, which we will describe in detail later. The most glaring evidence of that cover-up is found in the testimony of Shelley Davis, the IRS' only historian, who testified in front of Congress during the IRS Restructuring hearings in 1998 and whose testimony we captured for you to read later in section 6.9.9.1. She also wrote a book documenting the secret culture within the IRS entitled *Unbridled Power* which we highly recommend. Criminals, you will recall, don't want any historical information maintained about their misdeeds, and the IRS is one of the few organizations associated with the federal government that has no historical records, no current historian, and a concerted effort to provide as little information about their activities in their FOIA responses as possible. In most cases, you actually have to litigate against the IRS in federal court to get the information you want because they are so tight-lipped in their cover-up of their wrongdoing.

The most fruitful single source for information about the history of the Internal Revenue Service is found in a publication written by the Commissioner of Internal Revenue in 1948 entitled *The Work and Jurisdiction of the Bureau of Internal Revenue, 1948*, which we have published electronically and made freely available on our website at the below address:

http://famguardian.org/PublishedAuthors/Govt/IRS/WorkAndJurisOfTheBIR1948s.pdf

You will DEFINITELY want to download this large book (10.8 Mbytes) and read the history of the IRS right out of the horse's mouth. Below is a brief chronology of w the fraud was perpetrated over the years, as compiled from the many government publications at our disposal:

1. **1776: Declaration of Independence Signed.**
2. **1818: U.S. v. Bevans, 16 U.S. 336 (1818)**
   The U.S. supreme Court ruled that there are two separate and distinct jurisdictions within the United States of America:

   > "The exclusive jurisdiction which the United States have in forts and dock-yards ceded to them, is derived from the express assent of the states by whom the cessions are made. It could be derived in no other manner; because without it, the authority of the state would be supreme and exclusive therein," 3 Wheat., at 350, 351.
   > [U.S. v. Bevans, 16 U.S. 336 (1818)]

   This case is very significant, because it has never been overruled and when we read laws in the U.S. Codes, it is very important for us to establish which of these two jurisdictions apply. If it is the latter jurisdiction, the 50 union states, then the law applies to us. If it is the former jurisdiction, also called the "federal zone", then the law doesn't apply to the vast majority of citizens domiciled in the 50 union states. The Internal Revenue Code, incidentally, ONLY applies to the "federal zone"…not to you!

3. **1861-1865: Civil War**

4. **January 1, 1863: Emancipation Proclamation signed by President Lincoln**

5. **1862: The Nation's First Income Tax**
   5.1 President Lincoln introduced the first income tax to pay for the Civil War. Congress eliminated the tax in 1872.
   5.2 The Tax Act of 1862 was passed and signed by President Lincoln July 1 1862. The rates were 3% on income above $600 and 5% on income above $10,000. The rent or rental value of your home could be deducted from income in determining the tax liability. The Commissioner of Revenue stated "The people of this country have accepted it with cheerfulness, to meet a temporary exigency, and it has excited no serious complaint in its administration." This acceptance was primarily due to the need for revenue to finance the Civil War.
   5.3 Although the people cheerfully accepted the tax, compliance was not high. Figures released after the Civil War indicated that 276,661 people actually filed tax returns in 1870 (the year of the highest returns filed) when the country's population was approximately 38 million.
   5.4 With the end of the Civil War the public's accepted cheerfulness waned. The Tax Act of 1864 was modified after the war. The rates were changed to a flat 5 percent with the exemption amount raised to $1,000. Several attempts to make the tax permanent were tried but by 1869 "no businessman could pass the day without suffering from those burdens" From 1870 to 1872 the rate was a flat 2.5 percent and the exemption amount was raised to $2,000.
6. **1868: States Ratify the 14th Amendment**
   6.1 Citizenship was extended to Blacks. This was done in order to protect blacks, because southern states would give them no citizenship or rights under state law.
   6.2 Legislatures of the Southern States under gun point were forced to ratify the 14th Amendment.
   6.3 Just before the passage of the 14th Amendment, Congress passed a revision to the Statutes at Large which gave people a way out of being constitutional "citizens of the United States", 15 Stat. 223-224 (1868), R.S. § 1999, which stated that:

Chapter 6: History of Government Income Tax Fraud, Racketeering and Extortion in the U.S.A.

"*the right of expatriation is a natural and inherent right of all people, indispensable to the enjoyment of the rights of life, liberty, and the pursuit of happiness,*" *and decreed that* "*any declaration, instruction, opinion, order, or decision of any officers of this government which denies, restricts, impairs, or questions the right of expatriation, is hereby declared inconsistent with the fundamental principles of this government.*"

7. **1871: U.S. Inc. Federal Corporation Established**
   District of Columbia Organic Act of 1871, 16 Stat. 419-429 created a "municipal corporation" to govern the District of Columbia. Considering the fact that the municipal corporation itself was incorporated in 1801, an "Organic Act" (first Act) using the term "municipal corporation" in 1871 can only mean a private corporation owned by the municipality. Hereinafter we will call that private corporation, "Corp. U.S." By consistent usage, Corp. U.S. trademarked the name, "United States Government" referring to themselves. The District of Columbia Organic Act of 1871, 16 Stat. 419-429 places Congress in control (like a corporate board) and gives the purpose of the act to form a governing body over the municipality; this allowed Congress to direct the business needs of the government under the existent martial law and provided them with corporate abilities they would not otherwise have. This was done under the constitutional authority for Congress to pass any law within the ten mile square of the District of Columbia..

8. **1872: Nation's First Income Tax was Repealed**
   The Internal Revenue Act of 1862 was repealed, ending the nation's first income tax. The civil war was over and paid for and there was no longer any reason for the tax.

9. **1872: Office of the Assessor of Internal Revenue Eliminated**
   Functions of Assessor delegated to the Collector of Internal Revenue. See: 17 Statutes at Large, p. 401, 42nd Congress, Session III Chapter XIII (December 24, 1872).

10. **1875: U.S. v. Cruikshank, 92 U.S. 542 (1875). Supreme Court Confirms that there are Two Types of Citizens: federal and state**

    "*We have in our political system a Government of the United States and a government of each of the several States. Each of these governments is distinct from the others, and each has citizens of its own*

    ...

    "*Both before and after the Fourteenth Amendment to the federal Constitution, it has not been necessary for a person to be a citizen of the United States in order to be a citizen of his state.*"
    [Citing U.S. v. Cruikshank, 92 U.S. 542 (1875)]

11. **1894: Caha v. United States, 152 U.S. 211 (1894)**
    The U.S. supreme Court ruled that Congress can only make laws that apply to areas over which it has exclusive jurisdiction, which is the "federal zone", including the District of Columbia and other federal territories. It cannot make laws affecting activity within the states unless the Constitution explicitly grants that authority:

    "*The law of Congress in respect to those matters do not extend into the territorial limits of the states, but have force only in the District of Columbia, and other places that are within the exclusive jurisdiction of the national government.*"
    [Caha v. United States, 152 U.S. 211 (1894)]

12. **1895: Pollock v. Farmers' Loan & Trust Co., 157 U.S. 429, 158 U.S. 601 (1895)**
    12.1 U.S. Supreme court ruled that direct taxes on the income of individuals are unconstitutional and are forbidden.
    12.2 Here was the court's ruling:

    "*Nothing can be clearer than that what the constitution intended to guard against was the exercise by the general government of the power of directly taxing persons and property within any state through a majority made up from the other states. It is true that the effect of requiring direct taxes to be apportioned among the states in proportion to their population is necessarily that the amount of taxes on the individual [157 U.S. 429, 583] taxpayer in a state having the taxable subject-matter to a larger extent in proportion to its population than another state has, would be less than in such other state; but this inequality must be held to have been contemplated, and was manifestly designed to operate to restrain the exercise of the power of direct taxation to extraordinary emergencies, and to prevent an attack upon accumulated property by mere force of numbers.*

    ...

The Great IRS Hoax: Why We Don't Owe Income Tax, version 4.54
TOP SECRET: For Official Treasury/IRS Use Only (FOUO)   Copyright Family Guardian Fellowship

It is the duty of the court in this case simply to determine whether the income tax now before it does or does not belong to the class of direct taxes, and if it does, to decide the constitutional question which follows . . .

First. That the law in question, in imposing a tax on the income or rents of real estate, imposes a tax upon the real estate itself; and in imposing a tax on the interest or other income of bonds or other personal property, held for the purposes of income or ordinarily yielding income, imposes a tax upon the personal estate itself; that such tax is a direct tax, and void because imposed without regard to the rule of apportionment; and that by reason thereof the whole law is invalidated.

Second. That the law is invalid, because imposing indirect taxes in violation of the constitutional requirement of uniformity, and therein also in violation of the implied limitation upon taxation that all tax laws must apply equally, impartially, and uniformly to all similarly situated. Under the second head, it is contended that the rule of uniformity is violated, in that the law taxes the income of certain corporations, companies, and associations, no matter how created or organized, at a higher rate than the incomes of individuals or partnerships derived from precisely similar property or business; in that it exempts from the operation of the act and from the burden of taxation numerous corporations, companies, and associations having similar property and carrying on similar business to those expressly taxed; in that it denies to individuals deriving their income from shares in certain corporations, companies, and associations the benefit of the exemption of $ 4,000 granted to other persons interested in similar property and business; in the exemption of $4,000; in the exemption of building and loan associations, savings banks, mutual life, fire, marine, and accident insurance companies, existing solely for the pecuniary profit of their members,-these and other exemptions being alleged to be purely arbitrary and capricious, justified by no public purpose, and of such magnitude as to invalidate the entire enactment; and in other particulars. "
[Pollock v. Farmers' Loan & Trust Co., 157 U.S. 429, 158 U.S. 601 (1895)]

13. **1900: Knowlton v. Moore, 178 U.S. 41 (1900)**
The U.S. supreme Court defined the difference between direct taxes [income taxes on persons] and excise taxes:

    "Direct taxes bear immediately upon persons, upon the possession and enjoyment of rights; indirect taxes are levied upon the happening of an event as an exchange."
    [Knowlton v. Moore, 178 U.S. 41 (1900)]

14. **1901: Downes v. Bidwell, 182 U.S. 244 (1901): Corruption of our Tax System**
    14.1 The U.S. Supreme Court ruled that people domiciled in federal territories such as Puerto Rico, Guam, the District of Columbia, and the Virgin Islands, are NOT protected by the U.S. Constitution. Therefore, these people could be subjected to direct taxes on income because they were classified as citizens of the U.S.
    14.2 Below is an excerpt from that ruling:

    "CONSTITUTIONAL RESTRICTIONS AND LIMITATIONS [Bill of Rights] WERE NOT APPLICABLE to the areas of lands, enclaves, territories, and possessions over which Congress had EXCLUSIVE LEGISLATIVE JURISDICTION"
    [Downes v. Bidwell, 182 U.S. 244 (1901)]

    14.3 This lead subsequently to the imposition of direct taxes on the income of individuals who were U.S. Citizens following the fraudulent ratification of the 16th Amendment in 1913.
    14.4 This ruling was also behind why income tax returns after this case ask you: "Are you a U.S. Citizen?". Once you answer yes, you give up your constitutional rights! See sections 4.6 and 4.8 for further details on this.

15. **1909: Congress proposed the 16th Amendment and sent to states for ratification**
    15.1 The Senate approved it by an astounding vote of 77 to zero and the House followed suit with a roll call of 318 to 14.
    15.2 The measure then went to the states for ratification.

16. **1909: Corporate Excise Tax of 1909 was passed, 36 Stat 112.**
    16.1 This was the country's first income tax, where "income" was defined as corporate profit.
    16.2 All subsequent income tax laws and the Internal Revenue Code itself were based on this.
    16.3 The Supreme Court ruled in *Bowers v. Kerbaugh-Empire Co.*, 271 U.S. 170, 174 (1926) that:

    "Income has been taken to mean the same thing as used in the Corporation Excise Tax Act of 1909 (36 Stat. 112) in the 16th Amendment, and in the various revenue acts subsequently passed."
    [Bowers v. Kerbaugh-Empire Co., 271 U.S. 170, 174 (1926)]

17. **1911: Judicial Code of 1911:**

Chapter 6: History of Government Income Tax Fraud, Racketeering and Extortion in the U.S.A.

This act abolished the existing circuit courts and replaced them with Circuit Courts of Appeals. The District Courts of the United States became "United States District Courts". This left no Article III courts to hear cases involving constitutional rights. All district and circuit courts became, at that point, Article II courts which may only have jurisdiction within territories of the United States Government. These courts are part of the executive branch, not the judicial branch, of the U.S. government. The judges in these Art. II courts are civil service employees of the Office of Personnel Management, which is part of the Executive Branch. The judges are not judicial officers as required under Art. III of the Constitution, but federal employees.

18. **Feb. 12, 1913: 42nd state "allegedly" voted for approval of 16th Amendment, and the following words became a part of the United States Constitution:**

    "The Congress shall have power to lay and collect taxes on incomes, from whatever source derived, without apportionment among the several States, and without regard to any census or enumeration."

    Of course, we all know that the claim that the 16th amendment was ratified by the then secretary of state Philander Knox this was indeed one of the biggest "frauds" in history that has not to this day ever been questioned or investigated by a Congress that wants YOUR money. It ought to be quite obvious why the Supreme court won't touch this and the Congress has refused to investigate this fraud from the beginning. You can read about this fraud in a book called "Law That Never Was" by ordering the book from the following website:

    http://www.thelawthatneverwas.com/

19. **Oct. 3, 1913: Tariff Act**

    The Tariff Act of October 3, 1913, IIE, 38 Stat. 170 was passed, and it contained, perhaps somewhat surprisingly, a fairly expansive withholding provision. It was later repealed and replaced with the 1954 Code, 26 U.S.C. §6041 et seq.

20. **1913: Congress creates the Federal Reserve System with the Federal Reserve Act of 1913**
    20.1 Congress creates the FRS; permits the emission of FRNs, redeemable in "lawful money"; and declares FRNs to be "obligations of the United States", but *not* "legal tender". In practice, the Federal Reserve Banks and the United States Treasury redeem FRNs for gold coin on demand. FRNs are a *fiduciary* currency.
    20.2 Note that the Federal Reserve and the income tax were enacted at the same time because they cannot function without each other. If we are going to put our money supply in the hands of private bankers, then we need a way to sop up excess printed dollars with an income tax, or the economy will go out of control and inflation will spiral. Since both the income tax and the Federal Reserve are evil, we must eliminate both of them at the same time as well.

21. **1913-1917: Media heralded coming of the 16th Amendment**
    21.1 Announced after its alleged ratification that it was the basis for the new income tax which only the wealthy would pay. The camel now had its nose under the tent and all Congress had to do was raise the tax rates over time and let the camel all the way in.
    21.2 Who controlled the printed media in 1913? John D. Rockefeller and his bankers, through stock ownership.
    21.3 Most of the papers parroted what they were instructed to tell the people.
    21.4 To this day, a nationwide chorus of politicians, TV economists and Law school professors alike all repeat that the 16th Amendment authorized the imposition of an income tax on U.S. citizens. They are all mistaken.

22. **1916: Stanton v. Baltic Mining Co., 240 U.S. 103 (1916)**
    22.1 The U.S. Supreme Court ruled that the 16th Amendment conferred "***no new powers of taxation***"!
    22.2 Here are some excerpts. The 16th Amendment…:

    "…prohibited the … power of income taxation possessed by Congress from the beginning from being taken out of the category of indirect taxation to which it inherently belonged…"
    [Stanton v. Baltic Mining Co., 240 U.S. 103 (1916)]

    22.3 This was a big blow to the IRS. Shortly after that case Treasury Decision 2313 was issued as a form of "damage control".

23. **March 21, 1916: Treasury Decision 2313**

The Great IRS Hoax: Why We Don't Owe Income Tax, version 4.54

23.1 Thwarted by the *Brushaber* and *Stanton* decisions, the Department of Treasury issued Treasury Decision Number 2313. Here are a few excerpted quotes from T.D. 2313 in reference to the *Brushaber* decision:

> "...it is hereby held that income accruing to nonresident aliens in the form of interest...and dividends...is subject to the income tax imposed by the act of October 3, 1913. The responsible heads, agents, or representatives of nonresident aliens...shall make a full and complete return of the income therefrom on ...Form 1040..."

23.2 So there you have it. The Treasury Department has stated that you are to file Form 1040 on behalf of your "nonresident alien principal." So don't forget to do that next April 15th! Of course, since you'll be signing Form 1040 under penalties of perjury and stating that every material fact is 100% correct to the best of your knowledge, and since the commission of perjury is a felony that attaches criminal fines and penalties, be sure you really are filing Form 1040 on behalf of your "nonresident alien principal"!

23.3 By reading Internal Revenue Code section 871(a), we see that it imposes a tax of 30% on the amount received by non-resident aliens from sources within the United States. Code section 871(b) states that the nonresident alien shall be taxable under code section 1, thus authorizing the use of the charts in section 1 to compute and reduce his tax, so he can get a tax refund from the 30% which is withheld under the provisions of section 1441.

23.4 Also, under section 874(a), the nonresident alien is entitled to the benefit of deductions and credits filing or having his agent file, a 1040, as stated in TD 2313.

23.5 *Of course, this whole fiasco has nothing whatsoever to do with most Americans, who aren't liable for federal income taxes at all unless they make themselves liable by "volunteering"!*

24. 1920: Evans v. Gore, 253 U.S. 245 (1920); Supreme Court Declares Direct Taxes on Federal Judges to Not be Authorized by the 16th Amendment and Unconstitutional

24.1 In this case, the Supreme Court addressed the issue of whether a tax on salary was authorized:

> "After further consideration, we adhere to that view and accordingly hold that the Sixteenth Amendment does not authorize or support the tax in question. " [A direct tax on salary income of a federal judge]
>
> [Evans v. Gore, 253 U.S. 245 (1920)]

24.2 This case has a very thorough treatment of the 16th Amendment taxing issues, and discusses nearly all of the issues critical to the income tax, and by the way, fully supports the entire position advocated in this document with regards to the 26 U.S.C. §861 issues and taxable source issues.

25. 1922: Supreme Court Rules Against Socialism in the Case of Bailey v. Drexel Furniture Co., 259 U.S. 20 (1922)

25.1 This case was about the validity of Child Labor Tax law imposed by Congress. The Drexel Furniture Company filed suit because it didn't want to be forced to pay the Child Labor Tax to the IRS. The Supreme Court ruled that the Child Labor Tax Law was unconstitutional because it amounted to social engineering and exceeded the powers conferred by the Constitution on the federal government. In effect, they called it socialism and an abuse of the taxing and legal authority of Congress conferred by the Constitution and amounted to legislating socialism by legislatively plundering the employer profits for the benefit of the employees. The findings in this case are similar to the case of **Railroad Retirement Board v. Alton Railroad Co., 295 U.S. 330 (1935)**. The arguments used here apply equally well to the federal income tax, as we pointed out in the preface to this document.

> "Out of a proper respect for the acts of a co-ordinate branch of the government, this court has gone far to sustain taxing acts as such, even though there has been ground for suspecting, from the weight of the tax, it was intended to destroy its subject. But in the act before [259 U.S. 20, 38] us the presumption of validity cannot prevail, because the proof of the contrary is found on the very face of its provisions. *Grant the validity of this law, and all that Congress would need to do, hereafter, in seeking to take over to its control any one of the great number of subjects of public interest, jurisdiction of which the states have never parted with, and which are reserved to them by the Tenth Amendment, would be to enact a detailed measure of complete regulation of the subject and enforce it by a so-called tax upon departures from it. To give such magic to the word 'tax' would be to break down all constitutional limitation of the powers of Congress and completely wipe out the sovereignty of the states.*"
>
> [Bailey v. Drexel Furniture Co., 259 U.S. 20 (1922)]

25.2 Keep in mind the historical context of this ruling. The Federal Reserve had just been created by Congress AND the 16th Amendment had just been claimed fraudulently to have been ratified by Philander Knox, also in 1913. The tax code of 1921 had just been passed by 1922, which was a major rewrite of the code designed to conceal the unconstitutionality of income taxes on individuals. Now Congress was trying to expand its power even further by abusing its legislative authority to force employers to increase benefits to their workers!

26. 1925: Certiorari Act of 1925 Passed

26.1 Former President William Howard Taft, then acting as Chief Justice of the U.S. Supreme Court, helped author a bill called the Certiorari Act of 1925. Recall that William Taft had been the President who introduced the Sixteenth Amendment to the U.S. Congress in 1909 (see section 3.11.11.1 for further details on this). This Act authorized the U.S. Supreme Court to have discretion to deny the hearing of appeals from lower federal appeal courts. By refusing to hear an appeal, the Supreme Court in effect had the right to deny Constitutional rights of the appellants from the circuit courts if such rights had been violated by the lower courts or the then Bureau of Internal Revenue (now called the IRS). Justices of the Supreme Court take an oath to support and defend the Constitution against all enemies, foreign and domestic, and by denying appeals, they could in effect violate their oath and condone extortion by the BIR. This kind of scandal is called a sin of omission and its commonplace in the Supreme Court now.

26.2 When you think about it, the Certiorari Act of 1925 violates the separation of powers doctrine because the Judiciary and the Congress are supposed to be separate and sovereign powers within the federal government. How can one branch of government, the Congress in this case, authorize another *supposedly independent* branch of federal government, the Supreme Court in this Case, to violate the Constitutional rights of Americans by denying their appeals? They can't, because if the appeal involves constitutional issues, then they would not be upholding the constitution as their oath of office requires them to do!

26.3 As we explain subsequently in section 6.7.1, this bill was an important new tool that our corrupt government could use to uphold the federal income tax, because it allows the federal district and circuit courts to uphold and expand federal income taxes while allowing the U.S. Supreme Court to deny appeals from such cases, even if the findings of the lower court disagreed with numerous precedents set on previous Supreme Court cases that invalidate direct federal income taxes. It creates a schizophrenic, split personality federal government which, out of one side of its mouth, the Supreme Court, says income taxes are indirect excise taxes that are not authorized on natural persons as direct taxes, but then out of the other side of its mouth in the federal district and circuit courts, says direct income taxes are authorized by the Sixteenth Amendment. This represents not only hypocrisy of the highest order but also a violation of our fundamental right to due process under the Fourth, Fifth, and Seventh Amendments! How can you know what the Internal Revenue Code requires of you if the Supreme Court and the federal circuit courts can't even consistently agree and the Supreme Court refuses to hear appeals that contradict its own precedents?

27. 1933: FDR Amends the Trading With The Enemy Act of 1917 to Confiscate all Gold and Declare Emergency

27.1 Trading With The Enemy Act invoked to criminalize holding of gold. Penalty was $10,000 and imprisonment for 10 years. Act only applied on federal territories and possessions but not inside nonfederal areas of the 50 union states. However, FDR make it "appear" that it applied to EVERYONE.

27.2 Congress repudiates redemption of FRNs in gold for United States citizens, and declares that FRNs shall be "legal tender". The government continues to redeem FRNs in gold for foreigners; and United States citizens can redeem FRNs for "lawful money" (such as United States Treasury Notes and silver certificates), which is redeemable in silver coins. Therefore, FRNs remain a fiduciary currency, redeemable directly in gold internationally and indirectly in silver domestically.

28. 1935: FDR Proposes and Congress Passes the Social Security Act of 1935

28.1 FDR gave a pep talk to congress on January 17, 1935 trying to sell Social Security.

28.2 Congress passed FDR's Social Security Act of 1935 on August 14, 1935.

28.3 Once passed, socialism is officially "institutionalized" within our republican government. This marks the beginning of the end of "rugged individualism" in America. The tumor is planted and begins to grow. Eventually, this cancer will destroy the country.

28.4 Voluntary Social Security tax deductions begin.

29. 1935: Supreme Court Rules Against Socialism AGAIN in the Case of Railroad Retirement Board v. Alton Railroad Co., 295 U.S. 330 (1935)

29.1 After the Great Wall Street Crash in 1929, daily newspaper photographs of mile-long soup and bread lines persuaded a frightened public to eagerly embrace the introduction of the European style socialism in the form of Social Security, written and contrived in smoke-filled rooms by the same politician-puppets of the bankers who had engineered both the crash and the depression.

29.2 A public eager to exchange liberty for benefits would vote for those politicians who would promise to provide them with the greatest "fair share" of the public trough. Congress made its first attempt at socialist wealth redistribution when it passed legislation in 1934 to provide for the retirement of railroad workers. Here's what the Supreme Court had to say when they shot this act down as unconstitutional in their decision in ***Railroad Retirement Board v. Alton Railroad Company*** decided May 6, 1935:

> "The catalog of means and actions which might be imposed upon an employer in any business, tending to the comfort and satisfaction of his employees, seems endless.
>
> Provisions for free medical attendance and nursing, for clothing, for food, for housing, for the education of children, and a hundred other matters might with equal propriety be proposed as tending to relieve the employee of mental strain and worry.
>
> Can it fairly be said that the power of Congress to regulate interstate commerce extends to the prescription of any or all of these things?
>
> Is it not apparent that they are really and essentially related solely to social welfare of the worker, and therefore remote from any regulation of commerce as such? We think the answer is plain. These matters obviously lie outside the orbit of Congressional power."
> [Railroad Retirement Board v. Alton Railroad Co., 295 U.S. 330 (1935)]

29.3 There you have it--the high court informing Congress that it has no constitutional authority whatsoever to legislate for the social welfare of the worker. The result was that when Social Security was instituted, it had to be treated as strictly voluntary.

30. 1937: President Franklin D. Roosevelt "Stacks" the Supreme Court to Ramrod His Socialist Programs Down Our Throats!!!

Thwarted by resistance to his socialist programs, including Social Security, in 1937, President Franklin D. Roosevelt announced he was going to "stack" the Supreme Court (see http://www.hpol.org/fdr/chat/). This was called "the court packing plan". The Supreme court originally had 6 justices, and he doubled its size by adding several of his own "cronies" who would uphold and defend his socialist programs, including Social Security and the Victory Tax. He also proposed to replace all the justices over 70, which included 5 of the 6 justices then in office.

31. 1939: Congress Obfuscates the Tax Code by Removing References to Nonresident Aliens from the Definition of "Gross Income"

31.1 In particular, they removed the phrase "**in the case of a nonresident alien individual or of a citizen entitled to the benefits of section 262**" from the 1921 code, which was the predecessor to 26 U.S.C. §861 we have today. There was not fundamental change in the constitution or the law. They made these changes to further conceal the truth.

31.2 See section 6.3.7 "Cover-Up of 1939: Removed References to Nonresident Aliens from the Definition of 'Gross Income'" for details of how Congress obfuscated the tax code in this case.

32. Victory Tax Act of 1942, imposed by the Revenue Act of 1942, 172, 56 Stat. 884. Part of the 1939 Tax Code.

32.1 This act was a *voluntary* employer payroll deduction of income taxes required in order to fight World War II. It represented the start of employer withholding, but note that it was entirely voluntary.

32.2 As a part of the Victory Tax Act, President Franklin Delano Roosevelt created the Voluntary W-4 Withholding System, making income tax withholding mandatory for all citizens of the Union. This was a two year tax, and as expected, both the Victory Tax and the Voluntary W-4 Withholding were repealed by Congress in 1944. Unfortunately, they forgot to tell America.

32.3 Under the disguise of the 1913 Internal Income tax, the machinery of the Victory tax remained in operation. Voluntary compliance with the Federal internal income tax jumped from an anemic 5 percent to a robust 60 percent in a matter of a couple years via the repealed Victory tax system of tax collection. By using two illegitimate tax systems, Congress created the beast we have today, taxing us under rates and conditions exceeding those which prompted the Boston Tea Party and the Declaration of Independence.

32.4 The Victory Tax was replaced by the Current Tax Payment Act of 1943, 57 Stat. 126, and was repealed by the Individual Income Tax Act of 1944, 6 (a), 58 Stat. 234.

33. 1943: President Franklin Delano Roosevelt's Executive Order 9397 made Social Security Numbers a standard tracking mechanism across all federal agencies. Bye-bye privacy and Fourth Amendment!

33.1 Read Presidential Executive Order 9397 at:

http://resource.lawlinks.com/Content/Legal_Research/Executive_Orders/1940-1960/executive_order_9397.htm

34. 1947: U.S. v. Silk, 331 U.S. 704 (1947) Declares Social Security Taxes are Legitimate Excise Taxes On Businesses

34.1 FDR's stacking of the Supreme Court finally pays off!

34.2 The cancer of socialism begins to spread further with encouragement by the state.

34.3 Thomas Jefferson's warnings and predictions are realized:

> "In every government on earth is some trace of human weakness, some germ of corruption and degeneracy, which cunning will discover, and wickedness insensibly open, cultivate and improve."
> [Thomas Jefferson: Notes on Virginia Q.XIV, 1782. ME 2:207]

35. 1952: IRS Reorganization and elimination of the Office of Collector of Internal Revenue

35.1 Office of Collector of Internal Revenue abolished. See Reorganization Plans No. 26 of 1950 and No. 1 of 1952, and Notes under 26 U.S.C. §7804, "Amendments" at:

> https://www.law.cornell.edu/uscode/text/26/7804?qt-us_code_temp_noupdates=1#qt-us_code_temp_noupdates

35.2 As part of this reorganization, the government manufactured a scandal concerning the collectors. The real reason, however, was to make the code voluntary.

35.3 This office of the Collector of Internal Revenue made possible to protest a tax. Without a Collector of Internal Revenue, it is impossible to protest a tax because it has to be voluntary without a collector. If you don't make a demand in the law, then no one has to do anything. This reorganization made the process of tax collection into an administrative process, which allowed all U.S. District courts into administrative courts in regards to federal taxes. The only people who should go to these courts at this point are "taxpayers", which are people who volunteered to pay the tax.

35.4 Section 29 of the 1894 Revenue Act was the *last* federal law that imposed a legal duty to pay upon citizens and residents of the United States. The duty to pay the tax was subsequently eliminated by *Pollock v. Farmers' Loan & Trust Co., 157 U.S. 429 (1895)* and does not appear in any Revenue Law after that date.

36. 1954: Congress Rewrites the Tax Code Again to Hide Constitutional Limitations on The Right To Tax

36.1 Deleted any phrases referring to income that is, under the Constitution or fundamental law, not taxable by the government. This was done by changing the definition of gross income from "unless exempt from tax by law" to "unless excluded by law". There were no changes to the law or the Constitution that would necessitate deleting the reference to the Constitution; it was done for no other credible reason than to obscure the Constitutionally-limited application of the income tax, but without making the regulation technically incorrect - only deceiving and misleading.

36.2 They obfuscated locating taxable sources by adding double-negatives "list of sources that are NOT considered tax exempt". Why not just state what IS taxable, which is foreign income?

36.3 Removed from the regulations the phrase "in the case of nonresident alien individuals and foreign corporations engaged in trade or business within the United States" from the regulations in section 1.861-8. This made it appear that the applicability of the income tax was expanded. As Congress stated, the application of the law did not change in 1954, but some key phrases in the regulations were removed so as to make the truth less obvious.

36.4 The admission of the limited application vanished from the regulations defining "gross income," but remained in the regulations under 26 U.S.C. §861, and (to maintain literal accuracy) the regulations began to say that 861 and following and related regulations "*determine the sources of income for purposes of the income tax*." This change removed any chance of the regulations under Section 61 raising suspicions.

36.5 See section 6.8.12 "Cover-Up of 1954: Hiding Constitutional Limitations on the Right To Tax" for details of how Congress obfuscated the tax code in this case.

37. 1968: Congress Repudiates Redemption of All Forms of "lawful money" in silver

37.1 This turned FRNs into a *fiat* currency domestically *for the first time*.

38. 1971: President Nixon Repudiates Redemption of FRNs in Gold

38.1 This turned FRNs into a *fiat* currency internationally *for the first time*.

39. 1978: Congress Rewrites the Tax Code Again to Confuse the IRS Regulations on "Sources"

39.1 In 1978, the wording of 26 C.F.R. §1.861-8 was changed significantly, and the title was changed from "Computation of Taxable Income from Sources Within the United States" to "Computation of taxable income from sources within the United States **and from other sources and activities**." Some have suggested that the current title implies that one should not be using this section unless he has income both from within the United States and from "other sources and activities." The older title, as well as the text of the current regulations, shows that this is not the case.

39.2 See section 6.8.11 "Cover-Up of 1978: Confused IRS Regulations on 'Sources'" for details of how Congress obfuscated the tax code in this case.

40. 1979: The Zaritsky Report

40.1 Congressional Research Service report #79-131, written in 1979 by Howard Zaritsky and titled *Some Constitutional Questions Regarding the Income Tax Laws* agreed in stating:

> "...therefore it is clear that the income tax is an 'indirect' tax...subject to the rule of uniformity, rather than the rule of apportionment."

40.2 So the so-called "income tax amendment" that everybody and their uncle believe authorized the income tax and that many patriotic Americans object to since there is overwhelming evidence that it was never properly ratified by the States...changed absolutely nothing!

40.3 The 16th Amendment was constitutional window dressing and might as well have never been written. Why? In the original draft of the 16th Amendment, Senate Joint Resolution 39, as per page 3138 of the June 11, 1909 Congressional Record, included the word "direct." Fearing that the Supreme Court would again strike it down, Senator Nelson Aldrich, Chairman of the powerful Senate Finance Committee, and as you will recall, the host of the Jekyll Island conference, presented Senate Joint Resolution No. 40, entered on page 3900 of the Congressional Record of June 28, 1909, in which the word "direct" is omitted.

40.4 By deliberately omitting the word "direct" and then ending with the phrase, "...without apportionment among the several States", the language of the 16th was cleverly crafted to create the illusion that some new type of presumably direct, yet unapportioned tax was being imposed on "income."

40.5 But here's the problem. Article 1, Section 2, Clause 3, and Article 1, Section 9, Clause 4 requiring the apportionment of direct taxes, and Article 1, Section 8, Clause 1 requiring that indirect taxes be uniform had never been repealed and, at the time the 16th was drafted, they were still standing law. As the Supreme Court ruled in the famous *Marbury v. Madison* case in 1803, the Constitution cannot conflict with itself! An unapportioned income tax, as the 16th called for, would by very definition, have to be an indirect tax, because direct taxes still had to be apportioned.

40.6 The Supreme Court was alert to this ruse and chided Congress by deciding in *Stanton* that the inclusion of the phrase "without apportionment" could only mean that Congress intended to clarify that the income tax is indeed an indirect tax. The 16th Amendment to the United States Constitution did not repeal or alter Congress' power, or obligation, to impose the emergency direct tax should a deficit arise.

40.7 The power of Congress to impose a direct tax still exists, and direct taxes are still required to be apportioned among the states.

> *The fact that the 16th Amendment did not change one word or phrase in the Constitution has, for years, been one of the U.S. government's best kept secrets!*

Many college professors in our country's most prestigious institutions still teach that the income tax is neither a direct nor an indirect tax, but is a hybrid tax that falls somewhere between the two. Such a gross lack of understanding by those charged with teaching the Law to future lawyers is, in my opinion, unpardonable. It also explains many of the unexplained controversies and inconsistencies in the application of the Internal Revenue Code in the various circuit and district courts in section 3.20.1.

41. 1982: Congress Rewrites 26 U.S.C. to Remove Footnotes from IRC Section 61 Pointing to Section 861

41.1 The Code contains many footnotes and references to allow readers to search back and trace the origins and evolution of laws and regulations, since this often clarifies intent. IRC 61(a) on gross income used to have a footnote informing readers that it came from Section 22(a) of the 1939 Code and that the law hadn't been changed. The footnote said, "Source: Sec. 22(a), 1939 Code, substantially unchanged." ***That footnote was in the 1954 version of the Internal Revenue Code at least up to the 1982 edition, but then it vanished, making it difficult for tax professionals to understand how the wording has been deceptively altered, leading to misapplication of the law. Constitutional limitations discussed above were thus hidden***.

41.2 Deletion of the footnote has also made it much more difficult to notice and understand the close connection between IRC 61 and IRC 861 (or 26 C.F.R. § 1.61 and 26 C.F.R. §1.861), especially as 26 C.F.R. §1.861 is now thousands of pages distant from C.F.R. 1.61, and in the earlier versions, the section was not numbered 861, but 119.

41.3 See section 6.8.10 "Cover-Up of 1982: Footnotes Removed from IRC Section 61 Pointing to Section 861" for details of how Congress obfuscated the tax code.

42. 1986: *U.S. v. Stahl*, 792 F.2d. 1438 (1986), Federal District Court Refused to Hear Arguments on the Fraudulent Passage of the 16th Amendment, which Allegedly Authorized Income Taxes

This case was a major scandal for the Federal appellate court. The defendant Stahl presented credible evidence that the 16th Amendment to the U.S. Constitution was fraudulently claimed to have been ratified by the Secretary of State, Philander Knox, in 1913. The court refused to deal with the issue and ignored all the evidence presented. Instead, they said it wasn't their business to deal with the issue. Congress said the same thing. This leads to the conclusion that there is a federal judicial (as well as a Congressional) conspiracy to protect the income tax!

> "[Defendant] Stahl's claim that ratification of the 16th Amendment was fraudulently certified constitutes a political question because we could not undertake independent resolution of this issue without expressing lack of respect due coordinate branches of government...."

43. 1988: Congress Obfuscates the 26 U.S.C./IRC Further to Change the title of Part I, Subchapter N to Make it Refer Only to Foreign Income

43.1 Prior to 1988, the title of Part I of Subchapter N (which begins with Section 861) was "*Determination of sources of income*" (which is still the heading of the related regulations). In 1988, this title was changed to "*Source rules and other general rules relating to foreign income.*"

43.2 It should be mentioned that while the titles of parts may give an indication of what the part is about, the title has no effect on the actual legal application.

> "*...nor shall any **table of contents**, table of cross references, or similar outline, analysis, or **descriptive matter** relating to the contents of this title **be given any legal effect**.*"
> [26 U.S.C. §7806(b)]

43.3 So when the title was changed (but the text of the law was not), the application of the law did *not* change. What changed was the appearance of the table of contents.

43.4 When the title of Part I was changed, and the new title stated that the part was about "*foreign income*," it no longer appeared to be an obvious place for most people to look when determining their taxable income. This would certainly have the effect of drawing attention away from Section 861.

43.5 See section 6.8.8 "Cover-Up of 1988: Changed Title of Part I, Subchapter N to Make it Refer Only to Foreign Income" for details of how Congress obfuscated the tax code in this case.

44. 1993: IRS Removes References in IRS Publication 515 to Citizens Not Being Liable for Income Tax and Confused New Language.

44.1 Here's what was . Inside Publication 515, there appears a statement the IRS hopes you never see. Under the main heading "Withholding Exemptions and Reductions" and within the paragraph titled "Evidence of Residence", the IRS states in speaking to the payer of income:

> "*If an individual gives you a written statement stating that he or she is a citizen or resident of the United States, and you do not know otherwise, you do not have to withhold tax.*"

44.2 The 1994 version of Publication 515 varied somewhat. Instead of ending with "...you do not have to withhold tax", it continues:

> "*...you do not have to withhold tax under the rules discussed in this publication. Instead, get Publication 15, Circular E, Employer's Tax Guide.*"

44.3 This change was in response to tax protester groups, who at the time were citing this publication as proof that they weren't liable to pay taxes as citizens of the 50 union states with income from domestic sources!

44.4 See section 6.9.18 "Cover-Up of 1993: IRS Removed References in IRS Publication 515 to Citizens Not Being Liable for Tax and Confused New Language" for details of how IRS obfuscated their publications in this case.

45. 1995: IRS Modifies Regulations to Remove Pointers to Form 2555 for IRC Section 1 Liability for Federal Income Tax Under the Paperwork Reduction Act

45.1 The Paperwork Reduction Act of 1980 requires that every form used by the federal government to collect information from the public first be approved by the Office of Management and Budget ("OMB"). The regulations at 26 C.F.R. §602.101 contain a table listing the OMB-approved forms for each section of regulations. The regulations 26 C.F.R. §1.1-1 are entitled "*Income tax on individuals*," and correspond to 26 U.S.C. §1 (which imposes the "income tax"). Up until 1995, the first line in this table identified Form 2555, "**Foreign Earned Income**," as the only approved form under 26 C.F.R. §1.1-1.

45.2 In 1995, after many "tax resistance" groups had become aware of this, the listing for "1.1-1" was removed from the list, in order to avoid "confusion," according to the Department of the Treasury. The process of applying for, and receiving OMB approval for a form makes the possibility of an error extremely remote. The Department of the Treasury *requested* that Form 2555 be approved for 1.1-1, and the Office of Management and Budget *approved* it. When the entry drew too much attention, it was removed. At present no forms are approved for use with 26 C.F.R. §1.1-1.

45.3 See section 6.9.17 "Cover-Up of 1995: Modified Regulations to Remove Pointers to Form 2555 for IRC Section 1 Liability for Federal Income Tax" for details of how IRS obfuscated the regulations in this case.

46. 1998: IRS Restructuring and Reform Act of 1998

46.1 Because of widespread abuse of due process rights of Americans, the U.S. Congress passed the *IRS Restructuring and Reform Act of 1998* (http://www.irs.gov/irs/display/0,,i1%3D46%26genericId%3D23294,00.html). It was designed to remedy many of the abuses of the IRS, including:

  46.1.1 A shifting of the burden of proof from the Citizen to the IRS for certain circumstances. This eliminated the widespread perception by citizens that with regard to tax matters, citizens were "guilty until proven innocent".
  46.1.2 Illegal liens, levies, and seizures of the property of citizens.
  46.1.3 The labeling of Citizens as "illegal tax protesters".
  46.1.4 Creation of the Taxpayer Advocate office to resolve complaints of citizens.
  46.1.5 Prohibition of the IRS contacting third parties of the citizen without prior notice.
  46.1.6 Refunds of overpayments prior to final determination.
  46.1.7 Allowance for accountant-client privilege.
  46.1.8 Prohibition of threat of audit to coerce TRAC agreements.
  46.1.9 Severe penalties ranging between $100,000 and $1,000,000 for wrongful collection of taxes by revenue agents.
  46.1.10 Citizens allowed to quash 3rd party summons by IRS.

46.2 During the hearings prior to the enactment of this legislation, there was unbelievable publicized testimony of many different individuals who had been abused illegally by the IRS. The witnesses were so afraid of the IRS that they had to have their voices and identities concealed to avoid retribution. This was a clear indication that the IRS had way too much power.

46.3 You will note by examining the statistics in section 2.12 of the *Tax Fraud Prevention Manual*, Form #06.008 that IRS abusive behavior toward citizens was significantly curbed following the passage of this act. This act did exactly what it was supposed to do, which points to the fact that if we want real reforms of the tax system and the IRS, then ultimately it is up to us as citizens to vote and to be politically involved enough to make sure that our elected representatives know what we expect from them and from our tax system.

6.6 The Laws of Tyranny

This section contains a description of what is called The Laws of Tyranny. These laws describe the major techniques by which governments are systematically corrupted. As you read through the rest of this chapter, try to deduce for yourself how these laws apply to the specific instance of corruption described in each section. Nearly every section within this chapter can be associated with one of these laws.

The Laws of Tyranny

1. Any power that can be abused will be abused.
   1.1. The main mechanism for abusing law is through obfuscation of the law to turn it into a mechanism for terrorizing the ignorant and uninformed.
   1.2. Any law the electorate sees as being open to being perverted from its original intent will be perverted in a manner that exceeds the manner of perversion seen at the time.

1.3. Any law that is so difficult to pass it requires the citizens be assured it will not be a stepping stone to worse laws, will in fact be a stepping stone to worse laws.
1.4. Any law that requires the citizens be assured the law does not mean what the citizens fear, means exactly what the citizens fear.
1.5. Any law passed in a good cause will be interpreted to apply to causes against the wishes of the people.
1.6. Any law enacted to help any one group will be applied to harm people not in that group.
1.7. Everything the government says will never happen, will happen.
1.8. What the government says it could not foresee, the government has planned for.
1.9. When there is a budget shortfall to cover non-essential government services, the citizens will be given the choice between higher taxes or the loss of essential government services.
1.10. Should the citizens mount a successful effort to stop a piece of legislation, the same legislation will be passed under a different name or as a rider to a more popular measure.
2. All deprivations of freedom and choice will be increased rather than reversed. Abuse and tyranny will always expand to fill the limits of resistance to them.
3. If people don't resist the abuses of others, they will have no one to resist the abuses of themselves, and tyranny will prevail.

Frederick Douglas, an early American Civil Rights advocate, summed up these laws with the following statement:

> *Find out just what the people will submit to and you have found out the exact amount of injustice and wrong which will be imposed upon them; and these will continue until they are resisted with either words or blows, or with both. The limits of tyrants are prescribed by the endurance of those whom they oppress.*
> *[Frederick Douglass, civil rights activist, Aug. 4, 1857]*

6.7 Presidential Scandals Related to Income Taxes and Socialism

> *"The illegal we do immediately. The unconstitutional takes a bit longer."*
> *[Henry Kissinger]*

> *"Politicians are the same all over. They promise to build a bridge where there is no river."*
> *[Nikita Khrushchev]*

> *"The current income tax code is the chief source of political corruption in the nation's capitol. Tax reform is not for the timid."*
> *[Rep. Richard K. Armey, R-Texas]*

6.7.1 1925: William H. Taft's Certiorari Act of 1925

As we have stated repeatedly throughout this book, there is a judicial conspiracy to protect the income tax (see sections 6.12 and 1.7). The basic problem is that the federal district and circuit courts are acting as a protection racket for the IRS while the U.S. Supreme Court has been looking the other way by denying appeals to correct such abuses. How did we arrive at the point where the Supreme Court even had the discretion to deny such appeals? That is a scandal all by itself, as you will find out.

President Howard Taft is the single person most responsible for the federal income tax that we have today. He was a brilliant man and the _only_ person who had all the qualifications necessary to engineer an overthrow of our de jure government and the replacement of it with the de facto criminal government we have today. For instance, he is the only person who ever did all of the following:

1. Served as the President of the United States
2. Served as the Chief Justice of the Supreme Court
3. Served as a Collector of Internal Revenue in Michigan
4. Was able to get the Sixteenth Amendment into the hands of the states for ratification in 1909.
5. Was still in office when the Sixteenth Amendment was declared ratified and the Federal Reserve Act was passed.

Let's examine item 2 above in more detail. President Taft was the ONLY President who ever served as a Collector of Internal Revenue. Even as President of the United States and later as a Chief Justice of the U.S. Supreme Court, he apparently continued in that role. Here is what Wikipedia says on this subject:

Legal career

> After admission to the Ohio bar, Taft was appointed Assistant Prosecutor of Hamilton County, Ohio,[15][12] based in Cincinnati. In 1882, he was appointed local Collector of Internal Revenue.[16][13] Taft married his longtime sweetheart, Helen Herron, in Cincinnati in 1886.[17][12] In 1887, he was appointed a judge of the Ohio Superior Court.[18][12] In 1890, President Benjamin Harrison appointed him Solicitor General of the United States[19][12] As of January 2010, at age 32, he is the youngest-ever Solicitor General.[20][14] Taft then began serving on the newly created United States Court of Appeals for the Sixth Circuit in 1891.[21][12] Taft was confirmed by the Senate on March 17, 1892, and received his commission that same day.[22][15] In about 1893, Taft decided in favor of one or more patents for processing aluminium belonging to the Pittsburg Reduction Company, today known as Alcoa, who settled with the other party in 1903 and became for a short while the only aluminum producer in the U.S.[23][16] Another of Taft's opinions was Addyston Pipe and Steel Company v. United States (1898). Along with his judgeship, between 1896 and 1900 Taft also served as the first dean and a professor of constitutional law at the University of Cincinnati.[24][17]
>
> [SOURCE: Wikipedia: William Howard Taft; http://en.wikipedia.org/wiki/William_Howard_Taft, 4/28/2010]

Nearly all the financial corruption that exists in our country's money and tax systems was introduced during his tour of office as President and this corruption was later perfected and expanded during his nine year tenure as Chief Justice of the Supreme Court starting in 1921. If you would like to learn more about this man, we recommend *The Complete Book of U.S. Presidents*, by William A Degregorio, ISBN 0-517-18353-6.

In section 3.11.11.1 we revealed the legislative intent of the Sixteenth Amendment by showing you the Presidential Speech that introduced the Sixteenth Amendment for the first time, given by William H. Taft before Congress in 1909. That speech showed clearly that then President Taft understood that federal income taxes were excise taxes that could not be instituted against other than federal corporations. He introduced the Sixteenth Amendment to Congress in 1909 as a way to circumvent this restriction and broaden the application of federal income taxes to authorize a supposed direct income tax on private persons. Subsequent to the introduction of the Sixteenth Amendment for state ratification in 1909, Secretary of State Philander Knox committed fraud in 1913 by claiming that the Sixteenth Amendment had been properly ratified by ¾ of the states. Knox was Taft's hand-picked Secretary of State.

During his presidency, Taft made six appointments to the Supreme Court -- more than any other one-term President. Many think that when Taft named Edward White Chief Justice rather than the other obvious choice, Charles Evans Hughes, there was a political agenda to pave a way for his own later appointment as Chief Justice. Taft appointed White because White was twelve years older than Hughes. Naming White gave Taft a better shot at being Chief Justice one day himself -- in spite of Thomas Jefferson's famous complaint that "few [Justices] die and none resign.". You can read more about Taft's history from the speech given by Chief Justice Rehnquist on April 13, 2002, and which is posted on the Supreme Court website at:

---

[15] "William Howard Taft". National Park Service. 2004-01-22. http://www.nps.gov/history/history/online_books/Presidents/bio27.htm. Retrieved 2009-03-20.

[16] Herz, Walter (1999). "William Howard Taft". Unitarian Universalist Historical Society. http://www25.uua.org/uuhs/duub/articles/williamhowardtaft.html. Retrieved 2009-03-22.

[17] "William Howard Taft". National Park Service. 2004-01-22. http://www.nps.gov/history/history/online_books/Presidents/bio27.htm. Retrieved 2009-03-20.

[18] "William Howard Taft". National Park Service. 2004-01-22. http://www.nps.gov/history/history/online_books/Presidents/bio27.htm. Retrieved 2009-03-20.

[19] "William Howard Taft". National Park Service. 2004-01-22. http://www.nps.gov/history/history/online_books/Presidents/bio27.htm. Retrieved 2009-03-20.

[20] Cannon, Carl. "Solicitor general nominee likely to face questions about detainees". GovernmentExecutive.com. http://www.govexec.com/dailyfed/0405/042505nj1.htm. Retrieved 2010-01-03.

[21] "William Howard Taft". National Park Service. 2004-01-22. http://www.nps.gov/history/history/online_books/Presidents/bio27.htm. Retrieved 2009-03-20.

[22] "William Howard Taft (1857-1930)". U.S. Court of Appeals for the Sixth Circuit. http://www.ca6.uscourts.gov/lib_hist/courts/supreme/judges/taft/taft.html. Retrieved 2009-03-22.

[23] "Against the Cowles Company, Decision in the Aluminium Patent Infringement Case (article preview)". *The New York Times* (The New York Times Company). January 15, 1893. http://query.nytimes.com/gst/abstract.html?res=9904E3DE1731E033A25756C1A9679C94629ED7CF. Retrieved 2007-10-28. and Rosenbaum, David Ira (1998). *Market Dominance: How Firms Gain, Hold, or Lose It and the Impact on Economic Performance*. Praeger Publishers via Greenwood Publishing Group. pp. 56. ISBN 0-2759-5604-0. http://books.google.com/books?id=htQDB-Pf4VIC. Retrieved 2007-11-03.

[24] Cincinnati Law School: 2006 William Howard Taft Lecture on Constitutional Law.

http://www.supremecourtus.gov/publicinfo/speeches/sp_04-13-02.html

We know by reading excerpts from *Stanton v. Baltic Mining, 240 U.S. 103 (1916)* in section 3.17.11, that the Supreme Court, subsequent to the ratification of the Sixteenth Amendment in 1913, disagreed with President Taft about the effect of the Sixteenth Amendment by saying that it conferred "no new power of taxation" upon Congress. Here is what the U.S. Supreme Court said in 1916, three years after the ratification of the Sixteenth Amendment:

> "..by the previous ruling it was settled that **the provisions of the Sixteenth Amendment <u>conferred no new power of taxation</u> but simply prohibited the previous complete and plenary power of income taxation possessed by Congress from the beginning from being taken out of the category of indirect taxation to which it inherently belonged and being placed in the category of direct taxation** subject to apportionment by a consideration of the sources from which the income was derived, that is by testing the tax not by what it was -- a tax on income, but by a mistaken theory deduced from the origin or source of the income taxed."

President Taft, who would later leave office in 1913 to be appointed by President Harding to become Chief Justice of the Supreme Court in 1921, must have known this was going to happen when he introduced the Sixteenth Amendment in 1909. So how did he skirt this declaration by the Supreme Court that nullified the 16th Amendment to allow the fraud of federal income taxes to perpetuate anyway? The answer is quite interesting.

As Chief Justice of the U.S. Supreme Court, President Taft sponsored a bill called the Certiorari Act of 1925. In the year that Taft was appointed Chief Justice of the Supreme Court in 1921, the docket of the Supreme Court was reportedly 5 years behind, according to Chief Justice Rehnquist, so when Taft became Chief Justice, he complained to Congress and the President that the Supreme Court was hopelessly backed up in hearing appeals from lower courts and that the court needed the discretion to be able to deny appeals from lower courts. What sort of appeals might those be? How about federal income tax trials to begin with! Here is the way Chief Justice Rehnquist described this situation:

> "When he was appointed Chief Justice in 1921, the Court had fallen nearly five years behind in its docket. He resolved this caseload congestion in the Court by convincing Congress to pass the Judiciary Act of 1925 -- also known as the Certiorari Act -- which gave the Court discretion as to which cases to hear. Some members of Congress were doubtful -- why shouldn't every litigant have a right to get a decision on his case from the Supreme Court? Taft responded that in each case, there had already been one trial and one appeal. "Two courts are enough for justice," he said. To obtain still a third hearing in the Supreme Court, there should be some question involved more important than just who wins this lawsuit."

He must have figured that if the appeals courts below the Supreme Court would uphold the income tax and if the Supreme Court could deny appeals, then in spite of the Supreme Court precedents established earlier which nullified the Sixteenth Amendment, we could have a schizophrenic and split personality federal judicial system that on the one hand, would declare at the Supreme Court level that direct income taxes were unconstitutional, but at courts below the Supreme Court would declare them constitutional. As long as the Supreme Court under the Certiorari Act of 1925 could deny appeals, it wouldn't have to correct the abuses of the lower courts and the split personalities could continue. This sin of omission by the Supreme court which was authorized and even encouraged by Taft's unconstitutional Certiorari Act would then serve to perpetuate the income tax fraud. This would open the doors for the U.S. Congress to perpetuate the myth of income tax liability by lying to their constituents and telling them that they "must pay federal income taxes because the Sixteenth Amendment authorizes it". This, in a nutshell, is exactly the legacy and the heritage that we live with to this day, and we have President Taft in large part, to thank for it. The obscenely dishonest people in Congress who know the truth and yet continue to perpetuate this fraud are simply maintaining the system that Taft setup through his skullduggery.

Former President Taft served only four years as Chief Justice after the passage of the Certiorari Act of 1925, resigning from office in February 1930 because of illness and dying a month later. He must have figured he had accomplished the job he set out to do. E.B. White, his predecessor Chief Justice, served almost 10 years and Justice Fuller before him served 21 years.

To summarize the big picture, Chief Justice Taft must have known that the federal income tax fraud could not continue if the Supreme Court lacked the discretion to deny appeals, or Writs of Certiorari as they are called, from lower courts. If the Bureau of Internal Revenue, or BIR (now called the IRS) kept trying at the time to extort money from people and the Supreme Court consistently was saying that the Sixteenth Amendment didn't authorize them to do this, then people could eventually appeal all the way up to the Supreme Court and stop the unlawful assessment and collection, which would destroy federal revenues and keep the BIR in check. Allow the Supreme Court to deny appeals, however, and the situation would be very different. With his Certiorari Act passed by Congress in 1925 in place, President William Howard Taft had all the pieces in place needed to perpetuate and enlarge the federal income tax fraud:

1. A Supreme Court stacked with six of his own hand-picked justices during his term as President from 1909-1913.
2. The Sixteenth Amendment that Taft himself had introduced in 1909.
3. A fraudulent ratification of the Sixteenth Amendment by Philander Knox in 1913. Philander Knox was his own hand-picked Secretary of State.
4. The Federal Reserve Act of 1913, scandalously passed by just four members of Congress during a Christmas recess immediately after the Sixteenth Amendment was ratified and during Taft's administration.
5. The Certiorari Act of 1925 that authorized the Supreme Court to deny justice to people who had been defrauded of federal income taxes they didn't owe by the then Bureau of Internal Revenue (BIR).
6. Control of the Supreme Court for five years following the passage of the Certiorari Act, so he could get in place several circuit court rulings favorable to the income tax that the Supreme Court would deny writs to. Taft served as Chief Justice from 1921 to 1929 until his death in 1930.
7. At the end of Taft's term as Chief Justice, our country plunged into the Great Depression, which most knowledgeable people say was caused by a deliberate and systematic contraction of the money supply by the Federal Reserve in order to engineer the socialist reforms that FDR would later propose in the form of Socialist Security. Our purely capitalist economic system had to be made to look like it was failing by the banksters before most rugged individualist Americans would willingly accept anything as radical as Socialist Security or a government handout.

The fundamental defect in the Certiorari Act was the fact that the Supreme Court could:

1. Deny appeals without explaining why (and evade accountability for its decision). If the people are the sovereigns and the government is their servant, what gives the servant the right to tell the sovereign what to do with its appeal?
2. Deny appeals even though decisions of lower courts clearly conflicted with its precedents. This amounts to condoning government wrongs.
3. Deny appeals of parties whose constitutional rights were claimed to be injured. The ability to deny justice to parties whose constitutional rights had been violated clearly violates the oath that the justices take to "support and defend the Constitution against all enemies, foreign and domestic".

If the above three defects in the unconstitutional Certiorari Act of 1925 were remedied, we wouldn't have the split personality Dr. Jekyll and Mr. Hyde court system we have today and the fraud of the income tax, because they would be impossible to maintain with an accountable Supreme Court that was obligated to:

1. Correct rulings below it that violated or contradicted its precedents.
2. Correct rulings which violated constitutional rights without exception.
3. Explain why it would not hear the case or defend the constitutional rights of the injured party (be accountable).

The necessity of doing all the above has been described by the U.S. Supreme Court as "The Rule of Necessity" as follows:

> ### Rule of Necessity
>
> *The Rule of Necessity had its genesis at least five and a half centuries ago. Its earliest recorded invocation was in 1430, when it was held that the Chancellor of Oxford could act as judge of a case in which he was a party when there was no provision for appointment of another judge. Y. B. Hil. 214*214 8 Hen. VI, f. 19, pl. 6.[25] Early cases in this country confirmed the vitality of the Rule[26].*
>
> *The Rule of Necessity has been consistently applied in this country in both state and federal courts. In* State ex rel. Mitchell v. Sage Stores Co., *157 Kan. 622, 143 P.2d. 652 (1943) the Supreme Court of Kansas observed:*
>
> *"[I]t is well established that actual disqualification of a member of a court of last resort will not excuse such member from performing his official duty if failure to do so would result in a denial of a litigant's constitutional right to have a question, properly presented to such court, adjudicated." Id., at 629, 143 P. 2d, at 656.*
>
> *Similarly, the Supreme Court of Pennsylvania held:*

---

[25] Rolle's Abridgment summarized this holding as follows:

"If an action is sued in the bench against all the Judges there, then by necessity they shall be their own Judges." 2 H. Rolle, An Abridgment of Many Cases and Resolutions at Common Law 93 (1668) (translation).

[26] For example, in *Mooers v. White*, 6 Johns. Ch. 360 (N. Y. 1822) Chancellor Kent continued to sit despite his brother-in-law's being a party; New York law made no provision for a substitute chancellor. See *In re Leefe*, 2 Barb. Ch. 39 (N. Y. 1846). See also cases cited in Annot., 39 A. L. R. 1476 (1925).

> "The true rule unquestionably is that wherever it becomes necessary for a judge to sit even where he has an interest —where no provision is made for calling another in, or where no one else can take his place—it is his duty to hear and decide, however disagreeable it may be." Philadelphia v. Fox, 64 Pa. 169, 185 (1870).
>
> Other state[27] and federal[28] courts also have recognized the Rule.
>
> 215*215 The concept of the absolute duty of judges to hear and decide cases within their jurisdiction revealed in Pollack, supra, and Philadelphia v. Fox, supra, is reflected in decisions of this Court. Our earlier cases dealing with the Compensation Clause did not directly involve the compensation of Justices or name them as parties, and no express reference to the Rule is found. See, e. g., O'Malley v. Woodrough, 307 U.S. 277 (1939); O'Donoghue v. United States, 289 U.S. 516 (1933); Evans v. Gore, 253 U.S. 245 (1920). In Evans, however, an action brought by an individual judge in his own behalf, the Court by clear implication dealt with the Rule:
>
> > "Because of the individual relation of the members of this court to the question . . . , we cannot but regret that its solution falls to us . . . . But jurisdiction of the present case cannot be declined or renounced. The plaintiff was entitled by law to invoke our decision on the question as respects his own compensation, in which no other judge can have any direct personal interest; and there was no other appellate tribunal to which under the law he could go." Id., at 247-248.[29]
>
> 216*216 It would appear, therefore, that this Court so took for granted the continuing validity of the Rule of Necessity that no express reference to it or extended discussion of it was needed.[30]
>
> [United States v. Will Et Al, 449 U.S. 200 (1980)]

Now do you see how the pieces of the puzzle were cleverly and invisibly weaved together by conspiracies involving all three branches of the federal government over several years to create the totally unjust and extortionary slavery tax system we have now? Now do you understand why Thomas Jefferson said:

> "Single acts of tyranny may be ascribed to the accidental opinion of a day. But a series of oppressions, pursued unalterably through every change of ministers, too plainly proves a deliberate systematic plan of reducing us to slavery".
> [Thomas Jefferson]

Do you also now understand why Franklin Delano Roosevelt said?:

> "In politics, nothing happens by accident. If it happens, it was planned that way."
> [Franklin D. Roosevelt]

6.7.2   1933: FDR's Great American Gold Robbery

6.7.2.1   Money Background

Genuine money must have the following three qualities:

1. It must be a storehouse of intrinsic value.

---

[27] E.g., Moulton v. Byrd, 224 Ala. 403, 140 So. 384 (1932); Olson v. Cory, 26 Cal. 3d 672, 609 P. 2d 991 (1980); Nellius v. Stiftel, 402 A. 2d 359 (Del. 1978); Dacey v. Connecticut Bar Assn., 170 Conn. 520, 368 A. 2d 125 (1976); Wheeler v. Board of Trustees of Fargo Consol. School Dist., 200 Ga. 323, 37 S. E. 2d 322 (1946); Schward v. Ariyoshi, 57 Haw. 348, 555 P. 2d 1329 (1976); Higher v. Hansen, 67 Idaho 45, 170 P. 2d 411 (1946); Gordy v. Dennis, 176 Md. 106, 5 A. 2d 69 (1936); State ex rel. Gardner v. Holm, 241 Minn. 125, 62 N. W. 2d 52 (1954); State ex rel. West Jersey Traction Co. v. Board of Public Works, 56 N. J. L. 431, 29 A. 163 (1894); Long v. Watts, 183 N. C. 99, 110 S. E. 765 (1922); First American Bank & Trust Co. v. Ellwein, 221 N. W. 2d 509 (N. D.), cert. denied, 419 U. S. 1026 (1974); McCoy v. Handlin, 35 S. D. 487, 153 N. W. 361 (1915); Alamo Title Co. v. San Antonio Bar Assn., 360 S. W. 2d 814 (Tex. Civ. App.), writ ref'd, no rev. error (Tex. 1962).

[28] E. g., Atkins v. United States, 214 Ct.Cl. 186, 556 F.2d. 1028 (1977) cert. denied, 434 U.S. 1009 (1978); Pilla v. American Bar Assn., 542 F.2d. 56 (CA8 1976); Brinkley v. Hassig, 83 F.2d. 351 (CA10 1936); United States v. Corrigan, 401 F.Supp. 795 (Wyo. 1975).

[29] O'Malley cast doubt on the substantive holding of Evans, see n. 31, infra, but the fact that the Court reached the issue indicates that it did not question this aspect of the Evans opinion.

[30] In another, not unrelated context, Chief Justice Marshall's exposition in Cohens v. Virginia, 6 Wheat. 264 (1821) could well have been the explanation of the Rule of Necessity; he wrote that a court "must take jurisdiction if it should. The judiciary cannot, as the legislature may, avoid a measure because it approaches the confines of the constitution. We cannot pass it by, because it is doubtful. With whatever doubts, with whatever difficulties, a case may be attended, we must decide it, if it be brought before us. *We have no more right to decline the exercise of jurisdiction which is given, than to usurp that which is not given.* The one or the other would be treason to the constitution. Questions may occur which we would gladly avoid; but we cannot avoid them." Id., at 404 (emphasis added).

2. It must be a universal, portable medium of exchange.
3. It must have a common unit of account.
4. It must be immune to attempts by the government to lower its value by printing more and thereby use inflationary forces to "tax" all money in circulation. This ensures what we called earlier in section 2.8.9.2 "separation of money and state".

Black's Law Dictionary, 5th Edition, defines "**money**" as:

> "In its usual and ordinary explanation it means coins and paper currency used as circulating medium of exchange, and **does not embrace notes, bonds, evidences of debt** or other personal or real estate."

Gold and silver coins and the previous gold and silver certificates were a storehouse of "intrinsic" value. They actually increased in value with inflation. Therefore, they were a hedge against inflation.

LAWFUL MONEY is defined in Black's Law Dictionary, 2nd Ed., as:

> "Money which is legal tender in payment of debts; e.g. **gold** and **silver** coined at the mint."

The responsibility of coining gold and silver money was ceded to Congress in our Constitution; Article I, Section 8, Clause 5:

> "The Congress shall have the power...To coin money and regulate the value thereof..."

Because the Constitution is the Supreme Law of the Land, nothing but gold or silver coin is "lawful" money for the 50 union states. Because of heaviness of gold and silver coins, "Gold and Silver Certificates" were created by the Department of Treasury of the united States. These certificates were representative of actual gold and silver coins which were owned by the People holding the Certificates and maintained in the vaults of the banks and Fort Knox. These Gold and Silver Certificates were convertible to gold and silver coin, "PAYABLE ON DEMAND." It is important to understand that this gold and silver, represented by the Certificates, belonged to the **People** or Certificate Holders and NOT the banks or the government.

At one time, reference to the laws that made money "lawful" were printed directly on the face of our currency. The laws printed on the bills were enacted on March 14, 1900 and December 24, 1919.

66th Congress Sess. II Chapter 15, (December 24, 1919)-Public Law No. 103

CHAP. 15-An Act to make gold certificates of the United States payable to bearer on demand legal tender.

"Be it enacted by the Senate and House of Representatives of the United States of America in Congress assembled, that gold certificates of the United States payable to bearer on demand shall be and are hereby made legal tender in payment of all debts and dues, public and private.

§2 That all acts or parts of Acts which are inconsistent with this Act are hereby repealed."

Approved, December 24, 1919

The above law has NEVER been and CANNOT be repealed, as it is applicable to the 50 sovereign states, without amending the Constitution. Note that the Act, says "gold certificates payable to the bearer on demand 'shall be and are.'" This means not only when the Act was passed, but also ***into the future***!

§2 of the Act, repealing Acts or parts of Acts inconsistent with the above Public Law 103, would, therefore, not only be applicable to past Acts which were inconsistent with its intent but also future inconsistent Acts. It also says to be legal tender; the **certificates** MUST be **payable to bearer on demand**. Our current '**Federal Reserve Notes**' do not meet either of these lawful requirements for legal tender for the Citizens of the several states.

Perhaps Federal Reserve Notes are "legal tender" for the Territorial (federal zone) United States, under the EXCLUSIVE jurisdiction and not under Constitutional restrictions and protections. However, both the Constitution and the Law lead only to one inescapable conclusion, which is that:

Federal Reserve Notes certainly are NOT Constitutional tender or lawful money for the Citizens of the 50 sovereign states in these united states of America!

Because the Constitution prohibited the states from coining gold and silver (which would logically extend to the gold and silver certificates which were representative of the ownership of these coins) and because **We the People** specifically delegated monetary powers to Congress, it was not within the Congressional authority to transfer the issuing of gold and silver certificates and ultimately federal reserve notes to the private Federal Reserve.

Remember:

> "Congress may not abdicate ['to give up.. renounce or relinquish...authorities, duties...powers, or responsibility] to transfer to others its legitimate [delegated] functions"
> [Schechter Poultry v. U.S., 29 U.S., 495 U.S. 837, 842 (1935)]

Gold Reserve Act of March 14, 1900. "Be it enacted by the Senate and House of Representatives of the United States of America in Congress assembled, that the **dollar** consisting of twenty-five and eight tenths grains of gold, nine-tenths fine as established by section thirty-five hundred and eleven [§3511] of the Revised Statutes of the United States, shall be the standard unit of value, and all forms of money issued or coined by the United States, shall be the standard unit of value, and all forms of money issued or coined by the United States, shall be the standard unit of value, and all forms of money issued or coined by the United States shall be maintained at the parity of value with this standard, and it shall be the duty of the Secretary of the Treasury to maintain such **parity**.

Sec. 2. That United States notes, and Treasury notes issued under the Act of July 14, 1890, when presented to the Treasury for redemption, **shall be redeemed in gold coin** of the standard fixed in the first section of this Act..."

So where is our gold?...you ask. Where's our gold certificates?

Gold certificates were originally the idea of goldsmiths who would hold the gold of Citizens and issue much less bulky certificates as evidence of gold on deposit. The Certificate Holders could redeem their Certificates for their gold at any time. Greedy goldsmiths soon began to realize that the majority of the gold in their vaults just sat there because the Certificate Holders were using their certificates as a medium of exchange instead of the gold. Realizing this, the goldsmiths made up extra gold certificates and starting making loans, at interest, using OTHER Citizen's gold as backing. These loans were then repaid to the goldsmith in GOLD COIN! As long as all the gold owners didn't show up at once, the goldsmiths got away with their scheme. When the lawful owners of the gold got wise and demanded their gold back, the goldsmiths who couldn't produce it were hung from the nearest tree!

6.7.2.2 Outlawing of Gold Coin

Starting in 1933, FDR outlawed gold coin with the following sequence of executive orders:

1. Executive Order 6073: Regulations Concerning the Operation of Banks, March 10, 1933. Required banks trading in gold to be licensed by the Secretary of the Treasury.
   https://en.wikisource.org/wiki/Executive_Order_6073
2. Executive Order 6102: Forbidding the Hoarding of Gold Coin, Gold Bullion and Gold Certificates, April 5, 1933. Forbade withdrawals of gold from banks and made it a crime for STATUTORY U.S. citizens to hold gold.
   https://en.wikisource.org/wiki/Executive_Order_6102
3. Executive Order 6111: On Transactions in Foreign Exchange, April 20, 1933. Trading in gold for foreign exchange was prohibited.
   https://en.wikisource.org/wiki/Executive_Order_6111
4. Executive Order 6260: Relating to the Hoarding, Export, and Earmarking of Gold Coin, Bullion, or Currency and to Transactions in Foreign Exchange, August 28, 1933. Required an account of the old held that must be sent to the Collector of Internal Revenue.
   https://en.wikisource.org/wiki/Executive_Order_6260

In 1933, U.S. President Franklin D. Roosevelt issued Executive Order 6102, which outlawed the private ownership of gold coins, gold bullion, and gold certificates by American citizens, forcing them to sell these to the Federal Reserve. As a result, the value of the gold held by the Federal Reserve increased from $4 billion to $12 billion between 1933 and 1937.[31] This left the federal government with a large gold reserve and no place to store it. In 1936, the U.S. Treasury Department began construction of the United States Bullion Depository at Fort Knox, Kentucky, on land transferred from the military. The Gold Vault was completed in December 1936 for US $560,000. The site is located on what is now Bullion Boulevard at the intersection of Gold Vault Road. The building was listed on the National Register of Historic Places in 1988, in recognition of its significance in the economic history of the United States and its status as a well-known landmark.[32] It is constructed of granite mined at the North Carolina Granite Corporation Quarry Complex.[33]

The first gold shipments were made from January to July 1937. The majority of the United States' gold reserves were gradually shipped to the site, including old bullion and newly made bars made from melted gold coins. Some intact coins were stored. The transfer used 500 rail cars and was sent by registered mail, protected by the U.S. Postal Inspection Service, and the U.S. Treasury Department agents. In 1974, a Washington attorney named Peter David Beter circulated a theory that the gold in the Depository had been secretly removed by elites, and that the vaults were empty. A group of reporters was allowed inside in order to refute the theory, which had gained traction thanks to coverage in tabloid newspapers and on the radio. Other than this 1974 event, no member of the public has been allowed inside.[34]

During World War II, the depository held the original U.S. Declaration of Independence and U.S. Constitution. It held the reserves of European countries and key documents from Western history. For example, it held the Crown of St. Stephen, part of the Hungarian crown jewels, given to American soldiers to prevent them from falling into Soviet hands. The repository held one of four copies (exemplifications) of the Magna Carta, which had been sent for display at the 1939 New York World's Fair, and when war broke out, was kept in the US for the duration.

During World War II and into the Cold War, until the invention of different types of synthetic painkillers, a supply of processed morphine and opium was kept in the Depository as a hedge against the US being isolated from the sources of raw opium.[35]

6.7.2.3 The Trading With the Enemy Act: Day the President Declared War on His Own People and Confiscated all the Gold!

Many of the legal cites used in this section are taken from the tremendous research efforts of Dr. Eugene Schroder, who has authored a book called, Constitution: Fact or Fiction, published by Buffalo Creek Press, PO Box 2424 Cleburne, Texas 76033. Supporting documents and a video are also available from Dr. Schroder, c/o PO Box 89, Campo Colorado (81029). Dr. Schroder's research exposes Government corruption of insidious magnitude.

> Senate Report 93-549 (1973) states:
>
> "Since March 9, 1933, the United States has been in a state of national emergency. A majority of the people of the United States have lived their lives under emergency rule. For 40 years freedoms and government procedures, guaranteed by the constitution have, in varying degrees, been abridged by laws brought forth by states of national emergency…"
>
> "These hundreds of statutes delegate to the President extraordinary powers, ordinarily exercised by Congress, which affect the lives of American Citizens in a host of all-encompassing manners. This vast range of powers, taken together, confer enough authority to rule this country without reference to normal constitutional process."
>
> "Under the powers delegated by these statutes the President may: seize property, organize and control the means of production; seize commodities [i.e. the People's gold, silver, and currency] assign military forces abroad; institute martial

---

[31] *Ahamed, Liaquat (2009). Lords of Finance: The Bankers who Broke the World. London: Penguin Books. p. 474.* ISBN 978-1-59420-182-0.

[32] National Register of Historic Places Nomination Form: U.S. Bullion Depository, Fort Knox, Kentucky" *(PDF). October 20, 1987. Retrieved 2013-01-20.*

[33] *David W. Parham and Jim Sumner (November 1979).* "North Carolina Granite Corporation Quarry Complex' *(pdf). National Register of Historic Places - Nomination and Inventory. North Carolina State Historic Preservation Office. Retrieved 2015-05-01.*

[34] "Gold all there when Ft. Knox opened doors". Numismatic News. *Retrieved December 21, 2011.*

[35] *"Fort Knox: Secrets Revealed".* H2 History Channel. *2007.*

> law; seize and control all transportation and communication; regulate the operation of private enterprise, restrict travel; and, in a plethora of ways, control the lives of all American citizens."

Franklin D. Roosevelt was a shrewd banker, himself. In the 1920's, he made a considerable amount of money by floating millions of dollars in worthless German bonds. The artificially engineered Great Depression and a desperate country, paved the way for acceptance of the new unconstitutional socialistically oriented governmental policies of FDR. Families, desperate to survive, lost touch with the Constitution.

This section will provide powerful and irrefutable evidence that on March 9, 1933, the United States declared war on its own citizen subjects through Franklin D. Roosevelt, by amending the war powers, "Trading With The Enemy Act" of December 6, 1917, to include, as an enemy of the United States:

> *"any person within the United States or any place subject to the jurisdiction thereof"!!! [This was the Territorial United States or the federal zone, but **the People were not told this.**]*

The above trick is exactly the same trick our government is STILL playing on us with the whole of Subtitle A income taxes...fooling us into believing that the jurisdiction of the Subtitle A income tax extends into the borders of the sovereign 50 union states when it actually does NOT, according to 26 U.S.C. §7701(a)9-(a)10!

The purpose of this unconscionable and treasonous Act was to justify the theft and seizure of the People's gold by the Government and to cancel the contractual obligation of the bankers to redeem the People's Gold Certificates! This Act, if applicable to the Citizens of these united States, would have been a direct violation of Public Law 103 of Dec. 24, 1919, previously quoted, which stated, that only

> *"gold certificates of the United States payable to bearer on demand shall be and are legal tender in payment of all debts and dues, public and private."*

The amended Act also blatantly violated the Constitutional prohibition against making anything other than gold and silver legal tender for the payment of debts in the several states!

The Trading With The Enemy Act, called upon the extraordinary dictatorial war powers. These powers were only to be used in life-threatening circumstances and ONLY against the declared enemy of the United States. Obviously, the intent of the law was NEVER to seize the assets of American Citizens in the time of peace or war! These powers have been grossly abused to turn America from a free constitutional Republic into an enslaved statutory presidential dictatorship! We warned you this kind of scam would be used to rob you of your liberty in section 2.8.12 entitled "Surrendering Freedoms in the Name of 'Government Induced Crises'.

In other countries, emergency powers can suspend the Constitution. **Adolf Hitler used the Emergency Powers to suspend the German Constitution and institute an unfathomable dictatorial reign of terror!** The German Emergency Power Law was merely titled Article 48 and stated:

> *"If the public safety and order in the German Reich are seriously disturbed or endangered, the President of the Reich may...suspend in whole or in part the fundamental rights established [including] inviolability of person, inviolability of domicile, freedom of opinion and expression, freedom of assembly and association, secrecy in communication and inviolability of property."*

Even with the broad war powers, in America, where the Constitution is the supreme law of the land and ANY law contrary to it NULL and VOID, it is not within the power of the President, the Congress or the Judiciary to create a law or an emergency which suspends the Constitution and unalienable rights of the Sovereign People! Not even war can alienate the rights of the People in relationship to the government!

THE AMERICAN CONSTITUTION IS NON-SUSPENDIBLE!

> *"**No emergency justifies the violation of any of the provisions of the United States Constitution.**[36] An emergency, however, while it cannot create power, increase granted power, or remove or diminish the restrictions*

---

[36] As to the effect of emergencies on the operation of state constitutions, see § 59.

> *imposed upon the power granted or reserved, may allow the exercise of power already in existence, but not exercised except during an emergency.* [37]
>
> *The circumstances in which the executive branch may exercise extraordinary powers under the Constitution are very narrow.*[38] *The danger must be immediate and impending, or the necessity urgent for the public service, such as will not admit of delay, and where the action of the civil authority would be too late in providing the means which the occasion calls for.* [39] *For example, there is no basis in the Constitution for the seizure of steel mills during a wartime labor dispute, despite the President's claim that the war effort would be crippled if the mills were shut down.* [40]"
> [16 American Jurisprudence 2d, Constitutional Law, §52 (1999)]

Contrary to what the People were fraudulently mislead into believing, the Trading With the Enemy Act could not be, and therefore was not, applicable to the Citizens of the several states. In fact, in a section of the Trading With the Enemy Act, that was never amended, or repealed, the Citizens of these United States were specifically and logically exempted from being defined as the enemy. Therefore, the regulations and punishments of the Trading With the Enemy Act were not and could not later become applicable to the Citizens of the United States.

> *SIXTY FIFTH CONGRESS Sess. 1 Chapter 106, Page 411, October 6, 1917*
>
> *CHAP. 106—An Act To Define, regulate, and punish trading with the enemy, and for other purposes.*
>
> *Be it enacted by the Senate and House of Representatives of the United States of America in Congress assembled, That this Act shall be known as the "Trading With the Enemy Act."*
>
> *...SEC. 2. That the word "enemy" as used herein shall be deemed to mean, for the purposes of trading and of this Act—*
>
> *"...(c) Such other individuals or body or class of individuals, as may be natives, citizens, or subjects of any nation with which the United States is at war, **other than citizens of the United States...**"*

Again, it was the "persons" born in **Territories** over which the United States is exclusively sovereign and **NOT** the Citizens of the Sovereign states, who were the purported "Enemy" targets of the Trading With The Enemy Act. Even though the Citizens were **specifically excluded** from the Emergency War Powers Act, in the most heinous act of Government and Banker Fraud ever perpetrated, American Citizens were coerced by fear and defrauded into turning over all of their gold to the banks. They were threatened [coerced by fear] through the national media, with a $10,000 fine and 10 years in prison, if they refused to comply.

It is important to remember that the gold in the banks **was the property of the Citizens,** holding the gold certificates. **The gold did NOT belong to the Government or the Banks**. The Federal Reserve is a **PRIVATE CORPORATION** and gold certificates represented a **legitimate contractual obligation** to convert the certificates to an equivalent amount of gold, **payable on demand of the bearer, whenever** that demand might be! The Federal Reserve was required by law to maintain a 40% gold reserve and enough other liquid assets to meet the demands of all citizens who wanted to convert their certificates into gold.

Under normal circumstances, only a small percentage of Citizens would exchange their certificates for their gold. However, because of the depression, and well-founded rumors circulating that the private Federal Reserve was taking large amounts of gold belonging to the Citizens out of the country, people lined up at the bank to redeem their gold certificates for gold. This was the lawful prerogative of the People. The Citizens were merely demanding what was lawfully theirs. They had lawfully

---

[37] Veix v. Sixth Ward Building & Loan Ass'n of Newark, 310 U.S. 32, 60 S.Ct. 792, 84 L.Ed. 1061 (1940); Home Bldg. &Loan Ass'n v. Blaisdell, 290 U.S. 398, 54 S.Ct. 231, 78 L.Ed. 413, 88 A.L.R. 1481 (1934).

The Constitution was adopted in a period of grave emergency and its grants of power to the Federal Government and its limitations of the power of the states were determined in the light of emergency, and are not altered by emergency. First Trust Co. of Lincoln v. Smith, 134 Neb. 84, 277 N.W. 762 (1938).

[38] Halperin v. Kissinger, 606 F.2d. 1192 (D.C. Cir. 1979), cert. granted, 446 U.S. 951, 100 S.Ct. 2915, 64 L.Ed.2d. 807 (1980) and aff'd in part, cert. dismissed in part, 452 U.S. 713, 101 S.Ct. 3132, 69 L.Ed.2d. 367 (1981), reh'g denied, 453 U.S. 928, 102 S.Ct. 892, 69 L.Ed.2d. 1024 (1981) and on remand to, 542 F. Supp. 829 (D.D.C. 1982) and on remand to, 578 F. Supp. 231 (D.D.C. 1984), aff'd in part, remanded in part, 807 F.2d. 180 (D.C. Cir. 1986), on remand to, 723 F. Supp. 1535 (D.D.C. 1989), related reference, 1991 WL 120167 (D.D.C. 1991), remanded, 1992 WL 394503 (D.C. Cir. 1992).

[39] Mitchell v. Harmony, 54 U.S. 115, 13 How. 115, 14 L.Ed. 75 (1851).

[40] Youngstown Sheet &Tube Co. v. Sawyer, 343 U.S. 579, 72 S.Ct. 863, 96 L.Ed. 1153, 47 Ohio.Op. 430, 47 Ohio.Op. 460, 62 Ohio.L.Abs. 417, 62 Ohio.L.Abs. 473, 26 A.L.R.2d. 1378 (1952).

earned the gold certificates and gold which they represented and it was not within the power of the Government or the Bankers to take the sovereign American's property and substance, emergency or no emergency!

When FDR took office, he declared a national emergency. In Proclamation 2039, using the very words the Federal Reserve had written for him, He stated:

> "Whereas there have been heavy and unwarranted withdrawals of gold and currency from our banking institutions for the purposes of hoarding..."

"Hoarding???" Doesn't that mean "saving?" **It was the People's gold and not the bankers and, of course, it was their absolute prerogative to spend it or save it.** Most were spending it on SURVIVAL during a time of depression, which incidentally some informed economists blame as the cause a money supply that was deliberately contracted by the Federal Reserve! The President was certainly not delegated the power to ORDER the People not to "save" their own gold! When the smoke screen was removed, the real emergency was that the private federal reserve had breached its contract with American Citizens. They were repudiating their contractual obligation to redeem the People's gold Certificates and were removing the People's gold from the country. The Bankers were like the goldsmiths who had their corrupt scheme exposed. The emergency was that the People were ready to hang the bankers from the nearest tree! Demanding the return of the People's gold to the bankrupt private bankers was like having Americans return their cars if General Motors went bankrupt!

6.7.2.4 FDR Defends the Federal Damn Reserve

As representatives of the Citizens, the President's first duty was to the People who were the victims of banking fraud. Emergency legislation should have been passed, demanding an immediate and complete audit of the federal reserve (which has NEVER been audited). The 40% gold reserve should have been turned over to the People holding the gold Certificates and all of the bankers remaining assets should have been liquidated and converted to gold. This gold should have been returned to the holders of the gold certificates. If the audit found evidence of self-dealing and embezzlement of the People's gold, those involved should have been criminally prosecuted and their assets should have been seized. If an emergency currency needed to be issued, it should have been debt free currency, issued by the Treasury of these United States and People should have been compensated for their loss of gold. This is how a good President would have protected the People. **Instead, FDR was in the pocket of the Bankers!**

Let's go back to March 6-9, 1933 and find out what FDR did do. Instead of formulating a plan demanding that the Federal Reserve honor their contractual obligations to the People he instead consulted the Federal Reserve as to how they believed the crisis should be solved! Remember the REAL emergency was that the bankers did not want to honor their contractual obligation to convert the People's gold certificates to gold. The cats were consulted about what their punishment should be for eating mice. Of course, the cats ruled that they should be fed more mice! What did the private federal reserve conclude that their punishment should be for embezzling the People's gold and dishonoring their fiduciary responsibilities and legitimate contractual obligations? The cats at the FED decided that they should be fed more mice and the President was instructed to pass a law demanding that the People return ALL of their gold to the bankers or be subjected to a stiff fine and jail time. Roosevelt's Proclamations were taken word for word from the Resolution adopted by Federal Reserve.

> *Resolution Adopted by the Federal Reserve Board of New York.*
>
> "Whereas, in the opinion of the Board of Directors of the Federal Reserve Bank of New York, the continued and increasing withdrawal of currency and gold from the banks of the country has now created a national emergency..."

Remember, the controllers of the Federal Reserve were extremely well educated in law. History has shown them to be the brains behind all major Wars throughout the world. They create a conflict and then fund all sides. War is big business for banks. The fed understood how Congress can legislate for its Territorial subject "persons" through Art. I, Sec, 8, Clause 17, without regards to the Constitution (see also ***Downes v. Bidwell***, 182 U.S. 244 (1901)). These same scoundrels probably created the loophole! They also knew the difference between CONSTITUTIONAL citizens and STATUTORY citizens and they were well aware of the War Powers. Following is the original October 6, 1917 combined with the Amendments of March 9, 1933:

Note: **Bold faced** and single underlines are added by the author for emphasis and understanding. Double underlines and ~~strike-through deletions~~ are Amendments to the original "Trading With the Enemy Act" made in the Act of March 9, 1933.

<u>SIXTY FIFTH CONGRESS Sess. 1 Chapter 106, Page 411, October 6, 1917</u>

CHAP 106—An Act To define, regulate, and punish trading with the enemy, and for other purposes.

Be it enacted by the Senate and House of Representatives of the United States of America in Congress assembled, that this Act shall be known as the "Trading With the Enemy Act."

*SEC. 2. That the word "**enemy**" as used herein shall be deemed to mean, for the purposes of such trading and of this Act—*

*(a) Any individual, partnership, or other party of individuals, or any nationality, resident within the territory (including that occupied by the military and naval forces of any **nation with which the United States is at war** or resident outside the United States and doing business within such territory and any corporation incorporated within any country **other than the United States** and doing business with such [enemy] territory, and any corporation incorporated within such **territory with which the United States is at war** or incorporated within any country **other than the United States**.*

*(b) The government of any nation **with which the United States is at war**, or any political or municipal subdivision thereof.*

*(c) Such other individuals or body or class of individuals, as may be natives, citizens, or subjects of any nation **with which the United States is at war**, other than **citizens of the United States**, wherever resident or wherever doing business, as the President, if he shall find the safety of the United States or the successful prosecution of the war shall so require may, by proclamation, include within the term enemy"*

*[this section then continues to define an "ally of an enemy" in the same terms as the "enemy" and again states, "**other than citizens of the United States**,"]*

<u>Public Laws of the Seventy-Third Congress, Chapter 1, Title I, March 9, 1933 Sec. 2</u>

*Subdivision (b) of Section 5 of the Act of October 6, 1917 (40 Stat. L. 411), as amended, is **hereby amended** to read as follows:*

SEC. 5(b) "<u>During time of war or during any other period of national emergency declared by the President</u>, the President may <u>through any agency that he may designate, or otherwise</u>, investigate, regulate, or prohibit, under such rules and regulations as he may prescribe, by means of licenses or otherwise, any transactions of foreign exchange, export or earmarkings of gold or silver coin or bullion or currency, transfers of credits ~~in any form (other than credits relating solely to transactions to be executed wholly within the United States)~~ <u>between or payments by banking institutions as defined by the President, and export, hoarding melting, or earmarking of gold or silver coin or bullion or currency by any person within the United States or any place subject to the jurisdiction thereof;</u> ~~and transfers of evidences of indebtedness or of ownership of property between the United States and any foreign country, whether enemy, ally of enemy or otherwise, or between residents of one or~~ and ~~he~~ the President may require any ~~such~~ person engaged in any such transaction <u>referred to in this subdivision</u> to furnish under oath, complete information relative thereto, including the production of any books of account, contracts, letters or other papers, in connection therewith in the custody or control of such person, either before or after such transaction is completed. <u>Whoever willfully violates any of the provisions of this subdivision or of any license, order, rule or regulation issued thereunder, shall, upon conviction be fined not more than $10,000, or, if a natural person, may be imprisoned for not more than ten years, or both;'..."</u>

SOME DARE CALL IT TREASON!

Constitution for the United States, Article III, Section 3, Clause 1

"Treason against the United States shall consist only of levying war against them, or adhering to their enemies…"

The supreme Court decision of **Stoehr v. Wallace**, 255 U.S. 239 (1921) declared:

> *"The Trading With the Enemy Act, originally and as amended is strictly a war measure, and finds its sanction in the provision empowering Congress 'to declare war, grant letters of marque and reprisal and make rules concerning captures on land and water." Const. Art. 1, Sec. 8, Cl. 11*

How did FDR and the Federal Reserve get away with this treasonous robbery of the American People's substance? Probably for the same reason Congress is currently passing a multitude of un-American bills and Acts. Congress just does not read them! In the words of Congressman McFadden:

> *Congressman McFadden:* "*Mr. Speaker, I regret that the membership of the House has had no opportunity to consider or even read this bill. The first opportunity I had to know what this legislation is, was when it was read form the clerk's desk. It is an important banking bill. It is a dictatorship over finance in the United States, it is complete control over the banking system in the United States…It is difficult under the circumstances to discuss this bill. The first section of the bill, as I grasped it is the War Powers that were given back in 1917.*"

In spite of warnings of McFadden, the amended Trading With the Enemy Act was immediately passed by a trusting, uneducated and ignorant Congress.

What were the banking institutions as defined by the President?

> **TITLE II**
>
> *Sec. 202. As used in this title, the term "bank" means (1) any **national bank**. [Because this is federal legislation this would mean a U.S. national ie. U.S. Territorial bank, not a sovereign state bank.] (2) any bank or trust company **located in the District of Columbia** and operating under the supervision of the Comptroller of the Currency…*"

What is the collateral for federal reserve notes? To add insult to injury, it became the People's own property!

> *Congressman McGugin:* "**This money will…represent a mortgage on all the homes and other property of the people in the Nation.**"
>
> **Senate Document No. 43, 73rd Congress, 1st Session:** "*The ownership of all property is in the State [Remember, what the term "in the State" means?]; individual so called 'ownership' is only by virtue of Government, ie. Law, amounting to mere user; and use must be in accordance with law and subordinate to the necessities of the State.*"

6.7.3   1935: FDR's Socialist (Social) Security Act of 1935[41]

6.7.3.1   FDR's Pep-Talk to Congress, January 17, 1935

Below is a speech given January 17, 1935 by President Franklin Delano Roosevelt to Congress on the issue of advocating a proposed new program he called "Social Security". This speech resulted in the eventual passage of the Social Security Act of 1935 on August 14, 1935:

> *In addressing you on June 8, 1934, I summarized the main objectives of our American program. Among these was, and is, the security of the men, women, and children of the Nation against certain hazards and vicissitudes of life. This purpose is an essential part of our task. In my annual message to you I promised to submit a definite program of action. This I do in the form of a report to me by a Committee on Economic Security, appointed by me for the purpose of surveying the field and of recommending the basis of legislation.*
>
> *I am gratified with the work of this Committee and of those who have helped it: The Technical Board on Economic Security drawn from various departments of the Government, the Advisory Council on Economic Security, consisting of informed and public - spirited private citizens and a number of other advisory groups, including a committee on actuarial consultants, a medical advisory board, a dental advisory committee, a hospital advisory committee, a public - health advisory committee, a child - welfare committee and an advisory committee on employment relief. All of those who participated in this notable task of planning this major legislative proposal are ready and willing, at any time, to consult with and assist in any way the appropriate Congressional committees and members, with respect to detailed aspects.*
>
> *It is my best judgment that this legislation should be brought forward with a minimum of delay. Federal action is necessary to, and conditioned upon, the action of States. Forty - four legislatures are meeting or will meet soon. In order that the necessary State action may be taken promptly it is important that the Federal Government proceed speedily.*
>
> *The detailed report of the Committee sets forth a series of proposals that will appeal to the sound sense of the American people. It has not attempted the impossible, nor has it failed to exercise sound caution and consideration of all of the factors concerned: the national credit, the rights and responsibilities of States, the capacity of industry to assume financial responsibilities and the fundamental necessity of proceeding in a manner that will merit the enthusiastic support of citizens of all sorts.*

---

[41] Portions from article entitled "The Leviathan's Crown Jewel: The Beginning of Social Security" by Gregory Bresiger. Found at http://www.lewrockwell.com/bresiger/bresiger6.html.

It is overwhelmingly important to avoid any danger of permanently discrediting the sound and necessary policy of Federal legislation for economic security by attempting to apply it on too ambitious a scale before actual experience has provided guidance for the permanently safe direction of such efforts. The place of such a fundamental in our future civilization is too precious to be jeopardized now by extravagant action. It is a sound idea - a sound ideal. Most of the other advanced countries of the world have already adopted it and their experience affords the knowledge that social insurance can be made a sound and workable project.

Three principles should be observed in legislation on this subject. First, the system adopted, except for the money necessary to initiate it, should be self-sustaining in the sense that funds for the payment of insurance benefits should not come from the proceeds of general taxation. Second, excepting in old-age insurance, actual management should be left to the States subject to standards established by the Federal Government. Third, sound financial management of the funds and the reserves, and protection of the credit structure of the Nation should be assured by retaining Federal control over all funds through trustees in the Treasury of the United States.

At this time, I recommend the following types of legislation looking to economic security:

1. Unemployment compensation.

2. Old-age benefits, including compulsory and voluntary annuities.

3. Federal aid to dependent children through grants to States for the support of existing mothers' pension systems and for services for the protection and care of homeless, neglected, dependent, and crippled children.

4. Additional Federal aid to State and local public-health agencies and the strengthening of the Federal Public Health Service. I am not at this time recommending the adoption of so-called "health insurance," although groups representing the medical profession are cooperating with the Federal Government in the further study of the subject and definite progress is being made.

With respect to unemployment compensation, I have concluded that the most practical proposal is the levy of a uniform Federal payroll tax, 90 percent of which should be allowed as an offset to employers contributing under a compulsory State unemployment compensation act. The purpose of this is to afford a requirement of a reasonably uniform character for all States cooperating with the Federal Government and to promote and encourage the passage of unemployment compensation laws in the States. The 10 percent not thus offset should be used to cover the costs of Federal and State administration of this broad system. Thus, States will largely administer unemployment compensation, assisted and guided by the Federal Government. An unemployment compensation system should be constructed in such a way as to afford every practicable aid and incentive toward the larger purpose of employment stabilization. This can be helped by the intelligent planning of both public and private employment. It also can be helped by correlating the system with public employment so that a person who has exhausted his benefits may be eligible for some form of public work as is recommended in this report. Moreover, in order to encourage the stabilization of private employment, Federal legislation should not foreclose the States from establishing means for inducing industries to afford an even greater stabilization of employment.

In the important field of security for our old people, it seems necessary to adopt three principles: First, noncontributory old-age pensions for those who are now too old to build up their own insurance. It is, of course, clear that for perhaps 30 years to come funds will have to be provided by the States and the Federal Government to meet these pensions. Second, compulsory contributory annuities which in time will establish a self-supporting system for those now young and for future generations. Third, voluntary contributory annuities by which individual initiative can increase the annual amounts received in old age. It is proposed that the Federal Government assume one-half of the cost of the old-age pension plan, which ought ultimately to be supplanted by self-supporting annuity plans.

The amount necessary at this time for the initiation of unemployment compensation, old-age security, children's aid, and the promotion of public health, as outlined in the report of the Committee on Economic Security, is approximately $100,000,000.

The establishment of sound means toward a greater future economic security of the American people is dictated by a prudent consideration of the hazards involved in our national life. No one can guarantee this country against the dangers of future depressions but we can reduce these dangers. We can eliminate many of the factors that cause economic depressions, and we can provide the means of mitigating their results. This plan for economic security is at once a measure of prevention and a method of alleviation.

We pay now for the dreadful consequence of economic insecurity - and dearly. This plan presents a more equitable and infinitely less expensive means of meeting these costs. We cannot afford to neglect the plain duty before us. I strongly recommend action to attain the objectives sought in this report.

You can read this speech for yourself at the New Deal Network:

http://newdeal.feri.org/index.htm

A revolution was made when Social Security was enacted in 1935 and it radically changed our country. After remarkably little public and Congressional debate, Franklin Delano Roosevelt signed the Social Security Act into law on August 14, 1935. FDR knew that the welfare state wouldn't end with Social Security. Many of his disappointed allies had wanted much more. But FDR assured them this was just the beginning.[42]

FDR said, on signing the bill into law, that Social Security "represents a cornerstone in a structure which is being built but is by no means complete."[43] The federal government through programs such as Social Security would create its own business cycle, it would "flatten out the peaks and valleys of deflation and inflation,"[44] Roosevelt promised. Social Security was representative of national planning schemes – some of which had been tried during World War I – and which became popular again with intellectuals. Many of them believed that the government could wage war on poverty; that, by using the techniques of wartime planning so popular with progressives during World War I, the government could generate and control the business cycle.[45]

Social Security was a Keynesian device to ensure that buying power would remain strong in times of high unemployment. By Keynesian, I mean a kind of thinking that pre-dated Keynes by centuries, which held that injecting inflation into a weak economy would work miracles. Keynes, in the 1920s, 30s and 40s, was merely one member of this inflationist school. But his thought was influential in America in the 1930s. One of the founding fathers of Social Security has said that the contribution of Keynes was not appreciated.[46] Keynes' philosophy helped justify a massive welfare state.

The original Social Security package, for instance, was a lot more than so-called old age insurance. The program initially contained 10 programs and included 11 titles. Besides, pensions, the federal government was initiating vocational rehabilitation, unemployment insurance, aid to dependent children and public health programs, among others. Myriad additional programs would follow over the years because of the initial triumph of Social Security. It would help bring about a signal change in American culture and government: The federal government would take on many new powers and radically change our economy.[47]

But, most important of all, Social Security changed our culture in ways the authors of the original Social Security Act may or may not have realized: It would, among other things, also discourage savings, expand the state's reach into the family, redistribute income in ways no one imagined (quite often from the working poor and the lower middle-class to the upper middle-class because the latter group tended to have more political clout as exercised through organizations such as the AARP) and create a huge unprecedented peacetime bureaucracy, a bureaucracy that frequently pushed for more expansion under the guise of serving the people.[48]

The program also had a much more profound effect on American life: It invented the concept of a passive retirement in which individuals would stop working, stop making more than a few dollars a year, or what a Social Security advocate called "pin

---

[42] Although the Social Security system initially covered a relatively small part of the working force, FDR assured his allies it was just the beginning: "I see no reason why everybody in the United States should not be covered," FDR privately told Francis Perkins. "Cradle to the grave – from the cradle to the grave they ought to be in a social insurance system." See Arthur Schlesinger, Jr.'s *The Coming of the New Deal*, p. 308, (Houghton Mifflin Company, Boston, 1959).

[43] See *Policymaking for Social Security*, Martha Derthick, p5, (Villard Books, New York, 1991).

[44] *The Public Papers and Addresses of Franklin D. Roosevelt*, Samuel Rosenman, editor, IV, page 324-325.

[45] Some socialists said FDR was going in the direction of planning and economic nationalism. Said Stuart Chase: "National Planning and economic nationalism must go together or not all. President Roosevelt has accepted the general philosophy of planning." He added that the nation could confidently move toward autarchy. Also see George Soule's comments in Walter Lippmann's *The Good Society*, p 91, (Grosset & Dunlap, New York, 1936). "It is nonsense to say that there is any physical impossibility of doing for peace purposes the sort of thing we did for war purposes."

[46] *Madam Secretary: Frances Perkins*, by George Martin, p346, (Houghton Mifflin, Boston, 1976).

[47] Looking part at the achievements of FDR, Doris Kearns Goodwin writes: "No longer would government be viewed as merely a bystander and an occasional referee, intervening only in times of crisis. Instead, the government would assume responsibility for continued growth and fairness in the distribution of wealth." *No Ordinary Time; Franklin and Eleanor Roosevelt; The Home Front in World War II*, p 625, (Simon & Shuster, New York, 1994).

[48] The best example is one of the founding fathers of Social Security, Wilbur Cohen. With the Republicans back in power in 1953, the supposedly non-partisan Cohen quietly "wrote speeches and supplied information" for the Democrats. Says a friendly biographer: "It was not the first time that the non-partisan Social Security administration shaded into partisan politics." See *Mr. Social Security: The Life of Wilbur Cohen*, by Edward Berkowitz, p41, (University Press of Kansas, Laurence, 1995).

money[49]. To make more than pin money would mean Social Security penalties, an idea added to the original bill by the labor unions.

Social Security advocates implicitly convinced tens of millions of Americans that their golden years meant "taking it easy," withdrawing from the most challenging parts of their lives. That would free up millions of jobs, an important consideration in the midst of the Great Depression, an economic calamity in which FDR's policies failed even after six years of huge spending.[50] By 1940, an FDR historian would implicitly concede that the New Deal had failed to restore a strong economy. "The America over which Roosevelt presided in 1940 was in its eleventh year of depression. No decline in American history had been so deep, so lasting, so far reaching."[51] Clearly, America's recovery from the Great Depression did not begin until the buildup for World War II and the war itself. That's when FDR discovered his affinity for a military Keynesianism.[52]

Many changes triggered by Social Security. The changes triggered debates over basic social and economic issues such as personal responsibility vs. the general welfare, and who defines the nature of retirement, the individual or the government, as well as who should control the retirement assets of millions of people.

"Why, then was America so far behind? The first reason was out of the cherished ideal of rugged individualism."[53]

6.7.3.2   FDR and the Birth of Social Security: Destroying Rugged Individuality

Social Security has become the crown jewel of a welfare state, which is why its defenders are today so ardent in fighting any move to privatize any part of it. The welfare state will always be safe as long as Social Security survives. Social Security has continued to expand in good times and bad, under Democrats and Republicans, even though a few of the latter actually claimed that they would bring Social Security under control. Those who thought they would tame this huge program lost time and again. These politicians who once criticized Social Security, usually ended up praising it[54] or kept their criticisms to themselves.[55] And this was FDR's goal in designing the program: Insuring that no succeeding group of politicians could ever undo his work.[56]

Today those who would privatize or even reform Social Security[57] face a formidable task, a task as difficult as dismantling the military-industrial complex or selling off Amtrak. That's because decrepit government bureaucracies – as opposed to

---

[49] Barbara Armstrong, executive director of the Committee on Economic Security (CES), which wrote the Social Security plan said that retirement would mean "that you've stopped working for pay." See *The History of Retirement: The Meaning and Functioning of an American Institution, 1885-1978*, by William Graebner, p185, (Yale University Press, New Haven, Conn., 1980)

[50] By 1938, in the midst of a brutal recession, it was clear to many of FDR's advisers that the New Deal was failing. One of his political advisers, vice president John Nance Garner said that "I don't think the Boss has any definite programs to meet the business. I don't think much of the spending program. You can't keep spending forever. Some day you have to meet the bills." See *Jim Farley's Story. The Roosevelt Years*. P138, (McGraw Hill, New York, 1948). Roosevelt also complained when Secretary of Commerce Dan Roper told him that the economy was slipping into recession. "Dan, you've got to stop issuing these Hooverish statements all the time." Ibid, p101.

[51] The historian is Doris Kearns Goodwin. And clearly the implication of her writing was that FDR had failed just as Hoover had to reverse the depression. See *No Ordinary Time*, p. 42, (Simon & Shuster, New York, 1994)

[52] Roosevelt was "deliberately planning to use a great armament program as a means of spending money to create employment," the journalist John T. Flynn wrote in 1939. See *Prophets on the Right*, by Ronald Radosh, p207, (Simon & Shuster, New York, 1975). Also, Thomas Greer, in his *What Roosevelt Thought; The Social and Political Ideas of Franklin Roosevelt* quotes him in 1937 as saying Americans don't want to solve unemployment problems by huge armament program, yet Greer concedes that FDR resorted to a such an arms buildup. (East Lansing, Mich., Michigan State University Press, 1958) p 74.

[53] *Social Security in America* by William Lloyd Mitchell, p6, (Robert B. Luce, Washington, D.C., 1964).

[54] For instance Ronald Reagan, who had been a great critic of Social Security, would say, toward the end of his presidential years, that "Social Security has proven to be one of the most successful and popular [federal] programs." See *Social Security After 50: Sucesses and Failures*. Edward Berkowitz, editor, (Greenwood Press, New York, 1987).

[55] Any presidential candidate who proposed to tamper with Social Security was "a candidate for a frontal lobotomy," said Jack Kemp during the 1988 campaign. From *Social Insecurity*, by Dorcas Hardy, p16, (Villard Books, New York, 1991).

[56] "With those taxes in there, no damn politician can ever scrap my social security program," FDR said. See Schlesinger, p 309.

[57] The problem of privatizers is what are they to do with the huge unfunded liabilities of this system. It would cost billions, maybe trillions of dollars just for the transition costs to a private system. Meantime, according to economist Milton Friedman and observers such as Marshall Carter and William Shipman, the unfunded liabilities of the system are about $7 trillion. For more see my "Insecure Promise" in the November 1999 issue of *Financial Planning* magazine. Also, a former Social Security official likes to brag that the program is so entrenched that it would be also impossible to destroy. "Where does an 800-pound gorilla sit? Answer: anywhere it wants to. And where does the most popular government program sit? You got it." From Andy Landis's *Social Security, the Inside Story*, p3, (Crisp Publications, Menlo Park, California, 1997).

rotten private bureaucracies – have the power to tax and to preserve their existence. And the first rule of any bureaucracy is survival at any cost. The second rule is always try to expand.

The welfare state took much longer to take hold in the United States than in Europe, where socialism had a better name and a longer tradition.

By the early 1930s, Germany had a Social Security program for nearly a half century. Britain had a government pension scheme since before the World War I, when the Liberal/Labour government of Herbert Henry Asquith in 1911[58] laid the foundations of a welfare state that would be later carried out by the Labor and Conservative parties over the next two generations. Germany under Bismarck had passed a Social Security plan as part of an alliance with Social Democrats. Bismarck was ready for socialism[59]. Dozens of European countries had put Social Security schemes by the outbreak of World War I.

But in America, there was a tradition of "rugged individualism" that resisted most forms of collectivism. Even labor leaders like Samuel Gompers,[60] who had called for many other government initiatives, opposed a mandatory social insurance program, a concept that stressed an insurance that was not for profit, but was run for the benefit of society. But Gompers was wary of that idea. To him, it smacked of German socialism. "Compulsory social insurance," he complained, "is in essence undemocratic."[61] Foreshadowing the objections of those who would later complain that the government would mismanage the assets of a program, Gompers wanted workers to depend on themselves, private institutions, their unions – anything but the government.

The opposition to social insurance was owing to an American individualist tradition whose adherents held that individuals, families and community groups should take care of people in old age, not the government. And, most importantly, it was a voluntaryist tradition that resisted compulsory government programs.[62]

FDR, who was credited as the first major American politician to support a social security system, nevertheless had campaigned in 1932 in favor of limited government. He bitterly criticized Herbert Hoover's huge deficits. On the campaign trial he promised to roll back, not expand, the size of the federal government. "For three long years I have been going up and down this country preaching that government – federal government, state and local – costs too much. I shall not stop that preaching."[63]

FDR gave not the slightest indication that was he committed to a massive expansion of the power of the federal government. Later, as we will see, FDR would say that circumstances had changed. His supporters would argue that the Great Depression, and the more radical social insurance proposals of men like Huey Long, Upton Sinclair and Frances Townsend,[64] had led him to back this "moderate" program called Social Security.

Yet even before he took office, FDR was quietly committed to a social insurance program[65] as part of a program of counter-cyclical measures he believed would cure the problems of the business cycle. These initiatives were failures if one is to

---

[58] See *The Strange Death of Liberal England 1910-1914*, by George Dangerfield, pp7-30, (Capricorn Books, New York, 1961.

[59] See *Bismarck* by Alan Palmer, pp 206-207 and p250. (Charles Scribner's Sons, New York, 1976).

[60] See footnote 63.

[61] See *The Crisis in Social Security. Economic and Political Origins* by Carolyn Weaver, p28. (Duke University Press, Durham, North Carolina, 1982).

[62] "Voluntaryism, the right of citizens to define and pursue their goals, resulted in limited government and maximum liberty." See *The Struggle for Social Security, 1900-1935*, by Roy Lubove, p5 (University of Pittsburgh Press, 1986).

[63] See *The Roosevelt Myth*" by John T. Flynn, p37, (Devon-Adair Company, New York, 1961).

[64] *Social Security. The First Half Century*. Gerald Nash, editor, pp 35-36, (University of New Mexico Press, Albuquerque, 1988).

[65] *Social Security in the United States*, by Paul Douglas, p 15, (McGraw Hill, New York, 1936).

measure by unemployment numbers and traditional economic indices[66]. They did not restore prosperity, FDR was told by advisers six years into the New Deal.[67]

Social Security was a key part of his revolutionary corporativist economic policies. It was a revolution that shifted the responsibility for income maintenance from the private to the public sector, from the family to the state and from voluntary organizations to public bureaucracies. And it was a revolution carried out by elite groups of welfare workers, Social Democrats and other who believed European socialism could be imported to the United States on a step-by-step basis.[68] They believed in a "new liberalism." Classical liberalism would die in the United States in the 1930s through programs such as Social Security just as it had died in Britain some four decades before. A new liberalism celebrated the expanded powers of the federal government. The old American individualist tradition was distrustful of distant central governments and the bureaucracies they spawned.

"Americans assumed that their country was unique in assigning to private voluntary institutions a wide range of responsibilities which in other nations were relegated to governments or elite groups," writes one historian of Social Security.[69]

Almost everyone, FDR critics as well as admirers, agree that Social Security was a watershed event in our history. FDR said of the legislation that, if it was the only bill passed in the 1935-36 congressional session, Congress would have accomplished a lot.[70] Why was it so important to those such as FDR who scorned the individualist tradition? Social Security was the centerpiece of a revolution that one historian has said meant that "big government, modern government" was here to stay.[71]

When Social Security survived – and, in its earlier years, it was a dicey question if it would or not, requiring the most effective political skills that FDR and his allies could summon – Americans implicitly accepted the most essential part of a new social policy. Washington, not individuals, would now have huge powers over the individual citizen's retirement planning, unemployment insurance and welfare payments. When FDR signed the Social Security Act, the United States, for the first time in her history, would have "a significant, permanent social welfare bureaucracy."[72]

FDR assured his social democratic allies that the Social Security was just the beginning of an expanded role for the federal government. But it wasn't until toward the end of his life, in the Economic Bill of Rights speech that so "thrilled" his social democratic supporters[73], that he was ready to publicly walk away from the campaign promises of 1932 and the American individualist tradition.

Some four years after its creation, the structure of this landmark program was expanding. Some 12,000 employees would be working in the Social Security administration, which would become bigger and bigger . Once in place, there were calls for sister bureaucracies. American Socialists were disappointed that more people were not included in the 1935 act (such as servants and farm workers); that disability insurance wasn't initially covered, that health insurance had not been included. But many of those leftist critics, who had at the time claimed that it was too little, later would concede that Social Security's

---

[66] After some five years of the New Deal, another recession began in 1937. Two historians have written that "The resulting downturn began in August 1937 and continued through the winter and spring of 1938. It was nothing short of catastrophic." See *FDR*, Russell D. Buhite and David W. Levy, editors, p111 (Penguin Books, New York, 1992)

[67] FDR conceded there were problems in talks with Farley but blamed a conspiracy against him: "I know that the present situation is the result of a concerted effort by big business and concentrated wealth to drive the market down and just to create a situation unfavorable to me." See *Jim Farley's Story*, p101.

[68] "The vast expansion of public assistance functions and expenditures beginning in the 1930s was superimposed upon a long tradition of disdain totally incongruous with the political and economic power assumed by the public welfare sector." See *The Professional Altruist: The Emergence of Social Work as a Career, 1880-1930*, p54, (New York, Atheneum, 1969)

[69] See *The Struggle for Social Security, 1900-1935*, Roy Lubove, (University of Pittsburgh Press, 1986, p. 5 .

[70] FDR understood that Social Security's passage represented radical change: "If the Senate and the House of Representatives in this long and arduous session had nothing more than pass this Bill, the session would have been regarded as historic for all time." See *The New Deal: A Documentary History*. William E. Leuchtenburg, p 80, (Harper and Row, New York, 1968)

[71] Frances Perkins said "modern government" was here to stay when she saw the 1944 GOP platform, which accepted many of the welfare state initiative of FDR. The Republicans were in the process of becoming "a me too party." See *Frances Perkins: a Member of the Cabinet*." by Bill Severin, p. 223, (Hawthorn Books, New York, 1976).

[72] Goodwin, p 625.

[73] One of the CES' advisory board had contained a recommendation that health insurance should be included in the original Social Security package, but FDR cut that part out. See *Madam Secretary*, pp 347-348.

establishment, no matter how modest, opened the door for the government to do many other things.[74] All the measures left out of the original bill would be included within 30 years.

That is why even many of those socialists who scorned FDR, who said that he was a bumbling savior of capitalism, could still summon up some grudging praise for FDR. Socialism would be quietly achieved over generations as part of a mixed economy that seemed, on the surface, to be a traditional laissez-faire American economy.

Social Security, whether it was called social insurance or government pensions, was the first vital step on the road to the welfare state. How it finally happened in the United States, after decades of frustrating unsuccessful efforts by social democrats and professional bureaucrats, is a fascinating story. FDR went around Congress, which was too unpredictable and whose review process might not have given him what he wanted. FDR found his own experts that he knew would give him what he wanted, then would unveil a Social Security proposal that he expected to be adopted whole. Congress, generally intimidated by the experts, went along with few objections.

This process, this masterful strategy of building a welfare state in a country with a historic commitment to individualism, will be discussed in the next report.

6.7.4   1937: FDR's Stacking of the Supreme Court

President Franklin D. Roosevelt, during his long 12-year tenure in office in the 1930's, tried to ram his socialist programs down our throat. To name a few of these programs he tried to institute:

1. Social Security (1935).
2. Outlawing of the holding of gold by private individuals and forcing citizens to use paper currency.
3. Direct income taxes on individuals. These taxes were struck down by the following Supreme Court rulings:
    3.1. *1920: Evans v. Gore*, 253 U.S. 245 (1920) (struck down direct income taxes on federal judges).
    3.2. *1922: Bailey v. Drexel Furniture Co.*, 259 U.S. 20 (1922). The Supreme Court ruled that a federal income tax on child labor was unconstitutional.
    3.3. *1924: Cook v. Tait*, 265 U.S. 47 (1924) (ruled that direct taxes on individuals cannot be sustained based on income).
    3.4. *1938: Hassett v. Welch*, 303 U.S. 303 (1938). The Supreme Court ruled that all doubts about the construction of tax statutes, codes, and laws should be resolved in favor of taxpayers, not the government.
4. Social security numbers.
5. Railroad retirement (struck down in 1935 in the Supreme Court Case of *Railroad Retirement Board v. Alton Railroad Co., 295 U.S. 330 (1935)*).

Because of these rulings against his socialist programs, FDR was feeling thwarted by the Supreme Court. Therefore, on March 9, 1937, he announced his intention via radio to the entire country that he was going to "stack" the Supreme Court (see http://www.hpol.org/fdr/chat/). This was called "the court packing plan". The Supreme court originally had 6 justices, and he doubled its size by adding several of his own "cronies" who would uphold and defend his socialist programs, including Social Security and the Victory Tax. He also proposed to replace all the justices over 70, which included 5 of the 6 justices then in office. Here are some of FDR's own words, given during a radio address on March 9, 1937:

> *"But since the rise of the modern movement for social and economic progress through legislation, the Court has more and more often and more and more boldly asserted a power to veto laws passed by the Congress and by state legislatures in complete disregard of this original limitation which I have just read.*
>
> *[...]*
>
> *The Court in addition to the proper use of its judicial functions has improperly set itself up as a third house of the Congress - a super-legislature, as one of the justices has called it - reading into the Constitution words and implications which are not there, and which were never intended to be there.*
>
> *We have, therefore, reached the point as a nation where we must take action to save the Constitution from the Court and the Court from itself. We must find a way to take an appeal from the Supreme Court to the Constitution*

---

[74] One Democrat who noticed the transformation was FDR's fellow Democrat Al Smith. By the mid 1930s he was complaining that the "Brain Trusters caught the Socialists swimming and ran away with their clothes." See *Al Smith, Hero of the Cities*, by Matthew and Hannah Josephson, p459, (Houghton Mifflin Company, Boston, 1969). That's a good comparison given that the American Socialist Party of 1928 had called for a mandatory government pension system.

itself. We want a Supreme Court which will do justice under the Constitution and not over it. In our courts we want a government of laws and not of men.

[...]

What is my proposal? It is simply this: whenever a judge or justice of any federal court has reached the age of seventy and does not avail himself of the opportunity to retire on a pension, a new member shall be appointed by the president then in office, with the approval, as required by the Constitution, of the Senate of the United States.

That plan has two chief purposes. By bringing into the judicial system a steady and continuing stream of new and younger blood, I hope, first, to make the administration of all federal justice, from the bottom to the top, speedier and, therefore, less costly; secondly, to bring to the decision of social and economic problems younger men who have had personal experience and contact with modern facts and circumstances under which average men have to live and work. This plan will save our national Constitution from hardening of the judicial arteries.

[...]

Those opposing this plan have sought to arouse prejudice and fear by crying that I am seeking to "pack" the Supreme Court and that a baneful precedent will be established.

What do they mean by the words "packing the Supreme Court?" Let me answer this question with a bluntness that will end all honest misunderstanding of my purposes.

If by that phrase "packing the Court" it is charged that I wish to place on the bench spineless puppets who would disregard the law and would decide specific cases as I wished them to be decided, I make this answer: that no president fit for his office would appoint, and no Senate of honorable men fit for their office would confirm, that kind of appointees to the Supreme Court.

[...]

But if by that phrase the charge is made that I would appoint and the Senate would confirm justices worthy to sit beside present members of the Court, who understand modern conditions, that I will appoint justices who will not undertake to override the judgment of the Congress on legislative policy, that I will appoint justices who will act as justices and not as legislators - if the appointment of such justices can be called "packing the Courts," then I say that I and with me the vast majority of the American people favor doing just that thing - now.

Is it a dangerous precedent for the Congress to change the number of the justices? The Congress has always had, and will have, that power. The number of justices has been changed several times before, in the administrations of John Adams and Thomas Jefferson - both of them signers of the Declaration of Independence - in the administrations of Andrew Jackson, Abraham Lincoln, and Ulysses S. Grant.

[...]

Like all lawyers, like all Americans, I regret the necessity of this controversy. But the welfare of the United States, and indeed of the Constitution itself, is what we all must think about first. Our difficulty with the Court today rises not from the Court as an institution but from human beings within it. But we cannot yield our constitutional destiny to the personal judgment of a few men who, being fearful of the future, would deny us the necessary means of dealing with the present.

Could it be any clearer, after reading this and looking at the history of the Supreme Court rulings at that time following his "packing plan" that he was trying to stack the deck and ramrod his socialist programs down our throats?

Below is what the U.S. Senate Report 711 said about the packing plan, which they had a very dim view of:

Senate Report 711, June 7, 1937
http://famguardian.org/TaxFreedom/History/President/1937-SenRpt711-19370607.pdf

6.7.5   1943: FDR's Executive Order 9397: Bye-Bye Privacy and Fourth Amendment!

Below is a presidential Executive Order issued by our socialist President, Franklin Delano Roosevelt, in which the infamous Social Security Number became the standard number for monitoring all transactions of every citizen. This was the day we lost our privacy and gutted the Fourth Amendment. This infamous day marked the start of socialism in America and it was accomplished in a time of national crisis (World War II) and in the name of the public "good".

EXECUTIVE ORDER 9397

WHEREAS certain Federal agencies from time to time require in the administration of their activities a system of numerical identification of accounts of individual persons; and

WHEREAS some seventy million persons have heretofore been assigned account numbers pursuant to the Social Security Act; and

WHEREAS a large percentage of Federal employees have already been assigned account numbers pursuant to the Social Security Act; and

WHEREAS it is desirable in the interest of economy and orderly administration that the Federal Government move towards the use of a single unduplicated numerical identification system of accounts and avoid the unnecessary establishment of additional systems:

NOW THEREFORE, by virtue of the authority vested in me as President of the United States, it is hereby ordered as follows:

1. Hereafter any Federal department establishment, or agency shall, whenever the head thereof finds it advisable to establish a new system of permanent account numbers pertaining to individual persons, utilize exclusively the Social Security Act account numbers assigned pursuant to Title 26, section 402.502 of the 1940 Supplement to the Code of Federal Regulations and pursuant to paragraph 2 of this order.

2. The Social Security Board shall provide for the assignment of an account number to each person who is required by any Federal agency to have such a number but who has not previously been assigned such number by the Board. The Board may accomplish this purpose by

(a) assigning such numbers to individual persons,

(b) assigning blocks of numbers to Federal agencies for reassignment to individual persons, or

(c) making such other arrangements for the assignment of numbers as it may deem appropriate.

3. The Social Security Board shall furnish, upon request of any Federal agency utilizing the numerical identification system of accounts provided for in this order, the account number pertaining to any person with whom such agency has an account or the name and other identifying data pertaining to any account number of any such person.

4. The Social Security Board and each Federal agency shall maintain the confidential character of information relating to individual persons obtained pursuant to the provisions of this order.

5. There shall be transferred to the Social Security Board, from time to time, such amounts as the Director of the Bureau of the Budget shall determine to be required for reimbursement by any Federal agency for the services rendered by the Board pursuant to the provisions of this order.

6. This order shall be published in the Federal Register.

Franklin D Roosevelt
The White House
November 22, 1943

You can read this Executive Order for yourself on the web at the address below:

http://resource.lawlinks.com/Content/Legal_Research/Executive_Orders/1940-1960/executive_order_9397.htm

6.8 Congressional Cover-Ups, Scandals, and Tax Code Obfuscation

"I, _____, do solemnly swear (or affirm) that I will support and defend the Constitution of the United States against all enemies, foreign and domestic; that I will bear true faith and allegiance to the same; that I take this obligation freely, without any mental reservation or purpose of evasion; and that I will well and faithfully discharge the duties of the office on which I am about to enter. So help me God."
[Congressional Oath of Office]

> *"Suppose you were an idiot, and suppose you were in Congress, But I repeat myself."*
> *[Mark Twain]*

> *"If 'pro' is the opposite of 'con', a wise man once said, then 'progress' must be the antonym of 'Congress'."*

> *Late one night in the capitol city a mugger wearing a ski mask jumped into the path of a well-dressed man and stuck a gun in his ribs. "Give me your money!" he demanded.*
>
> *Indignant, the affluent man replied, "You can't do this - I'm a U.S. Congressman!"*

"In that case," replied the robber, "give me MY money!"

This section shall show conclusively the history of increasing obfuscation, confusion, and deception of our income tax laws from 1921 to the present. We will show that Congress has, with each successive revision of the U.S. Code and the Code of Federal Regulations, deliberately tried to make the law more confusing and deceptive by:

1. Removing focus of the law on "sources" or "taxable activities", by removing pointers to legitimate "sources" whenever discussing income in the Internal Revenue Code. This can lead to the mistaken assumption by the Citizen that ***all*** sources of income are taxable instead of just specific sources. But we know that Congress doesn't have the authority to tax people in China, so wherever there is an income, there must be an associated source.
2. Remove references to the fact that "foreign corporations" and only withholding agents for "nonresident aliens" are liable for income taxes and replace "foreigners" with "taxpayers". Thus, if American citizens (most of whom are NOT "U.S. citizens") can erroneously be convinced that they are "taxpayers", then they will think that the section applies to them.
3. Add more indirection by using new terms whose definition is not referred to where they are used. These terms include:
    3.1. "items of income"
    3.2. "statutory groupings"
    3.3. "operative sections"
4. Adding double negatives (in 26 C.F.R. §1.861-8T, for instance) instead of just referring to the positive of what can and cannot be taxed.
5. Changing the definitions of certain words to make them appear universal and yet in actuality they aren't. For instance, below are some confusing words in the tax code and their REAL definitions:
    5.1. "Employer": The Federal government as an employer of federal workers. There are repeated references to how employers are liable for taxes they don't withhold but little is said about the fact that the only people by the code who are liable for the deductions are Federal government agencies!
    5.2. "Taxpayer": A nonresident alien domiciled in the U.S. or a citizen living overseas.
    5.3. "The States": The District of Columbia and all federal States but not one of the Union states or several states.
    5.4. "trade or business in the United States": functions involving the holding of public office with the United States government (e.g. congressional office or presidential appointment).

We will argue that such an obfuscating evolution of the tax code as directed by lawyers (does anyone like lawyers?) in Congress would point to the fact that there is a conspiracy by the lawyers in Congress to defraud the citizens (notice we didn't say "taxpayers") illegally of their come by abusing the law and the tax code. This also points to the fact that we need better configuration management of the laws so that there is traceability for each modification of the law to a specific individual in Congress so that person can be prosecuted (and defamed and fired from office) appropriately when they either demonstrate a conflict of interest or try to obfuscate the code. We believe that a petition (under the First Amendment) and conviction of the government for the following crimes is inevitable based on current law and that it is only a matter of time before this issue ends up in front of the Supreme Court. Below are just a few of the crimes you will likely see the IRS and members of Congress convicted of based on the evidence presented here:

1. "Conspiracy against rights" (18 U.S.C. §241).
2. "Federally protected rights being violated" (18 U.S.C. §245).
3. "Illegally taking more money than is required by law" (26 U.S.C. §7214).
4. "Illegal extortion of taxes" (18 U.S.C. §872).
5. "Receiving the proceeds of extortion" (18 U.S.C. §880).

6. "Mailing threatening communications" (18 U.S.C. §876).
7. "Blackmail" (18 U.S.C. §873).
8. "Retaliating against a witness, victim, or an informant" (18 U.S.C. §1513).
9. "False writings" (18 U.S.C. §1018).
10. "Taking of property that is not based on law" (26 C.F.R. §601.106(f)(1)
11. "Retaliating against or harassing taxpayer" (Section 1203, IRS Restructuring and Reform Act of 1998.
12. "Unauthorized collection actions" (26 U.S.C. §7433).
13. "Fraud" (18 U.S.C. §1018).
14. "Fraud and swindling" (18 U.S.C. §1341).
15. "Sale or receipt of stolen goods" (18 U.S.C. §2315).
16. Running of a "continuing financial crimes enterprise" (18 U.S.C. §225).
17. "Engaging in monetary transactions in property derived from specified unlawful activity" (18 U.S.C. §1957).

6.8.1 No taxation without representation!

No taxation without representation!

This was one of the rallying cries before the American revolution. We have all heard it in high school and read it in the history books, and perhaps felt some sense of pride in it. But do we REALLY know what it means and if we still have it? The answer is, unfortunately, probably not. Because the Constitution SPECIFICALLY STATES that if *anyone* imposes a tax and tries to collect it, *it must be Congress!!*

This is what REPRESENTATION with TAXATION means. If you don't like a tax, you can vote against the people who passed it and who enforce it. *When was the last time you voted for an agent of the Internal Revenue Service?* Instead, our corrupt Congress as created a new executive agency, given it *no delegated authority* in the Internal Revenue Code, allowed it to write its own regulations to enforce the tax (a conflict of interest, I might add) and then hypocritically and habitually complained that it has overstepped its bounds, as if they had no responsibility for its existence! Here is the way Irwin Schiff insightfully describes this situation:

> *The government has done a masterful job at subterfuge. The same Congress that created the IRS is the one that complains about it. They complain about it like it is some evil and independent agency of the federal government with a life of its own and as though they have no control over it because it is outside the legislative branch, but it was created through the legislation of Congress in 26 U.S.C. §7805! Congress complaining about the abuses of the IRS is like people saying about me:*
>
> > *"You know Irwin Schiff is a really nice guy, but Oh.....HIS FIST. It really hurts and it's such an evil thing when it goes around hitting people all the time!"*
>
> *Don't let your Congressman suck you into his pity party! Tell him to get off his ass and fix the lawless behavior of the IRS!*

Congress and the Courts have, by allowing the current situation with the IRS to exist, *failed to live up to their oath of office to support and defend the Constitution, and thereby abdicated their powers to another branch of government.* Congress has abdicated their responsibility to collect taxes by delegating it to another branch of the government: The Department of the Treasury and the IRS are in the EXECUTIVE BRANCH! The Constitution does not allow the Congress to delegate or abdicate their duty to collect taxes! Punish the bastards by penalizing them for 2/3 of their salary until they fix this problem! Or better yet, cancel their retirement until they fix it. If we had a national referendum process, this would have happened hundreds of years ago!

> *"The accumulation of all powers, legislative, executive and judiciary, in the same hands ... may justly be pronounced the very definition of tyranny."* - James Madison (1751-1863)

> *"Taxation WITH representation ain't so hot either."* -- Gerald Barzan

6.8.2 The Corruption of Our Tax System by the Courts and the Congress: Downes v. Bidwell, 182 U.S. 244 (1901)

Recall that the Supreme Court in ***Downes v. Bidwell***, 182 U.S. 244 (1901) fracturing the United States into the equivalent of two countries: One with constitutional protections in the 50 union states, and the other one in the federal zone with no constitutional protections. We describe these two countries as:

> *"One nation [the 50 union states] under God. The other nation [the federal zone] under fraud."*

In discussing the supreme Court case of ***Downes v. Bidwell***, 182 U.S. 244 (1901), Judge Harlan, in the most eloquently expressed dissenting opinion, supported equal Constitutional protections for all territories and possessions of the United States, in the same manner that the 50 union states are protected. Following are excerpts from that opinion, along with Harlan's accurate predictions of the consequences of that decision:

> "*I take leave to say that, if the principles thus announced should ever receive the sanction of a majority of this court, a radical and mischievous change in our system of government will result. We will, in that event, pass from the era of constitutional liberty guarded and protected by a written constitution into an era of legislative absolutism..*
>
> *[...]*
>
> "*The idea prevails with some, indeed it has found expression in arguments at the bar, that we have in this country substantially two national governments; one to be maintained under the Constitution, with all of its restrictions; the other to be maintained by Congress outside the independently of that instrument, by exercising such powers [of absolutism] as other nations of the earth are accustomed to..*
>
> *[...]*
>
> *It will be an evil day for American liberty if the theory of a government outside the supreme law of the land finds lodgment in our constitutional jurisprudence. No higher duty rests upon this court than to exert its full authority to prevent all violation of the principles of the Constitution.*"
> [Downes v. Bidwell, 182 U.S. 244 (1901), Justice Harlan, Dissenting]

Judge Harlan's extremely prudent advice was ignored and his prediction of a "radical and mischievous change in our system" because of this ruling was right on target! This dual United States ruling is the root of the evil of the Internal Revenue Service, the Federal Reserve System, with its subsequent robbery of our gold and silver, and the many other unjust federal agencies that have abused American Right, confiscated their property, and strangled them with red-tape. A government established to protect the happiness of American people has become the root of their misery and the worst abusers of the Rights it was established to protect! Because of this ruling, Congress has been able to circumvent the Constitution for the united States of America, as follows:

1. The United States Government legally creates legislation, which may be unconstitutional for the 50 union states, under the authority and guise of legislating for the citizens and residents of the territories and possessions "belonging to" the United States, over which the United States has exclusive authority.
2. Such federal legislation is made applicable only to the citizens born and residing in Territories, possessions, instrumentalities and enclaves under the exclusive jurisdiction of the United States. These "individuals" are called "U.S. citizens" or "citizens of the United states, subject to its jurisdiction" in such legislation. The average American, of course, believes he or she is such a citizen (because it was never disclosed to them that our Congress legislates for two different types of citizens). Because that American has respect for the law, he or she voluntarily consents to obey this legislation that is contrary to the Constitution.

6.8.3 The Anti-Injunction Act statute, 26 U.S.C. §7421

This statute states:

> *Sec. 7421. Prohibition of suits to restrain assessment or collection*
>
> *(a) Tax*
>
> *Except as provided in sections 6015(e), 6212(a) and (c), 6213(a), 6225(b), 6246(b), 6331(i), 6672(b), 6694(c), and 7426(a) and (b)(1), 7429(b), and 7436, no suit for the purpose of restraining the assessment or collection of any tax shall be maintained in any court by any person, whether or not such person is the person against whom such tax was assessed.*
>
> *(b) Liability of transferee or fiduciary*
>
> *No suit shall be maintained in any court for the purpose of restraining the assessment or collection (pursuant to the provisions of chapter 71) of -*

> *(1) the amount of the liability, at law or in equity, of a transferee of property of a taxpayer in respect of any internal revenue tax, or*
>
> *(2) the amount of the liability of a fiduciary under section 3713(b) of title 31, United States Code [1] in respect of any such tax.*

The problem with this statute is that it is also commonly used as an excuse by our federal courts to NOT stop illegal assessment and collection of taxes for the government, which means that the IRS can act lawlessly and violate due process of Americans without a court order and cannot be restrained from illegally assessing and collecting the tax. The only recourse in any court above U.S. Tax Court is to pay the illegally assessed or collected tax and then sue the federal government. By that time, the plundered Citizen usually has so little property and cash left that he can't afford to defend his rights and an expensive lawyer will try to victimize and extort unreasonable fees from him to get him out of the predicament that this unconstitutional law put him in to begin with.

If you would like to know what the federal courts think about the Anti-Injunction Act, read the following cases:

- Willits v. Richardson, 497 F.2d. 240, 5th Circuit, (1974)
- Laing v. U.S., 423 U.S. 161 (1976): Upheld the Anti-Injunction Act.
- Enochs v. Williams Packing, 370 U.S. 1 (1961): Upheld the Anti-Injunction Act.

The state of California has enacted two laws that are similar to the Federal Anti-Injunction Act as follows:

- **California Constitution: Section 32**.

  > *No legal or equitable process shall issue in any proceeding in any court against <u>this State</u> or any officer thereof to prevent or enjoin the collection of any tax. After payment of a tax claimed to be illegal, an action may be maintained to recover the tax paid, with interest, in such a manner as may be provided by the Legislature. [New section adopted November 5, 1974].*

- **California Revenue and Taxation Code, Section 19081: Legal or equitable processes to enjoin assessment or collection of tax prohibited; Exception in residence cases**.

  > *No injunction or writ of mandate or other legal or equitable process shall issue in any suit, action, or proceeding in any court against this State or against any officer of this State to prevent or enjoin the assessment or collection of any tax under this part; provided, however, that any individual after protesting a notice or notices of deficiency assessment issues because of his alleged residence in this State and after appealing from the action of the Franchise Tax Board to the State Board of Equalization becomes final commence an action, on the grounds set forth in his protest, in the Superior Court of the County of Sacramento, in the County of Los Angeles or in the City and County of San Francisco against the Franchise Tax Board to determine the fact of his residence in this State during the year or years set forth in the notice or notices of deficiency assessment. No tax under this part based solely upon the residence of such an individual shall be collected from such individual until 60 days after the action of the State Board of Equalization becomes final and, if he commences an action pursuant to this section, during the pendency of such action, other than by way of or under the jeopardy assessment provisions of this part.*
  >
  > ***Cross References:***
  > *Duty of ascertaining correctness of tax return: §19254*
  > *Preventive relief: CC §§3420 et seq.*
  > *Injunctions generally: CCP §§525 et seq.*
  > *Action to determine fact of residence of individual claiming to be nonresident for purpose of Personal Income Tax Law: CCP §1060.5*
  > *Writ of mandate: CCP §§1084 et. seq.*
  > *State Board of Equalization: Gov.C. §§ 15600 et seq.*
  > *Franchise Tax Board: Gov.C. §§ 15700 et seq.*
  > ***Collateral References:***
  > *Witkin Summary (8th Ed.) p. 4220*
  > *Cal Jur 3d Income Taxes §§5, 58, 71*
  > *Corresponding federal statute: 26 USCS § 7421*

The thing to notice about the California version of the Anti-Injunction Act is the use of the term "this State" repeatedly throughout both the California Constitution and R&TC §19081. The important thing to remember is the meaning of the term "this State", which means federal enclaves within California. Recall that we said in section 5.2.6 that "State" is really just the federal enclaves within California as per California Revenue and Taxation Code Section 17018:

> 17018. "State" includes the District of Columbia, and the possessions of the United States.
> *[which don't include the 50 sovereign states but do include federal areas within those states]*

Also recall that California Revenue and Taxation Code, Section 6017 further defines the term "this State" explicitly to mean:

> 6017. *"In this State" or "in the State" means within the exterior [outside] limits of the [Sovereign] state of California and includes [only] all territory within these limits owned by or ceded to the United States*

So what they are saying here is that California's version of the Anti-Injunction act only applies in federal enclaves that are within California.

With respect to the comments in this section, the provisions of the Anti-Injunction Act may be easily circumvented if you know what you are doing. We describe how to do this in section 1.4.1 of the following:

> *Sovereignty Forms and Instructions Manual*, Form #10.005
> http://sedm.org/Forms/FormIndex.htm

6.8.4　Why the Lawyers in Congress Just Love the Tax Code

> *"All the Congress, all the accountants and tax lawyers, all the judges, and a convention of wizards all cannot tell for sure what the income tax law says."* -- Walter B. Wriston

Merriam Webster's New International Dictionary (unabridged, 2d ed.), defines the term "sentence" as follows:

> "**sentence**: 5. *A series of connected words extending from one period or full stop to another. See sense 8, below."*
>
> *"8. Gram. According to the degrees of complication in their structure, sentences are described as* simple, complex, compound, *and* compound-complex.*"*

A full, completed sentence ends with a period. The entire text of section 3121(b) of the federal Internal Revenue Code (IRC) contains only two completed sentences that end with a period. Printed below is the full text of section 3121(b) of the IRC. Inspection of the 1994, CCH Incorporated edition (volume 2) of the IRC reveals that the entire text of section 3121(b) required five pages to print in size 10 font. (This does not include the five additional pages that reference the "amendments" to section 3121(b).) A computer count of the entire text of section 3121(b) totaled some 19,098 characters, comprising some 3,834 words. The first completed sentence alone contained 18,880 characters or 3,788 words. According to Merriam Webster's ranking of the various degrees of complication that a sentence may take, those 3,788 words must surely classify that first sentence in section 3121(b) as a *compound-complex* sentence.

Below is printed the entire text of section 3121(b) comprised of 3,834 words which, properly and grammatically speaking, comprise only two completed sentences. Who said you can't have fun with the tax code!

> *"(b) Employment For purposes of this chapter, the term "employment" means any service, of whatever nature, performed (A) by an employee for the person employing him, irrespective of the citizenship or residence of either, (i) within the United States, or (ii) on or in connection with an American vessel or American aircraft under a contract of service which is entered into within the United States or during the performance of which and while the employee is employed on the vessel or aircraft it touches at a port in the United States, if the employee is employed on and in connection with such vessel or aircraft when outside the United States, or (B) outside the United States by a citizen or resident of the United States as an employee for an American employer (as defined in subsection (h)), or (C) if it is service, regardless of where or by whom performed, which is designated as employment or recognized as equivalent to employment under an agreement entered into under section 233 of the Social Security Act; except that such term shall not include - (1) service performed by foreign agricultural workers lawfully admitted to the United States from the Bahamas, Jamaica, and the other British West Indies, or from any other foreign country or possession thereof, on a temporary basis to perform agricultural labor; (2) domestic service performed in a local college club, or local chapter of a college fraternity or sorority, by a student who is enrolled and is regularly attending classes at a school, college, or university; (3)(A) service performed by a child under the age of 18 in the employ of his father or mother; (B) service not in the course of the employer's trade or business, or domestic service in a private home of the employer, performed by an individual under the age of 21 in the employ of his father or mother, or performed by an individual in the employ of his spouse or son or daughter; except that the provisions of this subparagraph shall not be applicable to such domestic service performed by an individual in the employ of his son or daughter if - (i) the employer is a surviving spouse or a divorced individual and has not remarried, or has a spouse living in the home who has a mental or physical condition which results in such spouse's being incapable of caring for a son, daughter, stepson, or stepdaughter (referred to in clause (ii)) for at least 4 continuous weeks in the calendar quarter in which the service is rendered,*

and (ii) a son, daughter, stepson, or stepdaughter of such employer is living in the home, and (iii) the son, daughter, stepson, or stepdaughter (referred to in clause (ii)) has not attained age 18 or has a mental or physical condition which requires the personal care and supervision of an adult for at least 4 continuous weeks in the calendar quarter in which the service is rendered; (4) service performed by an individual on or in connection with a vessel not an American vessel, or on or in connection with an aircraft not an American aircraft, if (A) the individual is employed on and in connection with such vessel or aircraft, when outside the United States and (B)(i) such individual is not a citizen of the United States or (ii) the employer is not an American employer; (5) service performed in the employ of the United States or any instrumentality of the United States, if such service - (A) would be excluded from the term "employment" for purposes of this title if the provisions of paragraphs (5) and (6) of this subsection as in effect in January 1983 had remained in effect, and (B) is performed by an individual who - (i) has been continuously performing service described in subparagraph (A) since December 31, 1983, and for purposes of this clause - (I) if an individual performing service described in subparagraph (A) returns to the performance of such service after being separated therefrom for a period of less than 366 consecutive days, regardless of whether the period began before, on, or after December 31, 1983, then such service shall be considered continuous, (II) if an individual performing service described in subparagraph (A) returns to the performance of such service after being detailed or transferred to an international organization as described under section 3343 of subchapter III of chapter 33 of title 5, United States Code, or under section 3581 of chapter 35 of such title, then the service performed for that organization shall be considered service described in subparagraph (A), (III) if an individual performing service described in subparagraph (A) is reemployed or reinstated after being separated from such service for the purpose of accepting employment with the American Institute in Taiwan as provided under section 3310 of chapter 48 of title 22, United States Code, then the service performed for that Institute shall be considered service described in subparagraph (A), (IV) if an individual performing service described in subparagraph (A) returns to the performance of such service after performing service as a member of a uniformed service (including, for purposes of this clause, service in the National Guard and temporary service in the Coast Guard Reserve) and after exercising restoration or reemployment rights as provided under chapter 43 of title 38, United States Code, then the service so performed as a member of a uniformed service shall be considered service described in subparagraph (A), and (V) if an individual performing service described in subparagraph (A) returns to the performance of such service after employment (by a tribal organization) to which section 105(e)(2) of the Indian Self-Determination Act applies, then the service performed for that tribal organization shall be considered service described in subparagraph (A); or (ii) is receiving an annuity from the Civil Service Retirement and Disability Fund, or benefits (for service as an employee) under another retirement system established by a law of the United States for employees of the Federal Government (other than for members of the uniformed service); except that this paragraph shall not apply with respect to any such service performed on or after any date on which such individual performs - (C) service performed as the President or Vice President of the United States, (D) service performed - (i) in a position placed in the Executive Schedule under sections 5312 through 5317 of title 5, United States Code, (ii) as a noncareer appointee in the Senior Executive Service or a noncareer member of the Senior Foreign Service, or (iii) in a position to which the individual is appointed by the President (or his designee) or the Vice President under section 105(a)(1), 106(a)(1), or 107 (a)(1) or (b)(1) of title 3, United States Code, if the maximum rate of basic pay for such position is at or above the rate for level V of the Executive Schedule, (E) service performed as the Chief Justice of the United States, an Associate Justice of the Supreme Court, a judge of a United States court of appeals, a judge of a United States district court (including the district court of a territory), a judge of the United States Court of Federal Claims, a judge of the United States Court of International Trade, a judge of the United States Tax Court, a United States magistrate, or a referee in bankruptcy or United States bankruptcy judge, (F) service performed as a Member, Delegate, or Resident Commissioner of or to the Congress, (G) any other service in the legislative branch of the Federal Government if such service - (i) is performed by an individual who was not subject to subchapter III of chapter 83 of title 5, United States Code, or to another retirement system established by a law of the United States for employees of the Federal Government (other than for members of the uniformed services), on December 31, 1983, or (ii) is performed by an individual who has, at any time after December 31, 1983, received a lump-sum payment under section 8342(a) of title 5, United States Code, or under the corresponding provision of the law establishing the other retirement system described in clause (i), or (iii) is performed by an individual after such individual has otherwise ceased to be subject to subchapter III of chapter 83 of title 5, United States Code (without having an application pending for coverage under such subchapter), while performing service in the legislative branch (determined without regard to the provisions of subparagraph (B) relating to continuity of employment), for any period of time after December 31, 1983, and for purposes of this subparagraph (G) an individual is subject to such subchapter III or to any such other retirement system at any time only if (a) such individual's pay is subject to deductions, contributions, or similar payments (concurrent with the service being performed at that time) under section 8334(a) of such title 5 or the corresponding provision of the law establishing such other system, or (in a case to which section 8332(k)(1) of such title applies) such individual is making payments of amounts equivalent to such deductions, contributions, or similar payments while on leave without pay, or (b) such individual is receiving an annuity from the Civil Service Retirement and Disability Fund, or is receiving benefits (for service as an employee) under another retirement system established by a law of the United States for employees of the Federal Government (other than for members of the uniformed services), or (H) service performed by an individual - (i) on or after the effective date of an election by such individual, under section 301 of the Federal Employees' Retirement System Act of 1986, section 307 of the Central Intelligence Agency Retirement Act (50 U.S.C. 2157), or the Federal Employees' Retirement System Open Enrollment Act of 1997 to become subject to the Federal Employees' Retirement System provided in chapter 84 of title 5, United States Code, or (ii) on or after the effective date of an election by such individual, under regulations issued under section 860 of the Foreign Service Act of 1980, to become subject to the Foreign Service Pension System provided in subchapter II of chapter 8 of title I of such Act; (6) service performed in the employ of the United States or any instrumentality of the United States if such service is performed - (A) in a penal institution of the United States by an inmate thereof; (B) by any individual as an employee included under section 5351(2) of title 5, United

States Code (relating to certain interns, student nurses, and other student employees of hospitals of the Federal Government), other than as a medical or dental intern or a medical or dental resident in training; or (C) by any individual as an employee serving on a temporary basis in case of fire, storm, earthquake, flood, or other similar emergency; (7) service performed in the employ of a State, or any political subdivision thereof, or any instrumentality of any one or more of the foregoing which is wholly owned thereby, except that this paragraph shall not apply in the case of - (A) service which, under subsection (j), constitutes covered transportation service, (B) service in the employ of the Government of Guam or the Government of American Samoa or any political subdivision thereof, or of any instrumentality of any one or more of the foregoing which is wholly owned thereby, performed by an officer or employee thereof (including a member of the legislature of any such Government or political subdivision), and, for purposes of this title with respect to the taxes imposed by this chapter - (i) any person whose service as such an officer or employee is not covered by a retirement system established by a law of the United States shall not, with respect to such service, be regarded as an employee of the United States or any agency or instrumentality thereof, and (ii) the remuneration for service described in clause (i) (including fees paid to a public official) shall be deemed to have been paid by the Government of Guam or the Government of American Samoa or by a political subdivision thereof or an instrumentality of any one or more of the foregoing which is wholly owned thereby, whichever is appropriate, (C) service performed in the employ of the District of Columbia or any instrumentality which is wholly owned thereby, if such service is not covered by a retirement system established by a law of the United States (other than the Federal Employees Retirement System provided in chapter 84 of title 5, United States Code); except that the provisions of this subparagraph shall not be applicable to service performed - (i) in a hospital or penal institution by a patient or inmate thereof; (ii) by any individual as an employee included under section 5351(2) of title 5, United States Code (relating to certain interns, student nurses, and other student employees of hospitals of the District of Columbia Government), other than as a medical or dental intern or as a medical or dental resident in training; (iii) by any individual as an employee serving on a temporary basis in case of fire, storm, snow, earthquake, flood or other similar emergency; or (iv) by a member of a board, committee, or council of the District of Columbia, paid on a per diem, meeting, or other fee basis, (D) service performed in the employ of the Government of Guam (or any instrumentality which is wholly owned by such Government) by an employee properly classified as a temporary or intermittent employee, if such service is not covered by a retirement system established by a law of Guam; except that (i) the provisions of this subparagraph shall not be applicable to services performed by an elected official or a member of the legislature or in a hospital or penal institution by a patient or inmate thereof, and (ii) for purposes of this subparagraph, clauses (i) and (ii) of subparagraph (B) shall apply, (E) service included under an agreement entered into pursuant to section 218 of the Social Security Act, or (F) service in the employ of a State (other than the District of Columbia, Guam, or American Samoa), of any political subdivision thereof, or of any instrumentality of any one or more of the foregoing which is wholly owned thereby, by an individual who is not a member of a retirement system of such State, political subdivision, or instrumentality, except that the provisions of this subparagraph shall not be applicable to service performed - (i) by an individual who is employed to relieve such individual from unemployment; (ii) in a hospital, home, or other institution by a patient or inmate thereof; (iii) by any individual as an employee serving on a temporary basis in case of fire, storm, snow, earthquake, flood, or other similar emergency; (iv) by an election official or election worker if the remuneration paid in a calendar year for such service is less than $1,000 with respect to service performed during any calendar year commencing on or after January 1, 1995, ending on or before December 31, 1999, and the adjusted amount determined under section 218(c)(8)(B) of the Social Security Act for any calendar year commencing on or after January 1, 2000, with respect to service performed during such calendar year; or (v) by an employee in a position compensated solely on a fee basis which is treated pursuant to section 1402(c)(2)(E) as a trade or business for purposes of inclusion of such fees in net earnings from self-employment; for purposes of this subparagraph, except as provided in regulations prescribed by the Secretary, the term "retirement system" has the meaning given such term by section 218(b)(4) of the Social Security Act; (8)(A) service performed by a duly ordained, commissioned, or licensed minister of a church in the exercise of his ministry or by a member of a religious order in the exercise of duties required by such order, except that this subparagraph shall not apply to service performed by a member of such an order in the exercise of such duties, if an election of coverage under subsection (r) is in effect with respect to such order, or with respect to the autonomous subdivision thereof to which such member belongs; (B) service performed in the employ of a church or qualified church-controlled organization if such church or organization has in effect an election under subsection (w), other than service in an unrelated trade or business (within the meaning of section 513(a)); (9) service performed by an individual as an employee or employee representative as defined in section 3231; (10) service performed in the employ of - (A) a school, college, or university, or (B) an organization described in section 509(a)(3) if the organization is organized, and at all times thereafter is operated, exclusively for the benefit of, to perform the functions of, or to carry out the purposes of a school, college, or university and is operated, supervised, or controlled by or in connection with such school, college, or university, unless it is a school, college, or university of a State or a political subdivision thereof and the services performed in its employ by a student referred to in section 218(c)(5) of the Social Security Act are covered under the agreement between the Commissioner of Social Security and such State entered into pursuant to section 218 of such Act; if such service is performed by a student who is enrolled and regularly attending classes at such school, college, or university; (11) service performed in the employ of a foreign government (including service as a consular or other officer or employee or a nondiplomatic representative); (12) service performed in the employ of an instrumentality wholly owned by a foreign government - (A) if the service is of a character similar to that performed in foreign countries by employees of the United States Government or of an instrumentality thereof; and (B) if the Secretary of State shall certify to the Secretary of the Treasury that the foreign government, with respect to whose instrumentality and employees thereof exemption is claimed, grants an equivalent exemption with respect to similar service performed in the foreign country by employees of the United States Government and of instrumentalities thereof; (13) service performed as a student nurse in the employ of a hospital or a nurses' training school by an individual who is enrolled and is regularly attending classes in a nurses' training school chartered or approved pursuant to State law; (14)(A) service performed by *an individual under the age of 18 in the delivery or distribution of newspapers or shopping news, not including delivery or distribution to any point for subsequent delivery or distribution; (B) service performed by an individual in, and at the time of, the sale of newspapers or magazines to ultimate consumers, under an arrangement under which the newspapers or magazines are to be sold by him at a fixed price, his compensation being based on the retention of the excess of such price over the amount at which the newspapers or magazines are charged to him, whether or not he is guaranteed a minimum amount of compensation for such service, or is entitled to be credited with the unsold newspapers or magazines turned back; (15) service performed in the employ of an international organization, except service which constitutes "employment" under subsection (y); (16) service performed by an individual under an arrangement with the owner or tenant of land pursuant to which - (A) such individual undertakes to produce agricultural or horticultural commodities (including livestock, bees, poultry, and fur-bearing animals and wildlife) on such land, (B) the agricultural or horticultural commodities produced by such individual, or the proceeds therefrom, are to be divided between such individual and such owner or tenant, and (C) the amount of such individual's share depends on the amount of the agricultural or horticultural commodities produced; (17) service in the employ of any organization which is performed (A) in any year during any part of which such organization is registered, or there is in effect a final order of the Subversive Activities Control Board requiring such organization to register, under the Internal Security Act of 1950, as amended, as a Communist-action organization, a Communist-front organization, or a Communist-infiltrated organization, and (B) after June 30, 1956; (18) service performed in Guam by a resident of the Republic of the Philippines while in Guam on a temporary basis as a nonimmigrant alien admitted to Guam pursuant to section 101(a)(15)(H)(ii) of the Immigration and Nationality Act (8 U.S.C. §1101(a)(15)(H)(ii)); (19) Service which is performed by a nonresident alien individual for the period he is temporarily present in the United States as a nonimmigrant under subparagraph (F), (J), (M), or (Q) of section 101(a)(15) of the Immigration and Nationality Act, as amended, and which is performed to carry out the purpose specified in subparagraph (F), (J), (M), or (Q), as the case may be; (20) service (other than service described in paragraph (3)(A)) performed by an individual on a boat engaged in catching fish or other forms of aquatic animal life under an arrangement with the owner or operator of such boat pursuant to which - (A) such individual does not receive any cash remuneration other than as provided in subparagraph (B) and other than cash remuneration - (i) which does not exceed $100 per trip; (ii) which is contingent on a minimum catch; and (iii) which is paid solely for additional duties (such as mate, engineer, or cook) for which additional cash remuneration is traditional in the industry, (B) such individual receives a share of the boat's (or the boats' in the case of a fishing operation involving more than one boat) catch of fish or other forms of aquatic animal life or a share of the proceeds from the sale of such catch, and (C) the amount of such individual's share depends on the amount of the boat's (or the boats' in the case of a fishing operation involving more than one boat) catch of fish or other forms of aquatic animal life, but only if the operating crew of such boat (or each boat from which the individual receives a share in the case of a fishing operation involving more than one boat) is normally made up of fewer than 10 individuals; or (21) domestic service in a private home of the employer which - (A) is performed in any year by an individual under the age of 18 during any portion of such year; and (B) is not the principal occupation of such employee. For purposes of paragraph (20), the operating crew of a boat shall be treated as normally made up of fewer than 10 individuals if the average size of the operating crew on trips made during the preceding 4 calendar quarters consisted of fewer than 10 individuals."*

The ridiculous, complex text of section 3121(b) leaves small wonder why Philadelphian, Orwellian type lawyers are able to spend their lifetimes arguing the federal tax code at the expense of "We the people."

> It's no wonder they call it "code"….because like the lawyers in Congress and like the safes in most banks, you need to be a ***thief*** to crack it and thereby extract the truth! Doesn't this kind of ruse amount to a violation of the Sixth Amendment right to due process of law?

Isn't it one of the first and foremost principles of due process that the law must be written simply and clearly enough that the defendant can read and understand it himself/herself without the aid of a lawyer and thereby know what behavior is prohibited by the law? However, who but some judge or lawyer with four or more years of college and three years of law school and several years practicing law can understand the above? We believe the lawyers in Congress have **deliberately** used legalese to hide the truth and thereby create a new (upper) class of society and an order of "priests and priestcraft" (in this case witchcraft!) that is the only one within our society qualified or allowed by law to read and interpret the laws. ***This is how they stole our birthright, our freedoms, and have systematically violated our fundamental due process rights! This is how they have nullified the value of serving as a juror…by ensuring that people like you and I serving on jury duty can't read and understand the law for ourselves and have to rely on the judge, who is a government employee and has the government's best interests in mind whenever he rules on cases or advises jurors.*** Jesus warned about this kind of insidious "lawyer abuse" and evil at the beginning of chapter 3, where we quoted from Luke 11:52 in the Bible. We also talk about this in section 6.12, where we discuss the judicial conspiracy to protect the income tax.

It's time for Citizens everywhere to remove this kind of ***pernicious evil trash*** and the unscrupulous lawyers who peddle it from our society once and for all, starting with throwing out *every one* of the bastards in Congress *every* election until they start paying attention to this issue. We should communicate this intent to them consistently and repeatedly and prevalently until they simplify the laws to give us our right to due process back.

1. I suggest that every person reading this document forward a web pointer to it (by snail mail) to his or her two senators and representative in the Congress and ask if they understand this tax statute, viz., 3121(b).
2. Ask them to explain to you what it means - if they know what it means.
3. If they admit that they don't know what it means, ask them to please rewrite it and all other laws that they don't know the meaning of until they themselves - the legislators - know the meanings of the laws they vote on.

6.8.5 Congressional Propaganda and Lies

> "When Congress talks about simplification, taxpayers may well be reminded of Emerson's comments regarding an acquaintance, 'the louder he talked of his honor, the faster we counted our spoons'."
> [Michael J. Graetz]

Congressmen frequently get correspondence from constituents about the illegality of the income tax. In response to these requests, they commissioned the Congressional Research Service to prepare a report entitled "Frequently Asked Questions Concerning the Federal Income Tax", CRS Report number 97-59A. The report is 29 pages and you can buy a copy of it for yourself from http://pennyhill.com for $29.95. Another way you can get this report is to write you Congressman with a question or an issue about income taxes. Oftentimes, they will write a short, one-page letter and attach the report. This document was recently updated on May 7, 2001. It is filled with lies, obfuscation, and deception. We got a copy of it, scanned it in and converted it to text, and then proceeded to write a rebuttal as part of the document itself. The rebutted version is a whopping 75 pages, more than twice the size of the original report. You can read this document yourself at:

> Rebutted Version of Congressional Research Service Report 97-59A: Frequently Asked Questions Concerning the Federal Income Tax
> http://famguardian.org/PublishedAuthors/Govt/CRS/CRS-97-59A-rebuts.pdf

We encourage you to download the complete version and look at it. We have posted it on the Taxes area of our website at:

> http://famguardian.org/Subjects/Taxes/taxes.htm

under the Main heading of "False Government Propaganda With Rebuttal", and the subheading "Congressional Research Report 97-59A: Frequently Asked Questions Concerning the Federal Income Tax." Reading the rebutted version of this report is very enlightening in explaining how Congressmen like to deceive their constituents. It is also useful in preparing for a confrontation with the IRS, for instance, during a summons or deposition. We strongly encourage you to download and read this report, and to send it to your Congressman to ask him to rebut any part of it. You probably won't get an answer. It's just too hot to touch! The direct address of the document is:

> http://famguardian.org/PublishedAuthors/Govt/CRS/CRS-97-59A-rebuts.pdf

6.8.6 Whistleblower Retaliation, Indifference, and Censorship

6.8.6.1 We The People Truth In Taxation Hearing, February 27-28, 2002

On February 27 and 28, 2002, the We the People Foundation for Constitutional Education held a Truth In Taxation Hearing. The hearing was a result of a hunger strike staged back in July 2001 by its founder, Bob Schulz, who indicated that he would starve himself to death on the steps of the U.S. Capitol unless Congress would have the Department of Justice and the IRS appear in a public hearing to answer questions they were legally obligated to answer under the petition clause of the First Amendment. Congressman Roscoe Bartlett of Maryland came to the aid of Bob Schulz a couple weeks into the fast and by July 20, had negotiated an agreement in writing with the DOJ and IRS to appear to answer the questions proposed by Bob Schulz. The hearing would be scheduled for September 27, 2001.

Bob Schulz then went immediately off his fast and assembled a group of tax researchers to put together the questions he was going to ask. They met initially in Las Vegas in August 2001 to coordinate and organize their research into questions that could be asked. At least 40 of the top researchers from around the country appeared at that meeting. The group began assembling their evidence and questions and had a complete package. However, because of the terrorist attack on September 11, 2001, the hearings were postponed until February 27-28 at the request of Bob Schulz. Subsequent to the postponement, Congressman Bartlett was contacted in November 2001 by the DOJ and IRS and told that the DOJ and IRS would not be participating in the hearing rescheduled for 27-28 Feb. 2002. Congressman Bartlett did not relay this fact to Bob Schulz until late January 2002. Apparently, he was waiting for Bob to commit some kind of faux pas that would justify the government pulling out without losing face.

Bob Schulz then launched his campaign called "Operation Wait and File Until The Trial" on January 12, 2002, where he encouraged Americans to wait to file their tax returns until after the Truth in Taxation Hearing on 27-28 Feb. This, he believed, would put pressure on the government to appear at the hearings. He posted a flyer on his website about it and sent that article to his mailing list. The article included the flyer to be published in newspapers and a letter to be direct mailed to about 300,000 individuals. Then he mailed or faxed the flier to:

- Members of the American Judges Association
- Judges of The Federal Circuit
- Mayors of Largest U.S. Cities
- Federal Tax Court Judges
- Supreme Court Justices
- Radio Station General Managers
- Radio Talk Show Hosts
- 550 Partners of the Big Five Accounting Firms
- Executive Cabinet Members and Cabinet Legal Advisors
- Members of the Association of Copy Editors

Subsequently on January 17, 2002, Congressman Roscoe Bartlett notified Bob that the government had pulled out of the hearings. Congressman Roscoe Bartlett's assistant Lisa Wright stated that the Congressman was "canceling the forum," and that he was "dismayed" by the "rhetoric" of the "Wait to File" ad and that he would not be party to any movement that tells people not to pay their federal income taxes. This, of course, was not what Bob Schulz was advocating. He never told people not to PAY income taxes, only to delay filing their returns until after the hearing, which they were perfectly and legally entitled to do. Bob tried to reason with her, but it was late and she was in no mood to listen.

Bob then decided to go ahead with the hearing anyway. He invited several expert witnesses to appear as a substitute for the government's witnesses. Subsequently, on February 10, 2002, he put a full page add in the New York Times regarding a Constitutional Crisis. Here is an excerpt from the add off his website at http://www.givemeliberty.org:

_____(BEGINNING OF ADD)_____

IRS & Department of Justice: Why Won't You Answer Our Questions?

On July 20, 2001, IRS Commissioner Charles Rossotti and U.S. Assistant Attorney General Dan Bryant <u>formally agreed</u> to have IRS and DOJ participate in a recorded, public hearing on Capitol Hill to officially answer questions under oath in response to a Petition For Redress Of Grievances from the American People. Our Citizen's Petition directly challenges:

- The jurisdiction and legal authority for the IRS
- The unlawful enforcement of the Internal Revenue Code against American citizens
- The pervasive abuse of the People's constitutional rights in the daily operations of the IRS

After agreeing in writing to publicly answer questions related to the unconstitutional origin of the IRS, and the devastating harm caused by the income tax system to the working men and women of our country, The Department of Justice and IRS on January 17, 2002, without explanation, <u>canceled the hearing</u>.

WE NOW HAVE A CONSTITUTIONAL CRISIS

What must a free People do when their government repeatedly refuses to honor its legal and moral obligation to respond to a proper Petition for Redress of Grievance as guaranteed by the 1st Amendment to the United States Constitution?

<u>We ask the People:</u> Is Alan Dershowitz Correct?

- We have NO unalienable rights?
- The Constitution is merely a piece of paper?
- Government should not be restrained because it can do good things for people?   9/27/00 debate at
  Franklin & Marshall

Can We The People simply accept that our Constitution has become a dead letter?

Must we resort to the same desperate measures that our Founders did to defend their unalienable rights to life, liberty and justice?

Do We Have a Constitution or Not?

For decades, the government has steadfastly refused to honor the petitions of a growing number of honorable, well-educated, professional legal researchers whose work has raised significant and legitimate questions about the Constitutional and statutory authority of the income tax system. These issues are of the utmost importance to the American People and to our Republic.

Our respectful petitions to our servant government have fallen on deaf ears, have been arbitrarily and unjustly thrown out of the courts, and have been used as grounds for criminal prosecution, asset seizure and other unlawful abuse by the IRS and DOJ.

Three years ago, We The People Foundation began a series of formal, public initiatives to convince the U.S. government to answer our questions regarding the jurisdiction and legal authority of the IRS and the personal income tax system. As the chronology of events outlined below demonstrates, we have worked diligently to show the American People the truth about the unconstitutional origin, abusive history and criminal conduct of the IRS, and the un-American nature of the personal income tax system.

Chronology of Evasion & Censorship

DATE	ACTIVITY	RESULT
July, 1999	Government is formally invited to a Foundation tax symposium in DC at National Press Club to publicly rebut and confront the tax and legal researchers.	• **No response from U.S.** • C-SPAN broadcasts the event live. Refuses all further WTP coverage.
Nov., 1999	Government invited to a Foundation tax symposium in DC at National Press Club.	• **No response from U.S.**
Apr., 2000	Government invited to a Foundation tax symposium in DC at National Press Club	• **No response from U.S.**
April, 2000	Formal Petition for Redress of Grievance delivered to President, House Speaker and Senate Majority leader. Petition is signed by thousands and is delivered to all 3 Branches by citizens from all 50 states.	In meetings in the White House and in the Capitol with senior aides to Clinton, Hastert and Lott, all three promise experts will attend the June 2000 conference at the NPC to discuss and debate the tax issues.
June, 2000	Government invited to Foundation tax symposium in DC at National Press Club	• **U.S. breaks its promise.** NO government officials attend. • Jason Furman, White House advises us *"The legality of the income tax system is not a high priority for President Clinton. We will not attend."*
July, 2000 through March, 2001	Foundation publishes the first of four full page ads in *USA Today* and the *Washington Times* to publicize the legal issues and questions and to publicly challenge the U.S. to answer the questions in a public forum.	• **No response from U.S.** • April 2001: USA Today refuses to accept any more advertising from the Foundation.
April, 2001	• U.S. Senate Finance Committee holds hastily called hearing on the full page ads, telling a room full of reporters that those who question the income tax laws have to be dealt with swiftly and harshly because they are "schemers, scammers and cons".	• Sen. Grassley refuses to allow the Foundation to testify at hearing on Foundation's ads because the Foundation's message *". . . would detract from the message the Committee was trying to convey."* Grassley refuses to enter Foundation's written statement into the record of the hearing.
July, 2001	Bob Schulz begins hunger strike <u>until his death or until government agrees to respond to the Petition</u> for Redress of Grievances as required by the Constitution (1st Amendment)	• On July 20, 2001, after 20 days with no food, after White House intervention and help from Rep. Bartlett (MD), **DOJ and IRS Formally agree** to answer the questions in a recorded public hearing on Capitol Hill, chaired by Bartlett. • Schulz ends his fast.
Sept, 2001	Due to 9/11, the September truth-in-taxation hearing is rescheduled for February, 2002 on Capitol Hill. Meeting is formally announced by Rep. Roscoe Bartlett (MD), who agrees to sponsor the hearing.	• Nov. 2001, IRS & DOJ quietly inform Rep. Bartlett they will not participate. • **On January, 17, 2002 Rep. Bartlett cancels the hearing.**

The Hearing Will Proceed

The Truth-in-Taxation Hearing will proceed <u>as scheduled on February 27 and 28</u> at the Washington Marriott in DC.

The Foundation has delivered to the IRS and DOJ, and also published, an initial set of 299 questions **with a demand that government officials attend the public hearing and answer the questions**. We The American People want to know whether we still have a Constitution that protects our unalienable rights to privacy, due process of law, equal justice and liberty for all.

For updated news and details see our website: www.givemeliberty.org

You Can Help

Please help us by contacting your government representatives and the media. Contact the IRS & DOJ and demand that they attend Truth-in-Taxation hearing. Make them "show us the law !"

- **Contact the President.**
  His "Comment Line" number is **202-395-3000**. Speak to a live operator. Tell him/her you expect straight answers from the government at the income tax trial on Feb 27th and 28th. Fax The President: Fax: **202-456-2461**.
  Write the President: **The White House, Washington, D.C. 20500**.
  E-Mail the President: president@whitehouse.gov

- **Contact the IRS and the Department of Justice**
  Demand that they "Show you the law!" at the hearing ! Demand that they uphold their oaths of office and the Constitution!

DOJ & Attorney General Ashcroft	E-Mail	**askdoj@usdoj.gov**
	Phone	**(202) 514-2000**
	Address	950 Pennsylvania Ave NW Washington, DC 20530
Treasury & Secretary O'Neil	E-Mail	**opcmail@do.treas.gov**
	Phone	**(202) 622-2000**
	Fax	**(202) 622-6415**
	Address	1500 Pennsylvania Ave NW Washington, DC 20220
IRS & Commissioner Rossotti	E-mail	**floyd.williams@irs.gov**
	Web Site	**www.irs.gov**
	Phone	**(800) 829-1040**
	Address	1111 Constitution Ave NW Washington, DC 20224

- **Contact Rep. Bartlett**
  Congressman Bartlett's, DC phone number: **(202) 225-2721**
  Fax: **(202) 225-2193**
  E-mail his press aide, **lisa.wright@mail.house.gov** and District office **sallie.taylor@mail.house.gov**

- **Contact your Congressmen.**
  Ask them to attend the hearing, then fix the tax problem.
  Phone the Capitol: **800-648-3516**. Ask to be connected to your congressman's office.
  Go to the website: **http://capwiz.com/washtimes/**. Under "Elected Officials", fill in your zip code. All contact information for your Senators and Representative will appear: phone, fax, addresses, and e-mail links.

- "Wait to File Until the Trial !"
  Print, copy, e-mail and distribute our **"Wait To File" flyers** from our website.
  Tell your co-workers, friends and family about the February 27th Hearing. Get the word out !
- Contact the media.
  Why are they NOT covering this story ?   Write a letter to the editor.
  Go to the website**: http://capwiz.com/washtimes/.** Under "Guide to the Media", fill in your zip code. The media contacts in your area will appear + Letters to the Editor.

This message was paid for by:

We The People Foundation for Constitutional Education
2458 Ridge Road   Queensbury, NY 12804
e-mail: bob@givemeliberty.org   phone: (518) 656-3578 Fax: (518) 656-9724

www.givemeliberty.org

_____(END OF ADD)_____

Bob Schulz then held the hearings and webcasted the event to 2,100 Americans throughout the country. There were about 100 people in the live audience as well. Although the mainstream media was informed of the event, only one representative, David Kay Johnston, appeared from the New York Times, and even he ducked out after the morning of the first day because he couldn't find anything to slander We The People with! There were two solid days of hearings, and representatives from around the country from various groups appeared in the audience, including J.A.I.L. For Judges, the Fully Informed Jury Association, the Libertarian party, and several other activists groups. The tax researcher group he had assembled had put together 540 questions to ask the government. 440 of these questions were asked at the hearings, which included about 130 questions assembled by the author relating to the Fourth Amendment and the First Amendment. All of the questions and the evidence used at the hearings and those that were not asked are posted on our website at:

http://famguardian.org/TaxFreedom/Forms/Discovery/Deposition/Deposition.htm

Each question included the evidence to back it up, and as each question was asked, the evidence was displayed on two large projection panels on either side of the meeting room. The evidence and complete text of the questions were also made available via the live webcast to the large audience so they could browse and examine it for themselves in digital form. It was a watershed and unprecedented event. Bob Schulz and the author, Family Guardian Fellowship, took turns asking the questions of a panel of various experts. These questions and the answers provided by experts stunned the audience and provided irrefutable proof of government fraud, extortion, and conspiracy to deprive sovereign Americans of their rights. Among the experts testifying included (some names not listed):

- Paul Rooney, a tax attorney with over 30 years' experience and who served as a U.S. Tax Court clerk for several years before going into private practice.
- Bill Benson, the person who investigated the Sixteenth Amendment and gathered overwhelming evidence supporting the conclusion that it was fraudulently ratified by a lame duck Secretary of State, Philander Knox. (http://www.thelawthatneverwas.com/)
- Joe Banister, X IRS agent from the IRS' Criminal Investigation Division (CID), who served there 5 years before resigning after finding out the truth (http://www.freedomabovefortune.com/).
- John Turner, former IRS Collection agent with 8 years experience.
- Sherry Jackson, former IRS Examiner with three years experience.
- Irwin Schiff, America's most famous de-taxing expert. (http://www.paynoincometax.com/)
- Larry Becraft, famous patriot Constitutional Attorney. (http://fly.hiwaay.net/~becraft/)
- Noel Spade, San Diego tax attorney.
- Vicky Osborne, a forensic CPA who had uncovered evidence of massive fraud in the administration of taxpayer IMF files

Subsequent to the event in March 2002, the IRS delivered a threatening CP-518 notice (Willful Failure to File) to the person who had handled the webcasting of the event, who shall remain nameless to protect his identity. This person was responsible for making the videotapes and CD's containing the evidence available for sale to the public. Apparently, they were trying to get some legal leverage on that person so they could blackmail him to suppress the release of the questions and evidence. Can you believe the kind of games the government played to suppress the truth from being heard?!

6.8.6.2 We The People Efforts: April 5, 2001 Senate Finance Committee Hearing

During the month of March 2001, We The People Foundation (http://www.givemeliberty.org/), a tax freedom and liberty advocacy, placed full page anti-income-tax adds in the USA Today Newspaper on March 2, and March 23, of 2001. The March 2, 2001 add featured a pointer to this book on our website. It talked about five employers who had stopped withholding federal income taxes from the pay of their employees. The March 23, 2001 add featured information about how income taxes violated the constitution. Subsequent to these adds, *60 Minutes* (CBS) decided to do a story on the anti-income tax movement on April 3, 2001, and featured a 20 minute segment on the activities of the employers featured in the March 2, 2001 add. The story was rather skewed, because they put a lot of credible people on the show from the opposing side, but wouldn't let spokespeople from We The People talk. They opened the story with a picture of a We The People meeting and even showed a picture of the We The People add, but didn't allow anyone from We The People to talk.

Shortly after the 60 Minutes story, our website started going crazy. In the following two days, we had about 500 downloads of this book. Then the U.S. Senate Finance Committee announced that it was going to have a hearing on April 5, 2001 at 10am. The subject of the hearing was "Tax Scams". We The People was one of the organizations they were going to talk about, and yet they denied a request by that organization to speak at the session! Bob Schulz, the leader of We The People, had the following to say about this situation:

> *A New York Times reporter, David Cay Johnston, telephoned us after 5 p.m. on Friday, March 30, 2001, to inform us of the fact that the Senate Finance Committee has scheduled a formal hearing for 10 a.m. on Thursday, April 5, 2001. Mr. Johnston said the subject of the hearing would be the full-page ads we have published in USA TODAY and that the Committee intended to have the ads on display during the hearing. Johnston said that our side of the story needs to be told, that we should try to get on the witness list and that all the major media outlets would attend any press conference we were to hold in the hallway outside the hearing room, if we were not allowed to testify before the Committee.*
>
> *Early Monday morning, April 2, 2001, we telephoned the Senate Finance Committee to request that we be added to the witness list. We were told that the witness list was closed before the Committee scheduled and publicly announced the hearing, but that we could fax a letter to the Committee Chairman to request that we be added to the list.*
>
> *On Monday morning we faxed our letter to Senator Grassley, requesting to be added to the witness list.*
>
> *Late Monday afternoon we received by fax a letter from Senator Grassley which reads: "Dear Mr. Schulz: Thank you for your letter requesting to be added to the witness list for the Senate Finance Committee Hearing on April 5, 2001. We will be unable to add you to our witness list. However, should your organization chose to submit a written statement regarding our hearing, 'Taxpayer Beware: Schemes, Scams and Fraud,' we will consider including it in the hearing record. Sincerely, Charles E. Grassley, Chairman Senate Finance Committee."*
>
> *It seems incongruous that the Senate would hold a hearing featuring our full-page ads and not invite us to testify. They apparently have a message that they want to convey, which is inapposite to our message. They apparently want to divert attention away from questions of whether the IRS is collecting taxes without legal authority by trying to portray those who raise such questions as scammers. In fact, those in the tax honesty movement see the IRS as the scammers! The question is not who is putting their money in an offshore trust, or who is not filing their tax return or which employers have stopped withholding from the paychecks of their employees. The primary question is: "What legal authority requires most Americans to file an income tax return and pay the income tax? There ought to be a moratorium on the IRS' enforcement activities, and all those people who are sitting in prison for not paying the income tax should be released, pending the determination of this fundamental question.*
>
> *Our government leaders apparently want to label anyone and everyone, including this Foundation, who are questioning the legal authority of the IRS to collect the individual income tax as schemers, scammers and frauds, while they continue to conduct their tax enforcement activities as usual, without addressing the compelling allegations of fraud and the illegal operations of the income tax system and without justifying their behavior.*
>
> *We have decided that we will hold a press conference in the hallway outside the Senate hearing room at 9:30 a.m. on Thursday. We will have press kits available which will include copies of letters inviting Commissioner Rossotti and the leaders of the executive and legislative branches of the government to identify their most knowledgeable people and have them participate with the experts in the tax honesty movement in the four symposiums and conferences we sponsored at the National Press Club to debate and discuss the issues. We will highlight the major allegations regarding the fraudulent ratification of the 16th Amendment, the demonstrable lack of evidence of any law that requires most citizens to file or pay the income tax, and the problems relating to routine violations by the IRS of the People's rights under the 4th, 5th, 6th and 13th Amendments in their day-to-day administrative procedures. We will point out that the government chose to evade the public forums and chose not to even acknowledge receipt of the invitations! We will also include a copy of the video tape of the April 13, 2000 meetings in the White House and in the Capitol with President Clinton's economic advisor Jason Furman, Speaker Hastert's policy advisor, Dr. William Koetzle and the Senate Majority Leader's policy director, Keith Hennessey. The tape shows these gentlemen meeting with Joe Banister and Bob Schulz and accepting a REMONSTRANCE for Clinton, Hastert and Lott. The tapes also show these men promising to have their experts review the research reports authored by Bill Benson, Joe Banister and William Conklin and to participate in our fourth attempt to get the two sides to meet on June 29, 2000, in a public forum, to debate the allegations of the fraudulent and illegal operations of the income tax system -- promises which were broken on June 2, 2000, when Jason Furman told Schulz; "The legality of the income tax is not a high priority matter for the White House and we will not be participating in any conference on the subject." The press kits will also include a copy of each ad we decided to publish in the wake of the government's reversal of its decision to review and then meet to discuss the research reports by Benson, Banister and Conklin.*
>
> *Our message will be a simple one: We want the government to answer the serious questions that have been raised by numerous tax researchers who say that the IRS is collecting the individual income tax without legal authority and that the IRS operates illegally when it tries to force citizens to pay taxes they do not owe. Instead of the Senate and House encouraging the IRS to increase enforcement of laws that apparently do not exist, wouldn't it be easier and better for them to have their experts meet with the tax researchers in a public forum, show them where they are wrong, embarrass them, and put it all to rest? Why is the government so averse to doing so? Are they worried that they can't show the researchers to be in error? When does evasion become admission?*

The government's dual actions of evading the public discussion of the issues while strengthening its steel-fisted, heavy-handed enforcement campaign of fear and terror only serves to strengthen the resolve and determination of a People who see themselves as free and sovereign, and who see all of government limited by a written constitution.

6.8.6.3 Cover-Up of Jan. 20, 2002: Congress/DOJ/IRS/ Renege on a Written Agreement to Hold a Truth in Taxation Hearing with We The People Under First Amendment

The We the People foundation (http://www.givemeliberty.org/), which was founded to fight government corruption, has been protesting the federal income tax for years. During July 2001, the leader of that organization, Bob Schulz, went on a 21 day hunger strike, telling the press and the government that he would *die of starvation* if the government would not grant him a hearing under the First Amendment to the U.S. Constitution to Petition the U.S. Government for Redress of Grievances related to the illegal enforcement of the federal income tax. On July 20, 2001, Congressman Rosco Bartlett negotiated a signed written agreement between the Department of Justice, the IRS, and Mr. Schulz to hold the requested hearing to address his concerns and questions. Prior to signing the written agreement, the DOJ and IRS insisted that the hearings be *private* (do you smell a cover-up here?), but Mr. Schulz said that this was a public matter of great concern to millions of Americans and that it must be open and the press must also be able to attend. The press was also invited. The hearing were to be in late Sept. 2001, but the terrorist attacks disrupted the meeting and it was postponed until Feb. 27, 2002 by Mr. Schulz.

Subsequent to the new hearing being scheduled, on January 20, 2002, Mr. Schulz launched a media campaign called "Wait and File Until the Trial", informing Americans that they should wait to file their tax returns until the Truth in Taxation hearing was over, because the income tax was on trial. He mailed out hundreds of thousands of fliers and emails to federal judges, congressmen, the IRS, and citizens. Immediately after the fliers went out, our website went crazy and we had five times the normal daily volume we usually have. Immediately after the start of the "Wait and File Until the Trial" campaign, Roscoe Bartlett cancelled the hearings, saying that he could not sponsor or support them because they were "encouraging Americans to not pay their income taxes", which was clearly not the case, as explained in Mr. Schulz' letter shown below. Later investigation by We the People revealed that in Nov. 2001, the IRS and DOJ both told Congressman Bartlett that they would not attend the hearings ever. Congressman Bartlett withheld this information, hoping that Bob Schulz would unilaterally cancel the hearings himself or commit a political faux pas that would eliminate the need to have them. When the Wait and File campaign started in earnest, Congressman Bartlett apparently thought he had enough excuse to terminate the meeting, but as Mr. Schulz' letter clearly explains, he was not justified in doing so and the comments about the Wait and File campaign were really just more deceptive and fraudulent government propaganda to discredit Mr. Schulz and further expand the government cover-up of the illegal operations of the IRS. Read the letter yourself below for enlightening information. Keep in mind that all Mr. Schulz has ever expected was for the government to honor his Constitutional, First Amendment right to a Petition for Redress of Grievance with the federal government.

We The People Foundation For Constitutional Education, Inc.
2458 Ridge Road, Queensbury, NY 12804
Telephone: (518) 656-3578 Fax: (518) 656-9724
www.givemeliberty.org

January 22, 2002

Hon. Roscoe G. Bartlett
Member of Congress
2412 Rayburn Building
Washington, DC 20515

Dear Congressman Bartlett:

On behalf of myself and the We The People Foundation for Constitutional Education, I want to thank you for all that you have done to support the People's Petition for Redress of our grievances related to the **fraudulent origin of the IRS and unlawful operations of the income tax system**. I thank you for your wisdom, your courage and your independence. Your steadfast and heroic efforts in defense of the American People's guaranteed constitutional right to have our government answer this historic petition are deeply appreciated by all of us who placed our trust in your integrity and leadership.

I know that you have tried your best in our behalf, and for that I am most thankful. I continue to hold you in high esteem. No matter what the future may hold, I will always remember your courageous defense of our Constitution.

Neither of us has shared with the general public the details of your actions and what happened behind the scenes in the days leading up to July 20, 2001. This was the day Assistant Attorney General Dan Bryant and IRS Commissioner Rossotti, as a result of your personal intervention and persuasion, contracted with the American people to have experts from their departments appear in a recorded, congressional-style, public meeting to answer the people's questions regarding the federal income tax system.

We also have not shared with the public the details of what has been happening behind the scenes since July 20, 2001. Under the present circumstances, it is appropriate that these details be made available to the American people. Following is a chronology of the facts related to our Petition for Redress of Grievances.

- On June 11, 2001, I personally delivered a letter to President Bush at the White House. Copies of the letter were also hand-delivered to Speaker of the House Hastert and Senate Majority Leader Daschle at the Capitol. The letter recited the numerous requests made by We The People Foundation For Constitutional Education to the Executive and Legislative Branches since May 1999 to answer our Petition For Redress of Grievances related to the income tax system. The letter also provided a factual account of the government's evasive and unresponsive behavior, which ultimately led to my decision to embark on a hunger strike until either I died or the federal government agreed to meet in a public forum to answer the people's questions regarding **the fraudulent origin of the IRS and the unlawful operations of the income tax system.**

- On July 1, 2001, I delivered a follow-up letter to President Bush, with copies to Speaker Hastert and Senator Daschle.

- On July 18, 2001, Lawrence B. Lindsey, Assistant to the President for Economic Policy and head of the National Economic Council, sent a letter to me which read, **"The President has asked me to thank you for your letters of June 11 and July 1 regarding the income tax system. I understand your concerns and the arguments you make. Your letter of June 11 outlines extensively the concerns of the We The People Foundation for Constitutional Education, Inc. with regard to the efficacy of the current income tax system. While I believe the best way to address your concerns is through the court system, I have taken the liberty of sharing your letters with the Internal Revenue Service for their review. A more substantive response will be forthcoming from this office once the IRS has had the opportunity to assess your grievances. I would be remiss if I did not suggest that you end your fast. Whether or not federal tax experts attend a meeting your organization has scheduled for September 18 will be determined based upon their substantive assessment of your** arguments. While your personal commitment to the cause of tax reform is dramatic, I hope that you will not endanger yourself physically in this cause. Please be assured that your letters will receive careful attention at the IRS.

Note: In reviewing my file and the events of last summer, I must now assume that when Commissioner Rossotti spoke with you by telephone on July 19th, and agreed to have his experts meet with our experts in a recorded public forum to answer our questions, he was responding to Mr. Lindsey's directive.

- On July 9, 2001, I delivered an updated version of the People's Petition for Redress of Grievances to one of President Bush's aides at the White House. I also met with you and three members of your staff, where we first discussed the issues related to **the fraudulent origin and unlawful operations of the IRS**, and you made the decision to help the American People in their quest for a response to this historic Petition.

- On July 17, 2001, you held a press conference on the House Triangle to announce the fact that you had placed top priority on getting the appropriate people in the government to agree to respond to our Petition. Rep. Ron Paul also strongly supported the fundamental right to be answered.

- It is now known that between July 9th and July 18th, 2001, management level personnel at DOJ and IRS were steadfast in their refusal to have their experts meet with representatives of the American People in a recorded public forum. For instance, Floyd Williams, the IRS Director of the Office of Congressional Affairs, stated the IRS would only agree to a private, unrecorded meeting between myself and the IRS Chief Counsel. Karen Wilson (Mr. Williams' counterpart at DOJ) suggested we submit our questions to DOJ and IRS in writing and wait for a response. She said she was otherwise in support of IRS' proposal for a private, unrecorded meeting. You replied that the proposal for a private, unrecorded meeting was totally unacceptable and that the questions had to be answered in a public forum. You emphasized the importance of allowing the public to see and hear the people asking the questions and those answering them. You strongly and effectively argued that to submit the questions in writing to DOJ and IRS would allow for delay, obfuscation and confusion, and would bring to ruin what you considered to be a proper, Constitutional Petition For a Redress of Grievances.

- From July 18th through July 20th you negotiated on the People's behalf, by telephone, with IRS Commissioner Rossotti and with DOJ's Assistant Attorney General Daniel Bryant. They expressed concerns about the security of a public meeting and wanted to know who would be "on the gavel" to control the meeting and keep it professional and orderly. After speaking with me about their concerns, you contacted Dan Bryant and Charles Rossotti and offered to hold the meeting on Capitol Hill and to personally gavel the meeting if Henry Hyde was not available.

- On or about July 19th, in a telephone conversation between you and Commissioner Rossotti, Rossotti agreed to have his experts participate in a recorded, public, congressional-style hearing on Capitol Hill, with appropriate controls. You telephoned me and asked to see me in your office. When I arrived, you told me of Commissioner Rossotti's agreement.

- On July 20th, Assistant Attorney General Dan Bryant also agreed, but told you he needed a formal request from you. He asked that you put your request for the meeting in writing. You telephoned me and asked to see me in your office. When I arrived, you prepared a hand-written letter to Dan Bryant. You then telephoned Mr. Bryant to tell him you had the formal request in hand and asked how soon he could meet with us. Bryant said he would see us right away in his office at the Department of Justice building. We met with Dan Bryant that afternoon. We fully discussed our written Petition for Redress of Grievances (he had previously received a copy of the Petition that was hand-delivered to the White House on April 13, 2000 and again on July 9, 2001). We also reviewed the terms and conditions of your offer to preside over the proposed congressional-style hearing on Capitol Hill. He penned a note at the bottom of your written request, agreeing to **"do everything within my power to ensure that the Dept. of Justice will provide appropriate representatives to participate in a congressional briefing hosted by Congressman Bartlett in connection with the above referenced matter."** Roland Croteau and Burr Deitz (a Director of the WTP Foundation) were also in attendance.

- Later that day, Friday, July 20, 2001, my office issued a press release and posted it on our web site, announcing the details of the agreement. Apparently, the news quickly found its way around the Internet.

- Between Friday, July 20th and Monday, July 23rd, as I would later learn from you, Dan Bryant apparently received a phone call or two from "higher ups," protesting his July 20th commitment to have DOJ answer our questions in a public forum.

- On July 23, 2001, I received an e-mail from your aide, Lisa Wright, which read: {"Congressman Bartlett asked me to contact you to inform you must take URGENT action in order to preserve the agreement as a result of your 7/20 meeting with Dan Bryant at USDOJ.1) Immediately pull down from the website the previous presentation of the meeting that begins with the subject – "The fast is over". 2) Replace it with a corrected version ASAP and distribute this to your list. Reference to Bryant must be limited explicitly to quoting only his handwritten comments. "I will do everything within my power. . ."Reference to Hyde -- that he will be invited -- NOT EXPECTED. Reference to a date -- to be determined, hopefully in mid to late September. 3) You must call Dan Bryant ASAP and apologize for the inaccuracies in the e-mail. This is his personal number -- 202-514-2141."}

  NOTE: On or about July 25th, I placed a call to Dan Bryant. He did not return the call.
- On July 30th, I issued a revised press release and posted it on our web site.
- On July 30th Lisa Wright of your office sent an e-mail to Dan Bryant at DOJ and Floyd Williams at IRS. It read: **"Mr. Bryant and Mr. Williams: Attached is a 7/30/01 news release from We the People Foundation for Constitutional Education which follows up a meeting Congressman Bartlett had on July 20 at DOJ w/ Asst. Atty. Gen. Dan Bryant and Bob Schulz concerning Mr. Schulz's Petition for Redress concerning the tax code and IRS enforcement of the tax code. Congressman Bartlett personally affirmed that this release is an accurate reflection of the July 20 meeting. Congressman Bartlett discussed the request for a public forum at which appropriate IRS representatives would participate in an earlier meeting with Floyd Williams of IRS and Karen Wilson of DOJ and subsequently in a phone conversation with IRS Commissioner Rossotti. Congressman Bartlett hopes that DOJ and IRS officials will contact Mr. Schulz directly concerning coordinating and ironing out the details for the public forum on Capitol Hill. Please feel free to contact Congressman Bartlett if you have any questions and so that we may procure the necessary space for the meeting."**
- On July 30th Lisa Wright forwarded to me a message from IRS' Floyd Williams. It read: **"Treasury/IRS has not agreed (either verbally or in writing) to participate in a public forum with Bob Schulz."**
- On August 13, 2001, Tax Notes published an article under the heading, "Backroom Deals, Fleeting Promises Put Income Tax Hearing in Jeopardy," by Warren Rojas. In the article, IRS spokesman Frank Keith is quoted as saying, "As of right now, no final agreements have been made."
- On August 29, 2001, your office issued the following statement; "Congressman Bartlett is continuing to actively pursue and secure participation by representatives of both the Department of Justice and the Internal Revenue Service at the September 25-26 forum organized by We the People," said Lisa Wright, a spokesman for Congressman Roscoe Bartlett. "He expects Dan Bryant, Assistant Attorney General for the Office of Legislative Affairs at the Department of Justice, and IRS Chairman Charles Rossotti to fulfill their personal commitments to him."(my emphasis).

- In early September, I met in your office with you and three of your aides, including Sallie Taylor and Lisa Wright. You said DOJ and IRS were trying to "wiggle off the hook" and that Sallie and Lisa had an "alternative proposal." Sallie and Lisa proceeded to describe their alternative proposal, which, instead of having the agree-upon public forum, would have me submit the Peoples' questions to you in writing. You would then post the questions on your web site and send them to DOJ and IRS for an answer. The answers would also be posted on your web site. I told Sallie and Lisa that their proposal was unacceptable to me and that you had already argued with DOJ and IRS (successfully) the futility of such an approach. Upon hearing my response you turned to an aide and asked him to call Dick Armey, the House Majority Leader, to request an immediate meeting with him. We were told to proceed to Mr. Armey's office. You, I, Sallie Taylor, and another of your aides (I don't remember his name) met with Dick Armey and one of his aides, who took extensive notes during the meeting. **You told Mr. Armey that DOJ and IRS were trying to wiggle off the hook and break their commitment to answer the People's questions in a public forum. Mr. Armey said it was important to have the hearing proceed as planned and that DOJ and IRS had to be "locked down." Armey said the way to do that would be to show DOJ and IRS that they were running the risk of offending many more Congressman than you if they broke their commitment. Mr. Armey then suggested that you prepare a letter to Attorney General Ashcroft and to Treasury Secretary O'Neil, which would thank them for their commitment to have the appropriate personnel from their departments participate in the income tax hearing and which would be signed by numerous members of the**

House of Representatives. Mr. Armey and you discussed a list of House members that both of you believed would sign the letter.

- On September 12, 2001, I communicated my request to you that the tax hearing be postponed due to the events of September 11th. I posted that message on our web site.
- On October 12, 2001, you delivered a letter and video message to me in which you announced that the event had been rescheduled for February 27 and 28, 2002. Your letter stated **"A letter of support and confirmation signed by myself and other members of Congress has been drafted, circulated, and will be sent to officials at the Department of Justice, Treasury and the IRS, informing them of the dates and times and requiring their attendance. I will personally chair the event and have invited other members of Congress to attend and sit on the panel…You have my word as an elected member of the United States Congress that I will do all within my power that this event go forward, the IRS and DOJ attend as they have promised to do, and are compelled to do by the Constitution."**(My emphasis).
- On January 7, 2002, Tax Notes published an article under the heading, "Schulz Hopes to Bury Tax Code at February Hearing," by Warren Rojas. In the article, Mr. Rojas wrote, "While the IRS has yet to officially confirm or deny its participation in the hearing, **a Bartlett press aide acknowledged receiving a letter from Justice around Thanksgiving stating plainly that the DOJ would not attend any Schulz-related events.**" (my emphasis). Note: I was never told about the "Thanksgiving letter." This was the first time any of the three government officials who were parties to the July 20th contract with the American People had put in writing that they were reneging on their agreement.
- On or about January 8, 2002, I telephoned Lisa Wright to tell her that I had read the Tax Notes article and was very concerned about the Thanksgiving letter from DOJ which informed you that DOJ would not attend the income tax hearing. I called to inform Ms. Wright that it was my intention to bring the February hearing to the attention of tens of millions of Americans, and ask them to wait to file their tax returns until they heard all of the questions and answers at the February hearing. I felt it was now time, as Mr. Armey had previously suggested, to do all I could to "lock the DOJ and IRS down" and demand that they keep their commitment to the American People. It was time to demand that they respond to our questions regarding **the fraudulent origin of the IRS and the unlawful operation of the personal income tax system.** I informed Ms. Wright that many thousands of Americans were already aware of the February hearing and were waiting for the answers to the questions before deciding how to file their tax returns. I explained that if DOJ and IRS were going to renege on their commitments, they were going to have to answer to a very large number of Americans. My call was passed through to Lisa's voice message system where I left a message. I asked her to call me.
- On January 11, 2002, Lisa returned my call. We discussed "Operation Wait to File Until the Trial." After we completed the call Lisa called back to say that if your name was mentioned in the "Wait to File" flyer/ad, she would like to approve the wording. I told her your name, together with those of Dan Bryant and IRS Commissioner Rossotti were mentioned in the first paragraph, which I then read to her. She said my use of the phrase "public hearing" was wrong, that the word "hearing" had a technical meaning on the Hill and that I should use the phrase "public forum." She also said that you did not have the power to force DOJ and IRS to attend the meeting. I replied that I understood that you had no more power at that time than you did on July 20, 2001, when you merely requested that Commissioner Rossotti and Assistant Attorney General Dan Bryant have appropriate personnel from their departments participate in the "public, recorded congressional-style briefing- hearing" on Capitol Hill to answer questions "concerning the legal jurisdiction and authority of the IRS." **At the July 20 meeting both Mr. Rossotti and Mr. Bryant agreed to your request and formally entered into a contract with the American people to have their "appropriate representatives participate in a congressional briefing hosted by Congressman Bartlett."**
- On January 12, 2002, in response to Lisa's one concern, I changed the phrase "public hearing" in the first paragraph of the Wait to File flyer/ad to "congressional-style hearing". We then launched "Operation Wait to File Until the Trial" by posting an article on our web site and by sending that article to our mailing list. The article included the flyer to be published in newspapers and a letter to be direct mailed to about 300,000 individuals.
- On Monday, January 14th I was in Milwaukee working with one of our attorneys on the questions for the hearing. I received word that Lisa had called my office and asked me to return the call. I tried several times on Monday and Tuesday to reach her by phone. I left voice messages on her machine, informing her that I would be returning to my office that afternoon at approximately 3 p.m. While en route from Milwaukee to Albany on Tuesday, January 15th I tried unsuccessfully to reach you by phone. I did manage to speak to Sallie Taylor. I told her to let Lisa and you know that I would be back in my office at 3 p.m. should either of you need to speak to me. I would not hear from anyone in your office until 8:20 p.m. Thursday evening, January 17th.

- On Monday, January 14th, Kim Herb, Legislative Assistant to Congressman John Linder sent an e-mail to "District Directors" which read,

  "Recently, it has been stated that there will be a Congressional hearing on the IRS. I wanted to dispel this rumor. There will be NO hearing. I repeat, there will be no Congressional hearing on the IRS in February. In response to a hunger strike by Mr. Robert Schulz, Congressman Roscoe Bartlett agreed to facilitate a meeting on IRS and tax topics. Accordingly, Mr. Bartlett arranged for "We the People" to have a public forum on the IRS, at which time "We the People" will debate such questions as the legality of the Sixteenth Amendment and the ratification process. However, no officials from the IRS or Justice Department will attend. Again, for emphasis, NO officials from either the IRS or Justice Department will be in attendance. The administration believes that these questions have been sufficiently addressed, and there is a fair amount of judicial precedence on this issue to confirm that assertion. Congressman Bartlett will likely give an opening statement, however, I understand that his comments will be limited to acknowledging that the "We the People" organization has a right to free speech and to voice their opinion. I recognize and support the Bush Administration's position. We have no interest in pursuing the ratification of the Sixteenth Amendment as a viable and legitimate argument in the fundamental tax reform movement. As such, I do not anticipate that Congressman Linder, as the official sponsor of the FairTax, will have any role in the February public forum organized by "We the People."

- At 3 p.m. Thursday, January 17th, as part of Operation Wait to File Until the Trial, I delivered several thousand letters and flyers to the personal fax machines of the following individuals:

  - Members of the American Judges Association
  - Judges of The Federal Circuit
  - Mayors of Largest U.S. Cities
  - Federal Tax Court Judges
  - Supreme Court Justices
  - Radio Station General Managers
  - Radio Talk Show Hosts
  - 550 Partners of the Big Five Accounting Firms
  - Executive Cabinet Members and Cabinet Legal Advisors
  - Members of the Association of Copy Editors

- At 8:20 p.m. on Thursday, January 17th I received a call from Lisa Wright. She stated that she had just forwarded via FedEx your letter informing me that you were "canceling the forum," and that you were "dismayed" by the "rhetoric" of the "Wait to File" ad and that you would not be party to any movement that tells people not to pay their federal income taxes. I tried to reason with her, but it was late and she was in no mood to listen.

I hope that you can understand how very disappointed I am with your actions. From the beginning of our discussions, I expected you to encounter great difficulty in holding both Mr. Rossotti and Mr. Bryant to their word regarding the February hearing. At this point, it is clear that neither DOJ nor IRS ever intended to keep their commitment to you or the American People. **Their refusal to answer these substantive questions regarding the fraudulent origin of the IRS and unlawful operation of the income tax system demonstrates the federal government's pervasive and arrogant disregard for the constitutional rights of the American People.** It is now clear, that on July 20, 2001, their objective was to stop the hunger strike and temporarily mollify the outrage of thousands of Americans who were demanding that our government agree to publicly answer the People's Petition For Redress of Grievances.

However, I shared your faith in our Constitution and your belief that at the top of our government were trustworthy men and women of moral integrity. Like you, I believed that no matter the practical difficulty, there were enough people of honor at the highest levels of our government, that the People's Constitutional Petition For Redress of Grievances would be heard. I did not believe that those who we have trusted to lead our country would turn their backs on the American People, disregard our Constitution and Bill of Rights, and hold in such low esteem the personal liberty so many of our countrymen have sacrificed and died to defend over the past 225 years. I believed that our highest government officials would honor their oaths of office to defend the United States Constitution, and its guarantee of every American's right to petition our government for a redress of grievances.

Congressman Bartlett, I wish you had told me sooner about the Thanksgiving letter from DOJ, and your apparent decision (if Kim Herb is to be believed) to merely give an opening statement at the February hearing, "limited to acknowledging that the 'We the People' organization has a right to free speech and to voice their opinion." I wish that you had told me then that our Petition was not going to be publicly and officially answered by the government.

You say in your letter to me dated January 17 that the newspaper ad is "misleading" and "has made it impossible for the forum to take place because the Internal Revenue Service (IRS) and the Department of Justice (DOJ) will not participate."

This is most offensive to me. There was no need to misrepresent the facts. As the paragraphs above demonstrate, the ad had nothing to do with the reluctance of DOJ and IRS to participate in the February income tax hearing. We now know that their decision not to participate was put in writing to you last Thanksgiving, nearly two months before the "Wait to File" campaign idea occurred to us. In fact, the Wait to File campaign is a direct result of learning from the January 7th edition of Tax Notes that you had received DOJ's Thanksgiving letter of withdrawal.

In your press release you say, "I will not be a party to advocating the non-payment of federal income taxes." This statement is also highly offensive, for it is nothing more than an unjustifiable, aggressive attack on my reputation and character. Your statement is also a misrepresentation of the facts and reflects a deliberate attempt to paint me and the Foundation as irresponsible law-breakers. In fact, the ad does not advocate the non-payment of federal income taxes. It suggests people do what the law allows them to do-- wait until February 27th to file their tax returns.

Neither I nor the Foundation have ever advocated, supported or encouraged anyone not to pay a tax they lawfully owe or not to file any tax return documents they are required by law to file. Ever. As we both know, the purpose of these important hearings is to have the government show us the law so that all Americans may be guided by specific requirements for filing.

In your letter and press release you say that you "remain[s] committed to ensuring the right of Bob Schulz and other citizens to exercise their constitutional rights under the First Amendment to get answers about federal tax policy from the government," and you propose, as an alternative to the public forum, that you deliver our questions to DOJ and IRS and that you post our questions and the answers on your web site. In fact, as you yourself argued so effectively last July, this would be tantamount to our agreeing not to have our questions answered. To use your own words, this approach "would allow for delay, obfuscation, confusion and to otherwise bring to ruin" what we have so patiently, intelligently, professionally and rationally developed into a proper petition for a remedy of the people's grievances.

I now fear for the future of our Constitutional Republic. A constitutional crisis has now developed. Whether we have a written Constitution that protects our unalienable rights as Americans is now a question. Whether the Constitution is any more than a piece of paper is now a question. Whether we have a federal government limited by a Constitution and Bill of Rights is now a question.

Here is what I have decided must now be done in response to the decision by DOJ and IRS not to participate in the public, recorded truth-in-taxation hearing on February 27-28, and also your decision last Thursday to withdraw your commitment to support this public forum.

First: Last week I spoke to your aide, Sallie Taylor, to request a meeting with you as soon as possible. She said your calendar would not allow such a meeting before Wednesday, January 23rd, and that she would have to speak with you to see if that is what you wanted to do. My purpose is to respectfully request that you reconsider your decision to cancel the February meeting.

Second: We plan to proceed with a recorded, public forum on February 27 and 28 in Washington DC. Because of the importance of this issue to the American People, we hope that you will decide to help us hold this event as planned in the secure location of the Science and Technology Committee Hearing Room. However, in the alternative, we have booked the Marriott Hotel for the two days.

Third: I am attaching to this letter our initial set of questions relating to the **fraudulent origin of the IRS and the unlawful operation of the income tax system**. These are the preliminary questions that we intend to present to the IRS and DOJ at the February meeting. We are releasing these questions several weeks earlier than planned. We have a number of additional questions currently being prepared that will be released upon completion. By copy of this letter to Attorney General Ashcroft, Treasury Secretary O'Neil and Mr. Lawrence B. Lindsey, we are demanding that experts from DOJ and IRS be present on

February 27 and 28 to answer the questions in a public forum. As you previously stated, the written exchange of questions and answers with DOJ and IRS would be utterly futile.

Fourth: We are posting the questions on our web site along with an invitation for all learned persons to answer these questions and participate in the February 27 and 28 hearing. We will request that interested parties contact us by e-mail using a prepared form.

Fifth: We will extend an invitation to the February 27 and 28 event to every organization, large or small, that is concerned about the protection, preservation and enhancement of human liberty in America, and that is interested in limiting the size, scope and costs of the federal government to the enumerated powers of the Constitution.

It is now imperative to summon all patriots in this cause for liberty and justice. It is time to ask all right thinking Americans to stand united and put a collective foot down against this arrogant disregard for our liberties, rights and freedoms, whether it be an erosion of our right to petition the government for a redress of grievances, our right to privacy, our right to property, our right to firearms, our right to fully-informed juries, our right to honest representation and voting, our right to a truly independent judiciary, our freedom from the influence of the "same hands" in all three branches, our right to honest checks and balances, our right to the fruits of our labor, our right not to have the government waste the fruits of our labor under the pretense of caring for us, our right to laws that do not favor public over private education, our right to home school our children, our right to have the war powers clauses adhered to, our right to have all treaties approved by the Senate, et al.

If the DOJ and the IRS do attend the event and provide honest, forthright answers to the people's questions relating to the authority of the IRS to force employers to withhold the income tax from the paychecks of their employees and to force most Americans to file a tax return and to pay the tax, we believe the probable outcome will be a more limited federal government, a cleansing of our political system and a restoration of power to the states and the people.

Sixth: We are calling on all patriotic Americans to help reveal the truth regarding the true limits to the federal taxing powers by standing up for our Country and its founding principles. In light of the decision by DOJ and IRS to ignore the People's fundamental, Constitutional right to petition our government for a redress of these grievances, we are respectfully requesting all Americans to:
> 1) Demand that the IRS and DOJ attend the February hearing and publicly answer the questions, as they committed to do last July.
> 2) Wait to file their tax returns at least until February 27th. If IRS and DOJ fail to appear at the citizens' hearing to answer the People's questions, we will then respectfully request every American citizen and business to defer filing of their tax returns and suspend employee withholding. The American People should not be obligated to pay a tax that the federal government will not, and cannot, publicly defend on lawful or moral grounds.
> 3) Stand together on the mall in Washington DC on **Sunday**, ~~March 31~~ **April 14, 2002**, and peacefully protest the unlawful income tax by filing their blank 1040 forms in metal waste drums.

Congressman Bartlett, do we still have a written Constitution in America? Do we still have a Bill of Rights? Do those documents still memorialize in writing what we believe most deeply in our hearts as Americans? Or have they become mere abstract concepts that have no real bearing on our moral conduct as country? What good is our Constitution and Bill of Rights if we do not treasure them and protect them?

It has been said that the limits of tyrants are prescribed by the tolerance of those whom they oppress.

I, for one, will not accept the decision by the DOJ and the IRS (our servant government) not to answer the People's questions in a recorded public forum---a decision that continues a longstanding history of unlawful, abusive and unaccountable conduct by our government. The refusal of DOJ and IRS to answer these questions in a public forum can only be interpreted as a glaring admission of guilt.

Congressman Bartlett, you gave your word to the American People. I respectfully ask that you keep your word to protect and defend our Constitution at this critical moment in America's history.

Wholeheartedly,

Robert L. Schulz
Chairman

cc: Hon. Lawrence B. Lindsey
Assistant to the President for Economic Policy
Department of Justice
950 Pennsylvania Ave N.W.
Washington, DC 20530

Hon. John Ashcroft
Attorney General of the United States
Department of Justice
950 Pennsylvania Ave NW
Washington, DC 20530

Hon. Paul O'Neil
Secretary
Department of the Treasury
1500 Pennsylvania Ave N.W.
Washington, DC 20220

6.8.7 Cover-Up of 2002: 40 U.S.C. §255 obfuscated

For over three years, this book made frequent reference to the original 40 U.S.C §255 to point out that there is no federal jurisdiction inside states of the Union. This section of the codes had remained intact and unchanged for over 62 years. Eventually, the Congress caught onto the fact that this section of code plainly showed the limits on their jurisdiction so in August 2002, they tried to hide the truth by splitting the section into two sections found in 40 U.S.C. §3111 and §3112 and by complicating the language in these two sections.

When the statute was broken up and restated, the notes section had the relevant quotes from the Supreme Court removed so that the implications of no federal jurisdiction within states of the Union would be less obvious and harder to find.

6.8.8 Cover-Up of 1988: Changed Title of Part I, Subchapter N to Make it Refer Only to Foreign Income

Prior to 1988, the title of Part I of Subchapter N (which begins with Section 861) was "*Determination of sources of income*" (which is still the heading of the related regulations). In 1988, this title was changed to "*Source rules and other general rules relating to **foreign** income*." It should be mentioned that while titles of parts may give an indication of what the part is about, the title has no effect on the actual legal application.

> "...nor shall any **table of contents**, table of cross references, or similar outline, analysis, or **descriptive matter** relating to the contents of this title **be given any legal effect**."
> [26 U.S.C. §7806(b)]

So when the title was changed (but the text of the law was not), the application of the law did *not* change. What changed was the appearance of the table of contents. Prior to the change, in light of the fact that the income tax applies to "***income*** from whatever **source** derived," the table of contents made the relevance of 26 U.S.C. §861 obvious:

> Subtitle A, "Income taxes"
> Chapter 1, "Normal taxes and surtaxes"
> Subchapter N, "Tax based on *income from sources* within or without the United States"
> Part I, "***Determination of sources of income***"
> Section 861, "*Income from sources* within the United States"
> (a) "Gross *income from sources* within the United States"
> (b) "Taxable *income from sources* within the United States"

When the title of Part I was changed, and the new title stated that the part was about "*foreign income*," it no longer appeared to be an obvious place for most people to look when determining their taxable income. This would certainly have the effect of drawing attention away from Section 861. Many tax professionals concede that Section 861 and the related regulations show income to be taxable only when it comes from certain activities related to international and foreign commerce. The new title gives the appearance that the part has no relevance to most people, and should not even be examined.

But this change resulted in a curious situation: a part whose title says it is about "*foreign income*" is identified as the part which (along with the related regulations) "*determine*[s] *the sources of income for purposes of the income tax*."

6.8.9 Cover-Up of 1986: Obfuscation of IRC Section 931

Since 26 U.S.C. §61 does not indicate the fact that "gross income" is restricted to specific property the I.R. Code had to detail this fact elsewhere. This is accomplished in section 931.

Prior to 1986, section 931 of the 1954 I.R. Code provided the exact terms as to what income is deemed to be "gross income" in the I.R. Code in this manner:

> Sec. 931. INCOME FROM SOURCES WITHIN POSSESSIONS OF THE UNITED STATES [provided in part]
>
> (a) General rule.
>
> *In the case of individual citizens of the United States,* gross income means only gross income from sources within the United States if *the conditions of both paragraph (1) and paragraph (2) are satisfied:*
>
> > *(1) 3-year period. If 80 percent or more of the gross income of such citizen...was* derived from sources within a possession of the United States; *and*

> *(2) Trade or business. If 50 percent or more of his gross income* was derived from the active conduct of a trade or business within a possession of the United States *either on his own account or as an employee or agent of another.*
>
> ...
>
> *(h) Employees of the United States*
>
> *For purposes of this section,* amounts paid for services performed by a citizen of the United States as an employee of the United States or any agency thereof shall be deemed to be derived from sources within the United States.

Chapters 4 and 5 laid the foundation for understanding that "within" and "without" in conjunction with the "United States" means within or without the United States Government. This section 931 confirms this by saying that "gross income" MEANS ONLY gross income from sources within a possession of the United States and from the active conduct of a trade or business within a possession of the United States. The 50 States of the United States of America are not possessions of the United States. But, Federal areas within the 50 States are deemed to be possessions (definition in chapter 14). The U.S. Congress can only pass laws for United States possessions and laws with regard to income only when the U.S. Government is the source of the income within its possession. This is the reason for having to state that the pay of employees of the United States is deemed to be derived from sources within the United States.

The old section 931 is provided to demonstrate the difference between it and the current section 931. In the 1954 I.R. Code, the source was emphasized, whereas in the 1986 I.R. Code the place is emphasized and the source of one's income is concealed. By adding vagueness, the intent could only be to mislead. This is part of the IRS humbug.

The 1986 I.R. Code section 931 reads in part:

> *Sec. 931. INCOME FROM SOURCES WITHIN GUAM, AMERICAN SAMOA, OR THE NORTHERN MARIANA ISLANDS*
>
> *(a) GENERAL RULE.--In the case of an individual who is a bona fide resident of a specified possession during the entire taxable year,* **gross income shall not include**---
>
> > (1) income derived from sources within any specified possession, and
> >
> > (2) income effectively connected with the conduct of a trade or business by such individual within any specified possession.
>
> *(c) SPECIFIC POSSESSIONS.--For purposes of this section, the term "specific possession" means Guam, American Samoa, and the Northern Mariana Islands.*
>
> *(d) SPECIAL RULES.--For purposes of this section--*
>
> > *(1) EMPLOYEE OF THE UNITED STATES.--***Amounts paid for services performed as an employee of the United States (or any agency thereof) shall be treated as not described** *in paragraph (1) or (2) of subsection (a).*

Inverse construction similar to that used in section 6012 is used here. Unlike the old section 931 (which made a definite statement restricting the meaning of gross income) section 931 in the 1986 I.R. Code excludes certain income from "gross income" and then, pursuant to section 931(d), excludes amounts paid to Federal Government employees from the exclusion. This accomplished the same result as section 931(h) of the 1954 I.R. Code where amounts paid to anyone for performance of personal services as an employee of the United States was deemed to be "gross income" without regard to any formulas put forth in section 931(a) of the 1954 I.R. Code for "individuals" employed by the U.S. Government by virtue of a trade or business effectively connected within the United States. Again showing that the term "within the United States" means within the U.S. Government and that income from sources other than the U.S. Treasury is foreign to the jurisdiction of the IRS.[75]

With section 931(a) and (d) of the 1986 I.R. Code, Congress is saying that "gross income" does not include income received by an individual (Federal Government employee) who is a bona fide resident of a specified possession when that income was derived from sources within the specified possession or if the income was effectively connected with the conduct of a trade

---

[75] 26 U.S.C. §7701(a)(31) defines that other sources of income are part of a "foreign estate and trust".

or business by such individual (Federal Government employee) within any specified possession unless the U.S. Government was the source of the income. Since there is equal treatment under the laws of the United States of America, this cannot be limited to persons who are bona fide residents of these specified possessions. The fact that "gross income" does not include what anyone receives from a source other than the U.S. Government applies to anyone. But, by emphasizing specified possessions, there is enough vagueness injected to cloud the fact the source of the income, not the place, is the controlling factor. The fact that the term "gross income" in the I.R. Code includes only income derived from the U.S. Government as compensation "for services performed as an employee of the United States or any agency thereof" is demonstrated here (also see section 3401(a) in chapter 6). You cannot enter into an employment agreement with a place, the employer must be the source. Again confirming it is legal kickback pursuant to employment agreements which control whether income is "gross income" subject to the I.R. Code laws.

6.8.10 Cover-Up of 1982: Footnotes Removed from IRC Section 61 Pointing to Section 861

The Code contains many footnotes and references to allow readers to search back and trace the origins and evolution of laws and regulations, since this often clarifies intent. IRC 61(a) on gross income used to have a footnote informing readers that it came from Section 22(a) of the 1939 Code and that the law hadn't been changed. The footnote said, "Source: Sec. 22(a), 1939 Code, substantially unchanged." ***That footnote was in the 1954 version of the Internal Revenue Code at least up to the 1982 edition, but then it vanished, making it difficult for tax professionals to understand how the wording has been deceptively altered, leading to misapplication of the law. Constitutional limitations discussed above were thus hidden***.

Deletion of the footnote has also made it much more difficult to notice and understand the close connection between IRC 61 and IRC 861 (or C.F.R. 1.61 and C.F.R. 1.861), especially as 26 C.F.R. §1.861 is now thousands of pages distant from 26 C.F.R. § 1.61, and in the earlier versions, the section was not numbered 861, but 119. In pre-1954 versions, the "gross income" regulations under Section 22(a) mentioned the taxable sources as income of nonresident aliens and foreign corporations doing business in the U.S. and its possessions and profits of citizens, residents, and domestic corporations derived from foreign commerce. The same sources were described in the regulations under IRC 119 "Income from sources within the United States."

The 1921 version was even more clear (and the law hasn't materially changed since then). It said explicitly "that in the case of a nonresident alien individual or of a citizen entitled to the benefits of section 262, the following items of gross income shall be treated as income from sources within the United States." (IRC 262 applied if at least 80% of a citizen's gross income was from a U.S. possession.)

In 1954, while the law still hadn't materially changed, the regulations were changed so that the "foreign" sources were omitted from the "gross income" description in C.F.R. 1.61(a), but remained in the regulations as C.F.R. 1.861 (renumbered from the regulations previously under IRC 119). Wording was put in those regulations stating that they "determine the sources of income for purposes of the income tax," and they stated that it was the foreign sources noted below that were the sources. These sources today are the ones listed in 26 C.F.R. §1.861-8(f)(1).

6.8.11 Cover-Up of 1978: Confused IRS Regulations on "Sources"

In 1978, the wording of 26 C.F.R. §1.861-8 was changed significantly, and the title was changed from "Computation of Taxable Income from Sources Within the United States" to "Computation of taxable income from sources within the United States **and from other sources and activities**." Some have suggested that the current title implies that one should not be using this section unless he has income both from within the United States and from "other sources and activities." The older title, as well as the text of the current regulations, shows that this is not the case.

Another change regarding 26 C.F.R. §1.861 that can only be seen as an intent to deceive occurred in 1978. 26 C.F.R. §1.861-8, which contains the key list of sources, went from less than one page before 1978 to more than forty pages. There was no underlying change in the law or even in the substance of the regulation, but the regulation became a maze of new phrases, such as "statutory groupings," or "operative sections," or "specific sources" that require much more effort to sort out, but lead to the same conclusion as before. There can no other explanation for such a masterpiece of regulatory obfuscation but the intent to confuse, obscure, deceive and defraud. Those who claim that IRC 861 is not relevant to citizens should explain why officials would go to such great lengths to obfuscate what would otherwise be a relatively little-used part of the Code. If it didn't apply to most citizens, such a masterful job of creating confusion would be a waste of lawyerly talent.

It's well worth the government's while to have the cleverest lawyers and officials try to keep playing with the wording of the income tax Code and regulations to further disguise the true meaning of the law without actually changing it, in order to make it appear that most citizens are required to file and pay even if they aren't. The payoff to the government is enormous - several hundred billion dollars a year.

6.8.12 Cover-Up of 1954: Hiding of Constitutional Limitations in IRC On Congress' Right To Tax

Here is a brief summary of what we will discuss in this section below, as far as what congress changed in the law:

1. Deleted any phrases referring to income that is, under the Constitution or fundamental law, not taxable by the government. This was done by changing the definition of gross income from "unless exempt from tax by law" to "unless excluded by law". There were no changes to the law or the Constitution that would necessitate deleting the reference to the Constitution; it was done for no other credible reason than to obscure the Constitutionally-limited application of the income tax, but without making the regulation technically incorrect - only deceiving and misleading.
2. Obfuscated locating taxable sources by adding double-negatives "list of sources that are NOT considered tax exempt". Why not just state what IS taxable, which is foreign income?
3. Removed from the regulations the phrase "in the case of ***nonresident alien individuals*** and foreign corporations engaged in trade or business within the United States" from the regulations in section 1.861-8. This made it appear that the applicability of the income tax was expanded. ." As Congress stated, the application of the law *did not change* in 1954, but some key phrases in the regulations were removed so as to make the truth less obvious.
4. The admission of the limited application vanished from the regulations defining "gross income," but remained in the regulations under 26 U.S.C. §861, and (to maintain literal accuracy) the regulations began to say that 861 and following and related regulations "*determine the sources of income for purposes of the income tax*." This change removed any chance of the regulations under Section 61 raising suspicions.

In 1954, the Code underwent a major rearranging and renumbering (and to some extent, rewording). This change-over did not substantially change the law itself, but simply rearranged it. While there have been several amendments, the current Code retains the same general structure, numbering and content of the 1954 Code. At the time of the 1954 "transformation" of the Code, several changes helped to conceal the truth about the limited application of the federal income tax.

As shown above, the regulations in 1945 specifically stated (twice) that some income not exempt by statute was nonetheless exempt from federal taxation because of the Constitution. The 1945 regulations under the definition of "gross income" began as follows:

> "Sec. 29.22(a)-1. What included in gross income.
> Gross income includes in general [items of income listed] derived from any source whatever, ***unless exempt from tax by law***." [1945 regulations]

Those regulations then went on to explain that this refers to income exempt by statute or "*fundamental law*," meaning the Constitution. The current corresponding regulations begin in a similar manner:

> "Sec. 1.61-1 Gross income. (a) General definition. Gross income means all income from whatever source derived, ***unless excluded by law***."
> [26 C.F.R. §1.61-1]

However, no mention of the Constitution remains. The phrase "*unless excluded by **law***" is now read as being synonymous with "unless excluded by **statute**." The Constitutional limitations still apply (there have been no subsequent constitutional amendments relative to the taxing power), but the present regulations under 26 U.S.C. §61 do not explicitly say that this is part of the "law" which exempts certain income. Instead, they use the general wording that leaves the reader free to assume that only income specifically exempted by *statute* is exempt from taxation.

But this was only one part of a major shift in the structure of the Great Deception that occurred in 1954. Prior to 1954, the regulations stated that "gross income" included everything not exempt, and then made clear that some types of income were not taxable by the federal government because of the Constitution. The regulations regarding "*What included in gross income*" then went on to say the following:

> "*Profits of citizens, residents, or domestic corporations derived from sales in **foreign commerce must be included in their gross income**; but special provisions are made for **nonresident aliens** and **foreign corporations***... and,

> *in certain cases... for citizens and domestic corporations **deriving income from sources within** possessions of the United States."*

This list of taxable activities is absent from the current regulations under 26 U.S.C. §61. However, something very similar is found in the current regulations under Section 861. The regulations under Section 861 twice define the term "*class of gross income*," saying that a "*class of gross income*" "*may consist of one or more **items**... of gross income enumerated in **section 61**.*" The regulations then refer the reader to "*paragraph **(d)(2)** of this section which provides that a **class of gross income** may include **excluded** income.*" In other words, the "*items*" of income listed in Section 61 are not necessarily taxable, but may be "exempt" or "excluded" from the federal income tax. Paragraph (d)(2) states only "*[Reserved]*" (meaning there is no current regulation) but refers the reader to paragraph (d)(2) of the temporary regulations at 26 C.F.R. §1.861-8T. This section describes what is meant by exempt income.

> *"(ii) Exempt income and exempt asset defined--(A) In general. For purposes of this section, the term **exempt income** means any income that is, in whole or in part, **exempt**, excluded, or eliminated for federal income tax purposes."*
> *[26 C.F.R. §1.861-8T(d)(2)(ii)]*

The section then goes on to specify what is not exempt. The following should be read carefully, since it starts with a double negative. If a certain kind of income is ***not*** exempt, it means it ***is*** subject to the federal income tax. Therefore, after being told that "*items*" of income (which make up "*classes of gross income*") may not be taxable, a list is given of the types of income which ***are*** subject to the federal income tax:

> *"(iii) Income that is **not** considered tax exempt. The following items are **not** considered to be **exempt**, eliminated, or excluded income and, thus, may have expenses, losses, or other deductions allocated and apportioned to them:*
> *(A) In the case of a **foreign** taxpayer...*
> *(B) In computing the combined taxable income of a **DISC or FSC**...*
> *(C) For all purposes under **subchapter N** of the Code... the gross income of a **possessions** corporation...*
> *(D) **Foreign earned income** as defined in **section 911** and the regulations thereunder..."*
> *[26 C.F.R. §1.861-8T(d)(2)(iii)]*

This is the entire list of non-exempt (taxable) income. The idea that other types of income are also taxable (not exempt), despite not being listed, is contradicted by the regulations stating that paragraph (d)(2) "*provides that a **class of gross income** [consisting of the "items" of income listed in 26 U.S.C. §61] may include **excluded** income.*" Unless those types of income not listed are exempt, paragraph (d)(2) does **not** show that the "*items*" of income listed in Section 61 may be exempt. (A basic principle of law is that such a list is assumed to be exclusive and complete, unless a phrase such as "*including, but not limited to...*" is used.)

While it is arranged and worded differently, this list of non-exempt income is essentially the same as the regulations under the old statute defining "gross income." It lists foreign earned income of citizens, income from within possessions, and income of foreigners. But while the 1945 regulations listed these "non-exempt" activities under the regulations defining "gross income," they are currently buried in dozens of pages of less prominent regulations under 26 U.S.C. §861. So while the 1945 statute and regulation defining "gross income" *by themselves* indicated the limited application of the law, the trail to find the truth in the current law is more involved (though the end conclusion is the same).

The basic shift in the Great Deception (in 1954) can be summed up as this: While the *older* version showed the limitations of the law in "step one" (the definition of "gross income"), the *current* statute and regulation defining "gross income" use the word "source" without further explanation, and *additional* steps must be followed to discover that the meaning of that term ("source") is determined by 26 U.S.C. §861 and following, and related regulations.

Prior to 1954, the regulations did not say that Section 119 (predecessor to the current 861) and its regulations "determined the sources of income for purposes of the income tax." Instead, the regulations under 22(a) (defining "gross income") list the *exact same activities* as Section 119 when discussing income from *within* the United States. In effect, both the regulations defining "gross income," *and* Section 119 and related regulations "determined the sources of income for purposes of the income tax."

(The regulations defining "gross income" mention "**nonresident aliens** and **foreign corporations** by sections 211 to 237, inclusive, and, in certain cases, by **section 251** for citizens and domestic corporations deriving income from sources within **possessions** of the United States." At the same time the regulations under 119 mention "**nonresident alien individuals**, **foreign corporations**, and citizens of the United States or domestic corporations entitled to the benefits of **section 251**.")

Chapter 6: History of Government Income Tax Fraud, Racketeering and Extortion in the U.S.A.

In 1954, the admission of the limited application vanished from the regulations defining "gross income," but remained in the regulations under 26 U.S.C. §861, and (to maintain literal accuracy) the regulations began to say that 861 and following and related regulations "***determine the sources of income for purposes of the income tax***." This change removed any chance of the regulations under Section 61 raising suspicions.

> (The way federal law works, there is no requirement that a section which *uses* a term point to where the definition or explanation of that term can be found. As ludicrous as it seems, it would be perfectly legal for Section 1 of some law to impose a tax "on the transfer of each automobile," and then have Section 14523(g)(4)(iii) say that "for the purposes of Section 1, the term 'automobile' means a blue Corvette owned by a foreigner." That is in essence how the Great Deception has been structured since 1954.)

While this makes the truth more difficult (but certainly not impossible) to demonstrate with the current statutes and regulations alone, in retrospect it strongly confirms the limited nature of the tax, by showing that while the structure of deception has changed, the conclusion remains the same.

But the regulations defining "gross income" were not the only place where the truth became less clear during the 1954 "transformation." When the statutes were being rearranged and renumbered, Section 119 of the 1939 Code became all of Part I of Subchapter N. The Senate report on the 1954 Code states the following:

> "SUBCHAPTER N - TAX BASED ON INCOME FROM SOURCES
> WITHIN OR WITHOUT THE UNITED STATES
>
> PART I - Determination of Sources of Income
>
> §861. *Income from sources within the United States*
> §862. *Income from sources without the United States*
> §863. *Items not specified in section 861 or 862*
> §864. *Definitions*

These sections, which are identical with sections 861-864 of the House bill, **correspond to section 119 of the 1939 Code**. **No substantive change is made**, except that section 861(a)(3) would extend the existing 90-day $3,000 rule in the case of a nonresident alien employee of a foreign employer to a nonresident alien employee of a foreign branch of a domestic employer."

Congress here states that the application of the law *did not change* (except for the specific detail mentioned). As would be expected, the statutes are nearly identical.

> *Sec. 119. [1939 Code] Income from sources within the United States*
> (a) Gross Income from Sources in United States.
> The following items of gross income shall be treated as income from sources within the United States:...
>
> *Sec. 861 [current Code]. Income from sources within the United States*
> (a) Gross income from sources within United States
> The following items of gross income shall be treated as income from sources within the United States:...

Section 119 of the old statutes and Section 861 of the current statutes use general terms that could easily be misread as applying to any income from within the United States. But *while the statutes did not change, the honesty of the regulations corresponding to these sections changed dramatically. The older regulations admitted the truth so plainly and so often that no step-by-step explanation is needed.* The following is the equivalent of the current 26 C.F.R. §1.861-1, *in its entirety*.

> "*Sec. 29.119-1. Income from sources within the United States.*
> *Nonresident alien individuals, foreign corporations*, and citizens of the United States or domestic corporations *entitled to the benefits of section 251* [this applies only to those who receive a large percentage of their income from within federal *possessions*] are taxable only upon income from sources within the United States. Citizens of the United States and domestic corporations entitled to the benefits of section 251 are, however, taxable upon income received within the United States, whether derived from sources within or without the United States. (See sections 212(a), 231(c), and 251.)
>
> The Internal Revenue Code divides the income of *such taxpayers* into three classes:
> (1) Income which is derived in full from sources within the United States;

> (2) Income which is derived in full from sources without the United States;
> (3) Income which is derived partly from sources within and partly from sources without the United States.
>
> The taxable income from sources within the United States includes that derived in full from sources within the United States and that portion of the income which is derived partly from sources within and partly from sources without the United States which is allocated or apportioned to sources within the United States."

Note that the second paragraph in the old regulations under Section 119 states that the Code (specifically Section 119) is for determining taxable income of "***such taxpayers***," meaning those deriving income from specific taxable activities or sources. The general language of the statutes is applicable *only* to those involved in certain types of international and foreign commerce.

The subsequent sections of the older regulations (like the current regulations) then deal with specific "items" of income. The sections of regulations following that (which correspond to the current 26 C.F.R. §1.861-8) then deal with determining taxable income from sources within the United States. Again, the regulations clearly show the limited application of the law.

> "Sec. 29.119-9. Deductions in general.
>
> The deductions provided for in chapter 1 shall be allowed to **nonresident alien individuals** and **foreign corporations** engaged in trade or business within the United States, and to citizens of the United States and domestic corporations **entitled to the benefits of section 251**, only if and to the extent provided in sections 213, 215, 232, 233, and 251.
>
> Sec. 29.119-10. Apportionment of deductions.
> From the **items** specified in sections 29.119-1 to 29.119-6, inclusive, as being derived specifically from sources within the United States there shall, in the case of **nonresident alien individuals** and **foreign corporations** engaged in trade or business within the United States, be deducted [allowable deductions]. **The remainder shall be included in full as net income from sources within the United States...**"

Regarding income from *within* the United States, the older regulations defining "*gross income*" describe the exact same taxable activities as the regulations of that time related to "*income from sources within the United States*" (namely, nonresident aliens and foreign corporations getting income from within the United States, and citizens and domestic corporations who receive much of their income from within federal possessions). "No substantive change" was made when Section 119 became Sections 861 and following, which implies that Section 119 and its regulations "*determine*[d] *the sources of income for purposes of the income tax*" (as the current regulations state). The older regulations did not need to say this, since the regulations defining "gross income" also specifically listed what activities could generate taxable income. So in 1945, the regulations defining "gross income" ***and*** the regulations under the old Section 119 "*determine*[d] *the sources of income for purposes of the income tax*." Today only the regulations under Section 861 list the taxable activities.

(There is a chart in section 3.15.5 of this document showing the outline and excerpts from Part I of Subchapter N and related regulations, and another chart showing the outline and excerpts from the corresponding statutes and regulations from before 1954.)

> QUESTION FOR DOUBTERS: *Do the older regulations under the predecessor of 26 U.S.C. §861 show income of U.S. citizens living and working within the 50 union states as taxable?*

Can it be considered an accident that the current regulations are so overly-complex and confusing, while the older regulations blurted out the truth in plain English in the very first sentence? The fact that the statutes apply only to income from certain "specific sources" (relating to international and foreign commerce) is still stated in the current regulations, but rather than being in first sentence, it is buried deep in the jumbled mess:

> "(ii) Relationship of sections 861, 862, 863(a), and 863(b). Sections **861, 862, 863(a), and 863(b)** are the four provisions applicable in **determining taxable income from specific sources**."
> [26 C.F.R. §1.861-8(f)(3)(ii)]

In fact, even here it does not specify to which "*specific sources*" it is referring; the meaning of that term has to be discovered by searching elsewhere in the regulations. (Three other sections of the regulations say that "*specific sources*" means the taxable activities described in the "operative sections" throughout Subchapter N.) The regulations prior to 1954 were short, plain, and very clear about who they applied to. (While many tax professionals are now aware of the correct application of Section 861 and its regulations, it certainly is not evident at first glance.)

When the regulations changed in 1954, they did *not* change directly into what the regulations are today. The current maze of "*statutory groupings*," "*specific sources*," "*operative sections*," etc. did not come about until 1978. Of particular note is how the regulations in 26 C.F.R. §1.861-8 appeared just after the change in 1954, and how the corresponding regulations appeared prior to 1954. The wording was only very slightly changed, but gives one of the most obvious examples of intent to deceive.

BEFORE 1954	AFTER 1954
29.119-10 Apportionment of deductions. From the **items specified in sections 29.119-1 to 29.119-6**, inclusive, as being derived specifically from sources within the United States there **shall, <u>in the case of nonresident alien individuals and foreign corporations engaged in trade or business within the United States,</u> be deducted** the expenses, losses, and other deductions properly apportioned or allocated thereto and a ratable part of any other expenses, losses, or deductions which cannot definitely be allocated to some item or class of gross income. **The remainder shall be included in full as net income from sources within the United States.** The ratable part is based upon the ratio of gross income from sources within the United States to the total gross income. Example. A **<u>nonresident alien individual</u>** engaged in trade or business within the United States whose taxable year is the calendar year derived gross income from all sources for 1942 of $180,000, including there-in: Interest on bonds of a domestic corporation $9,000 Dividends on stock of a domestic corporation 4,000 Royalty for the use of patents within the United States 12,000 Gain from sale of real property [in U.S.] 11,000 --------- Total 36,000 [remainder of example omitted]	1.861-8 Computation of Taxable Income from Sources Within the United States (a) General. From the **items of gross income specified in §§ 1.861-2 to 1.861-7**, inclusive, as being income from sources within the United States there **shall be deducted** the expenses, losses, and other deductions properly apportioned or allocated thereto and a ratable part of any other expenses, losses, or deductions which cannot definitely be allocated to some item or class of gross income. **The remainder, if any, shall be included in full as taxable income from sources within the United States.** The ratable part is based upon the ratio of gross income from sources within the United States to the total gross income Example. A **<u>taxpayer</u>** engaged in trade or business receives for the taxable year gross income from all sources in the amount of $180,000, one-fifth of which ($36,000) is from sources within the United States, computed as follows: Interest on bonds of a domestic corporation $9,000 Dividends on stock of a domestic corporation 4,000 Royalty for the use within the United States of patents 12,000 Gain from sale of real property [in U.S.] 11,000 -------- Total 36,000 [remainder of example omitted]

The wording is nearly identical, except for two changes. ***<u>The phrase stating that the whole section applies only to nonresident aliens and foreign corporations simply vanished!</u>*** In addition, while the specifics of the example in the regulation remained *identical*, the phrase "*a nonresident alien individual*" was replaced with "*a taxpayer*." As Congress stated, the application of the law ***did not change*** in 1954, but some key phrases in the regulations were removed so as to make the truth less obvious. A similar disappearance of a phrase occurred at the same time in the section of regulations dealing with the "item" of interest. The wording remained *identical* except for the disappearing phrase.

BEFORE 1954	AFTER 1954
29.119-2. Interest. There shall be included in the gross income from sources within the United States, **of nonresident alien individuals, foreign corporations, and citizens of the United States, or domestic corporations which are entitled to the benefits of section 251**, all interest received or accrued, as the case may be, from the United States, any Territory, any political subdivision of a Territory, or the District of Columbia, and interest on bonds, notes, or other interest-bearing obligations of residents of the United States, whether corporate or otherwise, except...	1.861-2 Interest. (a) General. There shall be included in the gross income from sources within the United States all interest received or accrued, as the case may be, from the United States, any Territory, any political subdivision of a Territory, or the District of Columbia, and interest on bonds, notes, or other interest-bearing obligations of residents of the United States, whether corporate or otherwise, except...

(Interest is the only "item" of income for which the regulations specifically mentioned who was receiving it. But the regulations cited above state that in the case of *all* of the "items" of income, the deductions and determination of taxable income can be done only by those engaged in the specific taxable activities.)

6.8.13   1952: Office of Collector of Internal Revenue Eliminated

The Office of the Collector of Internal Revenue abolished. See Reorganization Plans No. 26 of 1950 and No. 1 of 1952, and Notes under 26 U.S.C. §7804, "Amendments" at:

https://www.law.cornell.edu/uscode/text/26/7804?qt-us_code_temp_noupdates=1#qt-us_code_temp_noupdates

As part of this reorganization, the government manufactured a scandal concerning the collectors. The real reason, however, was to make the code voluntary.

This office of the Collector of Internal Revenue made it possible to protest a tax. Without a Collector of Internal Revenue, it is impossible to protest a tax because it has to be voluntary without a collector. Recall that earlier in section **Error! Reference source not found.**, we pointed out that a free people can only be free if they consent to their taxation. There are two ways to consent:

1. Indirectly consent by electing a Collector of Internal Revenue or have him appointed by a person who was elected.
2. Directly consent by sending a donation form called a "tax return", which gives the authority to the government to take your money by virtue of the liability that you assessed against yourself.

If you don't make a liability to pay a tax in the law, then no one has an obligation to do anything. This reorganization of the IRS made the process of tax collection into an administrative process which could only touch "volunteers" called "taxpayers". This made the U.S. District courts into administrative courts in regards to federal taxes. Administrative courts are "non-judicial" and are only there to hear cases where all parties appear by consent and confer jurisdiction on the court to resolve the matter by virtue of them appearing. The only people who should go to these courts are "taxpayers", which are people who *volunteered* to pay the tax. If you are a "nontaxpayer" or choose not to participate in income taxation, then you shouldn't appear in these courts and if you don't appear or are forced to appear involuntarily because you were extradited, simply refuse to plead and refuse to accept a public defender. That ends the jurisdiction of the court and they will eventually have to let you go because of the requirement for habeas corpus.

Recall that the original office of the Collector was in the House of Representatives, which is part of the Legislative Branch. The office of the Collector was created at 1 Stat. 65 of the Statutes at Large, before the Treasury Department even existed, so he was in the Legislative branch. From the founding of this country, tax Collectors were private parties who were bonded and who had to put their house up for surety with a federal lien while they were Collectors. If they collected unlawfully, then they could lose their house and would have to forfeit their bond in order to compensate those they hurt. The Collector was moved from the Legislative Branch to the Executive Branch in 1862, when the income tax was restructured during the Civil War and without explanation or fanfare. This was a violation of the legislative intent of the Constitution, which requires that taxation and representation must coexist with the same person, which could only be your Representative in the House of Representatives: Taxation WITH representation. Once the taxation and representation functions were separated to two separate branches of the government, then all of the corruption began because the separation of powers doctrine had been violated.

Section 29 of the Revenue Act of 1894 was the last federal law that imposed a legal duty to pay upon citizens and residents of the United States. The duty to pay the tax was subsequently eliminated by *Pollock v. Farmers' Loan & Trust Co., 157 U.S. 429 (1895)* and does not appear in any Revenue Law after that date.

6.8.14 Cover-Up of 1939: Removed References to Nonresident Aliens from the Definition of "Gross Income"

As shown above, some very telling phrases simply vanished from the regulations in 1954. But it was not only the regulations that lost some honesty along the way. The statutes found in the Revenue Act of 1921 show why the regulations said what they said up until 1954. But just as happened with the regulations, a telling phrase that existed in 1921 is no longer found in the statutes. The current Section 861 and its predecessors have remained basically the same for more than 70 years. The text begins *"The following items of gross income shall be treated as income from sources within the United States:"* The section then lists "items" of income (interest, dividends, compensation for labor, rents and royalties, etc.). In 1921 the section was very similar, but it began *"That **in the case of a nonresident alien individual or of a citizen entitled to the benefits of section 262**, the following items of gross income shall be treated as income from sources within the United States:..."*

(While Section 217 itself mentions only *individuals*, Section 232 of the Act states that "[i]*n the case of a foreign corporation or of a corporation entitled to the benefits of section 262 the computation shall also be made in the manner provided in section 217.*" As the current regulations and historical regulations state, the section is applicable to nonresident aliens, foreign corporations, and citizen or domestic corporations which receive much of their income from within federal *possessions*.)

1921 Code	1939 Code	Current Code
Net income of nonresident alien individuals Sec. 217. (a) That **in the case of a nonresident alien individual or of a citizen entitled to the benefits of section 262**, *the following items of gross income shall be treated as income from sources within the United States*: (1) Interest... (2) The amount received as dividends... (3) Compensation for labor or personal services performed in the United States. (4) Rentals or royalties... (5) Gains, profits, and income from the sale of real property... ------------------------------ (b) From the items of gross income specified in subdivision (a) there shall be deducted [allowable deductions]. **The remainder, if any, shall be included in full as net income from sources within the United States.**	Sec. 119. Income from sources within United States (a) Gross income from sources in United States. *The following items of gross income shall be treated as income from sources within the United States*: (1) Interest... (2) Dividends... (3) Personal services - Compensation for labor or personal services performed in the United States... (4) Rentals and royalties... (5) Sale of real property... (6) Sale of personal property... ------------------------------ (b) Net income from sources in United States From the items of gross income specified in subsection (a) of this section there shall be deducted [allowable deductions]. **The remainder, if any, shall be included in full as net income from sources within the United States.**	Sec. 861. Income from sources within the United States (a) Gross income from sources within United States *The following items of gross income shall be treated as income from sources within the United States*: (1) Interest... (2) Dividends... (3) Personal services - Compensation for labor or personal services performed in the United States... (4) Rentals and royalties... (5) Disposition of United States real property interest... (6) Sale or exchange of inventory property... (7) Amounts received as underwriting income... (8) Social security benefits... ------------------------------ (b) Taxable income from sources within United States From the items of gross income specified in subsection (a) as being income from sources within the United States there shall be deducted [allowable deductions]. **The remainder, if any, shall be included in full as taxable income from sources within the United States....**
(c) The following items of gross income shall be treated as income from sources **without** the United States:... ------------------------------ (d) From the items of gross income specified in subdivision (c) there shall be deducted [allowable deductions]. **The remainder, if any, shall be treated in full as net income from sources without the United States.**	(c) Gross income from sources **without** United States The following items of gross income shall be treated as income from sources **without** the United States:... ------------------------------ (d) Net income from sources without the United States - From the items of gross income specified in subsection (c) of this section there shall be deducted [allowable deductions]. **The remainder, if any, shall be treated in full as net income from sources without the United States.**	Sec. 862. Income from sources **without** the United States (a) Gross income from sources without United States The following items of gross income shall be treated as income from sources **without** the United States:... ------------------------------ (b) Taxable income from sources without United States - From the items of gross income specified in subsection (a) there shall be deducted [allowable deductions]. **The remainder, if any, shall be treated in full as taxable income from sources without the United States...**

(e) Items of gross income, expenses, losses and deductions, **other than those specified in subdivisions (a) and (c)**, shall be allocated or apportioned to sources within or without the United States...	(e) Income from sources partly within and partly without United States Items of gross income, expenses, losses and deductions, **other than those specified in subsections (a) and (c)** of this section, shall be allocated or apportioned to sources within or without the United States... (f) Definitions...	Sec. 863. Special rules for determining source (a) Allocation under regulations Items of gross income, expenses, losses, and deductions, **other than those specified in sections 861(a) and 862(a)**, shall be allocated or apportioned to sources within or without the United States... Sec. 864. Definitions and special rules... Sec. 865. Source rules for personal property sales...

Although it is obvious to whom this section applied in 1921, some may question whether this is at all relevant to current law. Treasury Decision 8687, in discussing what the regulations under the *current* 26 U.S.C. §863 should say (regarding sales of natural resources), specifically refer to Section 217 of the 1921 Code in trying to determine the "legislative intent" of Congress.

> "The legislative history to section 863's predecessor, section *217(e)* of the **Revenue Act of 1921**, also reflects an intention that..."
> [Treasury Decision 8687]

This Treasury Decision, passed in late *1996*, confirms that Section 217 of the Revenue Act of 1921 is the predecessor of the current Part I of Subchapter N, and shows that the IRS still refers to the 1921 Code to determine the proper application of the *current* Code. The Internal Revenue Manual shows that the courts, as well as the IRS, considers legislative history when determining the correct application of the law.

> "The courts give great importance to the literal language of the Code but the language does not solve every tax controversy. **Courts also consider the *history* of a particular code section...**"
> [Internal Revenue Manual, (4.2)7.2.1.1]

When the phrase disappeared from the statutes after 1921, the application of the law did not change. What changed was how easily the truth could be found.

6.8.15 1932: Revenue Act of 1932 imposes first excise income tax on federal judges and public officers

Congress knew from past court actions that Federal judges already in office would not permit impairment of their existing contracts. By changes in the wording in the Revenue Act of 1932, c. 209, to read:

> Sec. 22...In the case of Presidents of the United States and judges of courts of the United States taking office after June 6, 1932, the **compensation received as such shall be included in gross income; and all Acts fixing the compensation** *of such Presidents and judges* **are hereby amended accordingly.**

Congress managed to get the cooperation of Federal judges taking office after June 6, 1932. Cooperation is evidenced by acceptance of the job.

Note that this change in wording accomplished two things. First, by specifying that it applied to judges taking office after June 6, 1932 it did not affect existing employment contracts. Hence existing judges could not say it diminished their compensation. Secondly, the working of "all Acts are hereby amended accordingly" means that new judges are informed up front that their employment contract includes a kickback in the compensation. Just like other Federal Government employees, their compensation for labor was the amount arranged for under law by Congress less the kickback, which varies depending on the deduction benefits available to each judge.[76] Judges could have challenged the lawfulness based on unequal pay for like work, but then that argument would hold true for all other Federal Government employees as well.

The effect of this Act upon the compensation of judges who enter into a new employment agreement is brought out by the court cases after 1932. For example, in O'Malley v. Woodrough, 307 U.S. 277 (1939), Judge Woodrough brought action when his compensation as an Appeals Court judge was assessed. He had been a U.S. District Court judge prior to accepting his new position with the Appellate Court in 1933. The Supreme Court Justices decided that judges of courts of the United States taking office after June 6, 1932, had agreed to allow their salary to be deemed "gross income" and subject to a legal kickback. In other words, they agreed that, as a condition of employment, the salary of judges as set by Congress--as with all other Federal Government employees--includes their remuneration for personal service (income) and a kickback (gain) to the U.S. Government.[77] In essence, the Supreme Court said to Judge Woodrough--tough cookies, when you accepted a higher position, you agreed to a new employment contract and accepted the employment condition of kickback that all judges taking office after June 6, 1932 accepted.

---

[76] The Fourth Circuit Court of Appeals clarified this issue in Baker et al. v. Commissioner of Internal Revenue, 149 F.2d. 342 (1945) with the statement: "The necessary effect of the Woodrough case seems to us to be that *a judge who takes office under an established Congressional policy of taxing his salary becomes entitled only to the salary prescribed by statute less income taxes, and that in consequence his salary is not diminished by the tax..*"

[77] The kickback is some part of the gain portion of "gross income" or "wages." The amount depends upon the deduction benefits claimed by the Federal Government employee upon a "U.S. Individual Income Tax Return."

Chapter 7: Resources for Tax Fraud Fighters

As for periodic changes, it is no known if U.S. judges actually do agree and permit Congressional unilateral changes in their employment contracts through the varying rates and deduction benefits. It they do, it certainly is contrary to their tradition. To prove whether or not U.S. judges use current rates and deduction benefits or that which was in existence when they first took office would require review of their "U.S. Individual Income Tax Returns," which is a violation of their personal rights to privacy. So, it is something the public will never know, but the question is there.

6.8.16 1923: Classification Act, 42 Stat. 1488[78]

This act was passed on March 4, 1923 as H.R. 8928. Chapter 265 created several custom terms and definitions to be used throughout the government from that point on, including in subsequent Revenue Acts as well as the Internal Revenue Code, first codified in the U.S. Code in the Internal Revenue Code of 1939. Among the important terms defined and subsequently used in the I.R.C. include:

1. "department": "the term 'department' means an executive department of the United States Government, a governmental establishment in the executive branch of the United States Government which is not a part of an executive department, the municipal government of the District of Columbia, the Botanic garden, Library of Congress, Library Building and Grounds, Government Printing Office (GPO), and the Smithsonian Institution."
2. "position": "means a specific civilian office or employment, whether occupied or vacant, in a department other than the following: Offices or employments in the Postal Service; teachers, librarians, school attendance officers, and employees of the community center department under the Board of Education of the District of Columbia; officers and members of the Metropolitan police, the fire department of the District of Columbia, and the United States park police; and the commissioned personnel of the Coast Guard, the public Health Service, and the Coast and Geodetic Survey."
3. "employee": "means any person temporarily or permanently in a position."
4. "service": "means the broadest division of related offices and employments."
5. "compensation": "means *any salary, wage, fee, allowance, or other emolument paid to an employee for service in a position.*"

Nearly all of the above definitions would be very carefully used to deceive the American public in subsequent acts of Congress, because they would be misconstrued by the general public to have their common definition, rather than the very specific legal definition above. This act much better concealed the nature of the I.R.C., Subtitle A income tax as an excise tax upon the privileges incident to public office (e.g. "trade or business", see 26 U.S.C. §7701(a)(26)) by disguising hidden meanings within the terms "compensation" and "services" and "employee", all of which, by the above act, can ONLY be incident to service in the United States government as a public officer, whether elected or appointed.

The effect of this act carried over into the IRC's of 1954 and 1986 insofar as they merely restate relevant elements incorporated in the 1939 version. It is particularly important in the modern I.R.C. Section 61, "Gross Income Defined", wherein "compensation for services" is listed as a specific "item of income" and its misleadingly ambiguous distinction from "income derived", seen in the 1921 Revenue Act, is restored. The restoration was accompanied by a notation to the effect that the reconstruction of the 1928 language (which the 1939 code section duplicated) represented no substantial change in its meaning. Below is the content of 26 U.S.C. §61, "Gross Income Defined" so you can now apply the above definitions properly. We have boldfaced and underlined the words from the above definitions contained in the Classification Act and added bracketed material so you can clearly see the meanings:

> *TITLE 26 > Subtitle A > CHAPTER 1 > Subchapter B > PART 1 > § 61*
> *§ 61. Gross income defined*
>
> *(a) General definition Except as otherwise provided in this subtitle, gross income means all income from whatever source derived, including (but not limited to) the following items:*
> *(1) **Compensation** for **services [as a public official]**, including fees, commissions, fringe benefits, and similar items;*
> *(2) Gross income derived from [a trade or] business;*
> *(3) Gains derived from dealings in property [within the District of Columbia, see 26 U.S.C. 871];*
> *(4) Interest;*
> *(5) Rents;*
> *(6) Royalties;*
> *(7) Dividends;*
> *(8) Alimony and separate maintenance payments;*
> *(9) Annuities;*

---

[78] Adapted from *Cracking the Code, Pete Hendrickson, ISBN 0-9743936-0-6, pp. 52-53*.

(10) Income from life insurance and endowment contracts;
(11) Pensions;
(12) Income from discharge of indebtedness;
(13) Distributive share of partnership gross income;
(14) Income in respect of a decedent; and
(15) Income from an interest in an estate or trust [in the District of Columbia].

6.8.17 1918: "Gross income" first defined in the Revenue Act of 1918[79]

The Revenue Act of 1918, c. 18, 40 Stat. 1057, enacted by Congress on February 24, 1919, specifically placed the compensation for personal services of Federal judges and the U.S. President under the definition of "gross income" in an attempt to bring them into the existing kickback program. That statute reads:

> *Sec. 213. That for the purposes of this title...the term "gross income"-*
>
> *(a) Includes gains, profits, and income derived from salaries, wages, or compensation for personal service (including the case **of the President of the United States, the judges of the Supreme and inferior courts of the United States,** and all other officers and employees, whether elected or appointed, of the United States, Alaska, Hawaii, or any political subdivision thereof, or the District of Columbia, the compensation received as such), of whatever kind and in whatever form paid, or from professions, vocations, trades, businesses, commerce, or sales, or dealings in property, whether real or personal, growing out of the ownership or use of or interest in such property; also from interest, rent, dividends, securities, or the transaction of any business carried on for gain or profit, or gains or profits and income derived from any source whatever....[emphasis added]*

You will note that Congress is making reference to gross income where the U.S. Government is the source of that income. Again making it clear that ONLY the compensation for personal services for the labor of Federal Government employees is includible in "gross income." The compensation of a person working in the private sector or for a state or local government, which includes state judges, is not included. Therefore, the subject matter "gross income" in the I.R. Code only applies to Federal Government employees. Income not derived from the U.S. Government is not subject to the I.R. Code Laws. The sections of the current I.R. Code that provide this notice will be discussed in detail later.

The U.S. Government, like any other employer, can establish the terms of its own employment agreement. Legally the U.S Government cannot unilaterally impose new conditions or terms to existing employment agreements with Federal Government employees, which is confirmed by the stand the judges have taken and expressed in court opinions. Also, Congress cannot legally establish the terms of an employment agreement in the private sector or make the U.S. Government a party to such agreements.

6.8.18 1911: Judicial Code of 1911

This act abolished the existing circuit courts and replaced them with Circuit Courts of Appeals. The District Courts of the United States became "United States District Courts". This left no Article III courts to hear cases involving constitutional rights. All district and circuit courts became, at that point, Article II courts which may only have jurisdiction within territories of the United States Government. These courts are part of the executive branch, not the judicial branch, of the U.S. government. The judges in these Art. II courts are civil service employees of the Office of Personnel Management, which is part of the Executive Branch. The judges are not judicial officers as required under Art. III of the Constitution, but federal employees.

Below is the text of the act, excerpted from: http://air.fjc.gov/history/home.nsf/page/13b

> *The Judicial Code of 1911 (excerpted)*
> *March 3, 1911.*
> *36 Stat. 1087, 1167.*
>
> *CHAPTER THIRTEEN.*
>
> *GENERAL PROVISIONS.*
>
> *SEC. 289. The circuit courts of the United States, upon the taking effect of this Act, shall be, and hereby are, abolished; and thereupon, on said date, the clerks of said courts shall deliver to the clerks of the district courts*

---

[79] Adapted from *IRS Humbug: Weapons of Enslavement, Frank Kowalik, ISBN 0-9626552-0-1, 1991*, pp. 22-23.

of the United States for their respective districts all the journals, dockets, books, files, records, and other books and papers of or belonging to or in any manner connected with said circuit courts; and shall also on said date deliver to the clerks of said district courts all moneys, from whatever source received, then remaining in their hands or under their control as clerks of said circuit courts, or received by them by virtue of their said offices. The journals, dockets, books, files, records, and other books and papers so delivered to the clerks of the several district courts shall be and remain a part of the official records of said district courts, and copies thereof, when certified under the hand and seal of the clerk of the district court, shall be received as evidence equally with the originals thereof; and the clerks of the several district courts shall have the same authority to exercise all the powers and to perform all the duties with respect thereto as the clerks of the several circuit courts had prior to the taking effect of this Act.

SEC. 290. All suits and proceedings pending in said circuit courts on the date of the taking effect of this Act, whether originally brought therein or certified thereto from the district courts, shall thereupon and thereafter be proceeded with and disposed of in the district courts in the same manner and with the same effect as if originally begun therein, the record thereof being entered in the records of the circuit courts so transferred as above provided.

SEC. 291. Wherever, in any law not embraced within this Act, any reference is made to, or any power or duty is conferred or imposed upon, the circuit courts, such reference shall, upon the taking effect of this Act, be deemed and held to refer to, and to confer such power and impose such duty upon, the district courts.

SEC. 292. Wherever, in any law not contained within this Act, a reference is made to any law revised or embraced herein, such reference, upon the taking effect hereof, shall be construed to refer to the section of this Act into which has been carried or revised the provision of law to which reference is so made.

SEC. 293. The provisions of sections one to five, both inclusive, of the Revised Statutes, shall apply to and govern the construction of the provisions of this Act. The words "this title," wherever they occur herein, shall be construed to mean this Act.

SEC. 294. The provisions of this Act, so far as they are substantially the same as existing statutes, shall be construed as continuations thereof, and not as new enactments, and there shall be no implication of a change of intent by reason of a change of words in such statute, unless such change of intent shall be clearly manifest.

SEC. 295. The arrangement and classification of the several sections of this Act have been made for the purpose of a more convenient and orderly arrangement of the same, and therefore no inference or presumption of a legislative construction is to be drawn by reason of the chapter under which any particular section is placed.

SEC. 296. This Act may be designated and cited as "The Judicial Code."

6.8.19 1909: Corporate Excise Tax of 1909

Country's first income tax. The U.S. Supreme Court would later rule in Eisner v. Macomber, 252 U.S. 189 (1920) that the word "income" may not be defined by Congress, and that it can only be defined by the Constitution. It also ruled in the case of *Bowers v. Kerbaugh-Empire Co.*, 271 U.S. 170, 174 (1926) that:

> *"Income has been taken to mean the same thing as used in the Corporation Excise Tax Act of 1909 (36 Stat. 112) in the 16th Amendment, and in the various revenue acts subsequently passed."*
> [Bowers v. Kerbaugh-Empire Co., 271 U.S. 170, 174 (1926)]

All income tax acts under Internal Revenue Code, Subtitle A are based on the above, and are classified by the Supreme Court in *Stanton v. Baltic Mining Co., 240 U.S. 103 (1916)* as indirect taxes, which means they can only be excise taxes on privileges and may only fall on businesses and not directly on citizens:

> *"... [the 16th Amendment] conferred no new power of taxation... [and]... prohibited the ... power of income taxation possessed by Congress from the beginning from being taken out of the category of indirect taxation to which it inherently belonged..."*
> [Stanton v. Baltic Mining Co., 240 U.S. 103 (1916)]

6.8.20 1872: Office of the Assessor of Internal Revenue Eliminated

Functions of Assessor delegated to the Collector of Internal Revenue. See: 17 Statutes at Large 401, 42nd Congress, Session III Chapter XIII (December 24, 1872).

6.8.21 1862: First Tax on "Officers" of the U.S. Government[80]

The impairment of the Federal Government employee employment contracts began with the kickback program that Congress promulgated as law in the year 1862. Once the Federal Government kickback program was well established by forced acceptance, employees and employers in the private sector were forced to believe that the terms of the Federal Government employment agreements applied to them. Here is how it all happened.

Up until year 1862, Federal Government employees worked under the same kind of employment agreement as anyone who agrees to exchange their time and talent for the personal property of an employer. Then, in 1862, the Thirty-seventh Congress passed Ch. 119, 12 Stat. 472. Section 86 of that Public Law reads as follows:

> *SALARIES AND PAY OF OFFICERS AND PERSONS IN THE SERVICE OF THE UNITED STATES, AND PASSPORTS*
>
> *Sec. 86. And be it further enacted, That on and after the first day of August, eighteen hundred and sixty-two, there shall be levied, collected, and paid on all salaries of officers, or payments to persons in the civil, military, naval, or other employment or service of the United States, including senators and representatives and delegates in Congress, when exceeding the rate of six hundred dollars per annum, a duty of three per centum on the excess above the said six hundred dollars; and it shall be the duty of all paymasters and all disbursing officers, under the government of the United States, or in the employ thereof, when making any payments to officers and persons as aforesaid, or upon settling and adjusting the accounts of such officers and persons, to deduct and withhold the aforesaid duty of three percentum, and shall, at the same time, make a certificate stating the name of the officer or person from whom such deduction was made, and the amount thereof, which shall be transmitted to the office of the Commissioner of Internal Revenue, and entered as part of the internal duties; and the pay-roll, receipts, or account of officers or persons paying such duty, as aforesaid, shall be made to exhibit the fact of such payment. ...[Balance of section 86 applied to passports]*

First, you will note that it only applied to persons who received compensation for their services as an employee of the United States. Secondly, although Congress placed this into a Tax Act, and implies it is an indirect tax by the use of the word "duty," it cannot be a tax. A tax on labor would necessarily fall into the class of a direct tax that needs apportionment to be constitutional.

Note also that ***the only persons required*** to make an accounting of the kickback in section 86 were the officers who made the deductions and the Commissioner of Internal Revenue, not the Federal Government employee. As you continue to read, you will see that this is also true today.

The effect of section 86 identifies what it really is--a kickback of part of the property agreed under contract to be paid for labor of Federal Government employees [see chapter 1, footnote 3]. With this Act, the amount of compensation agreed to be paid was diminished by one party to the agreement (Congress) without the consent of the other (the Federal Government employee). A unilateral change in the employment contract of all persons then employed by the Federal Government was not legal just because Congress promulgated it as a law, and the conduct of U.S. judges proved this. The result of arranging for the withholding of 3 percent of the compensation due Federal Government employees under existing contracts was deprivation of liberty and property without due process of law, which is violative of the Fifth Amendment to the U.S. Constitution.

The facts presented above were expressed by the Supreme Court in *Pollock v. Farmers' Loan & Trust Co.*, 157 U.S. 429 (1895), where they said:

> *Subsequently, in 1869, and during the administration of President Grant, when Mr. Boutwell was Secretary of the Treasury and Mr. Hoar, of Massachusetts, was Attorney General, there were in several of the statutes of the United States, for the assessment and collection of internal revenue, provisions for taxing the salaries of all civil officers of the United States, which included, in their literal application, the salaries of the President and of the judges of the United States. The question arose whether the law which imposes such a tax upon them was constitutional. The opinion of the Attorney General thereon was requested by the Secretary of the Treasury. The Attorney General, in reply, gave an elaborate opinion advising the Secretary of the Treasury that **no income tax could be lawfully assessed and collected upon the salaries of those officers who were in office at the time the statute imposing the tax was passed,** holding on this subject the views expressed by Chief Justice Taney. His opinion is published in volume XIII of the Opinions of the Attorneys General, at page 161. I am informed that it has been followed ever since without question by the department supervising or directing the collection of the public revenue. [emphasis added]*

---

[80] Adapted from *IRS Humbug: Weapons of Enslavement*, Frank Kowalik, ISBN 0-9626552-0-1, 1991, pp. 18-21.

This "kickback" program illegally forced a 3 percent debt obligation upon Federal Government employees working under an existing employment agreement in 1862. However, the "kickback program" established by section 86 was legal when applied to the salary of persons who took employment with the Federal Government after that Act was passed because they were on notice that a 3 percent kickback was part of their employment agreement. Thus illegal and legal kickbacks existed then and, though they have changed in form, they exist today.

"Kickback" is defined in Webster's Dictionary as "a return of a part of a sum received often because of confidential agreement or coercion." Was not a "kickback" coerced from Federal Government employees when Congress promulgated a change in their employment agreement as if it were a tax when, in essence, it was, and is, a kickback program?

By presenting the "kickback" program in the form of "law," Congress (the legislative branch of government) provided the implied authority of law needed to get Federal Government employees in the executive branch of government (the IRS) to act illegally in depriving other Federal Government employees of property rightfully due them under existing contracts.

U.S. Supreme Court Judges understood this, and were legally and morally obligated to correct any illegal action of Congress or the IRS for all Federal government employees. The primary function of the Supreme Court is to provide opinions of public importance. Instead they chose, by misdirection and silence, to cooperate with Congress in the implementation of this kickback which forced a debt obligation upon all Federal Government employees except U.S. judges and the U.S. President. This was accomplished when Federal judges allowed the contracts of fellow Federal Government employees to be illegally impaired while seeing to it that their employment contracts remained intact. Does not such conduct demonstrate that the U.S. judges were partial to assuring that the illegal kickback scheme was implemented? Does not such indifference and cooperation violate their duty? Does their conduct not raise the question of concealment?[81]

6.9 Treasury/ IRS Cover-Ups, Obfuscation, and Scandals

> "The king establishes the land by justice,
> But he who receives bribes overthrows it."
> [Prov. 28:29, Bible, NKJV]
>
> "He who is greedy for gain troubles his own house,
> But he who hates bribes will live."
> [Prov. 15:27, Bible, NKJV]
>
> "There is never a wrong time to do the right thing."
> [Family Guardian Fellowship]

As we established in section **Error! Reference source not found.**, the Treasury Secretary, for whom the IRS Commissioner works, has NO lawful delegated authority to collect income taxes in the 50 union states. Below are some examples of illegal and unethical acts of extortion committed in the name of the Treasury Secretary in the absence of any legal authority to impose or enforce such income taxes.

---

[81] The U.S. Supreme Court said in *Boyd v. U.S.*, 116 U.S. 616 (1885) "...it is the duty of the courts to be watchful for the constitutional rights of the citizens, and against stealthy encroachment thereon."

"NO, WE HAVE NOTHING TO HIDE... WHY?"

6.9.1 Elements of the IRS Cover-Up/Conspiracy to Watch For

Here are a few things to watch out for as you see history being made by legislators and the IRS in the future relative to the income tax issue. These are the kinds of things that should clearly evidence to you that the IRS is part of a massive conspiracy to defraud U.S. citizens of their income by fooling them into thinking that income taxes are mandatory for citizens domiciled in the 50 union states with domestic income:

1. **IRS will refuse to answer questions about the following:**
    1.1 "What specific statute in either the U.S. Code (Internal Revenue Code), or the Code of Federal Regulations, makes me as a U.S. Citizen domiciled in the 50 union states and receiving nothing but income from within the 50 union states liable for paying taxes on that income?"
    1.2 "Please define what you mean by voluntary compliance?".
    1.3 IRS will not respond to invitations by tax freedom groups to discuss the legality of the income tax. This happened recently at a very public meeting where congress, the president, and the IRS were invited to attend. ALL declined! This was documented on the following website of a group called "We the People": http://www.givemeliberty.org/
    1.4 The IRS will refuse to define the term "United States" because then they would have to admit that the Internal Revenue Code doesn't apply in the 50 contiguous states to your average citizen who is by default NOT a federal/U.S.** citizen or government employee.
2. **IRS will try to manipulate the litigation of cases involving the issues raised in this document, including the 861/source issue by:**
    2.1 Keeping these cases in the U.S. Tax Court, where there is only one judge and no jury. It is easier to bribe or influence one judge rather than a whole jury.

- 2.2 Keeping these cases out of Federal Circuit courts where there might be juries, to avoid the risk of losing. They will do this by either fining individuals who raise the issue (violating the First Amendment right to free speech), or by encouraging the court to dismiss the case (motion to dismiss).
- 2.3 Keeping these cases out of the Supreme Court, because litigating them could shut down income taxes permanently and deprive the government of revenues. They will do this by either fining individuals who raise the issue (violating the First Amendment right to free speech), or by encouraging the court to dismiss the case, or by litigating so fiercely that the average Citizen can't afford the legal fees required to get their case to the Supreme Court level.
- 2.4 Abusing due process of litigants to the maximum extent possible by depriving them early on in their fight of financial resources needed to litigate the case to the Supreme Court. They will do this by seizing or levying the wages of tax freedom fighters as quickly as possible, rather than waiting till the end of litigation.
- 2.5 Doing complete tax background checks of any persons who act as jurors in these tax trials, to ensure that they choose only jurors who are ignorant of the Internal Revenue Code, have faithfully paid their "voluntary taxes", and who have contempt for people who don't. They need social security numbers to do this, so if you are acting as a juror in one of these trials, we strongly suggest that you NOT provide your social security number to anyone, because it is strictly voluntary. See section 2.9.19.1 of the *Tax Fraud Prevention Manual*, Form #06.008 entitled "Stacking the Deck During Jury Selection".
3. **Discovery Abuses**. Discovery is the process during tax litigation in which information is requested by a party to a legal action from the other side. Here are some of the ways you can expect the IRS to execute discovery abuse to cover up the conspiratorial nature of hiding the truth about the fact that income taxes are voluntary:
   - 3.1 Covering up truths about the voluntary nature of tax cases by requesting "protective orders" to oppress plaintiff citizens as part of the discover process who are serving requests for admissions and interrogatories on the IRS.
   - 3.2 Requesting that evidence related to the voluntary nature of income taxes be sealed and kept secret and only available to the court but not other individuals or citizens. This will prevent the truth from getting out about the voluntary nature of income taxes.
4. **IRS will try to get tax freedom organizations and individuals in trouble by:**
   - 4.1 Subsidizing "Tax Freedom" organizations to act as their operatives in attracting individuals and then giving them *bad advice* to get them into trouble. Remember that the IRS collects interest and penalties on back taxes if it can catch people "cheating" on taxes. Of course, we all now know that most citizens don't owe income taxes, but that never stopped the IRS from demagoguery, grand-standing, and avoiding legal issues in the presentation of their case in front of juries. CAVEAT EMPTOR!
   - 4.2 Paying their operative cronies to publish bogus books that tell tax freedom fighters the *wrong* methods to get out of income taxes as an inexpensive and ineffective way to have more people to make into examples to scare the rest of us into "voluntary compliance".
5. **IRS will try to confuse tax freedom groups who are focusing on the issues raised in this document**. For example, http://www.egroups.com/ has a group called "legality-of-income-tax" that is enlightening for people who are looking for tools and information to end their income tax. IRS agents regularly join into these groups anonymously and try to criticize and obfuscate the participants to keep themselves out of trouble.
6. **IRS will subsidize newspapers to slander individuals who legally stop paying income taxes**. For instance, read the article in section 9.3.1 by the New York Times. It was completely biased and didn't talk about the law at all. Even if the IRS didn't pay for this add, the secretive bankers at the Federal Reserve have more than enough reason to subsidize this in order to keep their interest payments on the national debt coming in.
7. **They will not maintain a historian position or will fire or retaliate against any historians who become whistleblowers to expose past cover-ups.**
8. **They will post confusing, misleading, and incomplete information on their website** at http://www.irs.gov/ about the voluntary nature of income taxes for citizens living and working in the 50 union states. For instance, look up the term "voluntary compliance" if you want some lawyer weasel words to obfuscate yourself with. Below is their definition of "voluntary compliance" from http://www.irs.gov/prod/taxi/taxterms.html - V:

> *"Your mom might order you to clean up your room. Well, the IRS doesn't have time to tell every single taxpayer to file taxes correctly and on time . . . there are millions of taxpayers in this country after all. This system relies on citizens to report their income, calculate tax liability and file tax returns on time. Everyone's gotta grow up sometime. Check out It's Payday! "*

9. There have been cover-ups over the years as the Internal Revenue Codes have been craftily modified to maximize their "confusion factor" and legalese content so that only legislators can understand them. As these laws have been "obfuscated" over the years, the IRS has systematically tried to cover its tracks by concealing the older laws, which are written much more clearly to state that income taxes are voluntary. Consequently, you can be sure that the IRS:

9.1 Would not want to keep any records of the old laws that citizens could use to show that they indeed don't owe income tax.
9.2 Would not want to make the older laws computer searchable.
9.3 Would not want to designate anyone to be a historian for the organization who could compile these old laws and publications. As a matter of fact, the IRS fired the only historian they had! Did she uncover the truth when she was compiling the archives to post on the website and tried to get the word out? Was she regarded as a "whistleblower"?

If you have heard of any of the above types of tactics by the IRS, please let us know so we can get the word out immediately and post the information on our website!

6.9.2 26 C.F.R. 1.0-1: Publication of Internal Revenue Code WITHOUT Index

The Dept. of the Treasury is responsible for writing most implementing regulations relating to federal income taxes. The first thing you notice about the Internal Revenue Code (I.R.C.) in the very first section is the information contained in its implementing regulation in 26 C.F.R. §1.0-1. This implementing regulation describes how the Internal Revenue Code is to be published by the government for consumption by the general public.

> *Sec. 1.0-1 Internal Revenue Code of 1954 and regulations.*
>
> *(b) Publication.*
>
> ***This Act shall be published*** *as volume 68A of the United States Statutes at Large, with a comprehensive table of contents and an appendix; but **without an index or marginal references**. The date of enactment, bill number, public law number, and chapter number, shall be printed as a headnote.*

The Internal Revenue Code itself is 9,500 pages, and publishment of anything that large *without* an index would deliberately create a situation for the public and the legal profession where it would be *very difficult* to find anything relevant to any subject of inquiry. This means that you can't order the code from the U.S. government printing office that has an index. How many commercial book vendors do you think would publish ANY book that large without an index? Their book wouldn't sell very many copies! If you want an index, then you have to order the publication from a private third party.

We would argue that devious act *deliberately obfuscates the tax code* and makes it much more difficult for most Americans to either read or understand the law. The lawyers in Congress want it that way because that is how they perpetuate the legal "priesthood" that maintains their power. They want to make it so people need special research tools and published sources for the code available only to legal professionals in order to locate information relevant to their inquiry. That way, ordinary citizens will be encouraged to read third party publications like the IRS' fraudulent publications in order to understand the tax code, and as we point out in section 3.19, these publications contain deliberate fraud. We expose this legal priesthood later in section 6.12 where we talk about the judicial conspiracy to protect the income tax and section 6.13, where we talk about legal profession scandals to protect the income tax.

The above regulation, by the way, violates an Act of Congress, which states in the Statutes at Large, 42nd Congress, Volume 17, Ch. 315, p. 258, Section 45. Unless the below act was repealed, the Secretary of the Treasury exceeded his authority to specify that the Internal Revenue Code should be published *without* an index:

> *"That the Secretary of the Treasury is hereby authorized and directed to revise and prepare for publication the internal-revenue laws in force after the passage of this act, with amendments incorporated in their proper places, conveniently arranged for reference, and with a proper index..."*
> *[Statutes at Large, 42nd Congress, Volume 17, Ch. 315, p. 258, Section 45]*

If you want a version of the code that includes an index, you can order a very nice one with an index and colored tabs for use in an audit or due process hearing from Irwin Schiff's website at:

http://www.paynoincometax.com/:

The cost is $38. Irwin sells the I.R.C. published by:

Research Institute of America (RIA)

800-950-1216
http://www.riahome.com

If you buy the latest edition of the above commercial version of the Internal Revenue Code and you examine the extensive index under "liability for tax", which is almost one page long by itself, you will see LOTS of entries. The January 2001 version of the code has this portion on page 201. Guess what? *If you look up "income taxes" or "citizen" or "American", you will not find a single entry*. Now do you understand why the Treasury directed that the I.R.C. not be published with an index? This is a very powerful argument to use in court, and the court and the Treasury sometimes will respond to this argument by making such excuses as:

> "Well, this commercial publisher is not a trusted source of information so your evidence isn't credible. Only government sources are credible."

And of course, there IS no government source that would ever publish such information because it is simply too incriminating! Wow!

6.9.3 Official/Qualified Immunity and Anonymity

> "**Counsel for the claimant,...makes a very ingenious argument... That the maxim of English constitutional law, that the king can do no wrong, is one which the courts must apply to the government of the United States, and that therefore there can be no tort committed by the government.....**
>
> *It is not easy to see how the first proposition can not have any place in our system of government.*
>
> *We have no king to whom it can be applied. The President, in the exercise of the executive functions, bears a nearer resemblance to the limited monarch of the English government than any other branch of our government, and is the only individual to whom it could possibly have any relation. It cannot apply to him, because the Constitution admits that he may do wrong, and has provided a means for his trial for wrongdoing,... by the proceeding of impeachment.*
>
> *It is to be observed that the English maxim does not declare that the government, or those who administer it, can do no wrong; for it is a part of the principle itself that wrong may be done by the government power, for which the ministry, for the time being, is held responsible; and the ministers personally, like our President, may be impeached; or, if the wrong amounts to a crime, they may be indicted and tried at law for the offense.*
>
> **We do not understand that either in reference to the government of the United States, or to the several States, or of any of their officers, the English maxim has an existence in this country.**"
> [*Langford v. U.S.*, 101 U.S. 341, 3423 (1879).]

Why do IRS agents get away with so many violations of due process with immunity? The answer is that they are protected from prosecution by our federal courts under the contemporary doctrine of "sovereign immunity". As you can tell by the quote above from the U.S. Supreme Court back in 1879, support for sovereign immunity was not always endorsed by the courts. As these courts have become corrupted over the years in the process of expanding and upholding the income very tax that pays their salaries, the corrupt black-robed lawyers in these courts have had to contradict historical precedent by protecting especially those who enforce and administer the income tax from personal liability for criminal wrongdoing and lawlessness. Below is an explanation of how agents of the government are insulated and protected from legal liability for wrongdoing:

1. According to one IRS revenue agent we spoke with IRS agents are told by their management that they are not allowed to reveal their first name, only their employee number. Without the full name and identifying information about the employee, it is more difficult to figure out who to serve with legal papers if you want to prosecute individual agents.

2. The IRS service bureaus for specific regions are usually located outside of the jurisdiction of the state they serve. For instance, Ogden Utah services large parts of California. Why isn't the service bureau for California inside of California? We would argue it is because that makes it much more difficult to personally serve agents who have broken the law or to prosecute them under the laws of your state, because they don't live in your state. Citizens who want to sue IRS agents or criminally prosecute them have to go outside of their state to serve the agent, which is much more difficult to coordinate, costly, and expensive.

3. The U.S. supreme Court has upheld the notion that persons acting as agents for the U.S. government have at least a limited immunity from prosecution because of illegal, unethical, or questionable acts they commit while on duty. This

is called *official immunity*. As we talked about in section 5.12 of the *Tax Fraud Prevention Manual*, Form #06.006 entitled "How the Federal Judiciary Stole the Right to Petition: Judicial Arrogance and Bias Against the Right to Petition", the federal judiciary has also for all intents and purposes destroyed our right to petition the government for redress of grievances and wrongs committed either by agents working for the government or by the government itself. One also cannot sue the U.S. government without their consent, and this is called judicial immunity or sovereign immunity. Why would they give their consent if you sued them for wrongful taking of federal income taxes? All of these factors conspire to make it very difficult if not impossible for the average sovereign American of the several states to protect his/her constitutional rights.

Below is a quote from the U.S. supreme Court on the subject of the types of *official immunity* in the case of *Nevada v. Hicks*, No. 99-1994 (U.S. 06/25/2001):

> "The doctrines of official immunity, see, e.g., Westfall v. Erwin, 484 U.S. 292, 296-300 (1988), and qualified immunity, see, e.g., Harlow v. Fitzgerald, 457 U.S. 800, 813-819 (1982), are designed to protect state and federal officials from civil liability for conduct that was within the scope of their duties or conduct that did not violate clearly established law. These doctrines short circuit civil litigation for officials who meet these standards so that these officials are not subjected to the costs of trial or the burdens of discovery. 457 U. S., at 817-818. For example, the Federal Employees Liability Reform and Tort Compensation Act of 1988, commonly known as the Westfall Act, allows the United States to substitute itself for a federal employee as defendant upon certifying that the employee was acting within the scope of his duties. 28 U.S.C. §2679(d). Nevada law contains analogous provisions. See Nev. Rev. Stat. §§41.032, 41.0335-41.0339 (1996 and Supp. 1999). The employee who successfully claims official immunity therefore invokes the immunity of the sovereign. When a state or federal official asserts qualified immunity, he claims that his actions were reasonable in light of clearly established law. Anderson v. Creighton, 483 U.S. 635 (1987). In those cases, we allow that official to take an immediate interlocutory appeal from an adverse ruling to ensure that the civil proceedings do not continue if immunity should be granted. Mitchell v. Forsyth, 472 U.S. 511, 524-530 (1985)."

> *[Nevada v. Hicks, No. 99-1994] (U.S. 06/25/2001)*

Below is a quote from the U.S. supreme Court on the subject of *official immunity* in the case of " *Westfall Et Al. v. Erwin Et Ux.*, 484 U.S. 292 (1988):

> "In Barr v. Matteo, 360 U.S. 564 (1959), and Howard v. Lyons, 360 U.S. 593 (1959), this Court held that the scope of absolute official immunity afforded federal employees is a matter of federal law, "to be formulated by the courts in the absence of legislative action by Congress." Id., at 597. The purpose of such official immunity is not to protect an erring official, but to insulate the decisionmaking process from the harassment of prospective litigation. The provision of immunity rests on the view that the threat of liability will make federal officials unduly timid in carrying out their official duties, and that effective government will be promoted if officials are freed of the costs of vexatious and often frivolous damages suits. See Barr v. Matteo, supra, at 571; Doe v. McMillan, 412 U.S. 306, 319 (1973). This Court always has recognized, however, that official immunity comes at a great cost. An injured party with an otherwise meritorious tort claim is denied compensation simply because he had the misfortune to be injured by a federal official. Moreover, absolute immunity contravenes the basic tenet that individuals be held accountable for their wrongful conduct. We therefore have held that absolute immunity for federal officials is justified only when "the contributions of immunity to effective government in particular contexts outweigh the perhaps recurring harm to individual citizens." Doe v. McMillan, supra, at 320.

And finally, below is a description of *qualified immunity* from the u.S. supreme Court in the case of *Harlow Et Al. v. Fitzgerald*, 457 U.S. 800 (1982):

> "Government officials whose special functions or constitutional status requires complete protection from suits for damages -- including certain officials of the Executive Branch, such as prosecutors and similar officials, see Butz v. Economou, 438 U.S. 478, and the President, Nixon v. Fitzgerald, ante, p. 731 -- are entitled to the defense of absolute immunity. However, executive officials in general are usually entitled to only qualified or good-faith immunity. The recognition of a qualified immunity defense for high executives reflects an attempt to balance competing values: not only the importance of a damages remedy to protect the rights of citizens, but also the need to protect officials who are required to exercise discretion and the related public interest in encouraging the vigorous exercise of official authority. Scheuer v. Rhodes, 416 U.S. 232. Federal officials seeking absolute immunity from personal liability for unconstitutional conduct must bear the burden of showing that public policy requires an exemption of that scope. Pp. 806-808."

6.9.4 Church Censorship, Manipulation, and Castration by the IRS

Churches are moral and social organizations. A big component of morality is social responsibility. However, the IRS has twisted the arms of churches by being empowered to pull their 501(c) tax exemption if they engage in socially responsible activities, such as eliminating bad laws, changing the laws, or advocating or opposing specific candidates for political office.

This effectively neutralizes any negative impact churches might have on the IRS, for instance, by advocating elimination of income taxes, like Jesus did (see section 1.10.1 entitled "Jesus Christ, The Son of God, was a Tax Protester!"). It also eliminates the possibility that churches will either sponsor or endorse godly men of principle for public office. Is it any wonder then why our politicians are so corrupt? This is a travesty and a disgrace. What good does it do to have free speech if you can't exercise it in the most important realm, which is the political and legislative realm? We would argue that under such circumstances, churches really don't have free speech.

IRS Publication 557, *Tax Exempt Status for Your Organization*, discusses the conditions under which churches can be tax-exempt. The Internal Revenue Manual (IRM) section 7.25.3, entitled "Religious, Charitable, Educational, Etc. Organizations" discusses how to qualify as an exempt church organization. The website below is where you can read this section:

http://www.irs.gov/irm/part7/ch10s03.html

The below excerpt from the IRM establishes a federal tax exemption for religious organizations:

> *[7.25.3] 3.6 (02-23-1999)*
> *Religion or Advancement of Religion*
>
> *IRC 501(c)(3) provides for the exemption of organizations organized and operated exclusively for "religious" purposes. Because activities often serve more than one purpose, an organization that is "advancing religion" within the meaning of Reg. 1.501(c)(3)-1(d)(2) may also qualify under IRC 501(c)(3) as charitable or educational organization.*

Below is an excerpt from the IRM that determines the conditions under which a church will LOSE its tax exemption:

> *Internal Revenue Manual*
> *[7.25.3] 3.3.4 (02-23-1999)*
> *Express Powers that Cause Failure of Organizational Test*
>
> *1. An organization does not meet the organizational test if its articles expressly empower it:*
>
>   *A. To devote more than an insubstantial part of its activities to influence legislation by propaganda or otherwise (Reg. 1.501(c)(3)-1(b)(3)(i));*
>
>   *B. Directly or indirectly to participate in, or intervene in (including the publishing or distributing of statements), any political campaign on behalf of or in opposition to any candidate for public office (Reg. 1.501(c)(3)-1 (b)(3)(ii));*
>
>   *C. To have objectives and to engage in activities which characterize it as an "action" organization (Reg. 1.501(c)(3)-1 (b)(3)(iii));*
>
>   *D. To carry on any other activities (unless they are insubstantial) which are not in furtherance of one or more exempt purposes (Reg. 1.501(c)(3)-1(b)(1)(i)(a)).*

In the IRS Regulations, 26 C.F.R. §1.501(c)(3)(ii), churches are prohibited from being action organizations:

> *(3) Action organizations. (i) An organization is not operated exclusively for one or more exempt purposes if it is an action organization as defined in subdivisions (ii), (iii), or (iv) of this subparagraph.*
>
> *(ii) An organization is an action organization if a substantial part of its activities is attempting to influence legislation by propaganda or otherwise. For this purpose, an organization will be regarded as attempting to influence legislation if the organization:*
>
> *(a) Contacts, or urges the public to contact, members of a legislative body for the purpose of proposing, supporting, or opposing legislation; or*
>
> *(b) Advocates the adoption or rejection of legislation.*

The implications of the above amount to silencing the churches in the political and legislative realm. This in effect completely neutralizes them and violates their First Amendment Right of Free speech. The federal courts, according to the IRS in their IRM, said this was *not* the case, which has made a travesty of justice, as indicated in the below excerpt from the IRM:

[7.25.3] 3.6.2 (02-23-1999)
Compliance with Statutory Requirements

1. Any religious organization, including a church, must satisfy the statutory requirements to be exempt under IRC 501(c)(3). As explained by the court in Christian Echos National Ministry. Inc. v. United States , 470 F.2d. 849 (10th Cir. 1972), cert . den ., 414 U.S. 864 (1973), in which the court upheld denial of tax exemption to a religious organization engaged in substantial legislative activity, **"[i]n light of the fact that tax exemption is a matter of grace rather than right, we hold that the limitations contained in Section 501(c)(3) withholding exemption from nonprofit corporations [that engage in substantial lobbying] do not deprive Christian Echoes of its constitutionally guaranteed right of free speech. The taxpayer may engage in all such activities without restraint, subject, however, to withholding of the exemption, or, in the alternative, the taxpayer may refrain from such activities and obtain the privilege of exemption."**

2. Exemption from state or local taxation is neither conclusive nor relevant to the determination whether an organization is operated exclusively for religious purposes under federal tax law. Universal Life Church v. U.S. , 721 U.S.T.C. 9467 (E.D. Cal. 1972).

Did you notice the above statement: "**[i]n light of the fact that tax exemption is a matter of grace rather than right, we hold that the limitations contained in Section 501(c)(3) withholding exemption from nonprofit corporations [that engage in substantial lobbying] do not deprive Christian Echoes of its constitutionally guaranteed right of free speech.**". *This is a devious tactic to make First Amendment religious rights into government privileges*. They are a privilege if they can be taken away arbitrarily by a government bureaucrat. We discuss this in section 4.3.12 "Government-instituted slavery using 'privileges'." We will repeat what we have said before in section 4.2.2 about rights in the Supreme Court case of *Harman v. Forssenius*, 380 U.S 528 at 540, 85 S.Ct. 1177, 1185 (1965):

> "It has long been established that a State may not impose a penalty upon those who exercise a right guaranteed by the Constitution." Frost & Frost Trucking Co. v. Railroad Comm'n of California, 271 U.S. 583. "Constitutional rights would be of little value if they could be indirectly denied,' Smith v. Allwright, 321 U.S. 649, 644, or manipulated out of existence,' Gomillion v. Lightfoot, 364 U.S. 339, 345."
> [Harman v. Forssenius, 380 U.S 528 at 540, 85 S.Ct. 1177, 1185 (1965)]

The above situation also applies to the federal government. We assert that removing a tax exemption as a penalty for exercising exercise a First Amendment right is unconstitutional because transforms *freedom of religion* from being a *right* into a *government-granted privilege*. The supreme Court has in effect legislated making a First Amendment right into a government privilege that can be taken away with their ruling, which courts are not supposed to be doing. Removal of tax exemptions because of political views or activities amounts to political persecution and censorship of the freedom of religious rights and speech of people attending churches and the churches themselves. Is it any wonder why churches have become silent on government abuses and violations of laws and the reforming of our laws? This kind of tyranny must end!

If you have done your homework and read Chapter 5, you know enough to explain how the Supreme Court and the IRS can get away with this kind of tyranny. We concluded in that chapter that Subtitle A income taxes are voluntary for natural persons. The only people who are "taxpayers" liable for tax are those who volunteer. Since they volunteered, then technically, the IRS isn't interfering with the exercise of First Amendment rights because the consequence of volunteering to become "taxpayers" is that they have no rights. It's their own fault for not knowing this, and do you think the Supreme Court would share this subtle fact with anyone? In effect what the Supreme Court said in Christian Echos National Ministry. Inc. v. United States , 470 F.2d. 849 (10th Cir. 1972), cert . den ., 414 U.S. 864 (1973) is similar to the following:

> "You *volunteered* to marry your spouse, so don't come whining to us that she is infringing on your First Amendment free speech rights by telling you she wants a divorce because you told her she is fat!"

Funny! Because of the above type of censorship being imposed by the IRS and the Supreme Court against churches and other charitable organizations, if reform is going to come of our income tax system, then it will need to come either from outside the churches and based on volunteer efforts, or it we will need to educate the churches about this book so that they understand that they don't have to pay taxes and therefore need not worry about losing their tax exemption. Those churches who can't be convinced of their nonliability to pay income taxes but who still wish to politically protest income taxes will need to take a different approach as shown below:

Church officers should pursue political activity as individuals during their own off-duty time and when they are not acting as an officer or agent of the church.
1. Church facilities or computers should not be used to do solicitation or political lobbying. Instead, members of the church should donate their own time and computers for the purpose instead.

2. If officers or agents of the church get up on the pulpit during a meeting, the pastor should say that he has no position on what the party is saying and does not necessarily advocate what he/she is saying, but wanted to offer that person an opportunity to speak about an issue he isn't familiar with.
3. Churches can offer to their congregations a section in their handouts for public announcements and then disclaim any association or affiliation with the people making the announcements. These announcements can list times to coordinate political activities or educational or fund-raising events to take political action.

6.9.5 Illegal Treasury Regulation 26 C.F.R. §301.6331-1

Treasury regulation 26 C.F.R. §301.6331 implements 26 U.S.C. §6331. Recall that the scope of a regulation may not exceed that of the statute it implements. Recall that 26 U.S.C. §6331(a) states:

> *(a) Authority of Secretary*
>
> *If any person liable to pay any tax neglects or refuses to pay the same within 10 days after notice and demand, it shall be lawful for the Secretary to collect such tax (and such further sum as shall be sufficient to cover the expenses of the levy) by levy upon all property and rights to property (except such property as is exempt under section 6334) belonging to such person or on which there is a lien provided in this chapter for the payment of such tax.* ***Levy may be made upon the accrued salary or wages of any officer, employee, or elected official, of the United States, the District of Columbia, or any agency or instrumentality of the United States or the District of Columbia, by serving a notice of levy on the employer (as defined in section 3401(d)) of such officer, employee, or elected official.*** *If the Secretary makes a finding that the collection of such tax is in jeopardy, notice and demand for immediate payment of such tax may be made by the Secretary and, upon failure or refusal to pay such tax, collection thereof by levy shall be lawful without regard to the 10-day period provided in this section.*

The purpose for this regulation is clear. It allows federal government employers to request that the agency employing a federal employee may withhold their wages for nonpayment of income taxes without the need for a court order. This also explains why under 26 U.S.C. §6331(e) allows for continuous levies upon federal wages without a court order even though this would otherwise violate the Fifth Amendment due process rights of the person levied upon. The process described in 26 U.S.C. §6331 is usually implemented using the IRS Form 668-A "Notice of Levy". However, the Notice of Levy may *not* be used against *private* employers or those who are not federal employers and instead requires a legal action and a corresponding court order before the levy may be instituted. The IRS very commonly and illegally misuses the "Notice of Levy form" against private employers, in part because the implementing regulation *illegally expands* the scope of the statute in 26 C.F.R. §301.6331-1 as follows:

> *"Levy may be made by serving a notice of levy on any person in possession of, or obligated with respect to, property or rights to property subject to levy, including receivables, bank accounts, evidences of debt, securities, and salaries, wages, commissions, or other compensation."*

The regulation should say that it only applies to federal employers, since the persons to be levied upon under 26 U.S.C. §6331(a) are only federal employees. Private employers who are not part of the federal government can safely disregard both the IRS Form 668A and 668B forms and only surrender property of their employees when they receive a valid court order. This is confirmed by the Legal Reference Guide for Revenue Officers, [MT 58[10][0]-14, Internal Revenue Service, which states in pertinent part:

> *332 (10-29-79)*
>
> *Constitutional Limitations*
>
> *(1) During the course of administratively collecting a tax, an occasion may arise where service of a levy or notice of levy is not adequate to seize property of the taxpayer. However,* ***it cannot be emphasized too strongly that constitutional guarantees and individual rights must not be violated. Property should not be forceably removed from the person of a taxpayer. Such conduct may expose a revenue officer to an action in trespass, assault and battery, conversion, etc. Larson v. Domestic and foreign Commerce Corp., 337 U.S. 682 (1949), rehearing denied, 337 U.S. 682 (1949). Maule Industries v. Tomlinson, 224 F.2d. 897, (5th Cir. 1949). If there is reason to suspect a failure to honor a notice of levy or an interference with levy, the matter should be referred for proper legal action against the offending party.*** *Remedies available to the Government, as contained in the Code and other statutes, are more than adequate to cope with the problem.*

The IRS also conveniently removes 26 U.S.C. §6331(a) from the back of the IRS Form 668-A(c)DO to hide the fact from private employers that they have no authority to demand property. It is only the ignorance of third party private employers and financial institutions that allows the IRS to seize assets through force using the "Notice of Levy" that they otherwise could not have gotten.

6.9.6 IRS Trickery on the 1040 Form to Get Us Inside the Federal Zone

For the purposes of the federal income tax we can lawfully be treated by the national government as though we were a "resident" (which is an alien) of the federal zone by actually being domiciled in the federal zone or by electing to be treated as though we do as a "person" married to a "U.S. citizen" pursuant to 26 U.S.C. §6013(g) and (h). When we file a 1040 income tax form without attaching an IRS Form 2555, for instance, we are fraudulently telling the federal government that we are an alien domiciled in the federal zone, insofar as the Internal Revenue Code is concerned, because we are claiming to be a "resident" of the U.S., which is to say from 26 U.S.C. §7701(a)(9) that we live in the District of Columbia or some other federal territory or part of the "federal zone" and that we are an "alien" as defined in 26 U.S.C. §7701(b)(1)(A). Why would we want to elect to be treated as an alien domiciled in the District of Columbia (federal zone) when there is absolutely no advantage to doing so on our tax forms? The only reason is because we have been tricked by our own government because of our own ignorance of the law into using the legally incorrect words and definitions they put in the IRS publications and on the 1040 form itself, which prominently says "U.S. Individual income tax return", which means we live in the U.S. (the District of Columbia). This fraud is encouraged and allowed to propagate because the IRS in its publications and especially in the 1040 booklet, never clarifies the three definitions of United States (see Hooven & Allison Co. v. Evatt, 324 U.S. 652 (1945), where we learned the three definitions of "United States") or which of the three we are using when we prepare the tax return.

Technically, as people domiciled outside the federal zone and inside the 50 union states, we live in the U.S.A. but NOT in the [federal] U.S**. for the purposes of the income tax, so we are already committing a fraud when we file the 1040 form and sign it under penalty of perjury. Do you think our own dishonest government would ever point that out when it advantages them financially in such a significant way? Pitman Buck, Jr. has written an entire book about this subject called *The Colossal Fraud of "Involuntary Perjury"*.

An interesting way to view this fraud is that it is an enticement into (financial) slavery, which violates 18 U.S.C. §1583, entitled "Enticement into slavery". 18 U.S.C. §1581 also prohibits arresting or apprehending anyone into slavery, which is exactly what the federal marshal does when they arrest someone who is convicted of a federal tax crime for cases in which they technically are not in actuality liable for any tax, but for which the court refuses to apply the law correctly. Such cases might occur, for instance, when the judge knows the accused is not liable for tax and knows the correct application of the Internal Revenue Code but because the accused did not address it or express his understanding of the law correctly, the judge sides with the government so that the tax system would not be undermined and so that his judgeship would not be terminated by the irate President or Congress who appointed him for "bad behavior".

6.9.7 IRS Form 1040: Irrational Conspiracy to Violate Rights

Many of the same arguments that as we present below in section 6.9.8 about the violations of our Constitutional rights with the IRS Form W-4 apply to the IRS Form 1040 as well. We won't repeat those arguments here, except to say that being compelled in any way to either submit or to sign a 1040 form violates our First Amendment right to NOT communicate with our government, our Fourth Amendment right to the privacy of our personal papers and effects (of which we could classify our tax returns and financial records as falling into the category of personal papers and effects), and our Fifth Amendment right to due process in the taking of our property and to not incriminate ourselves. All we have to prove in order to justify the conclusion that there are violations of rights is to demonstrate that there is any kind of penalty, compulsion, or punishment by the government for exercising these rights. Below are some of the possible statutory penalties imposed for exercising our right not to file a tax return, and these penalties are imposed as a result of statutes developed by the U.S. Congress and prosecuted by the Department of Justice.

Table 6-4: Unconstitutional IRS/Treasury Regulations Relating to form 1040

Statute	Condition when 5th Amendment is violated	Notes

26 U.S.C. §6702	Frivolous Income Tax Return	If the First and Fifth Amendments say you can't be compelled submit a return or testify against yourself in the return, then why can they criminally prosecute you for filling out a frivolous return, including one with no signature, a modified jurat statement above the signature, or incomplete or inaccurate information?
26 U.S.C. §7203	Willful failure to file return, supply information, or pay tax	If the First and Fifth Amendments say you can't be compelled to submit a return or to testify against yourself in the return, then why can the DOJ criminally prosecute you for not filing one and throw you in jail?
26 U.S.C. §7206	Fraud and false statements	If the First and Fifth Amendments say you can't be compelled submit a return or testify against yourself in the return, then why can they criminally prosecute you for what you do choose to say on the form without compulsion, as long as you don't represent that it is true or accurate by signing it?

The fact that the U.S. Congress wrote these statutes and the fact that they were debated, discussed, and voted on before they were passed makes theses statutes a "conspiracy against rights" under 18 U.S.C. Sec. 241, punishable by a fine or imprisonment not more than ten years, or both!

Consider the purpose of § 6702 of the Internal Revenue Code as stated by the appellate court in *Gary Holder v. Secretary of the Treasury*, 791 F.2d. 68, 72 (7th Cir. 1986), when an individual is penalized $500 under § 6702 for failing or refusing — based upon his belief that he is not liable for income taxes — to sign the Form 1040 jurat. The jurat reads:

> "Under penalties of perjury, I declare that I have examined this return and accompanying schedules and statements, and to the best of my knowledge and belief, they are true, correct, and complete."

Here is what the court in **Holder** said was the purpose of imposing a penalty under § 6702:

> "The purpose of §§ 6673 and 6702, like the purpose of Rules 11 and 38 and of § 1927, is to induce litigants to conform their behavior to the governing rules regardless of their subjective beliefs."

But hold on there, your honors! One of the governing rules is §7206 of the Internal Revenue Code, a rule whose purpose is to affect or regulate behavior by prohibiting perjury. Section 7206 reads:

> "Any person who- ... Willfully makes and subscribes any return, statement, or other document, which contains or is verified by a written declaration that it is made under the penalties of perjury, and which he does not believe to be true and correct as to every material matter ... shall be guilty of a felony and, upon conviction thereof, shall be fined not more than $100,000 ($500,000 in the case of a corporation) or imprisoned not more than 3 years, or both, together with the costs of prosecution." See also 18 U.S.C. § 1621 for definition of perjury.

Belief is defined in *Black's Law Dictionary* (Sixth Edition, p. 155) as:

> "A conviction of the truth of a proposition, existing subjectively in the mind, and induced by argument, persuasion, or proof addressed to the judgment."
> [Black's Law Dictionary, Sixth Edition, p. 155]

The *Holder* court's explanation of the purpose of § 6702 is ridiculous when applied to regulate the behavior of individuals with regard to their decision to sign or not to sign the jurat of Form 1040. The *Holder* explanation about the purpose of § 6702 is not applicable to the purpose of the governing rule § 7206 because the obvious purpose of § 7206 is to induce people to base their behavior upon their subjective belief. Thus, the purpose of § 7206 is the exact opposite of § 6702 as stated in Holder.

It must be obvious to all but the most obtuse of minds that an interpretation of law or the application of an interpretation of law that induces people to complete and sign the government's *prescribed* Form 1040 and its *prescribed* jurat *regardless* of their beliefs is absolutely irrational and preposterous! The stated purpose of § 6702 is to induce people to *disregard* their beliefs whereas § 7206 makes the act (behavior) of signing the Form 1040 jurat *dependent* upon the potential affiant's knowledge and belief. Under the First Amendment rights to freedom of belief and the expression thereof, no individual who believes he is not liable for income taxes is obligated to intentionally change his belief — if that were possible — so that, with his new belief that he is liable for income taxes, he could honestly fill in the blanks of the prescribed IRS Form 1040 and conscientiously sign its prescribed jurat. Plainly, the imposition of a $500 penalty under color of § 6702 in order to induce people to sign the Form 1040 regardless of their beliefs conflicts with the tax code rule that defines and punishes perjury, i.e., § 7206. Any attempt or coercion under color of law to induce individuals to take an oath or sign a jurat that is contrary to their knowledge and/or belief is nothing less than official oppression and intellectual tyranny. Welcome to George Orwell's 1984!

The Supreme Court in *Cheek v. United States, 498 U.S. 192, 111 S.Ct. 604 (1991)*, ruled that where one's belief is a relevant question to a situation or case, the question must be judged by a jury using the <u>subjective standard</u>. It is abundantly clear that a person's belief about whether he owes the federal government any income taxes is relevant to his conscientious ability to make and sign, under penalties of perjury, a Form 1040 tax return. By penalizing people under color of § 6702 when they fail or refuse to sign the Form 1040 jurat because of their belief (for example, the belief that they are not liable for income taxes), the IRS is presumptively making judgments about individuals' beliefs using the *Cheek*-discredited objective standard and without benefit of a jury. The signing of the government's prescribed Form 1040 jurat or a decision not to sign it is dependent upon one's knowledge and belief about the Internal Revenue Code. Section 7206 makes it so.

Clearly, an individual cannot make an honest and intelligent decision to sign or not to sign a document without recourse to his or her state of mind. The issue of penalizing individuals under 26 U.S.C. §6702 for failing or refusing to sign the Form 1040 jurat (based on their belief that they are not liable for income taxes) can never be properly settled as long as the IRS and courts, using twisted logic, rule that individuals must declare their knowledge and belief on the government's prescribed Form 1040 jurat while also ruling that under § 6702 — the statute under color of which individuals are penalized for not signing the jurat — their state of mind and good faith belief are irrelevant.

Belief is at once both subjective and a legal fact to be judged by a jury when it is relevant to behavior and in dispute. But the IRS, being the arbitrary, despotic, Gestapo-like agency that it is, and with the indulgence of the lower courts, insists on judging the subjective and factual question of one's belief using the objective standard and has yet to listen to reason. The obvious lesson taught by the IRS and the lower courts in this matter is, to say the least, extraordinary and quite remarkable: in order for individuals to escape the $500 penalty imposed under color of § 6702 for their failure or refusal to sign the jurat based upon their study and conscientious belief that they are not liable for income taxes, they should complete the government's prescribed Form 1040 and sign its prescribed jurat regardless of their beliefs and despite the perjury statutes!

6.9.8   IRS Form W-4 Scandals

This section discusses the fraud and the illegal or unconstitutional regulations and practices that the IRS and the Treasury have developed and used in the administration of the W-4 income tax forms, which are called the "Withholding Allowance Certificate". The purpose of these forms is for the Citizen to give permission to their employer to institute "voluntary" withholding of federal income taxes from their paychecks.

We'd like to remind you that throughout this book, we have used the 26 U.S.C. §861/source issues and other issues to prove beyond a reasonable doubt that the federal income tax system is truly voluntary for most of us and that citizens domiciled in the 50 union states with domestic rather than foreign income are not liable to pay these taxes. <u>*Because of this, the IRS and the Treasury basically has to commit fraud on the W-4 application to trick or deceive citizens into believing that they can be held criminally liable for the payment of income taxes*</u>. How do they do it? We'll explain here, and we'll show that they had to violate the law and the constitution to do it.

6.9.8.1   Fraud on the W-4 Form

The first fraud of the Treasury/IRS is in the naming of the IRS Form W-4 itself. Instead of *"Withholding Allowance Certificate"* the form really should be called a *"Voluntary Monthly Donation Certificate"* form, to remind people that the paying of federal income taxes is voluntary and cannot be coerced or compelled. This is in keeping with the Supreme Court Ruling in *Flora v. U.S., 362 U.S. 145 (1960)*:

> "Our tax system is based upon **voluntary assessment and payment**, not upon distraint".

For those of you who don't know, "distraint" means force or coercion. Such a name for the form would also reinforce that the for is NOT for the withholding of TAX, because taxes are something that citizens are assessed or made liable for, and most of us aren't liable for paying ANYTHING in federal income taxes. The few that are have foreign income or are nonresident aliens, and for those people, their permission isn't required, so you don't NEED an allowance form!

The second lie on the form is the definition of "employee", which they conveniently don't tell you on the IRS Form W-4, which we covered in section 3.12.1.4 and which also appears in 26 U.S.C. §3401(c):

> "the term "employee" includes [is limited to] an officer, employee, or elected official of the United States, a State, or any political subdivision thereof, or the District of Columbia, or any agency or instrumentality of any one or more of the foregoing. The term "employee" also includes an officer of a corporation."

Do you think anyone would complete this form if they were familiar with the proper legal definition of the term "employee"? Instead, the IRS publications expand the definition of employee well beyond this definition (see table 3-10 in section 3.5.12) without any constitutional authority whatsoever to do so! Why aren't they being prosecuted for exceeding the constitutional bounds of their authority? Remember that the IRS regulations that expand the definition of "employee" (see 26 C.F.R. §31.3401(d)-1) can be no more expansive than the U.S. Codes they are based on because these definitions must *implement* the codes!

If you look at the IRS Form W-4 itself, there are a number of questionable and misleading things on the form. Below is the first one we'd like to discuss that appears at the top of the form. You can view this form at:

> http://www.irs.gov/forms_pubs/forms.html

> "Routine uses of this form include giving it to the Department of Justice for civil and criminal litigation [AGAINST YOU!!!], to cities and states, and the District of Columbia for use in administering their tax laws".

This statement is there for a reason! *They are putting you on notice, rather blandly and innocuously, that you are waiving your 5th Amendment rights to not be compelled to incriminate yourself, which can only be done voluntarily and without coercion!* Of course, as a "resident" of the federal zone, you don't have fifth amendment rights, which is why they can make the warning so bland. This warning means that if you are a nonresident of the federal zone, you DON'T have to fill out this form and can't be compelled to do so! Remember that the main purpose of the Department of Justice is to PROSECUTE CRIMES, and the 5th Amendment says you can't be compelled to incriminate yourself. Don't let your employer incriminate you either by filling in any part of the form in for you! There's no law that says your employer has to do anything with the form or fill it out if you won't fill it out! The IRS, however, lies to you or doesn't tell you the whole truth because they don't tell you on the form that you *don't* have to fill out this form and can't be penalized in any way because of your failure to fill it out or submit it. Instead, they tell you on their website at:

> http://www.irs.gov/faqs/display/0,,i1%3D54%26genericId%3D16275,00.html

That:

> "You should inform your employees of the importance of submitting an accurate Form W-4. **An employee may be subject to a $500 penalty if he or she submits, with no reasonable basis, a Form W-4 that results in less tax being withheld than is required.** There is no penalty if your employee doesn't claim enough withholding allowances and has too much withheld."

It is obvious that the IRS is trying here to coerce your employer into coercing you to surrender your 5th Amendment rights on your behalf, which is a violation of several laws. Remember that the exercise of rights *can't* be fined or penalized, or they aren't rights (see section 4.2.2, "Fundamental Rights: Granted by God and Cannot be Regulated by the Government")! Remember the court ruling we quoted in that section for *Harman v. Forssenius*, 380 U.S 528 at 540, 85 S.Ct. 1177, 1185 (1965):

> "It has long been established that a State may not impose a penalty upon those who exercise a right guaranteed by the Constitution." Frost & Frost Trucking Co. v. Railroad Comm'n of California, 271 U.S. 583. "Constitutional rights would be of little value if they could be indirectly denied,' Smith v. Allwright, 321 U.S. 649, 644, or manipulated out of existence,' Gomillion v. Lightfoot, 364 U.S. 339, 345."

[Harman v. Forssenius, 380 U.S 528 at 540, 85 S.Ct. 1177, 1185 (1965)]

And yet, the IRS also coerces you again on the back of the IRS Form W-4 by saying:

> *"Failure to provide a properly completed form will result in your being treated as a single person who claims no withholding allowances; providing fraudulent information may also subject you to penalties."*

The "penalty" here for exercising your Fifth Amendment right is being compelled to give away your property against your will and without your consent, which is in effect THEFT! Then because they stole your property, they compel you later to fill out a ton of forms to "qualify" to get tax money back that you were never liable for to begin with, during which time you have to surrender your Fifth Amendment right AGAIN by signing a 1040 form AGAIN under penalty of perjury, and in effect becoming a compelled witness against yourself! The violation of the right the first time lead to a compelled SECOND violation of the same right! And then what about the violation of your 4th Amendment right to privacy because completing the 1040 form coerces you to reveal intimate details not only about your own financial life, but that of your loved ones as well when you complete the form, and the law says the IRS can use your tax form to criminally prosecute your spouse! This kind of tyranny has to stop! It could destroy your marriage and it is compelled!

Here are only a few of the laws and *rights* violated by the IRS during this process:

1. Your First Amendment Right NOT to speak to your government or to be compelled to speak (or write) to your government. The right of free speech includes the right NOT to speak if you don't want to!
2. Violation of your Fourth Amendment right to privacy (which you can petition the government to correct under the First Amendment to the Constitution, called the Petition clause).
3. Violating you Fifth Amendment rights (which you can petition the government to correct under the First Amendment to the Constitution, called the Petition clause).
4. 18 USC §242 provides that "whoever, under color of any law, statute, ordinance, regulation, or custom, willfully subjects any person in any State, Territory, Commonwealth, Possession, or District to the deprivation of any rights, privileges, or immunities secured or protected by the Constitution or laws of the United States ... shall be fined under this title or imprisoned not more than one year, or both."
5. 18 USC §245 "Violation of rights" provides that "Whoever, whether or not acting under color of law, intimidates or interferes with any person from participating in or enjoying any benefit, service, privilege, program, facility, or activity provided or administered by the United States; [or] applying for or enjoying employment, or any perquisite thereof, by any agency of the United States; shall be fined under this title, or imprisoned not more than one year, or both."
6. 42 USC §1983 provides that "every person who, under color of any statute, ordinance, regulation, custom, or usage, of any State or Territory or the District of Columbia, subjects, or causes to be subjected, any citizen of the United States or other person within the jurisdiction thereof to the deprivation of any rights, privileges, or immunities secured by the Constitution and laws, shall be liable to the party injured in an action at law, suit in equity, or other proper proceeding for redress."

6.9.8.2 Unconstitutional IRS/Treasury Regulations Relating to the W-4

To keep this corrupt tax system we have alive and well, in addition to committing fraud on the IRS Form W-4 documented above, the IRS/Treasury also have had to pass regulations that are clearly unconstitutional to administer the program. As we have emphasized before in section 3.15, the CFR's are the official regulations of the Treasury and the Commissioner of the IRS that implement Title 26 of the U.S. Codes. The bounds of authority of the IRS are explicitly and clearly defined in the U.S. Codes, and the implementing regulations in the CFR's *may not* exceed the strictly limited definitions and authority granted explicitly in these codes.

The right that is violated by the IRS/Treasury implementing regulations in 26 C.F.R. is once again the Fifth Amendment, which says in part:

> *No person shall be held to answer for a capital, or otherwise infamous crime, unless on a presentment or indictment of a Grand Jury, except in cases arising in the land or naval forces, or in the Militia, when in actual service in time of War or public danger; nor shall any person be subject for the same offence to be twice put in jeopardy of life or limb; <u>nor shall be compelled in any criminal case to be a witness against himself, nor be deprived of life, liberty, or property, without due process of law; nor shall private property be taken for public use, without just compensation.</u>*

Now we will put the IRS implementing regulations to the test. Below are a few regulations that will really get you steaming and which quite clearly penalize the exercise of one's Fifth Amendment right to not incriminate oneself and one's right to not be deprived of property without one's consent or a due process (court hearing). Remember, that in ALL of the IRS/Treasury regulations cited below:

1. The IRS is NOT required to obtain your consent or even consult or notify you *before* taking your property.
2. The IRS has no obligation to demonstrate a liability to pay federal income tax before it **STOLE YOUR MONEY**!!
3. The IRS is NOT a part of the federal judiciary, and that no jury trial is being held by the IRS before it orders/tells your employer to extort your property/money and give it to them without a trial.

You can read these regulations for yourself at:

http://squid.law.cornell.edu/cgi-bin/get-cfr.cgi?TITLE=26&PART=31&SECTION=3402(f)(2)-1&TYPE=TEXT

Table 6-5: Unconstitutional IRS/Treasury Regulations Relating to Form W-4

Regulation	Condition when 5th Amendment is violated
31.3402(f)(2)-1(a)	a) On commencement of employment. On or before the date on which an individual commences employment with an employer, the individual ***shall*** furnish the employer with a signed withholding exemption certificate relating to his marital status and the number of withholding exemptions which he claims, which number shall in no event exceed the number to which he is entitled, or, if the statements described in Sec. 31.3402(n)-1 are true with respect to an individual, he may furnish his employer with a signed withholding exemption certificate which contains such statements.
31.3402(f)(2)-1(a)	"The employer is required to request a withholding exemption certificate from each employee, but if the employee fails to furnish such certificate, such employee shall be considered as a single person claiming no withholding exemptions."
31.3402(f)(2)-1(e)	If an employer receives an invalid withholding exemption certificate, he shall consider it a nullity for purposes of computing withholding; he shall inform the employee who submitted the certificate that it is invalid, and shall request another withholding exemption certificate from the employee. If the employee who submitted the invalid certificate fails to comply with the employer's request, the employer shall withhold from the employee as from a single person claiming no exemptions (see Sec. 31.3402 (f)(2)-1(a))
31.3402(f)(2)-1(g)(v)	(v) The employer shall promptly furnish the employee who filed the defective certificate, if still in his employ, with a copy of the written notice of the Internal Revenue Service with respect to the certificate and may request another withholding exemption certificate from the employee. The employer shall withhold amounts from the employee on the basis of the maximum number specified in the written notice received from the Service. (vi) If and when the employee does file any new certificate (after an earlier certificate of the employee was considered to be defective), the employer shall withhold on the basis of that new certificate (whenever filed) as currently effective only if the new certificate does not make a claim of exempt status or of a number of withholding exemptions which claim is inconsistent with the advice earlier furnished by the Internal Revenue Service in its written notice to the employer. If any new certificate does make a claim which is inconsistent with the advice contained in the Service's written notice to the employer, then the employer shall disregard the new certificate, shall not submit that new certificate to the Service, and shall continue to withhold amounts from the employee on the basis of the maximum number specified in the written notice received from the Service.
31.3402(f)(2)-1(g)(vii)	(vii) If the employee makes a claim on any new certificate that is inconsistent with the advice in the Service's written notice to the employer, the employee may specify on such new certificate, or by a written statement attached to that certificate, any circumstances of the employee which have changed since the date of the Service's earlier written notice, or any other circumstances or reasons, as justification or support for the claims made by the employee on the new certificate. The employee may then submit that new certificate and written statement either to (A) the Internal Revenue Service office specified in the notice earlier furnished to the employer under this paragraph (g)(5), or to (B) the employer, who must then submit a copy of that new certificate and the employee's written statement (if any) to the Internal Revenue Service office specified in the notice earlier furnished to the employer. The employer shall continue to disregard that new certificate and shall continue to withhold amounts from the employee on the basis of the maximum number specified in the written notice received from the Service unless and until the Internal Revenue Service by written notice (under paragraph (g)(5)(iii) of this section) advises the employer to withhold on the basis of that new certificate and revokes its earlier written notice.

We didn't mention above, the hundreds of different types of penalties the IRS assesses against individuals who don't pay their taxes, which in most cases they don't owe anyway based on the 861/source argument. If you factor in these penalties, there are even greater reasons to believe that a massive "conspiracy to deprive of rights" (in this case 5th Amendment Rights) exists, in violation of 18 U.S.C. 241.

With this kind of background, can you see not why our prudent founding fathers prohibited direct taxes on citizens? There are so many constitutional conflicts that result when we violate the prohibition on direct taxes without apportionment specified in Article I, Section 2, Clause 3 of the Constitution!

6.9.8.3 Line 3a of W-4 modifies and obfuscates 26 U.S.C. §3402 (n)

26 U.S.C. §3402(n) is the section that determines the conditions under which persons may declare on their W-4 that they are exempt and have no tax liability. It states:

> *(n) Employees incurring no income tax liability—Notwithstanding any other provision of this section, an employee shall not be required to deduct and withhold any tax under this chapter upon a payment of wages to an employee if there is in effect with respect to such payment a withholding exemption certificate (in such form and containing such other information as the Secretary may prescribe) furnished to the employer by the employee certifying that the employee—*
>
> *(1) incurred no **liability** for income tax imposed under subtitle A for his preceding taxable year, and*
>
> *(2) anticipates that he will incur no liability for income tax imposed under subtitle A for his current taxable year.*
>
> *The Secretary shall by regulations provide for the coordination of the provisions of this subsection with the provision of subsection (f)*

However, on the W-4, it states on line 3:

> *3 I claim exemption from withholding because (see instructions and check boxes below that apply):*
>
> *a. ___ Last year I did not **owe** any Federal Income tax and had a right to a full refund of ALL income tax withheld, AND*
>
> *b. ___ This year I do not expect to owe any Federal income tax and expect to have a right to a full refund of ALL income tax withheld. If both a and b apply, enter "EXEMPT" here.*

You should notice that a different word is used on line 3a of the W-4 than is used in the code. Why did the IRS deviate from the wording in the statute when there is clearly no need for it? The law says nothing about tax refunds, and it speaks ONLY of tax "liability", not "owing" the tax. There can be no doubt that the W-4 was worded to conflict with the code in order to frustrate its proper application. If the IRS used the word "liable" instead of "owe" on the IRS Form W-4, they would draw attention to that word and people would start looking for it in the tax code and find that it isn't used anywhere in the context of any of the Subtitles A through C income taxes! They would virtually guarantee losing a court case over the use of this word if someone sued them, so they replace the word with "owe" to confuse things and so the word can't be interpreted literally in the code itself. In any case, natural persons who understand that there is not statute within Internal Revenue Code (26 U.S.C.) subtitles A through C making anyone *liable* for the payment of these voluntary donations (taxes), then they can safely write "EXEMPT" in the box and check boxes 3a and 3b. And since the tax was collected illegally on the basis of fraud and intimidation, all employees certainly have the "right" to a full refund—regardless of whether the federal mafia recognizes that right.

6.9.9 Whistleblower Retaliation

6.9.9.1 1998: IRS Historian Quits-Then Gets Audited[82]

---

[82] *Losing Your Illusions*, Gordon Phillips, p. 20.

Former official historian for the Internal Revenue Service, Shelley Davis, quit her post in protest over how the agency is systematically destroying its historical documents, presumably to break the trail of any possible investigation into the numerous ways that the internal revenue laws are being violated.

The IRS has also stated in 1999 (?) that it is abolishing the position of historian. The IRS has announced it wanted to audit Ms. Davis' tax returns, who was a former IRS historian. Yes, the IRS will turn on anyone, including one of its own.

In the 1998 senate hearings that resulted in the approval of the IRS Restructuring and Reform Act (RRA) during which IRS abuses were exposed, the IRS agents who were blowing the whistle on the agency repeated over and over that they felt they were doing a service by testifying against the agency, but that their biggest concern was now becoming targets of retaliation by the IRS or Department of Justice.

Sure, and if they close their eyes and wish real hard, Tinkerbell will appear. As you may have surmised, if you've been paying attention, I personally do not have the "highest confidence in the integrity" of the Internal Revenue Service. Yet, in spite of Ms. Richardson's (the former IRS commissioner who quit over compliance issues) heartwarming sentiment and Publication 1's reassuring rhetoric about the "voluntary" nature of the income tax, just like the creature in the movie "Alien" that won't stop until it has located and devoured your property--assuming you own property titled in your own name, of course--and has totally destroyed you, both financially and personally. Remember, like the Alien, the government is hungry. It must eat to survive and it will destroy you to feed itself if it has to, in blatant violation of your constitutionally protected rights as an American. See:

> *Night of the Living Government*, Andrew Klavan
> https://www.youtube.com/embed/aUwTyycRoCQ

Below is the text of Ms. Davis' prepared testimony in front of the Congressional Committee that investigated the IRS in 1998. We downloaded this speech off the About.com website under "Police Conduct: Internal Revenue Service" at http://civilliberty.about.com/cs/irs/:

> *PREPARED STATEMENT OF*
> *SHELLEY L. DAVIS*
> *BEFORE THE SENATE FINANCE COMMITTEE*
> *OVERSIGHT HEARING ON THE INTERNAL REVENUE SERVICE*
> *TUESDAY, SEPTEMBER 23, 1997*
>
> *Mr. Chairman and Members of the Senate Finance Committee, I am pleased to be able to share a few of my thoughts and experiences with you today as you explore specific issues of IRS abuse of those the tax agency likes to call its "customers" -- American taxpayers.*
>
> *For 16 years I worked as an historian for the federal government. Nine of those years were with the Department of Defense and the final seven were spent as the first and unfortunately, the last, official historian for the Internal Revenue Service. At the end of 1995, I resigned from my federal career in protest over the unwillingness of the IRS, or the Treasury Department Inspector General, to investigate my complaint of illegal document destruction by the IRS. I learned that the same federal investigator to whom I originally reported my concerns regarding this, had turned around and opened an investigation of me on unfounded and false charges of "wrongful release of confidential information." Later, I learned that this is a common tactic used against IRS employees who dare to speak up against management. I knew then that I had no alternative but to resign and try to raise awareness of the intransigence, arrogance, and abusive patterns of behavior that I found all too common inside the headquarters of the IRS. I decided to write a book which was published earlier this year entitled, "Unbridled Power."*
>
> *My testimony today will touch briefly on three areas:*
>
> *1.) The cultural climate of the IRS;*
>
> *2.) List keeping at the IRS;*
>
> *3.) The IRS definition of "tax protester."*
>
> *My introduction to the culture of the IRS came during my earliest days with the tax agency, in the fall of 1988. Although I had been hired as the first historian for the IRS, I found little interest or support for my efforts. I found even less history. By history I mean both an awareness of the heritage of the IRS as well as the raw material (the documentation) from which narrative history is distilled. Neither the documents nor the heritage were to be found.*

Initially, I found this curious. Later, I found it alarming. At the IRS National Headquarters, there seemed little connection between the work of employees and actual tax collection--what I presumed to be the mission of the IRS. Rather than possessing any basic curiosity about the past, the IRS employees I encountered exhibited a wariness, a suspicion--assuming that anyone looking for records must have some definite agenda. An agenda presumed to be negative.

This reluctance to think about the past translated into routine day-to-day operations, meaning that all documents were tossed, shredded, whatever, when a program was completed--or shut down, as in the case of many IRS computer projects. No records. No paper trail. No history.

As time went on, I realized that this not only made my job as historian virtually impossible, but that it guaranteed that the IRS could never be held accountable for its actions. With a sense of historical development, I came up with my own interpretation of this phenomenon. One could easily pass off the reluctance of the IRS to acknowledge its past as a reaction to a constant barrage of criticism. But the IRS is certainly not the only federal agency subjected to criticism from the press, Congress, or the public.

Instead of reflecting on positive actions in response to criticism, the IRS proclaims that any criticism of the agency is "IRS bashing" and "will only lead to more tax protesters." Rather than respond with solid information, historical examples, and analysis, the IRS jumps around skittishly, telling Congress that this reorganization, or that new position, or another new task force will remedy the current problem. The IRS has learned that its most effective response to inquiring questions from Congress, from the press, or from the American people is to hide behind the privacy laws. These are the laws meant to protect taxpayers. But by endlessly citing restrictions on its authority to comment on taxpayer cases, the IRS deflects criticism for any and all actions. In essence, the response of the IRS to question about anything and everything is, "Trust us. We're doing the right thing. We just can't tell you what that is because we're protecting American taxpayers."

A corollary to this defensive shield is the penchant of the IRS to destroy its paper trail. There were virtually no records of IRS actions throughout the twentieth century in any of the repositories where one would normally find federal records: the IRS itself, the National Archives (including the permanent archives in Washington, D.C., the 10 records centers around the country, or the Presidential libraries.)

In my early years with the IRS, a good question to ask was, "Where are the records?" What I learned was shocking. The records had been destroyed. Gone. Shredded. Tossed. They no longer exist due to a lack of attention to, or concern for, the law which requires all federal agencies to preserve records of what they do. It is as though the IRS assumed that laws which apply to the FBI, to the CIA, to every other part of the federal establishment can be ignored.

No other agency of our government could get away with this. I questioned the reason why it had taken so long for anyone to realize that the records were not just missing, but destroyed. I believe the answer is based on fear. As taxpayers, why would we ever question the one agency that can truly bite back? Our fear of suffering a personal attack from the IRS generally keeps most of us in check. Our fear of being audited has allowed the IRS to theoretically eliminate any potential smoking guns by trashing its own records. This ensures that it can never be held accountable for its actions. How can you prove any wrongdoing when the evidence is already destroyed?

The IRS has learned that the privacy protections are its best weapon in its war against its "customers." There is an "us against them" mentality which is far too common among IRS employees. I witnessed and experienced this attitude firsthand for over seven years working at the IRS headquarters. When I questioned the lack of record keeping by the IRS, it was made clear to me that I was a "lone ranger," a "loose cannon," and "not a team player." Is it any wonder they investigated me?

I'll conclude this section with a stark example from my personal experience. After my protest resignation at the end of 1995, admittedly I was not on the "most favored" list of IRS. But when I went to the IRS National Office on Monday, April 15, 1996, to meet a friend who had invited me for lunch to celebrate my birthday, I did not expect to be threatened with arrest. But that is what happened.

While waiting for my friend to meet me at the entrance of the building, I was pulled aside by an IRS internal security agent who told me to leave immediately because I was officially "banned" from the building.

I thought this was odd as I was standing in the front entrance, a public space. When I asked for an explanation, I was told that I was "banned" because I "did not turn in my official identification badge when I resigned four months earlier."

This was untrue.

When the agent detaining me prepared to call for Federal Protective Service agents to carry out her threat to arrest me, I knew I had to make a quick decision: let them carry through with this absurd threat, or turn and leave. I left. To this day, I wish I had stayed and made them carry through with their threat. The IRS brought false charges against me, used government resources to pursue a false investigation of me, and continued to harass me even after I had resigned. With the IRS, as I am sure you will hear from others today, retaliation is prompt, swift and catastrophic.

My years with the IRS were spent exclusively in the National Office, the headquarters of the tax agency. Throughout my tenure at the IRS, I often heard stories that different types of codes were used to identify taxpayers and returns.

I have specific knowledge of one type of list maintained inside the IRS. It is a product of a secretive, cloistered unit of the IRS which existed from 1969 through 1973, known by the name "Special Services Staff," or SSS.

The SSS list had approximately 11,000 individuals and organizations designated as possible audit targets by the IRS. Who were these people and organizations? Some were names you will recognize: Shirley MacLaine, Joan Baez, John Lindsay, the Black Panthers, and the Student Nonviolent Coordinating Committee(SNCC).

But most of those who made it onto the list were not household names but were individuals the SSS determined were of questionable character as determined by the SSS.

Ten employees of the SSS dutifully clipped newspaper articles each day. The FBI willingly sent over its own files on political dissidents and protesters, and subscriptions were taken to radical publications which were perused for names and other leads. All in all, the SSS targeted individuals with no known tax problems for audit simply because of their political activities.

The commissioner who abolished the SSS, Donald Alexander, actually testified before Congress in 1975 that he believed the SSS records should be taken "out on the mall and burned."

Yet, despite the fact that the SSS files remain intact at the IRS (at least through my resignation at the end of 1995), the IRS steadfastly refuses to release the files to researchers or even to the National Archives for safekeeping. Why? Because they contain "taxpayer information." Who is protecting whom, one has to wonder? What has all this got to do with the present? Today I believe there exist thousands of names of American taxpayers whose Master Files are coded as TC-148, which brands them as "Illegal Tax Protesters." Whether this is a list, or compilation of files which bear that designation, is semantics. Just how many Americans bear this designation?

At the very least, we need to know if we are on that list, We reserve that right. The IRS says we can't know and don't have a right to know while simultaneously claiming Congress wants it this way.

The only thing being protected in this scenario is the IRS. Just what is a tax protester? Your definition, like mine, is probably different from the IRS definition. I learned that while inside the IRS.

A tax protester, in my definition, is not someone who may oppose our system of taxation, but pays his taxes nonetheless. A tax protester is not someone who says that our tax system is broken and must be dismantled, but still files a Form 1040. A tax protester is not someone who merely criticizes the IRS. A tax protester is not someone who challenges an IRS assessment. But in the mind of the IRS, all of the above ideas fit the unofficial IRS profile of a tax protester. In the cloistered environment of the IRS, criticism of the IRS, or the income tax, equals tax protester. Anyone who has the misfortune of bearing that title is most likely going to witness first hand just what "taxpayer abuse" really means.

Don't get me wrong. I am not in any way condoning the actions of those who, by one manner or another, attempt to cheat or not live up to their financial responsibilities as a U.S. citizen. But I do recognize the use of the label of "Illegal Tax Protestor" as another powerful weapon of the most powerful agency in America. It is time for Congress to compel the IRS to be more forthcoming about its audit procedures, even though the IRS would like us to believe that our system of taxation will collapse if the American people know how their tax collector goes about his or her business.

The IRS gains too much benefit from the privacy laws to come clean on its own. The culture of the IRS, built over decades of learning to hide behind the privacy laws, will not change on its own. Without intervention from Congress, it will not happen. Last year, a top career IRS executive testified before Congress that, "There is the general view that the more mysterious tax enforcement is, the more likely taxpayers will voluntarily comply." Mystery breeds distrust and contempt. It also breeds fear, which compels many taxpayers to comply with the tax laws because they are afraid of the consequences, but it does not breed voluntary compliance or trust.

The arrogance of the IRS is outrageous and harmful. We lose more than we gain by allowing the IRS to operate in this manner. Congress must demand accountability from the IRS. Congress must shine the spotlight on the IRS and never switch the power off.

Thank you.

6.9.9.2 1993: IRS Raided the Save-A-Patriot Fellowship[83]

Unlike many so-called "tax groups" which are nothing more than boiler room operations, often moving from State to State to avoid detection, the Save-A-Patriot Fellowship has been at the same physical location at 12 Carroll Street, Westminster, Maryland, and at the same telephone number (410) 857-4441, since opening their doors in 1984.

Fellowship Fiduciary, John Kotmair, has employed individuals for thirteen years without applying for an employer identification number, and therefore has not withheld taxes of any kind from those within the employ of the Fellowship in all of this time.

The IRS raided the Fellowship in 1993, and one of the allegations was that he had no employer identification number and was not withholding taxes. After requesting the requirement to do so in court, the IRS dropped the allegation.

Eventually they were ordered to return the property taken, which they did, and the federal court ruled on December 18, 1996, against the IRS's allegation that the Fellowship could not exist without being regulated by the government. Judge Garbis of the United States district Court for the District of Maryland ruled on December 18, 1996 that the Fellowship is in fact:

> "...an unincorporated association and, as such, is legally capable of owning property",

needing no permission to exist and independent of government regulation. This ruling amounts to being given the "Good Housekeeping Seal of Approval" by a federal court.

So why does the IRS "allow" the Fellowship to stay in business? Why haven't we been shut down? It wasn't for lack of trying.

On December 10, 1993, the Internal Revenue Service conducted a raid on our national offices at 12 Carroll Street, Westminster, Maryland. The Fellowship had suspected for some time that there were many misperceptions within the IRS as to the purpose and goals of the Fellowship, and that under the circumstances it would be appropriate to explain their position in order to ensure that it was not misrepresented either in the public forum or certain branches of the IRS. To accomplish this, the Fellowship wrote to the Acting Commissioner of Internal Revenue, Michael Dolan, on July 19, 1993, expressing their concern. In that letter they extended an invitation to the Commissioner or any of his designates to visit the Fellowship's national headquarters and observe firsthand their activities.

The same invitation was extended to all of the federal judges and magistrates in this district, and public notice of the invitation was printed in the Carroll County Times, a local Maryland newspaper, on three consecutive Mondays. The Fellowship was glad to see local Federal Magistrate Paul M. Rosenberg respond to our invitation and comment that we were doing "an admirable job."

So on October 27, 1993, the Fellowship wrote to the new Commissioner of Internal Revenue, Margaret Milner Richardson, and repeated their invitation. This time, because of their growth and national prominence, they even suggested a permanent IRS liaison for the office, but instead of any spirit of cooperation, the IRS response was to notify them that the matter was turned over to the Criminal Investigation Division in Baltimore. Magistrate Rosenberg, who was fully aware of the Fellowship's intent, knew of the invitation. Therefore, he also knew that the Fellowship was not "concealing" anything.

Nevertheless, on December 8,1993, Magistrate Rosenberg signed a search warrant stating:

> "...property is now concealed on the premises.. and if the ...property be found there to seize same."

After making every effort to communicate their purpose and extending the above invitation, the Fellowship was accused of "concealing" something, of what they are not sure. The fact is, it is believed that the IRS had ulterior motives.

Since the Fellowship documents the systematic denial of due process in the various assessment and collection procedures and the fraudulent practice of various IRS agents, it is entirely possible that the seizure of such documents was intended to thwart the association's investigations into such affairs, in other words, to cover up corruption at the highest levels.

---

[83] Portions from *Losing Your Illusions*, Gordon Phillips, pp. 138-141.

The public should call for an investigation by the Justice Department into the circumstances surrounding the warrant and subsequent raid, rather than to tacitly assume that the individuals responsible for this "raid" are above reproach.

The events leading up to the raid would further seem to support this hypothesis. They began on December 1, 1993, when John B. Kotmair, Jr. the fiduciary of The Save-A-Patriot Fellowship, was subpoenaed to appear at a grand jury investigation in Sioux Falls, South Dakota. The affidavit supporting the subpoena contained false statements made by an IRS Special Agent, so Mr. Kotmair naturally notified the Court to inform them of the defect.

Nevertheless, the Federal District Court of South Dakota insisted that he appear in Sioux Falls on December 9, 1993, to testify. During his testimony, John provided the Grand Jury with copies of the documentation showing the perjurious statements of the IRS Special Agent.

The U.S. Attorney conspired with the perjurious Special Agent in an obvious attempt to obtain the indictment against Mr. Kotmair.

Also during the proceedings, the U.S. Attorney asked Mr. Kotmair:

> "..isn't it true that anyone who disagrees with an IRS assessment can pay the tax and then sue for a refund in court?"

The implication was that Mr. Kotmair was "selling" the public a false information in the form of a "non-existent legal remedy."

Mr. Kotmair responded by explaining to the jury that suing for a refund was only one option. He said:

> "If the IRS claimed you owed a million dollars, could you afford to pay the tax then sue for a refund?"
>
> "What about $25,000?
>
> "Could you afford to pay $25,000 and then sue for a refund?"

He then gave them a brief history lesson and explained that during the War Between the States, Congress passed the Anti-Injunction Act that prevented the courts from enjoining (stopping) the collection of a tax. He told them that because of this Anti-Injunction Act, a bureaucrat could literally pluck a figure out of thin air, (like a million dollars), claim you owe it, and there would be no judicial remedy because the courts no longer had jurisdiction over such matters.

Then he explained why the U.S. Attorney was wrong and cited "the other option under the IR Code", section 6404, the section that the IRS does not like to talk about! He explained that people with errant assessments have an administrative remedy that the IRS was ignoring and/or denying in violation of due process requirements, and then he explained that he assisted people in pursuing this administrative remedy and in requesting abatements if and when they believed an assessment had been made in error.

There was no need to go through the expensive and often prohibitive process of appealing to a tax court. He added that he had helped thousands of people and that at the present time he was helping a 72 year-old man in Alaska who had never even paid him a dime!

The grand jury evidently agreed with the information about the Save-A-Patriot Fellowship! Mr. Kotmair was able to take a late flight home and arrived just in time for the scheduled raid at the Fellowship shortly after 9AM the next day, December 10, 1993.

The whole affair reeks of shame, and the alleged liability of Mr. Kotmair appears to be nothing more than a ploy designed to make the IRS's actions palatable to an increasingly suspicious public. They no doubt hoped to make a public spectacle out of the indictment and subsequent raid.

As to what actually happened--one of the Fellowship's caseworkers had already arrived at the office and was busily working at his computer. Hearing a noise from behind, he turned around only to find four 9-millimeter semi-automatic handguns pointed at his head. In a calm, quizzical voice he asked, "What seems to be the problem?"

As luck would have it, this particular staff member was a former treasury agent himself, and by the purest of coincidences, he was wearing his personalized "treasury" jacket.

The swat team was intimately familiar with the apparel and immediately asked him where he had obtained it. The staff member replied, "I used to be one of you boys until I learned the truth!"

He was promptly ordered out of the building with his hands on his head. Federal agents then began to sort through the Fellowship's property and loaded it onto trucks. To show just how ridiculous the raid was, the computers stored only information pertaining to correspondence that had already been sent to the IRS as the Fellowship maintains no membership lists on the premises.

Considering that the IRS already had copies of these documents, and considering the costs involved with performing the raid, not a mention how much the subsequent litigation is going to cost the IRS in terms of money and embarrassment, we just cannot fathom why some IRS special agent would be dumb enough to cause the IRS all of the problems that this raid is going to cause for them.

It may be that the raid was to be the "icing on the cake" to the indictment that never came down, and that someone forgot to inform the Baltimore IRS to call off the raid. But regardless, it should be pointed out that the warrant only authorized the seizure of property belonging to Mr. Kotmair, and not to the Fellowship. But Mr. Kotmair is only the fiduciary for the association. He does not own the property.

Therefore, since the warrant specified only property belonging to John Kotmair, the Save-A-Patriot property that was taken, was taken illegally, regardless of whether the warrant was justified or not.

Unfortunately, the travesty of justice doesn't stop there. At the same time as the raid on the office, agents forcibly entered Mr. Kotmair's home with weapons drawn. His wife, Nancy, was in her nightgown and turned to get her bathrobe to open the door after she heard the knocks, but agents immediately smashed the front door in with a sledge hammer before she could get her bathrobe on. His son was asleep and awoke to find a shotgun close to his head.

Mrs. Kotmair was not even allowed to change clothes to put on something warmer. Instead, she was confined to a chair near the broken front door with cold winter air coming in on her. After about an hour she was allowed to put on her bathrobe. When she needed to use the bathroom a female agent would go with her and refused to leave for "her own protection" they told her. She observed agents quarreling over what property they would take but was not allowed to be involved in their determination of what was applicable property to be seized pursuant to the warrant.

Witnesses reported that the rude, arrogant, confrontation attitude of the fifty gun-waving IRS agents turned to confusion when they were not met with angry or hostile "opponents". They were apparently given false information of what to expect, quite possibly, to provoke an "incident" which could be used to justify the raid in the mind of the public.

A few of Mr. Kotmair's perfectly legal handguns were laid out on the ground and photographed as though to suggest that he was some sort of drug king pin. Considering that John spent nearly a decade in the 1950's as a police officer in Baltimore, Maryland, it would not be unusual for him to have a legal gun collection.

This was all part of the public spectacle to justify this travesty of justice, resulting from a faulty warrant and subsequent raid that should have been called off, all because the IRS doesn't want John Kotmair helping innocent people whom the IRS wants to destroy.

Both "raids" were certainly unnecessary expense that, by the time the matter is litigated, will cost the people of this country millions of dollars. But the saddest part of this story is how innocent people are subjected to the threat of harm or even death at the hands of uniformed bureaucrats whose mercenary employees justify their actions by saying, without any personal conscience, "...we're just following orders."

The failure of the IRS to publicly defend their actions establishes the presumption that their activities are either unlawful or that the agency incorrectly believes itself to be above the Law and under no obligation to the public.

The people certainly have the right to the truth and the government has the duty to respond to all inquiries regarding the truth, as required in IRS Publication 1.

During the raid, the IRS broke federal laws by opening and reading sealed correspondence between the Fellowship and our members, and took numerous computers, copy machines, fax machines, laser printers, file cabinets, etc. The IRS failed completely in their effort to discredit the Fellowship and demoralize the staff.

A national alert for help went out and within days, money, new computers and other office equipment streamed into headquarters. Ten days after the raid, the Fellowship was back in full operation, and membership swelled as a result of solidarity on the part of patriotic Americans nationwide.

About nine months later, the IRS returned unannounced in a rental truck, dressed in plain clothes, and returned all of the Fellowship's property with the exception of $60,000 stolen from a safe. Needless to say, the Fellowship has filed numerous lawsuits against the IRS which are ongoing. That was in 1993.

Since that time enrollment has soared with members pouring in from across the country. One of our member, nationally known talk radio personality Zoh Hieroniumus, hosts her own ten-thousand watt radio talk show on Baltimore AM radio station WCBM every weekday morning from 9AM to Noon.

Zoh covered the raid live on the air. Among numerous other guests, she has on many occasions interviews Fellowship founder John Kotmair and other staffers on the air, beaming 10,000 watts of truth about the proper limited application of the income and employment sections of the Internal Revenue Code directly into the beltway inside Washington, D.C.

We have knowledge that the IRS and other State and federal government officials are tuning in to Zoh. And for good reason! She is ruthless at uncovering the truth about any issue she covers, and is an unusually gifted speaker. The Fellowship has researched and developed legal defenses to protect the liberty and property of its members from those within the government who would ignore the law, violate due process, and rob honest Americans.

I hate to use so strong a word as rob when speaking of the actions of a government I was raised to love and respect, but the extortion of property from U.S. citizens through decades of deception and misinformation in clear violation of the written Law can only be called what it really is--robbery.

Apparently the Supreme Court aggress. In the 1874 case, *Loan Association v. Topeka, 20 Wall. 655 (1874)*, they said:

> *"To lay with one hand the power of government on the property of the citizen, and with the other to bestow it on favored individuals.. is none the less robbery because it is.. called taxation."*

The "bottom line" is that the Save-A-Patriot Fellowship successfully withstood an IRS raid and then prevailed against the IRS in Federal District Court's Judgment to t the United States Court of Appeals for the Fourth Circuit, Case No. 97-1303, and on March 13th, 1997, filed with that Court a Motion for Dismissal of Appeal--with prejudice.

Since the day the Fellowship opened its doors on February 24, 1984, John B. Kotmair, Jr., Founder and Fiduciary, has never withheld a dime in income or employment taxes from any of the approximately two dozen staffers who work at the Fellowship's Maryland headquarters.

The IRS knows full well that there is no law that requires the withholding of such taxes from a U.S. citizen working and living within the 50 union states. Furthermore, the IRS has never in nearly fourteen years made any attempt to levy on the pay of any of the above staffers. If you want to *be* free, you have to live free.

Liberty works! End of Story!!

6.9.10 IRS has NO Delegated Authority to Impose Penalties or Levies or Seizures for Nonpayment of Subtitle A Personal Income Taxes!

6.9.10.1 What Particular Type of Tax is Part 301 of Treasury Regulations?

Part 301 of the Regulations (26 C.F.R.) warrants a detailed explanation, because it is these Regulations that the IRS fraudulently misapplies to Citizens of the 50 [nonfederal] states as their purported authority to charge interest and penalties and seize property and levy compensation. All 301 Policies and Procedures cannot be and are not applicable to ALL subject matters of taxes.

Note: A "cross reference" and the word "see," in statutory construction, are used as a means of clarification only and have no legal applicability.

> **IMPORTANT**!: A Part 301 Regulation, by itself, has no legal force to promulgate or implement Part 1, "Income Tax" provisions. A Part 301 Regulation is merely a cross reference added, in the interest of completeness, not as the lawful "authority."

The 1939 and 1954 Title 26 Internal Revenue Codes for Income Taxes, which were never repealed and are the basis and nucleus of our current system of taxation, did not contain a Part 301! From 1939 until 1961, there was NO Part 301 "Procedure and Administration" outlining procedures for interest, penalties, property seizures, and levies! The preface to the 54 Regulations (February 16, 1954) states:

"This book [1954 Internal Revenue Code] contains rules and regulations constituting Parts 1 to 79 of Title 26…"

Following is a sample excerpt from the Table of Contents for the 1954 Regulations [26 C.F.R.]:

Table of Contents

Title 26:
   Chapter I –Internal Revenue Service, Department of the Treasury
    (Parts 1-79)...3

[Note the conspicuous absence of Part 301!]

So where did Part 301 come from? Where was Part 301 in the 1954 Regs? The first time Part 301 mysteriously appeared was in a specially published 1961 edition of C.F.R. Title 26. The Preface to these Regulations solved the mystery of the origin of Part 301, stating:

"Title 27 (Alcohol, Tobacco, and Firearms), formerly included..Part 300 to the end..."

What Particular Types of Taxes were these "Procedures and Administrations" applicable to? Alcohol, Tobacco, and Firearms! Part 301 was NOT written for Title 26 Voluntary Income Taxes! These Part 300+ provisions carry severe penalties for noncompliance, because Alcohol, Tobacco and Firearms Tax is a "regulated" revenue taxable industry imposing a Mandatory Tax upon which criminal sanctions and property seizures could be imposed!

The "Publisher's Note," which was added to the first page of the 1954 microfiche of the CFR, after its publication, makes a reference to this suspicious alteration, stating:

"No Federal Register citation covering this change was discoverable."

Again, the IRS cannot lawfully impose civil and criminal penalties on a voluntary tax because noncompliance is one of the options! That is why there is nowhere in the Regulations that a Part 1 Voluntary Tax cross references to a 301 Regulation applicable to penalties, interest, levies, seizure, or summons!

Any attempted enforcement by the IRS of a Code relating to voluntary tax, without a Part 1 Implementing Regulation, is a denial of due process for the American Citizen in violation of 26 C.F.R. §601.106!

6.9.10.2   Parallel Table of Authorities 26 C.F.R. to 26 U.S.C

The following is taken from the Parallel Table of Authorities in the back of the Title 26 Code of Federal Regulations [CFR]. It is a list of the ONLY Part 301 Regulations that derive their Authority for implementation from Title 26 USCS or 26 IRC [Income Taxes]. Note the conspicuous absence of any penalty, interest, levy or seizure for the Title 26 Voluntary Income Tax. Again, it is inconceivable that the Congress would legislate penalties for the individual income tax, since the supreme Court and the IRS have both substantiated that such a Tax is voluntary and NOT based upon distraint. It would be absurd to impose penalties for non-compliance, when such an option is what made the tax voluntary to begin with!

Table 6-6: Parallel Table of Authorities 26 C.F.R. to 26 USCS

| CFR to USCS ||
Treasury Regulations	Internal Revenue Code
26 Part 301	26 §6011
26 Part 301	31 §3720A
26 Part 301	26 §6245
26 Part 301	26 §7805
26 Part 301	26 §6233
26 Part 301	26 §6326
26 Part 301	26 §6404
26 Part 301	26 §§6324A-6324B
26 Part 301	26 §6241
26 Part 301	26 §§6111-6112
26 Part 301	26 §6223
26 Part 301	26 §6227
26 Part 301	26 §6230-6231
26 Part 301	26 §6033
26 Part 301	26 §6036
26 Part 301	26 §6050M
26 Part 301	26 §6059
26 Part 301	26 §2032A
26 Part 301	26 §7624
26 Part 301	26 §3401
26 Part 301	26 §§6103-6104
26 Part 301	26 §1441
26 Part 301	26 §7216
26 Part 301	26 §6621
26 Part 301	26 §367
26 Part 301	26 §6867
26 Part 301	26 §6689

You can look at the Parallel Table of Authorities yourself at:

http://www.access.gpo.gov/nara/cfr/parallel/parallel_table.html

Keep in mind that the above table is not considered an exhaustive or authoritative source by the courts, as we mention later in section 5.16 of the Tax Fraud Prevention Manual, Form #06.008.

6.9.11 Service of Illegal Summons

It is quite common for the IRS to send out illegal summons in order to go on "fishing expeditions" in trying to uncover mud to sling at a law-abiding Citizen. 26 U.S.C. §7603 governs the issuance of summons. The vast majority of IRS summons are illegal and do not comply with the requirements of this section because:

- The summons did not identify the code section establishing a tax liability. It MUST do so to be enforceable. Since there is no section in the I.R.C. that established a tax liability for Subtitles A through C, if the summons relates to these taxes, it cannot be validly issued. You might want to ask the agent the following:

    "In referring to an unspecified and alleged 'tax liability', does this refer to the tobacco tax liability contained in Section 5703 (yes or no)?"
    Ask the same question about sections 5005, 4374, and 4401(c) of the I.R.C. and then if the answer is no, ask:

    "Then what section of the Internal Revenue Code establishes the liability for which this summons is being issued?"
- The agent did not personally serve the person being summoned
- The agent did not specify the precise books and records being requested.

- The agent who issued them does not have a "Delegation Order" which allows him to issue the summons form.
- The wrong form or not form at all was used.
- The summons was not signed by the agent, or in most cases *anyone*.

If you receive a summons from an IRS that contains any of the above defects, then you have been illegally served and need not appear at the summons, but should notify the IRS of the defect in their notice promptly (usually within 10 days). For more information about summons, see:

http://famguardian.org/TaxFreedom/Evidence/Discovery/IRSSummons.pdf

6.9.12 IRS Publication 1: Taxpayer rights…Oh really?

IRS Publication 1, entitled *Your Rights as a Taxpayer*, is supposed to tell you what your rights are, but why doesn't the IRS title it "*Your rights as an American regarding taxes?*" Have you ever thought of that? *Is the implication here that you have to pay money to the government to have rights?* Under such circumstances, doesn't the government really just become a big mafia protection racket, where we pay money to keep them off our back and keep IRS computers from sending us automated anonymous and harassing letters? This is what we meant earlier in section 4.3.12 entitled "Government-instituted slavery using privileges", where we said that the government has illegally tried to turn rights into taxable privileges, and here that very reality is staring you right in the face if you are paying attention!

Think hard about this: If you are a "taxpayer", then by definition, you are *liable* for tax and we already know that you don't have any rights under those circumstances! We pointed this out earlier in section 3.12.1.21. The only reason you have *any* liberties at all as a "taxpayer" is because the government didn't take ALL of your income so you had enough left over after being raped to go out and have some fun. Let's face it: The whole bill of rights goes straight down the toilet when you are liable for *any* income taxes. The attitude of most passive "taxpayers", the people we call "sheeple", is:

> "Go ahead and take [steal] whatever money you want, but please don't hit me!"

If the IRS replaced "Taxpayer" with "American" in their Publication 1, however, they would have to explain what law *makes the average American liable* for income tax and why you owe it to begin with. This question is a question the IRS knows they *can't* answer because there *aren't* any statutes in all of Subtitles A and C that make natural persons liable for income taxes. We even have a letter form a Congressman on Congressional letterhead stating this! Click here to view it (http://famguardian.org/TaxFreedom/Evidence/Congressional/IncomeTaxLiability.pdf). So instead the IRS deceptively names their publication using the word "Taxpayer" to keep attention off the real issues, which are jurisdiction and liability! Therefore, the audience this publication is written for are those people who already mistakenly believe they are liable. However, the only way you as a natural person can have rights is to *not* pay income taxes and not be liable for income taxes. The name of this publication is therefore an oxymoron if we ever saw one. It's like saying any of the following similarly self-contradictory oxymorons:

- Military intelligence
- Government organization
- Honest politician

Next time you call the IRS, ask them if they have a publication that tells people who *don't* believe they are liable what their rights are. You will probably be discarded like a hot potato by the agent once he finds out what you are up to!

Ironically, the State of California pulls the same trick with the word "taxpayer". Their Publication 70 "Your Rights as a Taxpayer" uses the same kind of sneaky word play to deceive and evade the truth.

6.9.13 Cover-Up of March 2004: IRS Removed List of Return Types Authorized for SFR from Internal Revenue Manual (I.R.M.), Section 5.1.11.6.8

The We The People Truth in Taxation Hearing held 27-28 February 2002 in Washington, D.C. had an area of inquiry, section 13, entitled: 26 U.S.C. §6020(b) Substitute for Returns. You can view that area of inquiry at:

http://famguardian.org/TaxFreedom/Forms/Discovery/Deposition/Section%2013.htm

That area focused on IRS efforts at performing illegal Substitute for Returns against people who technically are not "taxpayers". Prior to that hearing, a group of 40 researchers, including former IRS agents, assembled evidence to be used at the hearing. Among that evidence compiled for the hearing was an excerpt from section 5.1.11.6.8 of the IRS Internal Revenue Manual, which is the manual that describes proper procedures for doing assessments within the IRS. You can view that evidence at:

http://famguardian.org/TaxFreedom/Forms/Discovery/Deposition/Evidence/Q13.009c.pdf

Below is what that section said, as demonstrated during the hearing:

> 5.1.11.6.8 (05-27-1999)
> IRC 6020(b) Authority
>
> 1. The following returns may be prepared, signed and assessed under the authority of IRC 6020(b):
>   A. Form 940, Employer's Annual Federal Unemployment Tax Return
>   B. Form 941, Employer's Quarterly Federal Tax Return
>   C. Form 943, Employer's Annual Tax Return for Agricultural Employees
>   D. Form 720, Quarterly Federal Excise Tax Return
>   E. Form 2290, Heavy Vehicle Use Tax Return
>   F. Form CT–1, Employer's Annual Railroad Retirement Tax Return
>   G. Form 1065, U.S. Return of Partnership Income.
>
> 2. Pursuant to IRM 1.2.2.97, Delegations of Authority, Order Number 182 (rev. 7), dated 5/5/1997, revenue officers GS-09 and above, and Collection Support Function managers GS-09 and above, have the authority to prepare and execute returns under IRC 6020(b).

We showed earlier in section **Error! Reference source not found.** that the IRS has no legal authority to assess natural persons with a tax liability under Internal Revenue Code, Subtitle A. The above section of the Internal Revenue Manual clearly proves that conclusion. Notice that the form 1040 is NOT listed as one of the forms that the IRS can do a Substitute for Return (SFR) on.

Following the hearings, the IRS apparently read these materials and starting in March 2004, they removed the above content from section 5.1.11.6.8 of their Internal Revenue Manual. This evidence was so damning that the IRS apparently decided to remove it from their website after we made a big public spectacle about it. Now that section is empty! Apparently, they don't want to be held accountable for obeying 26 U.S.C. §6020(b) and want to encourage their employees to improperly administer that very important part of the Internal Revenue Code that allows the illegal flow of money to continue.

6.9.14 Cover-Up of Jan. 2002: IRS Removed the Internal Revenue Manual (IRM) from their Website Search Engine

Apparently frustrated by our website and dedicated patriots everywhere who have been reading the law and the IRS publications to defend their legal and Constitutional rights to not pay direct taxes, the IRS completed redesigning their website (http://www.irs.gov) to remove key portions from their search engine, thereby making it more difficult for patriots to find help on important subjects and understand their responsibilities using the IRS website.

The most valuable portion of their website, the Internal Revenue Manual (IRM), was moved from the Tax Professional's Corner to the FOIA area of their website and conspicuously removed from their search engine. The FOIA area of most government websites is reserved for things the government doesn't want to disclose to people but has to anyway under the Freedom Of Information Act (FOIA). The IRM is several thousand pages long and *removing it from the website search engine makes it extremely difficult and inconvenient for patriots and freedom advocates to locate relevant information and properly comply with the Internal Revenue Code*. We would be willing to bet that their internal intranet accessible only to IRS employees has the document added to their search engine for more convenient use by its *own* employees. We'd recommend doing an FOIA request to find this out to gather evidence to document this hypocritical scam. Please send us a copy of your FOIA response from the IRS if you do so.

The IRS also deleted the area below telling where to file FOIA requests, as though they no longer want any!:

http://www.irs.gov/prod/preview/foia/offices.html

IRS: Is THIS what you call improving customer service and satisfaction and better meeting your mission statement, which says(?):

*"Provide America's taxpayers top quality service by **helping them understand and meet their tax responsibilities** and by applying the tax law with integrity and fairness to all."*

We'd say this strategic move conflicts with your mission statement and makes it *more, not less* difficult for people to understand and meet their legal tax responsibilities! Instead, it simply makes them more dependent on your fraudulent IRS publications and less able to understand the law.

Nice try, IRS, but we were ready for you when you pulled this stunt! Don't fret, patriots! If you want an indexed, searchable version of the IRM as of Sept. 2001, you can go to our site below:

http://famguardian.org/Publications/IRM-020311/0,,i1=5&genericId=21023,00.html

The search box is at the end of the table of contents. However, the search function only works on our home site and not on our mirror sites.

6.9.15 Cover-Up of 2002: W-8 Certificate of Foreign Status Form Removed from the IRS Website December 2000 and replaced with W-8BEN

The IRS website, up until December of 2000, contained a copy of the form W-8 available for download. The form was simple to use and could exempt you from both employment withholding and tax withholding of banks on accounts. After that date, the form was removed, presumably because so many people were using the simple nonresident alien approach advocated in this book and by other authors. Remember that nonresident aliens have no requirement to pay any income tax or file returns if they have no income from inside the federal United States, which includes the District of Columbia, the federal territories, and federal enclaves within states of the Union. Without a tax liability, nonresident aliens domiciled in the 50 Union states don't have to file a tax return or provide any information about themselves to the IRS! How then does the IRS track these people and find out about them so they can use their computers to harass them and extort money out of them? They deceive them into thinking that they are required to file returns and pay tax, and that they are required to get a Taxpayer ID Number or T.I.N. (as a substitute for a Social Security Number).

After December 2000, the IRS replaced the W-8 form with the W-8BEN form, and they did so, it would appear, to once again to create a *false presumption* in the minds of most Americans, using the form itself, that even nonresident aliens are "liable" to pay income tax and to file a return, which wasn't previously the case with the W-8 form. They did this at a time when there were no changes in the laws that would add this new requirement and when a lot of people were using the W-8 forms. Apparently, the IRS wanted to try, without legal authority we might add, to close the nonresident alien loophole being used by so many patriots to exit the income tax system by modifying the IRS Forms. Once again, they did their dirty work using sneaky definitions just like they did with the Internal Revenue Code. The instructions for the form define "beneficial owner" as follows:

> "**Beneficial owner**. *For payments other than those for which a reduced rate of withholding is claimed under an income tax treaty, **the beneficial owner of income is generally the person who is required under U.S. tax principles to include the income in gross income on a tax return…***"

The W-8BEN form clearly implies that even the nonresident alien in this case:

1. "Is required" to file a tax return;
2. "Is required" to show even foreign income on the tax return

We know from *Non-Resident Non-Person Position*, Form #05.020, Section 6.4 (entitled "Tax Liability and Responsibilities of Nonresident Aliens") that these assertions aren't true and that nonresident aliens with no U.S.**/federal zone source income clearly aren't liable for income tax, nor do they have "gross income", and they also aren't required to file a tax return. This fact is abundantly confirmed by examining 26 U.S.C. §861(a)(3)(C)(i). The insidious and misleading changes in the W-8BEN form, however, creates a false presumption that advantages the IRS! We must continually remember from our discussion in section 3.19 (entitled "IRS Publications and Internal Revenue Manual (IRM)), however, that the IRS publications are NOT to be relied upon to sustain a position and you are wasting your time to rely on them.

Not only are the instructions for the W-8 insidious and damaging to the freedoms of nonresident alien Sovereign Natural Born Citizens, but the W-8BEN form itself is also misleading and creates a false presumption. The title is "Certificate of Foreign Status of Beneficial Owner for United States Tax Withholding". This creates the impression that the withholding is occurring in the "United States"**/federal zone, which clearly isn't the case in the 50 union states! Also be careful when filling in block 6, because it says "U.S. taxpayer identification number". If you put ANYTHING in this box, then you are claiming you are a taxpayer, which you are not as a nonresident alien domiciled in the 50 union states.

6.9.16 Cover-Up of 1999: IRS CID Agent Joe Banister Terminated by IRS For Discovering The Truth About Voluntary Nature of Income Taxes!

The story below was taken from the personal testimony of Joe Banister given to me at the Freedom Rally held April 7, 2001 in Irvine hosted by the Freedom Law School (http://www.livefreenow.com). Joe also maintains his own website at:

http://freedomabovefortune.com/

Joe Banister has a BS degree in accounting and spent three years at KPMG Peat Marwick on their professional staff as a senior tax specialist and staff auditor. He went to work for the IRS in 1993 and was a licensed Certified Public Accountant. He enforced tax codes for the IRS, and quickly achieved high status and many awards within the government during his five year career with the IRS. Joe was an agent of the IRS Criminal Investigative Division in San Jose, CA for five years. In December 1996, he heard a talk show radio program with Geoff Metcalf in San Jose, and overheard Devvy Kidd being interviewed. She was claiming that the federal income tax was voluntary. Since Joe made his domiciled investigating criminal violations of the taxing statutes, he listened intently to the radio program. His life has never been the same since then!

Subsequently, Joe wrote Devvy and asked for some materials. He received a package in January 1997 from Devvy containing two books approximately 50 pages in length. The books were entitled *Why a Bankrupt America* and *Blind Loyalty*. The books were filled with very shocking claims about the United Nations, the federal income tax system, and the federal banking and monetary systems, among other topics. He read the books thoroughly and found a more detailed explanation of the allegations she made on the radio. There were three allegations that he found the most profound and unbelievable:

1. *Allegation 1*: Due to Limitations Imposed By The U.S. Constitution, Filing of Federal Income Tax Returns and Payment of Federal Income Tax Is Voluntary, Not Mandatory.
2. *Allegation 2*: The 16th Amendment To The U.S. Constitution, The Amendment Which Precipitated The Federal Income Tax, Was Never Legally Ratified.
3. *Allegation 3*: The U.S. Government Finances Its Operations Form the Unconstitutional Creation of Fiat Money, not with Revenue From Income Taxes.

Kidd's allegations were so shocking to Mr. Banister and contrary to everything he had been taught that he spent many months simply thinking and meditating about what he had read. In the latter part of 1997, he read the book, *The Creature From Jekyll Island*, authored by G. Edward Griffin. Griffin's book shared some of the same subject matter as Kidd's books, which prompted Joe to pick Devvy's books up a second time. During this second review, he noticed an unusual aspect about Kidd's books that he had paid little attention to the first time through. Kidd had a practice of including telephone numbers of the people responsible for the evidence she provided. It was at this point that Joe realized he could simply telephone these men and make direct inquiries about the evidence supporting their allegations. In December 1997, Joe decided to contact them personally in order to determine the truth.

During the ensuing two years, Joe did his own research on his private time to try to verify the truth of the three allegations. Eventually, he convinced himself that Devvy's claims were entirely true, and after two years of research, he submitted a preliminary report of his findings to his supervisor at the IRS. That supervisor forwarded the report up the chain. **Joe asked his I.R.S. supervisor to help him refute the claims so he could have a clear conscience about continuing to work at the IRS. Instead of helping correct Joe in the error in his findings or set the record straight, his supervisor asked him to either desist or tender his resignation. Joe Banister decided to leave the IRS and quit on the anniversary of the signing of the 16th Amendment, February 25, 1999.** He eventually joined the tax freedom movement! He also joined the We The People Foundation (http://www.givemeliberty.org) soon after his resignation and supported the efforts of employers to stop withholding. Part of his story was featured on a 60 Minutes II episode aired on CBS on April 2, 2001 in connection with a story entitled "Tax Revolt". He was described as helping employers to legally stop income tax withholding of their employees. Joe defended the legal position of the employer during the 60 Minutes interview. He was very convincing. He has also been exposed to this book and I have personally met with him and obtained an autographed copy of his book about the illegality of the federal income tax. He is also a frequent speaker with the Freedom Law School and appears at their annual Freedom Rallies, usually held in April of each year in Irvine, CA (contact Peymon Mottahedeh, the President, at http://www.livefreenow.com/).

We encourage you to read more about Joe Banister's story on his website shown above. You can also get a copy of his report off his website, entitled *Investigating the Federal Income Tax: A Preliminary Report*. The cost is $20.

6.9.17 Cover-Up of 1995: Modified Regulations to Remove Pointers to Form 2555 for IRC Section 1 Liability for Federal Income Tax

The Paperwork Reduction Act of 1980 requires that every form used by the federal government to collect information from the public first be approved by the Office of Management and Budget ("OMB"). The regulations at 26 C.F.R. §602.101 contain a table listing the OMB-approved forms for each section of regulations. The regulations at 26 C.F.R. §1.1-1 are entitled "*Income tax on individuals*," and correspond to 26 U.S.C. §1 (which imposes the "income tax"). Up until 1995, the first line in this table identified Form 2555, "*Foreign Earned Income*," as the only approved form under 26 C.F.R. §1.1-1. In 1995, after many "tax resistance" groups had become aware of this, the listing for "1.1-1" was removed from the list, in order to avoid "confusion," according to the Department of the Treasury. The process of applying for, and receiving OMB approval for a form makes the possibility of an error extremely remote. The Department of the Treasury *requested* that Form 2555 be approved for 1.1-1, and the Office of Management and Budget *approved* it. When the entry drew too much attention, it was removed. At present no forms are approved for use with 26 C.F.R. §1.1-1.

6.9.18 Cover-Up of 1993--HOT!!: IRS Removed References in IRS Publication 515 to Citizens Not Being Liable for Tax and Confused New Language

A key piece of the puzzle that unraveled the IRS' Great Deception was formerly found in 26 C.F.R. §1.1441 and in IRS Publication 515. Recall that we have been saying all along that foreign earned income is the only thing to be counted as "gross income" for the purposes of 26 U.S.C. §861?

Call 1-800-TAX-FORM and request a copy of IRS Publication 515, titled "Withholding of Tax on Nonresident Aliens and Foreign Entities". Now, you might look this up and ask yourself, "what on Earth does that have to do with me?"

Here's what. Inside Publication 515, there appears a statement the IRS hopes you never see. Under the main heading "Withholding Exemptions and Reductions" and within the paragraph titled "Evidence of Residence", the IRS states in speaking to the payer of income:

> "If an individual gives you a written statement stating that he or she is a citizen or resident of the United States, and you do not know otherwise, you do not have to withhold tax."

The 1994 version of Publication 515 varied somewhat. Instead of ending with "...*you do not have to withhold tax*", it continues:

> "...you do not have to withhold tax under the rules discussed in this publication. Instead, get Publication 15, Circular E, Employer's Tax Guide."

Of course our friends at the IRS fail to clarify that Circular E, Employer's Tax Guide has to do with *employment* taxes under subtitle C, and has nothing whatsoever to do with the withholding of *income* tax under subtitle A, the subject of Publication 515. Isn't that interesting?

> *Considering the deluge of recent requests from Patriotic Americans for a copy of Publication 515, do you suppose that this creative suggestion to go get Circular E instead and read about employment taxes could have been added to misdirect or confuse anyone?*

Remember, the "S" in IRS stands for "Service"!

And what is the statement of citizenship? It's simply an affidavit, notarized and signed under penalties of perjury stating that "I, John Doe, am a Citizen of the United States." It's that simple. So, the bottom line is that, according to the IRS, if you agree a "Citizen or resident of the United States", the payer of your income does not have to withhold tax. Imagine that!

Chapter 7: Resources for Tax Fraud Fighters

Now ask yourself this question: If a United States citizen every really were liable for tax withholding, why would the IRS ever have printed this statement anywhere? Why would it even exist in writing?

It exists because the Law behind the Statement of Citizenship is 26 C.F.R. §1.1441-5 "Claiming to be a person not subject to withholding", paragraph (a) of which states:

> "For purposes of Chapter 3 of the Code, an individual's written statement that he or she is a citizen or resident of the United States may be relied upon by the payer of the income as proof that such individual is a citizen or resident of the United States."

And where is Chapter 3 of the Code? In Subtitle A, income tax. 1.1441-5, paragraph (c) states:

> "The duplicate copy of each statement and form filed pursuant to this section shall be forwarded with a letter of transmittal to Internal Revenue Service Center, Philadelphia PA 19255. The original statement shall be retained by the withholding agent."

And why must the Statement of Citizenship be sent to Philadelphia, and not the local IRS office or regional service center? Because Philadelphia is the IRS' international service center--the *foreign* service center, which makes perfect sense since the income tax is a tax on foreign activity only!

The IRS Philadelphia office has never been known to reject a Statement of Citizenship from a withholding agent. It also does not acknowledge receipt of the Statement of Citizenship, which confuses some people. The reason for this is simple. If the statement were inaccurate or off-point, there would be a rebuttal from Philadelphia. Silence, in this case, is acceptance.

> *Because of a deluge of requests and attention focused on IRS Publication 515 and 26 C.F.R. §1.1441-5 by patriotic Americans who didn't want to have to pay or file income taxes legally in 1998, 26 C.F.R. §1.1441-5 was rewritten in 1993!!! The cover-up expands! Instead, all we are left with is a confusing pointer back to Circular E, the Employer's Tax Guide, and no mention of how to handle nonresident aliens!! Apparently, the truth got just a little too close for comfort so the Great Deceiver bureaucrat lawyers in Congress and at the IRS had to bury it a little deeper in legalese to confuse the scent for us tax freedom hound dogs!! BARK, BARK!!! Sick-em!*

6.9.19 Obfuscation of 2004: IRS Publication 519 added deceptive reference to "United States" to deceive and confuse readers

IRS Publication 519, Starting in year 2004, introduced the following language to infer that the term "United States" as used in the Internal Revenue Code, includes the 50 states of the Union for the purposes of jurisdiction to tax under Internal Revenue Code, Subtitle A:

> *Substantial Presence Test*
>
> *Example. You were physically present in the United States on 120 days in each of the years 2003, 2004, and 2006. To determine if you meet the substantial presence test for 2005, count the full 120 days of presence in 2006, 40 days in 2004 (1/3 of 130), and 20 days in 2003 (1/6 of 120). Because the total for the 30 year period is 180 days, you are not considered a resident under the substantial presence test for 2005.*
>
> "The term United States includes the following areas.
>
> - "All 50 states and the District of Columbia."
> - "The territorial waters of the United States"
>
> *[...]*
>
> "The term does not include U.S. possessions and territories or U.S. airspace."
> *[IRS Publication 519 (2005), p. 4*
> *SOURCE: http://famguardian.org/TaxFreedom/Forms/IRS/IRSPub519-2005.pdf]*

We have several points to make about the above reference:

1. The above cite was added to the publication in about 2004 in an apparent response to the content of this book, as a way to deceive the readers and stop the spread of the Non-Resident Non-Person Position.
2. The definition comes from an IRS Publication, which the IRS Internal Revenue Manual admits is UNTRUSTWORTHY and not guaranteed to be accurate:

> "IRS Publications, issued by the National Office, explain the law in plain language for taxpayers and their advisors... While a good source of general information, publications *should not be cited to sustain a position.*"
> [Internal Revenue Manual (I.R.M.), Section 4.10.7.2.8 *(05-14-1999)*]

See also:
> *Federal Courts and the IRS' Own IRM Say the IRS is NOT RESPONSIBLE for Its Actions or its Words or for Following Its Own Written Procedures*, Family Guardian Fellowship
> http://famguardian.org/Subjects/Taxes/Articles/IRSNotResponsible.htm

3. The text above is an EXAMPLE which does not infer or imply or specify the context in which it may suitably be used. There are actually THREE and not ONE context in which the term "United States" could be referring to or implied and only *one* of them is used in the above example, which is the *third* one listed below:
    3.1. The meaning of the term "United States" within the Internal Revenue Code, Subtitle A.
    3.2. The meaning of the term "United States" within ordinary speech, which most people associate with the COUNTRY to include states of the Union.
    3.3. The meaning of "United States" in the context of jurisdiction over aliens (not "citizens" or "nationals") temporarily present in the *country* "United States", which in this context includes all 50 states *and* the District of Columbia.

In the context of item 3.3 above, the U.S. Supreme Court has repeatedly affirmed the plenary power of Congress over aliens in this country, *wherever they are located to include areas within the exclusive jurisdiction of states of the Union*:

> *In accord with ancient principles of the international law of nation-states, the Court in The Chinese Exclusion Case, 130 U.S. 581, 609 (1889), and in Fong Yue Ting v. United States, 149 U.S. 698 (1893), held broadly, as the Government describes it, Brief for Appellants 20, that **the power to exclude aliens is "inherent in sovereignty, necessary for maintaining normal international relations and defending the country against foreign encroachments and dangers - a power to be exercised exclusively by the political branches of government . . . ." Since that time, the Court's general reaffirmations of this principle have [408 U.S. 753, 766] been legion. 6 The Court without exception has sustained Congress' "plenary power to make rules for the admission of aliens and to exclude those who possess those characteristics which Congress has forbidden." Boutilier v. Immigration and Naturalization Service, 387 U.S. 118, 123 (1967). "[O]ver no conceivable subject is the legislative power of Congress more complete than it is over" the admission of aliens. Oceanic Navigation Co. v. Stranahan, 214 U.S. 320, 339 (1909).***
> *[Kleindienst v. Mandel, 408 U.S. 753 (1972)]*

> *While under our constitution and form of government the great mass of local matters is controlled by local authorities, **the United States, in their relation to foreign countries and their subjects or citizens, are one nation, invested with powers which belong to independent nations, the exercise of which can be invoked for the maintenance of its absolute independence and security throughout its entire territory.** The powers to declare war, make treaties, suppress insurrection, repel invasion, regulate foreign commerce, secure republican governments to the states, and admit subjects of other nations to citizenship, are all sovereign powers, restricted in their exercise only by the constitution itself and considerations of public policy and justice which control, more or less, the conduct of all civilized nations. As said by this court in the case of Cohens v. Virginia, 6 Wheat. 264, 413, speaking by the same great chief justice: **'That the United States form, for many, and for most important purposes, a single nation, has not yet been denied. In war, we are one people. In making peace, we are one people. In all commercial regulations, we are one and the same people. In many other respects, the American people are one; and the government which is alone capable of controlling and managing their interests in all these respects is the government of the Union.** It is their government, and in that character they have no other. America has chosen to [130 U.S. 581, 605] be in many respects, and to many purposes, a nation; and for all these purposes her government is complete; to all these objects, it is competent. **The people have declared that in the exercise of all powers given for these objects it is supreme. It can, then, in effecting these objects, legitimately control all individuals or governments within the American territory."***

> *[. . .]*

> *"**The power of exclusion of foreigners being an incident of sovereignty belonging to the government of the United States as a part of those sovereign powers delegated by the constitution**, the right to its exercise at any time when, in the judgment of the government, the interests of the country require it, cannot be granted away or restrained on behalf of any one. **The powers of government are delegated in trust to the United States, and are incapable of transfer to any other parties.** They cannot be abandoned or surrendered. **Nor can their exercise be hampered, when needed for the public good, by any considerations of private interest. The exercise of these public trusts is not the subject of barter or contract.**"*

[Chae Chan Ping v. U.S., 130 U.S. 581 (1889)]

Therefore, in regard to control over aliens present anywhere within the American confederation, the general government legislates over all the territory of the American Union, including those of the states. Consequently, for the purposes of determining "permanent residence" of aliens ONLY, the term "United States" as used in item 3 above must be interpreted to include the 50 states of the Union as the IRS indicates above. HOWEVER:

1. The Presence Test indicated does *not* refer to "citizens" or "nationals". The Presence Test is found in 26 U.S.C. §7701(b)(3) and references ONLY "aliens" as defined in 26 U.S.C. §7701(b)(1)(A) and not "nonresident aliens" defined in 26 U.S.C. §7701(b)(1)(B) or "citizens" defined in 26 C.F.R. §1.1-1(c). Therefore, an alien domiciled in a state of the Union could be a "resident" within the meaning of the presence test while neither a "citizen" nor a "national" would be considered a "resident" under the *SAME* test when located in the SAME place. Under the I.R.C., one cannot be a "resident" (which is an alien with a domicile) and either a "citizen" or a "national" at the *same* time. This is confirmed by the Law of Nations, which the Founding Fathers used to write the Constitution:

    > "**Residents, as distinguished from citizens, are aliens who are permitted to take up a permanent abode in the country.** Being bound to the society by reason of their dwelling in it, they are subject to its law so long as they remain there, and being protected by it, they must defend it, although they do not enjoy all the rights of citizens. They have only certain privileges which the law, or custom, gives them. Permanent residents are those who have been given the right of perpetual residence. They are a sort of citizens of a less privileged character, and are subject to the society without enjoying all its advantages. Their children succeed to their status; for the right of perpetual residence given them by the State passes to their children."
    > [Law of Nations, Vattel, p. 87
    > SOURCE: http://famguardian.org/TaxFreedom/CitesByTopic/Resident-LawOfNations.pdf]

2. Remember that the only context in which "residence" is defined or described anywhere in the Internal Revenue Code is in the context of "aliens", and not in the context of either "citizens" or "nationals". See 26 C.F.R. §1.871-2 and section 4 of the article below:

    > *Why Domicile and Becoming a "Taxpayer" Require Your Consent*, Form #05.002
    > http://sedm.org/Forms/FormIndex.htm

    Therefore, a person who is a "national" but not a "citizen" and a "nonresident alien" can NOT have a "residence" as defined anywhere in the Internal Revenue Code.

3. For the purposes of determining *tax liability and not residency of all persons*, we must defer to the definition of "United States" found in 26 U.S.C. §7701(a)(9) and (a)(10), which is limited to the District of Columbia and nowhere expanded in the Internal Revenue Code, Subtitle A to include any other place.

Based on the foregoing, we must conclude that the IRS' statement above is a deception and a ruse intended to compel false presumption under the influence of CONSTRUCTIVE FRAUD that will maximize the illegal flow of PLUNDER to the federal government. It is provided as an example and cannot mean the legal definition of "United States" used in the Internal Revenue Code. If they wish to imply that ALL THREE of the contexts in which the term "United States" could be used are *the same*, then they should say so and provide statutory and regulatory authority for saying so. Until then, we must defer to the definition of "United States" found within 26 U.S.C. §7701(a)(9) and (a)(10). This is a consequence of the following doctrine of the Supreme Court:

> "Keeping in mind the well-settled rule that **the citizen is exempt from taxation unless the same is imposed by clear and unequivocal language, and that where the construction of a tax law is doubtful, the doubt is to be resolved in favor of those upon whom the tax is sought to be laid.**"
> [Spreckels Sugar Refining Co. v. McClain, 192 U.S. 297 (1904)]

6.9.20 Cover-Up of 2012: IRS removed exemption for withholding and reporting for "U.S. persons" on the W-9 form even though it is still in the regulations

2011 was the last year that the Form W-9 clearly showed the exemption for U.S. persons from withholding and reporting. That exemption from withholding and reporting is found in the regulations at 26 C.F.R. §1.1441-1(d)(1) and TD8734 (62 F.R. 53391, SEDM Exhibit #09.038). Below is a snapshot of the form for that year:

Figure 6-4: IRS Form W-9, 2011

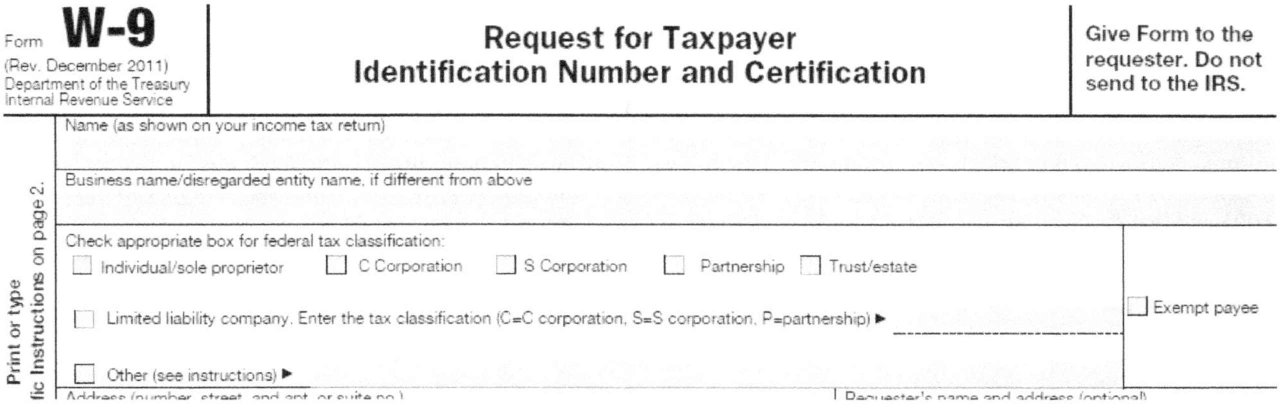
Form **W-9**
(Rev. December 2011)
Department of the Treasury
Internal Revenue Service

Request for Taxpayer Identification Number and Certification

Give Form to the requester. Do not send to the IRS.

Print or type
...ic Instructions on page 2.

Name (as shown on your income tax return)

Business name/disregarded entity name, if different from above

Check appropriate box for federal tax classification:
☐ Individual/sole proprietor ☐ C Corporation ☐ S Corporation ☐ Partnership ☐ Trust/estate

☐ Limited liability company. Enter the tax classification (C=C corporation, S=S corporation, P=partnership) ▶

☐ Exempt payee

☐ Other (see instructions) ▶

Address (number, street, and apt. or suite no.) | Requester's name and address (optional)

The current version of the IRS Form W-9 eliminates the "Exempt payee" from the above, even though such status is and exemption still referenced in the regulations at 26 C.F.R. §1.1441(d).

Figure 6-5: IRS Form W-9, 2017

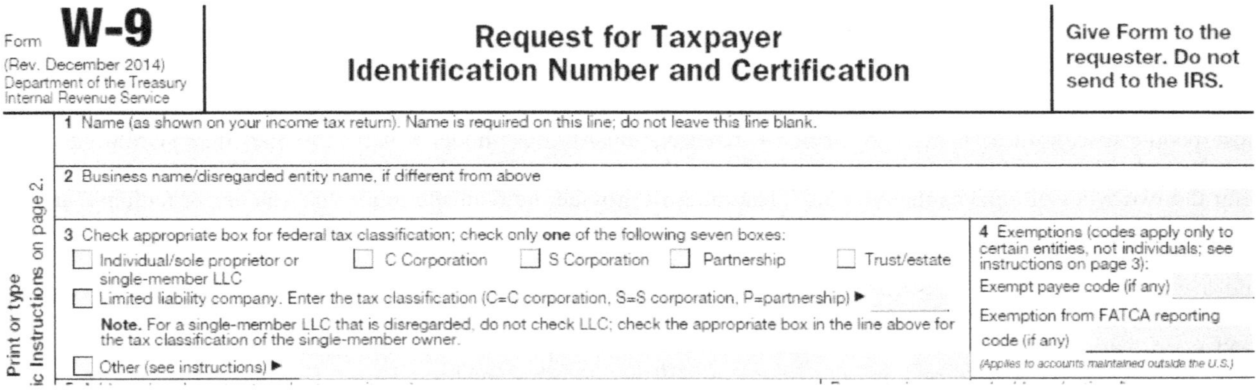
Form **W-9**
(Rev. December 2014)
Department of the Treasury
Internal Revenue Service

Request for Taxpayer Identification Number and Certification

Give Form to the requester. Do not send to the IRS.

Print or type
...ic Instructions on page 2.

1 Name (as shown on your income tax return). Name is required on this line; do not leave this line blank.

2 Business name/disregarded entity name, if different from above

3 Check appropriate box for federal tax classification; check only **one** of the following seven boxes:
☐ Individual/sole proprietor or single-member LLC ☐ C Corporation ☐ S Corporation ☐ Partnership ☐ Trust/estate

☐ Limited liability company. Enter the tax classification (C=C corporation, S=S corporation, P=partnership) ▶

Note. For a single-member LLC that is disregarded, do not check LLC; check the appropriate box in the line above for the tax classification of the single-member owner.

☐ Other (see instructions) ▶

4 Exemptions (codes apply only to certain entities, not individuals; see instructions on page 3):
Exempt payee code (if any)
Exemption from FATCA reporting code (if any)
(Applies to accounts maintained outside the U.S.)

Notice the block to the right says "(applies to accounts maintained outside the U.S.)". 26 C.F.R. §1.1441-1(d) currently provides an exemption for accounts WITHIN the U.S., and used to appear in that block, but was removed. By "U.S.", we obviously mean that defined in 26 U.S.C. §7701(a)(9) and (a)(10) and 4 U.S.C. §110(d), which means federal territory subject to the exclusive jurisdiction of Congress and not within the exclusive jurisdiction of any state of the Union.

If you want to be exempt on the current form, you have to check the "Other" block and write the following:

> *"Exempt payee. See 26 C.F.R. §1.1441-1(d). No withholding or reporting. See: https://sedm.org/Forms/04-Tax/0-CorrErrInfoRtns/CorrErrInfoRtns.pdf"*

This scam is obviously designed to cause people who are NOT subject to the income tax when within the "United States" (federal zone) to pay anyway.

6.10 Department of State (DOS) Scandals Related to Income Taxes

We say earlier in section 2.8.13 that the federal courts commonly but erroneously "presume" that all people are "U.S. citizens" under 8 U.S.C. §1401 in order to illegally expand federal jurisdiction. Here is an example:

> *"Unless the defendant can prove he is **not** a citizen of the United States, the IRS has the right to inquire and determine a tax liability."*
> *[U.S. v. Slater, 545 Fed.Supp. 179,182 (1982).]*

Therefore, it is very important to establish proof that you are not a statutory "national and citizen of the United States** at birth" under 8 U.S.C. §1401. Consequently, the *Sovereignty Forms and Instructions Manual*, Form #10.005 in section

4.5.3.13 suggests that readers obtain what is called a "Certificate of non-citizen National Status" as certified proof that they are not "U.S. citizens", and we recommend using this as proof in any judicial proceeding. We also recommend getting certified proof of your "non-citizen national status" into your IRS administrative record long before you involve yourself in any judicial proceeding, so that the judge may not keep it out of evidence or out of view of the jury to prejudice your case.

Well, the government is catching on to this and obstructing justice by the following devious means. A number of our readers have contacted us to report that they have attempted to obtain a "Certificate of non-citizen National Status" under the authority of 8 U.S.C. §1452 as suggested in sections 4.5.3.13 and 5.6.12 in the *Sovereignty Forms and Instructions Manual*, Form #10.005 and that the Secretary of State of the United States positively refuses his duty under this statute to issue the requested certificate. The person we talked to indicated that now the Secretary of the State has posted a notice on their website indicating that they have changed their policy and are no longer issuing such certificates, although they did not explain why. Here is the notice:

http://travel.state.gov/noncit_cert.html

There's obviously a cover-up going on here folks. The slaves have figured out how to remove their legal chains and leave the federal plantation, so our crooked government is blocking their exit by depriving them of the evidence needed to prove that they are not "U.S. citizens" under the Internal Revenue Code. There is still a way to force the Secretary of State to do his duty under 8 U.S.C. §1452 by providing the requested certificate, but it takes a separate lawsuit in a federal court to do so, and that lawsuit is called a "writ of mandamus". A writ of mandamus is simply a request that the court compel a public servant to perform his duty under the law. Not only that, but the conspiracy against rights surrounding the citizenship issue gets MUCH worse.

If you read the above link to the Department of State website, you will find out that the Department of State recommends that for those people who want a "Certificate of non-Citizen National Status" under 8 U.S.C. §1452, they should get a U.S. Passport instead. There is a big problem with that, because the passport simply says "citizen/national" rather than identifying which of the two types of citizens that you are. That doesn't provide the requisite proof that you are a "national" under 8 U.S.C. §1101(a)(22)(B). It's certified, but it doesn't distinguish in the way you need at a tax trial.

To find a way around this political roadblock to emancipation, we applied for a U.S. Passport as they recommended. However, before we did, we amended the DS-11 application form electronically so as to indicate that *both* of our parents *and* our spouse are "nationals" rather than "U.S. citizens" in blocks 14, 15, and 16. This removes the incorrect presumption on the form. We also filled out the form without a Slave Surveillance Number and turned it in. The clerk didn't even pause, but processed the application and gave us a passport a few hours later. When we came to pick up the passport, we asked the clerk if we could have a copy of the approved DS-11 application form and we asked to have it certified. We wanted it certified so that we could use it as evidence admissible in court of our true status as a "non-resident on-persons" and "nationals" under 8 U.S.C. §1101(a)(21). Guess what? Here is what the clerk told us, which is more foot dragging and really surprised us:

> *"It is our policy NOT to provide copies of the application form. If you want a certified copy, then the only way you can get it is through a Privacy Act request."*

To make things worse, we asked WHY they have this requirement and from what legal authority it derives, and we got evasive comments back. Therefore, we have written a Privacy Act request that you can reuse which demands a copy of the approved DS-11 Passport Application form from the Department of State, along with several other key documents. You can find that document either in section 3.6.13 of the *Sovereignty Forms and Instructions Manual*, Form #10.005. That form is also available online below:

http://famguardian.org/TaxFreedom/Forms/Emancipation/DOSFOIA-Non-CertDS11.htm

One of our readers who attempted to procure the Certificate of "non-citizen National Status" by mail using the form provided in section 5.6.12 of the *Sovereignty Forms and Instructions Manual*, Form #10.005 also received the following letter back from the Department of State in response to his correspondence:

http://famguardian.org/TaxFreedom/Evidence/Citizenship/dos-AmCitizenResponse.pdf

Based on the crooked behavior of the Department of State in this instance, the government obviously doesn't want to cooperate with people in obtaining proof of their true citizenship status. They know that if the word gets out that this works, and everyone does it, we will have a country of "nontaxpayers" and "nonresident aliens" as we clearly show in section **Error! Reference source not found.** and following! He.. he…he! Scumbags!

6.11 Department of Justice (DOJ) Scandals Related to Income Taxes

> *"Evil men do not understand justice,*
> *But those who seek the Lord understand **all**."*
> *[Prov. 28:5, Bible, NKJV]*

> *"He who justifies the wicked, and he who condemns the just,*
> *Both of them alike are an abomination to the Lord."*
> *[Prov. 17:15, Bible, NKJV]*

As we established in section **Error! Reference source not found.**, the Department of Justice has NO delegated authority to prosecute IRC Subtitle A Income Tax Crimes. Below are some examples of some of the illegal and unethical things they have done in the absence of that authority.

6.11.1 Prosecution of Dr. Phil Roberts: "Political Tax Prisoner"

In the opening of this book, section 1.9 entitled "Political 'Tax' Prisoners" talked about an unfortunate victim of legal abuse by the Department of Justice (DOJ) named Dr. Phil Roberts. Phil is a respected member of the community, a physician, and an intelligent and principled man. We have summarized his case (Federal District Court in Fort Smith, Arkansas, case # 00-20018-001) in that section using information provided by his attorney and relatives. We also have the entire transcript (over 700 pages!) of his criminal tax trial posted on our website for you to read (http://famguardian.org, look in Tax Freedom and then under the heading "Case Studies"). The transcript and the Trial Notes are instructive educational aids for you to learn how many different constitutional rights of Dr. Roberts were arrogantly and illegally violated by the Department of Justice conspiring with the judge of that court. It is obvious that many laws were violated, and below are just a few of the violations:

1. **_Department of Justice_**:
    1.1. Taking of property not based on law (26 C.F.R. §601.106(f)(1).
    1.2. Retaliating against a witness, victim, or informant (18 U.S.C. §1513).
    1.3. Blackmail (18 U.S.C. §873).
    1.4. Extortion (18 U.S.C. §872)
2. **_Judge_**:
    2.1. Federally protected rights being violated (18 U.S.C. §245).
    2.2. Conspiracy against rights (18 U.S.C. §241).
    2.3. Conflict of interest (28 U.S.C. §455).

In the year 2000, Dr. Phil Roberts was prosecuted and eventually imprisoned for willful failure to file under 26 U.S.C. §7203, after he took the IRS to court on three different occasions because they kept harassing him about filing his tax return but refused to produce any evidence or a legal basis why they thought he had any tax liability whatsoever. Among the incredible treachery foisted upon him by the judge, we are told, was the following, reported directly to us by his attorney, Oscar Stilley and appearing in the trial transcript itself:

1. Tried to deny Dr. Roberts the right to counsel of his choice because the judge didn't like his attorney.
2. Would not allow his attorney to cross-examine prospective jurists during voir dire (his attorney told us this on the phone).
3. Slipped three pre-selected jurists into the courtroom at the last minute.
4. Rigged the drawing box for selecting jurists.
5. Judge kept the instructions he gave to the jury OFF THE RECORD (so he couldn't be prosecuted for jury tampering). See items 69 and 247.
6. At his arraignment, the court allowed Dr. Roberts to be forced by the DOJ in front of the jury, to sign his tax return (like making Jesus carry his cross before they nailed him to it). All along, they knew he had refused to sign his return, but not to submit it, because he wanted to be made aware what specific law made him liable to pay income tax! How can you prosecute someone for wanting an answer to that question and being stonewalled all the way up to trial by the IRS, who refused to answer the question?
7. Judge would not allow any laws to be discussed in front of the jury. (item 35).
8. Would not allow Dr. Roberts to demand or expect the DOJ to produce the law he violated.

9. Told his attorney that his license would be revoked if he tried to discuss the law because the ability to practice law was a "privilege" granted by the court (see item 232).
10. Refused to allow Dr. Roberts to discuss the legal basis for his reasonable cause belief that he had no income tax liability. Ignored repeated requests from his counsel throughout the trial to discuss the Internal revenue Code (a violation of his Sixth Amendment rights).
11. Overruled most of the defense's objections and almost none of the Department of Justice's.
12. Insisted that the defense tell him the questions he wanted to ask of witnesses in a sidebar BEFORE he actually asked them.
13. Ignored Dr. Robert's Fifth Amendment right to not incriminate himself by filing a tax return.

And the punishment for exercising his First Amendment right to not talk to his government, his Fifth Amendment right to not incriminate himself by not filing a tax return was a prison sentence of about 1 year and a half. Remember that we said that what makes something a right is that the exercise of the right cannot be penalized, regulated, or punished in any way when one freely chooses to exercise the right. Do we really have any rights with such a prejudicial and conspiratorial court system and a Department of Justice that instead of defending criminals, makes us ALL into criminals for exercising our constitutional rights? Below are some of the ridiculous statements made by the judge during the trial, all of which you can read yourself on our website in the actual trial transcript. The following Trial Notes were prepared by Dr. Roberts' brother, Robert Roberts, to summarize the over 700 pages of transcript on the case. This transcript is very effective at showing that there is indeed a judicial conspiracy to protect the income tax, and that the judge was conspiring with the DOJ to make an example out of Dr. Roberts. They wanted to get him into jail so they could use the fear factor to continue intimidating other citizens to continue "volunteering" to pay taxes for which they weren't liable. The numbers in the left margin come from the Trial Notes, and are there so we can refer to specific comments afterward:

35   Court informs the potential jurors that he will tell them **the law** and that they must follow his instructions whether they agree or not. P59, 21-25 & P60, 1
49.   Judge implies to potential jurors that **everyone must pay the correct amount of Federal Income Tax.** P78, 5-10
69.   **Jury instructions given but not entered into the transcript.** P120, 18
78.   Statement objected to by prosecution, "Yeah" agrees the court, and court states **"Let's not argue the law."** P131, 1-7
80.   Court tells defense **"You know, don't argue the law."** P131, 22-23
83.   Court states **"Let's not argue the law..." "Don't argue the law!"** P133, 12-14
88.   Defenses' opening statement is again objected to and the court calls for a bar side conference where the counsel is directed to change his opening statement to the jury. Objection sustained. P137, 17-25, P138 - P143 (all)
89.   Defense tells jury that the prosecution must show the statute of law requiring a person to make and file and income tax return. P143, 9-15
90.   Defense tells jury that defendant wrote a letter to the IRS requesting that they show him the law...P143, 24-25 & P144, 1-2
91.   Defense objects to the introduction of previous tax returns as evidence of knowledge by the prosecution., P147, 1-7
92.   Objection overruled. P147, 8-9
93.   Court states **"In this matter, you know, if you're making similar objection, I'm probably going to overrule those, too."** P147, 16-18
95.   Prosecution moves to enter exhibit (previously filed tax return). Court states: **"Same objection Mr. Stilley? It will be admitted over your objection."** P149, 5-6
102.   Defense counsel cross examines asking if the witness can **"... tell us what law required Dr. Roberts to file a tax return?"**
OBJECTED to and sustained by the court.P156, 1-6
103.   Sidebar called for by the court. P156, 9-10
104.   Court asks the prosecution if they have already been over this, prosecution gives a thorough argument why it feels that the court should not allow this line of questioning and the court agrees. P156, 15-23
112.   Defense asks witness on cross if he perhaps knows the law that requires the defendant to file... Objected to and sustained by the court. P191, 10-13
113.   Defense asks if the terms **"make"** and **"file"** meant the same thing... OBJECTED TO AND SUSTAINED BY THE COURT. P193, 14-18
116.   Court states **"Let's not get into the definition of income."** Orders defense off of the question. P219, 18-23

120. Defense asks that prosecution witness, Tom Bryan be excluded from the court room while Magistrate Jones-Stites is questioned. Court refuses stating that Bryan "**... is the representative of the government and he's not going to be excluded.**"   P278, 17-22
122. Court sustains prosecutions objection to Jones-Stites being required to testify in court for the defense stating: "**I'm going to sustain the objection to it. You've made your offer of proof and that will be a part of the record available to the Eighth Circuit <u>when you appeal this matter.</u>**" P289, 10-14
124. Defense asks the court if the witness admits to selective prosecution against the defendant and the court interjects that "**I'm not going to let you put her up there to ask that. What else are you going to put her up there and ask her?**" P292, 4-6
131. Under cross examination, the defense asks her, Jefferee Bolen, if she has ever seen the law that requires you to file a tax return.
OBJECTED TO AND SUSTAINED by the court as an improper question. P332, 14 -17
132. Court tells the defense counsel that "**We're not going to have any questions, you know, about laws and tax returns and whatever.**" P332, 19-21
138. Witness, Brian Miller (IRS Agent), states that "**... nobody's an expert on all the tax law, but I'm pretty familiar with certain parts of it.**" P346, 22-23
139. In cross examination of the witness, Brian Miller, he states that the requirement to file can be found in the IRC, section 6012 and section(s) 61,63, and   P349, 10-25 & P350, 1-8
140. Defense then asks the witness if the IRC, when opened to Section 6012, will show the law that requires a person to file a tax return.
OBJECTED to by the prosecution and sustained by the court. P350, 9-13
141. Defense asks the courts permission to approach the witness and the court states, "**No, you may not approach the witness. You can approach the Bench. I want to see you up here right now...**"P350, 15-19
142. Court tells defense counsel " **... I don't want you to go there...**" "**... you're not to go there on this.**"P351, 8-11
146. Court answers by telling the defense that if it asks an improper question, "**... I'm going to clear this courtroom.**" P352, 22-23
149. The defense asks the expert witness that if the jury wanted to see the law, how would they see it. P355, 18-19 Court interrupts saying "**... let's not go there, sir.**"   P355, 20
151. Defense asks the court if he can read part of the IRC Section 6012 to the witness and the court says "**No, Sir, you may not.**" " **No, sir. You cannot. You cannot. You can't read a snippet, can't read a word....**" P357, 9-14
152. Court again asks the defense if it is attempting to cause a mistrial (jury is out of the room). Court then tells the defense counsel " **If you have an objection to it and if you think the Court's wrong, when this trial is over, it can be appealed...**" P358, 11-18
153. Court tells the defense counsel "**... You may not be permitted to ask any more questions, ever, if you're not careful in this case...**"   P361, 4-5
154. Court demands that the defense present its questions to the court prior to asking them in open court.   P361, 16-24
155. Court again tells the defense counsel to approach the bench prior to asking any additional questions of the witness, Brian Miller, IRS agent. P363, 8-11
156. Court admonishes the defense counsel for asking to approach the bench. Court states, " **... I also need to advise you that you don't need to make comments like that in front of the jury.**"   P370, 5-7
157. Court tells defense that it can ask any question that if wants to. Defense states that he wants to ask what law would be needed... . The prosecution objects and the court sustains the objection. P373, 18-24
158. Court orders the defense counsel to tell the court what other questions he is going to ask (at sidebar). P374, 10-12
159. Court authorizes the defense to ask two questions. P371, 15
160. Court refuses to allow the defense to ask a question regarding the penalties of perjury clause and tells the defense counsel "**... Your cross examination is over, sir, you may be seated.**" P379, 8-18
166. Court tells the defense counsel, at sidebar, that the "**... difference between making and filing I think is a matter of semantics that I'm not going to let you go into with this witness.**" P440, 9-12
170. Court tells defense counsel " <u>I don't want to hear the word "LAW</u>" mentioned again from this witness. Do you understand me?**"** P444, 15-17
171. Expert witness, Tom Bryan (IRS Agent), states that he doesn't "... really like to respond to a lot of things in writing." "... I don't want to get into a letter writing campaign such as this." Regarding letters written to him by the defendant. P449, 9-14
172. (Sidebar) Court demands that the defense counsel disclose his questions to the court at sidebar. "**Tell me what questions you're going to ask.**" P452, 18
173. Court threatens to end the defenses' cross examination and demands to know what questions counsel will pose to this witness. P452, 22-24

174.	*Court again admonishes the defense not to discuss the law*. P453, 19-20
180.	Regarding the testimony of defense witness, Brenda Gray, the court tells the defense, " **I don't doubt you're trying to lay a foundation. I just wonder if we hadn't already removed that foundation... .**" P486, 5-7
186.	Defendant is asked to whom else he had presented his questions regarding his requirement to file and he asks if he must divulge the name of the US Magistrate. (Magistrate Jones-Stites). The prosecution objects and the court sustains the objection telling the defendant "**... you'll not be permitted to answer that. Ask your next question.**" P528,13-22
187.	At sidebar, the court tells the defense counsel, concerning Magistrate Jones-Stites testimony before a jury less court room the day before, " **I ain't going to let you - - we ain't going there.**" "**...It's prejudicial, and we're not going there.**" " **I don't want any conversations with the US Magistrate, we're not going there. That's improper.**" P528, 9-22
188.	Court continues to demand that the defense counsel present its questions for the witness to the court at sidebar for approval or disapproval without the jury hearing any of it. P530, 4-11
189.	Prosecutor threatens the defense counsel, "You want to go for sanctions, you just keep it up." P531, 11-12
190.	Court tells the attorneys that, **"We're not going to introduce anything on the Internal Revenue Code."** P531, 23-24
191.	Court tells the defense counsel, "**... you're not functioning just exactly right. I don't know if you're not hearing or you're not comprehending...**" P532, 10-12
192.	Still at sidebar, the court tells the defense in response to the defense counsel's question about how to get the defendants' understanding of the law from his head to the jury, "**I don't know, but you're not going to do it with the Magistrate. You're not going to do it with reading the law to him either.**" P532, 14-20
193.	Speaking of the defendant, the court states, " **Let's try to get rid of this witness. After he finishes, what other witness do you have?**" P533, 16-18
194.	Defense informs the judge that this is the defendant and the court responds, " **Let's finish it then today.**" P533, 21-22
198.	At sidebar again, the court threatens to clear the jury from the room because the defense counsel is talking too loudly. P540, 11-13
199.	Court continues to insist, at sidebar, that the defense must present all of its Exhibit list for approval/ disapproval by the court before it can be offered in open court before the jury. P541, 14-20
200.	Court continues to disallow defense Exhibits at the sidebar. Court states that. " *... we're not going to talk about statutes to the jury ...*" P544, 11-13
201.	Court restates to the defense that "*... you're not going to be permitted to talk about any statutes, any acts, any law...*" P545, 7-8
202.	Court dismisses the jury for the day and asks the defense if some of its Exhibits weren't developed after the years 93/94. P548, 20-22
220.	Court reminds the defense counsel, "**... And I'm taking you at your word as an <u>officer of this court</u> that you're not going to ask something that we've already discussed time and time again, Sir.**" P628, 10-12
221.	Defense questions to the witness (defendant) with regards to discussions he had with a Magistrate judge are interrupted by the court and the court tells the defense counsel three (3) times "**... and we're not going there, Mr. Stilley. ...**" P629, 22-23 "**... You're not to go there, Mr. Stilley.**" P630, 1 "**... You're not to go there, Mr. Stilley. Ask another question, sir, if you have another question.**" P630, 3-4
222.	Defense counsel asks the defendant (witness) if he has ever filed a lawsuit in order to get a declaratory judgment as to his rights and duties under the law. Objected to and sustained by the court. The court then instructs the defense counsel, **"Don't argue with me in front of the jury, Mr. Stilley. If you need to argue, come forward, but we've already resolved that."** P622, 22-25 & P633, 7-9
223.	Court states that if it hadn't ruled previously, with regard to bringing up the lawsuits filed by the defendant, that, **"Well, if I didn't, I am now. I am telling you it is sustained on nothing concerning any civil lawsuits he may have filed. That's improper. And I'm going to prohibit you from asking any question about it, and your record is about as clear as it can be. ..."** P634, 18-23
224.	Court asks the defense counsel, "**... Are you getting -- making any progress in getting him off the stand?**" He is referring to the defendant who is testifying in his own behalf. P635, 6-7

225.	When the defense responds that he hasn't gotten there yet, the court responds, **"Well, you may not ever get there if you keep asking questions about that have already been -- you know, about issues that have already been resolved."** P635, 10-12
226.	The prosecution's cross examination of the defendant appear to be irrelevant and most of the questions concern the years outside of the years in question, 1993 and 1994. Defense objections are overruled by the court. P643 - P675 (all)
229.	Court interrupts the defendants testimony in order to limit it. The prosecution had raised no objection. P682, 15-17
230.	Court tells the defense counsel, **"Mr. Stilley, don't argue with me."** P683, 6
232.	At sidebar, the Court tells the defense counsel, **"... This is the most improper-- this is the worst conduct I've ever seen of a lawyer, Mr. Stilley. ..." "... (W)e're going to visit this further at length, Mr. Stilley. _The practice of law, sir, is a privilege, especially in Federal Court. You're close to losing that privilege in this court, Mr. Stilley._"** P685, 5-11
234.	At sidebar, the defense counsel asks again if he can ask questions regarding the defendants attempts to get a declaratory judgment to ascertain his responsibilities and is told by the Court, **"Absolutely not, N O T, period."** The defense states that he objects highly and the court responds, **"Fine. I want you to object as highly as you need to be, but what else do you have?"** P687, 1-6
235.	Court demands, at sidebar, that the defense tell the court where else it's going. P688, 3-4
236.	At sidebar, the defense explains that many people disagree about matters of tax law without being kooks. The Court responds, **"Mr. Stilley, you have -- you're not going there, sir. What else?"** P688, 18-22
237.	At sidebar still, the court asks the defense if that is going to be its last question. The defense answers no and the court responds, **"Well, it very well could be, unless you tell me what they are. Now, the jury has been waiting over there for about five minutes and they're getting impatient and so am I, Mr. Stilley."** P699, 19-25
238.	Court continues to deny the defense's proposed questions at the sidebar stating, **"That's improper. He's not to do that." "I'm not going to permit it. What else you got?"** P690,6 &12-13
240.	Court states that it believes that the jury has been abused. P700, 12
241.	Defense tells the Court that it objects to any instruction to the jury with regard to income until it is defined. Court notes the objection and overrules it. P706, 21-25
242.	Court states, absent the jury, that regarding willfulness, **"... I don't know what the law is. I'm going to go look it up."** P716, 20-21
243.	Court states that closing arguments are just that, arguments. Court states, **"... I don't ever like to interrupt closing arguments..."** P718, 2-7
244.	Defense is giving its closing argument and asks if there is a law that requires a single person under the age of 65 to make a Federal income tax return for 1994. Prosecution objects and the court sustains the objection stating, **" ... You are not to argue the law, Mr. Stilley."** P739, 14-19
245.	When the prosecution makes its closing argument and the defense objects to statements made by the prosecution, the Court overrules the objection stating, **"It's overruled. This is closing arguments. Be seated, sir."** P748, 9-15
246.	Defense objects again and the court overrules the objection stating, **" You're overruled. Sit down, sir."** P748, 22-24
247.	JURY INSTRUCTIONS FROM THE COURT ARE NOT TRANSCRIBED INTO THE TRIAL TRANSCRIPT. P752, 6-7
248.	Jury gives its verdict to the two charges of the Indictment. Guilty on both counts. P753 (all) & P754 (all)
249.	Court instructs the jury saying, **"... We have a rule in the Western District of Arkansas that you're -- that jurors cannot be contacted, and that rule is going to remain in effect. I would say if you are contacted by anybody in connection with this case, you need to notify the Court immediately. ..."** P755, 8-12
250.	Prosecuting attorney, Blackorby, tells the Court regarding the defendant, *"He doesn't have a Fifth Amendment privilege now. It's been waived by the conviction."* P756, 7-8
251.	Court states, **" I'm going to continue the bond at present through sentencing. ..."** P756, 9-10

After reading item 232, I wonder why ANYONE would want to hire an attorney to represent them in a trial in Federal Court! What a farce!! That's why this document places such an emphasis on helping to develop in you the skills to masterfully litigate your own case—so you can tell the tax emperor he has no clothes without having your livelihood and your ability to earn a living threatened by a covetous so –called judge with a criminal conflict of interest in violation of 18 U.S.C. §208, 28 U.S.C. §144, and 28 U.S.C. §455!

Throughout the trial, the judge emphasized that *they couldn't talk about the law*. What the hell else are courts and the lawyers in them supposed to talk about...hearsay and what we *think* the law says?(!) All that's left if the judge manipulates and abuses the jury and the law isn't discussed is a kangaroo court that's on a witch hunt to convict and burn the defendant, which is precisely what they did in this case! What a miscarriage and abuse of justice if I ever saw one! The judge, by refusing to discuss the law, has violated the Sixth Amendment because he has made it impossible for a defendant to clearly know what the law says and what the charges against him are—instead, the court devolved into a subjective exercise of whatever the judge *thinks* the law says or wants the law to say! We are supposed to be a society of *laws* and not of *men* but this judge has made sure it is the other way around. This kind of tyranny MUST be stopped!

The court stated in item 240 that the "jury has been abused". That's right, and you know *who* abused them?.. THE JUDGE! And his abuse of them led to an involuntary abuse of Dr. Phil Roberts by the jury! Do we live in a *mobocracy*, I mean democracy, or a *republic*? Fire the bastard and strip him of his federal retirement and benefits for plundering the citizenry! THIEF! Now we know why judges wear black robes,.. because they are the executioner in most federal tax trials. When you go into federal court as the defendant, you have TWO prosecutors: The Judge and the U.S. attorney. The deck is stacked against you.

6.11.2 Fraud On The Court: Demjanuk v. Petrovsky, 10 F.3d. 338

If any reader doubts that officials of the United States government, even U.S. attorneys in the United States Department of Justice, are capable of perpetrating "fraud on the court" by engaging in "misconduct," the case of Demjanjuk v. Petrovsky, 10 F.3d. 338 (6th Cir.1993) should remove that doubt. Mr. Demjanjuk was wrongly identified as "Ivan the Terrible" and charged with murdering thousands of Jews during WW2. The appellate court found that some U.S. attorneys committed "fraud on the court" and "engaged in prosecutorial misconduct by failing to disclose to the courts and to the petitioner [Demjanjuk] exculpatory information in their possession during litigation culminating in extradition proceedings, which led to the petitioner's forced departure from the United States and trial on capital charges in the State of Israel." The record shows that "no fewer than eight government attorneys worked on the Demjanjuk denaturalization case...." The "exculpatory information" that U.S. attorneys possessed but failed to reveal to the courts (that heard and ruled on Demjanjuk's denaturalization and extradition proceedings) and to Demjanjuk's attorneys was reasonable evidence that Demjanjuk was not the man that the U.S. attorneys claimed him to be, "Ivan the Terrible."

As readers may recall, Mr. Demjanjuk was extradited to Israel where he was found guilty of the "mass murder of Jews" and sentenced to hang. But the persistent search for truth and justice by Mr. Demjanjuk's attorneys and his son-in-law through discovery requests and Freedom of Information Act requests and litigation finally paid off. Fortunately for Mr. Demjanjuk, upon appeal of his death sentence the Supreme Court of Israel learned from the withheld documents and statements of guards at Treblinka that "clearly identified" Ivan Marchenko--not John Demjanjuk--as "Ivan the Terrible." It is significant that it was the Supreme Court of Israel and not an American court that ultimately saved the life of John Demjanjuk. The Demjanjuk case proves that some U.S. attorneys had little interest in learning the true identity of a man they were prosecuting for mass murder or the attainment of justice when Demjanjuk's life was assumed to be at risk. Shamefully, such attorneys' apparent, chief interest is in obtaining convictions and "winning" cases. It would be interesting to know if the U.S. attorneys who perpetrated fraud on the court in the Demjanjuk case were punished and if the U.S. Department of Justice still employs any of them. With such grave, egregious and unethical misconduct as was practiced in Demjanjuk by U.S. attorneys who swore to uphold the law, there is small wonder why so many Americans have come to have so little faith in this country's judiciary system.

6.12 Judicial Scandals Related to Income Tax

> *"He who justifies the wicked, and he who condemns the just, both of them alike are an abomination to the Lord."*
> *[Prov. 17:15, Bible, NKJV]*
>
> *"Getting treasures by a lying tongue*
> *Is the fleeting fantasy of those who seek death.*
> *The violence of the wicked will destroy them,*
> *Because they refuse to do justice."*
> *[Prov. 21:6-7, Bible, NKJV]*
>
> *"If a ruler pays attention to lies,*
> *All his servants become wicked."*
> *[Prov. 29:12]*
>
> *"And you shalt take no bribe, for a bribe blinds the discerning and perverts the words of the righteous."* *[Exodus 23:8, Bible, NKJV]*

> *"Under a government which imprisons any unjustly, the true place for a just man is also a prison."*
> [Henry David Thoreau]

In 1789 Thomas Jefferson warned that the federal judiciary, if given too much power, might ruin our REPUBLIC, and destroy our RIGHTS! Based on the content of the following subsections and the behavior of the IRS, we believe the very tyrannical situation that Thomas Jefferson warned us about below has come true!

> *"The new Constitution has secured these [individual rights] in the Executive and Legislative departments: but not in the Judiciary. It should have established trials by the people themselves, that is to say, by jury."*

> *"The Judiciary of the United States is the subtle corps of sappers and miners constantly working under ground to undermine the foundations of our confederated fabric." (1820)*

> *"...the Federal Judiciary; an irresponsible body (for impeachment is scarcely a scarecrow), working like gravity by night and by day, gaining a little today and a little tomorrow, and advancing its noiseless step like a thief, over the field of jurisdiction, until all shall be usurped from the States, and the government of all be consolidated into one....when all government ... in little as in great things, shall be drawn to Washington as the center of all power, it will render powerless the checks provided of one government on another and will become as venal and oppressive as the government from which we separated." (1821)*

> *"The opinion which gives to the judges the right to decide what laws are constitutional and what not, not only for themselves in their own sphere of action, but for the legislative and executive also in their spheres, would make the judiciary a despotic branch.*

> *"...judges should be withdrawn from the bench whose erroneous biases are leading to dissolution. It may, indeed, injure them in fame or fortune; but is saves the Republic..."*

The U.S. Supreme Court described succinctly how the government most often acts unconstitutionally and illegally, and we should heed and learn from their description below:

> *"It may be that it...is the obnoxious thing in its mildest and least repulsive form, but illegitimate and unconstitutional practices get their first footing in that way; namely, by silent approaches and slight deviations from legal modes of procedure. This can only be obviated by adhering to the rule that constitutional provisions for the security of person and property should be liberally construed. A close and literal construction deprives them of half their efficacy, and leads to gradual depreciation of the right, as if it consisted more in sound than in substance. It is the duty of the courts to be watchful for the constitutional rights of the citizens, and against any stealthy encroachments thereon. Their motto should be obsta principalis." [Mr. Justice Brewer, dissenting, quoting Mr. Justice Bradley in boyd v. United States, 116 U.S. 616, 29 L.Ed. 746, 6 Sup.Ct.Rep. 524"*
> *[Hale v. Henkel, 201 U.S. 43 (1906)]*

It is therefore the job of the courts to be watchful over our liberties and to act as a check and balance against unconstitutional acts by either the Executive or Legislative branches of government. This is a fiduciary duty they have for the citizens and inhabitants they serve within their jurisdiction. We'll let you be the judge in this section of how well they have fulfilled that duty.

Whole books have been written just about judicial conspiracy and tyranny. We have tried to narrow the scope of this section to summarize the picture for you only within the context of the income tax. If you would like to dig deeper into this subject of judicial tyranny, the best book we have found is:

- *Government by Judiciary: The Transformation of the Fourteenth Amendment*, Raoul Berger, Second Edition, 1997, Liberty Fund, Inc.; 8335 Allison Pointe Trail, Suite 300; Indianapolis, Indiana 46250-1684; ISBN 0-86597-143-9 (hardcover).

6.12.1 Abuse of "Case Law"[84]

In any court of law, an understanding of the legal relationship between statutory law and case law (i.e. court decisions) is crucial. The following U.S. Supreme Court case of *Consumer Products Safety v. GTE Sylvania*, 447 U.S. 102, establishes that the statute takes precedence over the case law backing the statute:

---

[84] Paraphrased from *The Federal Mafia*, 2000 edition, ISBN 0-939374-09-6, Irwin Schiff, pp. 124-125.

> *"We begin with the familiar canon of statutory construction that the starting point for interpreting a statute is the language of the statute itself. Absent a clearly expressed legislative intention to the contrary, the language must ordinarily be regarded as conclusive.*

So if and only if there is doubt about the meaning of the statute is there a need to refer to case law to resolve the controversy. This is especially true of the Supreme Law of the Land, which is the Constitution. In actual practice, however, corrupt judges and the federal courts where they occupy the bench commonly subvert this requirement in order to expand federal fiscal and monetary power, and in the process, conspire against the rights of Americans in illegally enforcing a *voluntary* tax, the Subtitles A through C personal income tax. To give you an example, take the case of **Griffith v. C.I.R.**, 598 F. Supp. 405, where one Charles Griffith attempted to prevent the IRS from illegally seizing his assets without due process in order to collect a $500 penalty that had been assessed against him for allegedly filing a false W-4. As stated in that court decision:

> *"According to plaintiff's complaint, on September 3, 1982, the Internal Revenue Service (IRS) sent plaintiff a letter claiming that his W-4 did not meet the requirements of the Internal Revenue Code Sec. 3402 and informing him that his employer be directed to disregard [notice the court did not say "ordered" to] the W-4 form and withhold monies from his paycheck as if he were single and claiming one (1) withholding allowance. By letter dated September 14, 1982, plaintiff informed the IRS of his reasons for completing the W-4 in alleged illegal manner. However, the IRS notified his employer to proceed withholding as if plaintiff were single...and was assessed a penalty of five hundred dollars ($500) under 26 U.S.C. §6682(a).*

Note that the court suggests that Griffith completed his W-4 in an "allegedly illegal manner." How exactly does one complete an IRS Form W-4 in an "illegal manner"? Did Griffith hit the personnel clerk over the head with a hammer, strip the clothes off and then complete his W-4 on her naked body? And if it were completed in an "allegedly illegal manner," why wasn't he arrested? It is clear that Griffith's W-4 did "meet the requirements of Section 3402." Griffith obviously knew (as you also know) that he was not liable for income taxes, and so probably claimed "exempt" in accordance with 26 U.S.C. §3402(n). Note that the court states that the "plaintiff informed the IRS of his reasons for completing the form." So why didn't the court state those reasons in its decision, since Section 6682 only applies when such reasons are not "reasonable"? But not only did the court refuse to consider whether Griffith's reasons were "reasonable," it refused to even mention them! I wonder why? Who, therefore, decided that Griffith "reasons" were not "reasonable"? An IRS cleaning lady?

In finding against Griffith the DIShonorable Judge White wrote:

> *Plaintiff's claim that the manner of collection of the penalty violates his Fifth Amendment rights is without merit. He has attempted to show that the government cannot prevail in the collection of the penalty because to do so prior to a hearing would deprive him of his Fifth Amendment constitutional rights. Case law dictates otherwise...The power of the government to levy is essential to the **self assessment tax system** because it encourages **voluntary** compliance.*

So the court, in deciding to allow the IRS to seize Griffith's property without any hearing whatsoever, admits that it does so on the basis of what "case law dictates"—never mind what the statute itself "dictates" or what the Constitution "dictates", which the judge took an oath "to support and defend"! Section 6682 only allows the penalty if there is no "reasonable basis" for the claim, which the court here refuses to even consider!

It should also be pointed out in this case that Griffith represented himself against the government as a pro per. He undoubtedly believed he could do so, since he was convinced (and rightly so) that he had several statutes, the Constitution, and logic all on his side. But he learned (as we all do sooner or later), that these often do not count much in federal court because of the massive corruption and outright tyranny that exists there. Incidentally, did you happen to get the feeling when you read the above, that you were reading right out of *Alice in Wonderland*?

Clearly, Griffith's argument is not only "not without merit"; it is legally correct. But federal judges can easily dispatch such arguments by labeling them "frivolous" or stating they are "without merit" and not explaining the basis for that determination. This leaves the average pro per litigant, not to mention most attorneys, without any recourse except to shake their head and file a lawsuit for breach of fiduciary duty and corruption against the judge.

6.12.2 The Federal Mafia Courts Stole Your Seventh Amendment Right to Trial by Jury!

The Federal Mafia Courts stole your Seventh Amendment right to trial by jury. Here is what the Seventh Amendment says about the right of trial by jury:

> *In Suits at common law, where the value in controversy shall exceed twenty dollars, **the right of trial by jury shall be preserved**, and no fact tried by a jury, shall be otherwise re-examined in any Court of the United States, than according to the rules of the common law.*
> *[Seventh Amendment]*

And here is what the U.S. Constitution, Article 3, Section 2, Clause 3 says about the right of trial by jury:

> ***"The Trial of all Crimes**, except in Cases of Impeachment, **shall be by Jury**; and such Trial shall be held in the State where the said Crimes shall have been committed; but when not committed within any State, the Trial shall be at such Place or Places as the Congress may by Law have directed."*
> *[Article III, Section 2, Clause 3, U.S. Constitution]*

Here is what the tyrants in the Fifth Circuit court of federal appeals said about your Seventh Amendment right to jury trial in the case of *Mathes v. Commissioner of Internal Revenue*, 576 F.2d. 70 (1978) in relation to a civil tax trial held in U.S. Tax Court:

> *Taxpayers also assert they were denied their Seventh Amendment right to trial by jury before the Tax Court. **The Seventh Amendment preserves the right to jury trial "in suits at common law." Since there was no right of action at common law against a sovereign, enforceable by jury trial or otherwise, there is no constitutional right to a jury trial in a suit against the United States.** See 9 C. Wright & A. Miller, Federal Practice & Procedure § 2314, at 68-69 (1971). Thus, there is a right to a jury trial in actions against the United States only if a statute so provides. Congress has not so provided when the taxpayer elects not to pay the assessment and sue for a redetermination in the Tax Court. For a taxpayer to obtain a trial by jury, he must pay the tax allegedly owed and sue for a refund in district court. 28 U.S.C. §§ 2402 and 1346(a)(1). The law is therefore clear that a taxpayer who elects to bring his suit in the Tax Court has no right, statutory or constitutional, to a trial by jury. Phillips v. Commissioner, 283 U.S. 589, 599 n. 9, 51 S.Ct. 608, 75 L.Ed. 1289 (1931); Wickwire v. Reinecke, 275 U.S. 101, 105-106, 48 S.Ct. 43, 72 L.Ed. 184 (1927); Dorl v. Commissioner, 507 F.2d. 406, 407 (2d Cir. 1974) (holding it "elementary that there is no right to a jury trial in the Tax Court.").*
> *[Mathes v. Commissioner of Internal Revenue, 576 F.2d. 70 (1978)]*

Therefore, we only get a trial by jury when litigating against the U.S. government for wrongful taking of taxes if Congress gives its permission by statute! Do you think they will ever do that? Fat chance! The Constitution no longer guarantees a trial by jury if the matter being litigated is taxes and the litigant is suing the federal government. We have the wranglings of corrupt judges like the one above to thank for that. Such abuses directly contradict the U.S. Constitution, which states:

> *Article 1, Section 9, Clause 8: "No Title of Nobility shall be granted by the United States: And no Person holding any Office of Profit or Trust under them, shall, without the Consent of the Congress, accept of any present, Emolument, Office, or Title, of any kind whatever, from any King, Prince or foreign State."*

In this case, the Title of Nobility is "Sovereign"! Here's what the definition of Nobility is, right from Black's Law Dictionary, Sixth Edition, p. 1047:

> *"In English law, a division of the people, comprehending dukes, marquises, earls, viscounts, and barons. These had anciently duties annexed to their respective honors. **They are created either by writ, i.e., by royal summons to attend the house of peers, or by letters patent, i.e., by royal grant of any dignity and degree of peerage; and they enjoy many privileges exclusive of their senatorial capacity**. Since 1963 no new hereditary ennoblements have been created."*
> *[Black's Law Dictionary, Sixth Edition, p. 1047]*

In the above case, the "royal decree" creating the "Title of Nobility" is a judgment by the courts, and the "exclusive privilege" granted to the government (by itself, which by the way is a conflict of interest) is that of:

1. *Not* being directly accountable to a jury or the people it is elected to represent *like everyone else* for its wrongdoing
2. *Not* being able to be sued by the *real* sovereigns (the people) without its own consent.

> *"While sovereign **powers** are delegated to ... the government, **sovereignty itself remains with the people**.."*
> *[Yick Wo v. Hopkins, 118 U.S. 356, page 370]*

Hypocrisy and lawlessness! With the above startling realizations in mind, do you think it is EVER possible to guarantee a fair trial or a balance of power if you are litigating against the IRS or the federal government in their own federal court? Absolute power corrupts absolutely, and there is no better example of that philosophy in action than in the federal courts. The deck in federal court is obviously stacked, which explains why so many irrational and unconstitutional rulings occur in the context of income tax litigation in the federal courts. Another thing that this section ought to convince you of is that it is more productive in a federal court to go after the *individual government officials* involved for corruption, fraud, and extortion under the color of office than it is to go after the government. If they violate the law, they can be held *personally liable*, and because you are not suing a sovereign, the United States Government, you can be assured your right to a Trial by Jury.

Do you STILL think we live in a free country? Our government is no different than having a monarch with absolute power to do whatever it wants with sovereign immunity from prosecution for wrongdoing granted by our corrupt federal courts!

6.12.3 You Cannot Obtain Declaratory Judgments in Federal Income Tax Trials Held in Federal Courts

Your wonderful Congress legislated away your right to obtain a Declaratory judgment in a federal income tax trial. A declaratory judgment is one where there are no disputes over fact and the only relief sought is a declaration of status or rights of the plaintiff under law. No jury trial occurs and the court (judge) makes the declaration of status or right by motion and without a trial. An example might be a declaration of your status by the court as a nonresident alien, a person not liable for federal income tax, etc.

Congress knows that people don't like to pay taxes and that they will be likely to litigate to protect their Constitutional rights, so they put a statutory roadblock in front of patriots who use Constitutional rights to avoid paying taxes and who want to litigate to get a declaratory judgment identifying them as persons not liable for income taxes. This roadblock guarantees that those who don't know what they are doing will lose in federal court, especially in cases where issues of status as a nonresident alien or personal liability for tax are asserted. That roadblock is 28 U.S.C. §2201 as follows, and it prevents federal courts from declaring the rights or status of a plaintiff to remedy a wrong related to taxes or illegal taking of taxes by the federal government in a federal court:

> *United States Code*
> *TITLE 28 - JUDICIARY AND JUDICIAL PROCEDURE*
> *PART VI - PARTICULAR PROCEEDINGS*
> *CHAPTER 151 - DECLARATORY JUDGMENTS*
> *Sec. 2201. Creation of remedy*
>
> (a) **In a case of actual controversy within its jurisdiction,** except with respect to Federal taxes *other than actions brought under section 7428 of the Internal Revenue Code of 1986, a proceeding under section 505 or 1146 of title 11, or in any civil action involving an antidumping or countervailing duty proceeding regarding a class or kind of merchandise of a free trade area country (as defined in section 516A(f)(10) of the Tariff Act of 1930), as determined by the administering authority,* **any court of the United States, upon the filing of an appropriate pleading, may declare the rights and other legal relations of any interested party seeking such declaration**, *whether or not further relief is or could be sought. Any such declaration shall have the force and effect of a final judgment or decree and shall be reviewable as such.*
>
> *(b) For limitations on actions brought with respect to drug patents see section 505 or 512 of the Federal Food, Drug, and Cosmetic Act.*

What this means is that a federal court can't issue a declaratory judgment relating to federal taxes or declare your rights or status (e.g. the Bill of Rights, and the first ten Amendments to the U.S. Constitution) or the status of its own jurisdiction to hear your case with respect to federal income taxes. So in other words, declaratory judgments based on lack of jurisdiction or based on citizenship or assertion of constitutional rights *cannot be decided* in federal court solely by a judge! Such cases must be heard in *state court* or a *common law court*!

When you think about this statute, it actually makes sense. The statute doesn't allow a federal judge to solely decide rights or jurisdiction or citizenship status on a federal income issue because it would present a conflict of interest that would not serve the interests of justice and would violate 28 U.S.C. 455. Why? Because the judge's paycheck comes from the matter he is deciding on! Do you think he is going to rule in favor of the Citizen by saying he doesn't have to pay income taxes? The Congress therefore required an outside entity, such as a state court, to decide on issues of status. Don't be discouraged by the above, however. There is a way around this statutory trap. Below is the way around the roadblock:

While income tax arguments are barred under this rule - actions proving lack of citizenship, domicile, and residence are specifically allowed. The issue is not income tax but jurisdiction over the person. Lack of jurisdiction is proved by FRCP Rule 44 and 44.1 - You go to the proper jurisdiction to resolve the matter by taking the following steps:

1. Acquire domicile and residence in a common law jurisdiction.
2. File notice in the clerk's office in state and federal courts.
3. Argue this in Federal court using as evidence the filings filed at common law, state court and federal courts.
4. Appeal at common law under Federal Rule of Civil Procedure 60 last line "by independent action".

You are then not arguing jurisdiction in front of that court - you are using evidence to prove that jurisdiction already exists in another court. Read 28 U.S.C. §2201 and it states that it must be argued in the proper manner - and that is by not letting the US court decide that issue - go to common law and plead condition precedent under FRCP rule 8.(The citizenship was already decided before the action began).

This argument is in agreement with all of the cites herein and the argument that dual citizenship can exist. State law tells you the procedure for noticing the state courts that you have acquired a new residence and domicile.

6.12.4 The Changing Definition of "Direct, Indirect, and Excise Taxes"

> *"Dishonest scales are an abomination to the Lord, but a just weight is His delight."*
> *[Prov. 11:1, Bible, NKJV]*

> *"Judicial verbicide is calculated to convert the Constitution into a worthless scrap of paper and to replace our government of laws with a judicial oligarchy."*
> *[Senator Sam Ervin, during Watergate hearing]*

> *"By mercy and truth iniquity is purged: and by the fear of the LORD men depart from evil."*
> *[Prov. 16:6, Bible, NKJV]*

> *"Thus says the Lord: 'Execute judgment in the morning; and **deliver him who is plundered [illegally by the IRS]** out of the hand of the oppressor, lest my fury go forth like fire and burn so that no one can quench it, because of the evil of your doings."*
> *[Jeremiah 21:12, Bible, NKJV]*

The purpose of this section is to provide evidence to support the conclusion that there is a conspiracy of massive proportions by the federal judiciary to defend and uphold federal income taxes. We hinted at the existence of this conspiracy in section 5.6.11.9 entitled "Why Hasn't the 861 Issue Been Challenged in Court Already?". Now we will prove the existence of this conspiracy by researching actual cases and by reading from judgments of the federal courts at various levels over the years.

Because the judiciary is authorized by the Constitution to "legislate", federal judges and the legal profession have crafted a different approach to support and expand the operation of the federal income tax. It's called "redefining the meaning of words". Over time, they have redefined such words as "direct tax", "excise tax", and "indirect tax" to expand the applicability of federal taxes and, by implication, the jurisdiction of the federal government to tax its citizens. Our own ignorance of the concept of "stare decisis", also called "precedent", and our lack of attentiveness to their transgressions through the political process has allowed them to get away with this devious fraud. We will therefore take a look at how the definitions of these terms have evolved and have been "optimized" over the years by federal judges as a way to maximize illegal government revenues from income taxes. This notion of changing the definition of words is not new. Instead, it is just another devious trick that covetous lawyers use to enslave us by hiding and obfuscating the truth over time. Instead of using language as a way to empower and free people and respect their liberties, lawyers abuse words as a way to trick, enslave, confuse, and control people. We talked about this devious approach in section 2.11.3, entitled "How to Teach Your Child About Politics", when we said:

> *"When your child has matured sufficiently to understand how the judicial system works, set a bedtime for him and then send him to bed an hour early. When he tearfully accuses you of breaking the rules, explain that you made the rules and you can interpret them in any way that seems appropriate to you, according to changing conditions. This will prepare him for the Supreme Court's concept of the U.S. Constitution as a "living document."*
>
> *[...]*
>
> *This brings me to the most important child-rearing technique of all: lying. Lie to your child constantly. Teach him that words mean nothing - or rather that the meanings of words are continually 'evolving', and may be tomorrow the opposite of what they are today.*
>
> *Some readers may object that this is a poor way to raise a child. A few may even call it child abuse. But that's the whole point: Child abuse is the best preparation for adult life under our form of GOVERNMENT."*

If the above quote doesn't make the judicial conspiracy, I don't know what does! The below humorous anecdote carries this violation of due process to its extreme, and isn't too far from the truth!:

> **NEW RULES FOR LAW**
>
> SMUCKWAP NEWSSERVICE, Washington: The Supreme Court ruled today that judges can do whatever the hell they want. In a landmark case, Black-Robed Lawyers vs. Everyone Else, the justices handed down their inestimable judgment that since lawyers in general and judges in particular are such fine examples of humanity, not to mention smart enough to get through law school, judges can do whatever they please.
>
> "The Rule of Law has ended," proclaimed Supreme Court Justice Arrogant B. Astard, "and the Rule of Judges begins!"
>
> Turning their shiny black backs on the rest of America, the justices decided to toss out two hundred years of Constitutional law and indeed, to rid themselves completely of having to heed the Constitution.
>
> "The law is what we say it is," said Justice Whiney I. Diot. "It has been this way for some time now, but with Black-Robed Lawyers vs. Everyone Else, we are coming out of our judicial closet. No more arguments will be allowed from anyone, and we don't want to hear any more of your complaining about your rights. In fact, any mention of so-called rights will guarantee you 100 years, hard labor."
>
> Justice K. Rupt Assin concurred in his opinion that "judicial oligarchy has now fully come into its place in American history and will be fully enforced by an iron rule of law, and remember, law is whatever we say it is."
>
> The Center for People Who Want to Leave This Country Because It Is Beginning to Look Too Much Like Nazi Germany analyzed the justices' decision.
>
> "Judges now legally can put anyone in prison for any reason they want, for as long as they want," states the analysis. "Judges can also put jurors in prison for 'obstructing justice' and for anything else, including not handing the judge whatever money they may have on them at the time. Jurors who don't behave exactly as the judge desired have been persecuted in the past, but "now they can receive prison terms much longer than their own lifespan added to the lifespan(s) of the defendant(s) in any trial.
>
> The report also mentioned the justices' decision that anyone who says anything disagreeable in their courtroom can be immediately arrested and jailed, their property confiscated, and their spouses and children taken as "wards" of the court under the justices own personal pleasure ... or... supervision.
>
> The concept of separation of powers was addressed in the Center's report on the decision.
>
> "There is no separation of powers," it reads, "when not only all the justices are lawyers, so are all Congressmen and the President, his wife, his cabinet, the entire Department of Justice, most lobbyists and almost everyone else in Washington, D.C."
>
> When questioned about what effect the decision would have on all Americans, the spokesman for the Center said, "I can't be certain. I suspect that emigration rather than immigration will become a major concern. Those Americans who are lawyers will be fine, for the most part. No one will ever again show up for jury duty. But if we thought we had an overcrowded prison problem before, we're in for a *major* shock!"

Another way the federal judiciary has conspired with Congress to usurp such arbitrary and unconstitutional authority over time has been for Congress to write the laws in a deliberately vague way in order to leave a lot of undue discretion to the courts to interpret and misapply and broaden the applicability of these laws. Here are the two main ways this has deliberately been done in the case of the tax codes:

1. Title 26 of the U.S. Codes, which are written by Congress, don't clearly define "income." Does it mean "profit"? Does it mean "wage"? What about "sources" of income? If it means profit, then we must deduct from our wages the cost of sustaining our life, which includes food, clothing, housing, insurance, etc., since we must view ourselves as producers of labor for sale, which is not free but involves a cost to sustain and maintain the ability to provide that labor.
2. The purpose of the laws is to clearly define or to limit the authority of the government and to define precisely and unambiguously which actions are criminal. Congress has written the tax codes in such a way that they do not satisfy this requirement, but instead expand and enlarge the authority of the federal government to tax in a way that can't be completely defined or even understood by the common man. They have done this by deliberately monkeying with the definition of the word "includes" found in 26 U.S.C. §7701(c). This word in normal usage is a term of _limitation_, but as we showed in section 3.12.1.8, Congress has used it as a term of _enlargement_, as if to say:

> *"The Internal Revenue Code laws aren't a limiting factor and do not bound or define the authority of Congress to tax. Instead, these laws mean <u>whatever</u> the judge says they mean at the time, which can arbitrarily change over time without explanation or justification. Our powers to tax are <u>unlimited</u> and beyond your ability to comprehend or understand and beyond our obligation to explain to you. We don't care if this violates the Fifth, Sixth, and Tenth Amendments and your due process rights. <u>Always remember</u> that WE'RE the government and WE are in complete control and the ONLY ones who are sovereign or empowered or who know what the laws that we write really say! We don't work for you, YOU are OUR financial slaves and YOU will do exactly and only what you are told to do by our chief priests in the federal courts, who are the only ones qualified to interpret the law, who we appoint, and who can only hold office as long as they do exactly what we tell them to do by keeping tax dollars they extort from you under duress flowing into our Treasury.*
>
> *And by the way, your lawyer can't help you in challenging our sovereign authority to tax because we license him to practice law both in this state and in this court and if he in any way questions or threatens our authority to tax or our jurisdiction, we will simply pull his license and blacklist him with the IRS, and he will therefore cease to be able to earn a living and be subject to the same kind of financial terrorism, harassment, and intimidation that you are undergoing. You can't win this war, my friend, because our power is absolute and we will squash you like a bug if you don't 'voluntarily comply'! Nevertheless, you can do whatever you want because we live in a 'free' country and you are a free man, and we are here to benevolently protect that freedom. The minute you start complaining about losing that freedom, then we'll turn your 'rights' into government 'privileges' and charge you an additional tax to have these privileges upheld and respected in our courts."*

You will note that a remedy is suggested for this kind of government arrogance, legal abuse, and terrorism in section 4.5, of the *Sovereignty Forms and Instructions Manual*, Form #10.005 when we talk about "What would it take for the IRS and the US Congress to 'come clean'" by saying that Congress needs to reform their definition of the word "includes", which *even they* don't use in a consistent fashion in the case of 26 U.S.C. §61, which says in part:

> (a) *General definition* - ... **gross income** means all **income** from whatever <u>source</u> derived, **including (but not limited to)** the following **items**:
>
> [...]

Isn't that interesting? If 26 U.S.C. §7701 (c) indeed says the word "includes" is not a limiting term, then why do the shyster lawyers in Congress and the IRS need to use the phrase "including (but not limited to)"? I'll tell you why, because they don't want you to understand what the law really means or know what you are expected to do, but would rather see you terrorized into submission to whatever it is their arbitrary whims dictate. This legal terrorism and the fear it generates is foisted upon us with our own extorted tax dollars by lawyers in the Department of (In)Justice and the courts in the process of illegally enforcing (no Delegation of Authority orders to the DOJ to support litigation of voluntary income taxes) laws that are so vague that they violate the "void for vagueness" criteria we described in section 5.12.3, entitled "Why the 'Void for Vagueness Doctrine' Should be Invoked By The Courts to Render the Internal Revenue Code Unconstitutional in Total". This has to be one of the biggest frauds and scams in history and the tyranny won't end until We The People remedy this most basic violation of our right to due process guaranteed by the Fifth and Sixth Amendments. We must do this first at the ballot box, then the jury box, and finally with the cartridge box (guns) if need be to coerce the government to respect our Constitutional rights!

6.12.4.1 Definition of terms and legal framework

Recall from Chapters 3 and 5 that we spent a lot of time talking about "direct taxes" and "excise taxes" and the relationship between the two. Another synonym for an excise tax is "privilege tax". In particular, we compared and contrasted these two types of taxes in section **Error! Reference source not found.**, which we will not repeat here. Understanding the relationship between these two types of taxes is foundational to understanding why income taxes are unconstitutional as they are implemented by the IRS, and why they are upheld by the federal district/circuit courts in some cases. We also talked about the five types of constitutional taxes in section 5.1

Much of the deliberately-induced confusion created in the courts results from the rather basic misunderstanding in most people's minds over the term "United States". We talked this issue in sections 4.7 entitled "The Three 'United States'" and section 3.12.1.23 entitled "'United States' (in 26 U.S.C. §7701)'". You have to remember that the judicial conspiracy to protect the income tax can only be upheld and spread if the courts avoid discussing the true definition of this term within the meaning of 26 Title U.S.C. and the nature of the limited application of the income tax to federal/U.S.** (federal zone) citizens). Within the I.R.C, the term "United States**" actually means the "federal zone", which includes the District of Columbia and the federal territories and possessions within the contiguous 50 union states, but not the 50 sovereign states themselves. The courts, however, don't want your average sovereign natural born Citizen of the 50 union states knowing that the federal income tax only applies within the federal zone to people who claim to be U.S.** citizens, so they have done things in their rulings such as:

1. Not mention or confuse the U.S. citizenship or residency status of the defendant. The most famous case of this was the case of *Brushaber v. Union Pacific Railroad Co., 240 U.S. 1 (1916)*, in which Frank Brushaber claimed to be a Sovereign naturalized citizen of the New York Republic (state) and NOT a U.S./federal citizen. The government tried to confuse his status as a nonresident alien for tax purposes by claiming that he was a French immigrant who never obtained state citizenship.
2. Avoid discussing jurisdictional issues. For instance, ignoring claims by a Citizen that the U.S. government lacks jurisdiction to prosecute a Citizen for not paying income taxes.
3. Make cases won by the Citizen rather than the IRS unpublished so other Citizens don't find out the most effective tactics to litigate the income tax issues.

In this section, we will trace several U.S. supreme and appellate court cases to show that primarily the federal appellate and district the courts have established a new and changing definition for these terms that conflicts both with the original definition of the terms used by the founding fathers, the rulings of the Supreme Court, *and* with the modern-day definition that the "common man" understands of these terms. We will show how they have done this on their own accord and without any authority derived from the Constitution, congress, the rulings of the supreme Court, or the law itself. *We will show that the definitions of the terms "direct" and "excise" taxes over time has been slowly modified by the courts in such a way that revenues from income taxes for the federal government have not only been increased, but MAXIMIZED*. We will show that this approach violates the important concept of "stare decisis" that is foundational to our republic and our whole legal system. We will show that this behavior by the courts is consistent with their alleged role as part of the "federal mafia", whose mission is to expand the plunder and extortion of the property of private citizens in disregard of the U.S. Constitution. Simply by changing the definitions and interpretation of these two terms in their judgments, the federal courts have, in effect, "legislated" by setting new precedents, to uphold and expand the federal income tax system.

So let's start with a definition of the terms "stare decisis" and "precedent":

> **STARE DECISIS**: *Lat: to abide by, or adhere to, decided cases. Policy of courts to stand by precedent and not to disturb settled point. Neff v. George, 364 Ill. 306, 4 N.E.2d. 388, 390, 391. Doctrine that, when court has once laid down a principle of law as applicable to a certain state of facts, it will adhere to that principle, and apply it to all future cases, where facts are substantially the same; regardless of whether the parties and property are the same. Horne v. Moody, Tex.Civ.App., 146 S.W.2d. 505, 509, 510. Under doctrine a deliberate or solemn decision of court made after argument on question of law fairly arising in the case, and necessary to its determination, is an authority, or binding precedent in the same court, or in other courts of equal or lower rank in subsequent cases where the very point is again in controversy. State v. Mellenberger, 163 Or. 233, 95 P.2d. 709, 719, 720. Doctrine is one of policy, grounded on theory that security and certainty require that accepted and established legal principle, under which rights may accrue, be recognized and followed, though later found to be not legally sound, but whether previous holding of court shall be adhered to, modified, or overruled is within court's discretion under circumstances of case before it. Otter Tail Power Co. v. Von Bank, 72 N.D. 497, 8 N.W.2d. 599, 607. Under doctrine, when point of law has been settled by decision, it forms precedent which is not afterwards to be departed from, and, while it should ordinarily be strictly adhered to, there are occasions when departure is rendered necessary to vindicate plain, obvious principles of law and remedy continued injustice. The doctrine is not ordinarily departed from where decision is of long-standing and rights have been acquired under it, unless considerations of public policy demand it. Colonial Trust Co. v. Flanagan, 344 Pa. 556, 25 A.2d. 728, 729. The doctrine is limited to actual determinations in respect to litigated and necessarily decided questions, and is not applicable to dicta or obiter dicta. See also Precedent,; Res (Res judicata)*
> [Black's Law Dictionary, Sixth Edition, p. 1406]

> **PRECEDENT**: *An adjudged case or decision of a court, considered as furnishing an example or authority for an identical or similar case afterwards arising or a similar question of law. Courts attempt to decide cases on the basis of principles established in prior cases. Prior cases which are close in facts or legal principles to the case under consideration are called precedents. A rule of law established for the first time by a court for a particular type of case and thereafter referred to in deciding similar cases. See also Stare decisis.*
>
> *A course of conduct once followed which may serve as a guide for future conduct. See Custom and usage; Habit.*
>
> [Black's Law Dictionary, Sixth Edition, p. 1176]

From these definitions, we can see that ***stare decisis*** and ***precedent are*** very important aspects of law that constrain what the federal courts can do. Together, they establish that cases must follow precedents unless there is a compelling reason not to, and that the reasons for overruling past precedents ought to be clearly explained so that the lower courts will understand how to apply the new paradigm.

Now let's move to the words themselves. We'll start off by examining the definition of "**excise tax**" found in Merriam Webster's Dictionary of Law[85]:

> ['ek-'siz, -'sis]
>
> 1: a tax levied on ***the manufacture, sale, or consumption of a commodity***
> (compare income tax, property tax)
> 2: any of various taxes on privileges often assessed in the form of a license or other fee
> (see also Article I of the Constitution)
> (compare direct tax)
>
> [emphasis added]

Similarly, Barron's Law dictionary defines "**excise**" as follows:

> "Broadly, "any kind of tax which is not directly on property or the rents or incomes from real estate." 4A. 2d 861, 862. "An inland impost upon articles of manufacture or sale and also upon licenses to pursue certain trades, or to deal in certain commodities." 184 U.S. 608, 617. It is imposed directly and without assessment and is measured by amount of business done and other means. 161 So. 735, 738. See tax [EXCISE TAX][86]
>
> "a federal tax imposed upon the purchase of certain items. See excise."

Excise taxes are commonly referred to as "indirect" taxes within the meaning of the U.S. Constitution (see section 5.1 for further details). From the preceding discussion, it ought to be clear that excise taxes apply to businesses involved in trade and the amount of tax is to be determined by any measure related to activity that the legislature determines. For instance, the (fraudulently ratified) 16th Amendment allows excise taxes to be measured by income, but does NOT allow for direct taxes without apportionment as ruled in the case of *Stanton v. Baltic Mining* (240 U.S. 103), 1916. In particular, the court said in that case that the 16th Amendment merely:

> "...prohibited the ... power of income taxation possessed by Congress from the beginning from being taken out of the category of indirect taxation to which it inherently belonged..."

A good definition of "excise taxes" is found in the Supreme Court case of *Flint v. Stone Tracy Co., 220 U.S. 107 (1911)*:

> "**Excises** are taxes laid upon the manufacture, sale or consumption of commodities within the country, upon licenses to pursue certain occupations and upon corporate privileges; the requirement to pay such taxes involves the exercise of the privilege and if business is not done in the manner described no tax is payable...it is the privilege which is the subject of the tax and not the mere buying, selling or handling of goods."
> [Flint v. Stone Tracy Co., 220 U.S. 107 (1911)]

The Supreme Court case of *Bromley v. McCaughn*, 280 U.S. 124 (1929) provides another good definition of the operation of "excise taxes":

> "While taxes levied upon or collected from persons because of their general ownership of property may be taken to be direct, Pollock v. Farmers' Loan & Trust Co., 157 U.S. 429, 15 S.Ct. 673; Id., 158 U.S. 601, 15 S.Ct. 912, this court has consistently held, almost from the foundation of the government, that a tax imposed upon a particular use of property or the exercise of a single power over property incidental to ownership, is an excise which need not be apportioned, and it is enough for present purposes that this tax is of the latter class. Hylton v. United States, supra; cf. Veazie Bank v. Fenno, 8 Wall. 533; Thomas v. United States, 192 U.S. 363, 370, 24 S.Ct. 305; Billings v. United States, 232 U.S. 261, 34 S.Ct. 421; Nicol v. Ames, supra; Patton v. Brady, 184 U.S. 608, 22 S.Ct. 493; McCray v. United States, 195 U.S. 27, 24 S.Ct. 769, 1 Ann. Cas. 561; Scholey v. Rew, 23 Wall. 331; Knowlton v. Moore, supra. See, also, Flint v. Stone Tracy Co., 220 U.S. 107, 31 S.Ct. 342, Ann. Cas. 1912B, 1312; Spreckels Sugar Refining Co. v. McClain, 192 U.S. 397, 24 S.Ct. 376; Stratton's Independence v. Howbert, 231 U.S. 399, 34 S.Ct. 136; Doyle v. Mitchell Brothers Co., 247 U.S. 179, 183, 38 S.Ct. 467; Stanton v. Baltic Mining Co., 240 U.S. 103, 114, 36 S.Ct. 278.

---

[85] Merriam-Webster's Dictionary of Law ©1996.

[86] *Law Dictionary*, Barron's, Copyright 1996, ISBN 0-8120-3096-6, p. 180.

> *It is a tax laid only upon the exercise of a single one of those powers incident to ownership, the power to give the property owned to another. Under this statute all the other rights and powers which collectively constitute [280 U.S. 124, 137] property or ownership may be fully enjoyed free of the tax. So far as the constitutional power to tax is concerned, it would be difficult to state any intelligible distinction, founded either in reason or upon practical considerations of weight, between a tax upon the exercise of the power to give property inter vivos and the disposition of it by legacy, upheld in Knowlton v. Moore, supra, the succession tax in Scholey v. Rew, supra, the tax upon the manufacture and sale of colored oleomargarine in McCray v. United States, supra, the tax upon sales of grain upon an exchange in Nicol v. Ames, supra, the tax upon sales of shares of stock in Thomas v. United States, supra, the tax upon the use of foreign built yachts in Billings v. United States, supra, the tax upon the use of carriages in Hylton v. United States, supra; compare Veazie Bank v. Fenno, supra, 545 of 8 Wall.; Thomas v. United States, supra, 370 of 192 U. S., 24 S.Ct. 305.*
>
> *It is true that in each of these cases the tax was imposed upon the exercise of one of the numerous rights of property, but each is clearly distinguishable from a tax which falls upon the owner merely because he is owner, regardless of the use of disposition made of his property. See Billings v. United States, supra; cf. Pierce v. United States, 232 U.S. 290, 34 S.Ct. 427. The persistence of this distinction and the justification for it rest upon the historic fact that taxes of this type were not understood to be direct taxes when the Constitution was adopted and, as well, upon the reluctance of this court to enlarge by construction, limitations upon the sovereign power of taxation by article 1, 8, so vital to the maintenance of the national government. Nicol v. Ames, supra, 514, 515 of 173 U. S., 19, S.Ct. 522."*

Merriam Webster's Dictionary of Law defines "direct tax" as follows[87]:

> *"a tax imposed on a taxpayer himself or herself or on his or her property (compare excise)"*

The Supreme Court did a good job describing "direct taxes" in the case of *Veazie Bank v. Fenno, 75 U.S. 533* (1869):

> *"This review shows that personal property, contracts, occupations, and the like, have never been regarded by Congress as proper subjects of direct tax.*
>
> *...*
>
> *It may be rightly affirmed, therefore, that in the practical construction of the Constitution by Congress, direct taxes have been limited to taxes on land and appurtenances, and taxes on polls, or capitation taxes."*

We believe that these are good definitions that are consistent with the wishes of the founding fathers.

6.12.4.2 The Early Supreme Court View of Direct vs. Indirect/Excise Taxes Prior to Passage of the 16th Amendment 1913

With the legal definitions complete, let's examine the historical background for the subject of direct and indirect/excise taxes by the Supreme Court prior to the (fraudulent) passage of the 16th Amendment. We'll start off with the case of *Pacific Ins. Co. v. Soule, 74 U.S. 433* (1868), which is a very good reference on the definition of "direct taxes" and "indirect taxes":

> *The ordinary test of the difference between direct and indirect taxes, is whether the tax falls ultimately on the tax-payer, or whether, through the tax-payer, it falls ultimately on the consumer. If it falls ultimately on the tax-payer, then it is direct in its nature, as in the case of poll taxes and land taxes. If, on the contrary, it falls ultimately on the consumer, then it is an indirect tax.*
>
> *Such is the test, as laid down by all writers on the subject. Adam Smith, who was the great and universally received authority on political economy, in the day when the Federal Constitution was framed, sets forth a tax on a person's revenue to be a direct tax. 5 Mill,6 Say,7 J. R. McCulloch,8 Lieber,9 among political economists, do the same in specific [74 U.S. 433, 438] language. Mr. Justice Bouvier, in his learned Law Dictionary, defines a capitation tax, 'A poll tax; an imposition which is yearly laid on each person according to his estate and ability.'*
>
> *Indeed, it is obvious that an income tax, levied on the profits of any business, does not fall ultimately on the consumer or patron of that business, in any other sense than that in which a poll tax or land tax may be said ultimately to fall, or be charged over by the payer of those taxes upon the persons with whom and for whom they do business, or to whom they rent their lands. The refinement which would argue otherwise, abolishes the whole distinction, and under it all taxes may be regarded as direct or indirect, at pleasure.*

---

[87] Merriam-Webster's Dictionary of Law ©1996.

> *But, if the distinction is recognized (and it must be, for the Constitution makes it), then it follows, that an income tax is, and always heretofore has been, regarded as being a direct tax, as much so as a poll tax or as a land tax. If it be a direct tax, then the Constitution is imperative that it shall be apportioned.*
>
> *If it be argued that an income tax cannot be apportioned, then, it cannot be levied; for only such direct taxes can be levied as can be apportioned.*
>
> *But an income tax can be apportioned as easily as any other direct tax; first, by determining the amount to be raised from incomes throughout the United States, and then by ascertaining the proportion to be paid by the people of each State. An income tax, in the matter of its apportionment, is not embarrassed by any other difficulties than those which grow out of apportionment, in the admitted cases of poll taxes and land taxes."*

According to the Supreme Court, there can be only these type types of taxes: direct or indirect/excises:

> *"And although there may have been from time to time intimations that there might be some tax which was not a direct tax nor included under the words "duties, imposts and excises," such a tax has yet remained undiscovered, not withstanding the stress of particular circumstances has invited thorough investigation into sources of revenue."*
> *[Pollock v. Farmers' Loan & Trust Co., 157 U.S. 429, 158 U.S. 601 (1895), 557, Thomas v. United States (1903) 192 u.s. 363, 370]*

6.12.4.3 Common Manifestations of the Judicial Conspiracy

This section summarizes the common elements of the judicial conspiracy to uphold the federal income tax. Below are a list of some of the more common tactics used by the courts following the passage of the 16th Amendment to prejudice any litigation that would undermine the income tax. These are things that you should be watching vigilantly for and loudly blowing the whistle when you see them:

1. **Political moves:**
   1.1. Congress making federal judgeships into political appointees instead of elected offices. This causes the judges to be more partial toward their political benefactors than they are in favor of citizens or the law.
   1.2. Congress or presidents appointing judges who will participate actively in the judicial conspiracy to uphold the federal income tax.
   1.3. Congress or presidents appointing judges who aren't confrontational (YES men) and who are unlikely to make any rulings that would have big political implications, like overthrowing illegal and fraudulent income taxes.
2. **Counsel:**
   2.1. Refusing to allow the counsel of the Citizen to represent him in the court because of his views about taxes, but at the same time, pretending like it is due to his lack of a license to practice law in a particular federal court or jurisdiction.
   2.2. Only granting pro-tem (temporary) judgeships (during the absence of the normal judge, during vacation, for instance) to lawyers who are in favor of the income tax, so that they have more authority and leverage against lawyers who are against in any case.
3. **Jury selection:**
   3.1. Including a "mole" or planted individual (perhaps a lawyer who is a tax advocate) on the jury who is outspoken and biased against the Citizen and biased in favor of income taxes. This most often happens when the government or judge "slips" new candidates of the government's choosing into the courtroom at the last minute during jury selection or voir dire. This is what happened to Dr. Phil Roberts failure to file case, for instance, and it biased his case and led to a unfair criminal prosecution. Visit our website if you like, to learn about this despicable miscarriage of justice that happened in his case.
   3.2. When it comes time to draw names out of a box to select jurists, the box will be populated (rigged) outside the courtroom by the government and the judge will not allow either the defense or prosecution to examine the contents of the box prior to drawing names. For all they know, the unbiased or better-informed jurists or the ones who have been convicted of tax crimes, are removed from the box. Dr. Phil Robert's attorney, Oscar Stilley, thinks this is what happened in Dr. Phil Robert's case.
   3.3. Not allowing the counsel (threatening with contempt) of the Citizen who is contesting the taxes to interview or question the prospective jurors or the government's lawyers. Cross-examination allows biases to be uncovered. This is what happed in Dr. Phil Robert's case.
   3.4. Asking the prospective jurists to reveal their social security number prior to jury selection and investigating their tax payment history. Then, only choosing jurists who have a history of paying taxes and who would be more likely to get indignant about people who either don't file or don't pay income taxes, even if they aren't obligated to.

Having the jurists social security numbers also affords the IRS an opportunity to harass and audit them if they don't rule in the government's favor.

4. **During Trial:**
    4.1. Hiding the nature of the citizenship and residency of the accused. Remember that according to Downes v. Bidwell, 182 U.S. 244 (1901), citizens of the District of Columbia or the Federal Zone have no constitutional rights. The court won't make it clear what the citizenship and residency of the accused is so that they can make it appear that all citizens are liable to pay income taxes on all income. Go back to section 4.11 for a clarification of citizenship issues
    4.2. Fining or punishing litigants who raise issues about which the court doesn't want to address, such as:
        4.2.1. Fraudulent ratification of the 16th Amendment ($5,000 fine currently in some federal courts for filing claims regarding this issue).
        4.2.2. Fifth Amendment issues related to taxes (putting litigants in jail for failure to file).
        4.2.3. Government conspiracy claims related to taxation filed by citizens.
        4.2.4. Claiming a case deals with frivolous issues when in fact it doesn't and then forcing the litigant to pay the attorney fees of the government to defend against this.
        4.2.5. Assessing the fines or fees without a due process hearing, which violates the Fifth and 14th Amendments.
    4.3. Judges granting the IRS' frequent motion in most tax cases to dismiss a valid filing by a tax protester. This has the effect of censoring the litigant and violating his First Amendment rights.
    4.4. Not allowing (threatening with contempt) the Citizen or his counsel to discuss or reveal the law regarding income taxes. Instead, trying to convince them that they must follow the judge's orders and interpretation of the law, rather than revealing the actual law and letting the jurists decide both the facts and the law for themselves. This gives the judge far more power than he should have.
    4.5. Holding pro per litigants to the same standards as attorneys, which is illegal.
    4.6. Delaying the judgment for controversial issues. For instance, in the case of *William T. Conklin vs. IRS*, case no. 89 N 1514 in the Tenth Circuit, a famous tax protester sued the government because he thought his fifth amendment rights were being violated by being compelled to file and sign a tax return under penalty of perjury and thereby be a witness against himself. The judge (Judge Nottingham) took SEVEN YEARS to reach a decision, because he had such a difficult time reconciling the constitutional issues involved! He was probably hoping he could put it off so he would retire first! The judge deviously chose to censor this judgment by making it unpublished so the truth wouldn't leak out. Nevertheless, the judge also sanctioned Mr. Conklin $6,000 by making him pay the IRS' legal fees, and without the ability to even litigate or challenge the fees. This he may have done to discourage him from litigating further.

5. **After trial:**
    5.1. Making cases dealing with controversial aspects of federal income taxes "unpublished". This means that after there is a judgment on a controversial tax case that exposes fraud or wrongdoing of the government, the federal judge ensures that the findings *aren't* available in most federal case databases or indexes and copies can only be obtained by writing directly to the clerk of the specific court where the case was heard, and the reproduction is costly and long delays in obtaining the documents are commonplace. This amounts to censorship, in violation of the First Amendment to the U.S. Constitution, which says that we have a right to speak freely and to petition the government for redress of grievances. This would also imply that we have a right not to have our court case regarding income taxes be censored or discriminated against from publication based on our views or the tax issues we are litigating. For instance, a notable tax freedom fighter, William Conklin, filed at least six different federal cases against the IRS and won several of them. The focus of his cases was related to the unconstitutionality of being compelled in the process of filing income tax returns to be a witness against oneself in violation of the 5th amendment. In the majority of his cases, the judges refused to publish his cases. For instance, the case of *Conklin vs. United States of America*, No. 94-1213 in the Tenth circuit, was unpublished. This kind of censorship is unconscionable!

6.12.4.4 Judicial Conspiracy Following Passage of 16th Amendment in 1913

With the definitions and historical legal background prior to the passage of the 16th Amendment (in 1913) fresh in our minds, we'll now try to start answering some questions:

1. How did taxes on businesses as excise/indirect taxes which fall on the consumer evolve into direct taxes on the labor of individuals (which are property) after the passage of the 16th Amendment?
2. How does the court justify a deviation from precedents already established by the U.S. Supreme Court in a way that is consistent with the U.S. Constitution?

3. How did the courts distort the interpretation of the law to expand the reach of the income tax to become direct taxes on citizens living outside of the federal zone (how did they "get away with it?")?

To answer these questions, we have to look at later cases and see how the courts redefined "excise taxes" or "indirect taxes", since the following case firmly established that taxes on income allowed under the 16th Amendment are limited to indirect or excise taxes:

> "..[The 16th Amendment] .prohibited the ... power of income taxation possessed by Congress from the beginning from being taken out of the category of indirect taxation to which it inherently belonged..." [in describing **Brushaber v. Union Pacific Railroad Co., 240 U.S. 1 (1916)**, 17-19]
> [Stanton v. Baltic Mining, 240 U.S. 103]

Most of error and distortion in the meaning of the Internal Revenue Code, and the judicial conspiracy to protect and expand the income tax, it turns out, comes ***not*** from the U.S. Supreme Court, but from the federal appellate/circuit courts immediately below the Supreme Court. Indirectly, the Supreme Court has contributed to the misdirected verdicts of the circuit courts by refusing to hear (not granting a "writ of certiorari") to cases which relate to direct income taxes on individuals. Most of that distortion, we argue, came after the passage of the 16th Amendment, and results from a misapplication and misunderstanding of the Internal Revenue Code by the circuit courts. It also results indirectly from voters adopting the socialist policies instituted by President Franklin D. Roosevelt during his long term in office.

We'll start the exposition by examining the case of *Evans v. Gore*, 253 U.S. 245 (1920):

> "After further consideration, we adhere to that view and accordingly hold that the Sixteenth Amendment does not authorize or support the tax in question. " [A direct tax on salary income of a federal judge]

This case quite clearly shows that a direct tax on the income of a federal judge is unconstitutional. The case was then subsequently overturned by the U.S. Supreme Court in *O'Malley v. Woodrough*, 307 U.S. 277 (1939). However, the Supreme Court in that case declined to address whether the tax on income of federal judges was a "direct" or an "indirect" tax or the nature of its constitutionality relative to the 16th Amendment, and therefore they skirted entirely the issue of whether taxes on income of citizens could or should be included in "gross income". Instead, by fiat, the justices simply said without any real legal analysis of facts, that the tax was constitutional because everyone regarded it as "unpopular". This, of course was a cop-out and there was a long dissenting opinion that advocated a more rational view that is more consistent with this document. Here's an excerpt from the findings of the court in that *O'Malley* case:

> "However, the meaning which **Evans v. Gore**, supra, imputed to the history which explains Article III, 1 was contrary to the way in which it was read by other English-speaking courts.[88] The decision met wide and steadily growing disfavor from legal scholarship and professional opinion. Evans v. Gore, supra, itself was rejected by most of the courts before whom the matter came after that decision[89]"

This decision, it is to be noted, occurred during a period of depression and recovery from depression, in which Franklin Roosevelt was pushing his socialist "Social Security" agenda. President Roosevelt held office for three terms, or 12 years. During that time, FDR wanted to ramrod his socialist agenda (Social Security, the Federal Reserve, Income Taxes, outlawing of ownership of gold coin, forced use of paper money) through Congress and the courts and get it firmly entrenched in our system of government before he left office. Therefore, FDR had to "stack" the Supreme Court by *doubling* its size from six to twelve justices. We talked about this in section 6.1 and even quoted FDR's own words about the "supreme court packing plan" in our analysis. This was unprecedented in American history and he was able to do it successfully because the Constitution didn't specify the size of the Supreme Court! The court that made the ruling above was therefore a "rigged" court. This ruling was the beginning of a long string of unfavorable rulings at the federal appellate level that would eventually mean the spread of the unconstitutional fraud we know today as the income tax. We'll now examine some of these circuit court cases. If you examine Supreme Court cases following *Evens vs. Gore* and search for the word "direct tax" and "excise tax", you will find nothing that relates to income taxes on citizens domiciled in the 50 union states. Consequently, when the IRS wants to defend the validity of the income tax, it usually cites *Brushaber v. Union Pacific Railroad* as its precedent.

It is very important to note a fact that in the *Brushaber* decision, the person subject to tax was a nonresident alien principal, who was receiving income from a railroad through a trustee, rather than directly. Treasury decision 2313, which was published just after this decision was rendered, reveals this:

---

[88] The opinion is set forth in a footnote at page 160 et seq., of 3 Cranch.

[89] Printed in 157 U.S. at page 701.

> "..it is hereby held that income accruing to nonresident aliens in the form of interest...and dividends ..is subject to the income tax imposed by the act of October 3, 1913. The responsible heads, agents, or representatives of nonresident aliens...shall make a full and complete return of the income therefrom on...Form 1040..."

So there you have it. The Treasury Department stated that you are to file Form 1040 on behalf of your "nonresident alien principal". So don't forget to do that next April 15th! This is a fact the IRS doesn't like to discuss, for obvious reasons!

6.12.4.5   The Federal District/Circuit Court Conspiracy to Protect the Income Tax

Recall that the Supreme Court declared in *Stanton v. Baltic Mining Co., 240 U.S. 103 (1916)* that the only constitutional income taxes were <u>excise taxes</u>. The federal circuit/appellate courts, following the passage of the 16th Amendment in 1913, and the Supreme Court decisions that followed, suddenly got very creative in their definitions of "excise tax" in order to fit a square peg into a round hole made by the 16th Amendment. This was encouraged by the fact that the Supreme Court refused to hear cases involving direct taxes on income (looked the other way). Such cases are referred to as "cert denied". However, *it is an important principal of law that the fact that a cert was denied is NOT necessarily an affirmation of a particular federal circuit court ruling by the Supreme Court.* This lack of attentiveness by the Supreme Court in not correcting errors by the circuit courts gave the circuit and district courts carte blanche authority to do <u>*anything they wanted*</u> and to ignore the constitution entirely relative to income taxes. The result was a broadened application of income taxes to what should have been excepted subjects, like Americans living outside the federal United States but inside the United States of America. We'll examine some of these cases to show you how the courts "legislated" the income tax by redefining the word "excise", and in some cases also boldly claiming, quite wrongfully, that the 16th Amendment authorized "*direct income taxes without apportionment*" (see the case of *U.S. v. Collins*, 920 F.2d. 619, 1990, mentioned in section 6.4.5). In all cases, we emphasize that the devious tactics mentioned in section 6.12.4.3 "Common Manifestations of the Judicial Conspiracy" apply.

The first case we want to look at is *Simmons v. United States*, 308 F.2d. 160, 8/28/1962:

> *A direct tax is a tax on real or personal property, imposed solely by reason of its being owned by the taxpayer. A tax on the income from such property, such as a tax on rents or the interest on bonds, is also considered a direct tax, being basically a tax upon the ownership of property.*[90] *Yet, from the early days of the Republic, a tax upon the exercise of only some of the rights adhering to ownership, such as upon the use of property*[91] *or upon its transfer,*[92] *has been considered an indirect tax, not subject to the requirement of apportionment. The present tax falls into this latter category, being a tax upon the receipt of money and not upon its ownership.*
>
> *This tax is similar to others held to be indirect. In the case which on its facts most nearly resembles the present one, Scholey v. Rew, 90 U.S. (23 Wall.) 331, 346-348, 23 L.Ed. 99 (1875), the Supreme Court upheld a federal death tax, placed upon persons receiving real property from a deceased under a will or by intestate succession, against the claim that the tax was an unapportioned direct tax on property. In that case, as in the present, the tax was borne directly by the recipient, but was held to be merely upon the transfer of property. The Scholey case was by name reaffirmed in Knowlton v. Moore, 178 U.S. 41, 78-83, 20 S.Ct. 742, 44 L.Ed. 969 (1900), and by implication in New York Trust Co. v. Eisner, 256 U.S. 345, 349, 41 S.Ct. 506, 75 L.Ed. 963 (1921), both cases upholding federal estate taxes imposed, not upon the beneficiary but upon the decedent's estate. A tax upon the donor of an inter vivos gift was held to be an indirect tax in Bromley v. McCaughn, 280 U.S. 124, 135-138, 50 S.Ct. 46, 74 L.Ed. 226 (1929). If a tax on giving property is indirect, so would be a tax on receiving it, regardless of its source. That no distinction may be drawn between giving and receiving was pointed out in Fernandez v. Wiener, 326 U.S. 340, 352-355, 361-362, 66 S.Ct. 178, 90 L.Ed. 116 (1945), where the Supreme Court upheld as an indirect tax the federal estate tax on community property at the death of one spouse: "If the gift of property may be taxed, we cannot say that there is any want of constitutional power to tax the receipt of it, whether as a result of inheritance [citation omitted] or otherwise, whatever name may be given to the tax * * *. Receipt in possession and enjoyment is as much a taxable occasion within the reach of the federal taxing power as the enjoyment of any other incident of property."*[93]
>
> *While the distinctions drawn in these cases may seem artificial, the necessity for making them stems from the structure of the Constitution itself, which distinguishes between direct and indirect taxes. The Supreme Court has*

---

[90] Pollock v. Farmers' Loan & Trust Co., 157 U.S. 429, 15 S.Ct. 673, 39 L.Ed. 759, on rehearing, 158 U.S. 601, 627-628, 15 S.Ct. 912, 39 L.Ed. 1108 (1895).

[91] Hylton v. United States, 3 U.S. (3 Dall.) 171, 1 L.Ed. 556 (1796) (tax on carriages for the conveyance of persons).

[92] Fernandez v. Wiener, 326 U.S. 340, 352-355, 361-362, 66 S.Ct. 178, 90 L.Ed. 116 (1945) (estate tax on community property at death of one spouse).

[93] 326 U.S. at 353, 66 S.Ct. at 185. Analogous too are cases holding that a tax on the gross receipts of a business is an indirect tax, but, being a tax on business, this is more like the traditional excise tax, expressly treated by the Constitution as not direct. Spreckels Sugar Ref. Co. v. McClain, 192 U.S. 397, 410-413, 24 S.Ct. 376, 48 L.Ed. 496 (1904); Stanton v. Baltic Mining Co., 240 U.S. 103, 114, 36 S.Ct. 278, 60 L.Ed. 546 (1916) (alternate holding); Penn Mut. Indem. Co. v. Commissioner, 277 F.2d. 16, 18-20 (3d Cir. 1960), affirming 32 T.C. 653 (1959).

> *restricted the definition of direct taxes to the above-enumerated well-defined categories, and we have no warrant to expand them to others.*
>
> *Even if we were to assume that the tax upon Simmons is direct, it comes within the Sixteenth Amendment, which relieved direct taxes upon income from the apportionment requirement. We need look no further than the two most recent Supreme Court cases in this area. In Commissioner of Internal Revenue v. Glenshaw Glass Co., 348 U.S. 426, 75 S.Ct. 473, 99 L.Ed. 483 (1955), the Court upheld the inclusion in gross income of money received by the taxpayers as punitive damages, stating that "[here] we have instances of undeniable accessions to wealth, clearly realized, and over which the taxpayers have complete dominion." 348 U.S. at 431, 75 S.Ct. at 477. This test was specifically reaffirmed in James v. United States, 366 U.S. 213, 81 S.Ct. 1052, 6 L.Ed.2d. 246 (1961), where the Court considered the taxability of embezzled money. The plunder was held to be income solely because it came into the taxpayer's possession and control and despite the fact that he had no right to it and indeed was under a legal obligation to return it to its rightful owner. This obligation to repay was deemed irrelevant, for a gain "constitutes taxable income when its recipient has such control over it that, as a practical matter, he derives readily realizable economic value from it."[94] As is apparent from the quoted statements, and as illustrated by the diverse factual situations in these cases, it is the status in the recipient's hands of the money being taxed which is the crucial factor, while the source of the money is not relevant.*

The above case of *Simmons v. United States* taxed receipt of income (which in this case was a gift) by a citizen not related to the conduct of a business or trade, as an occasion for an excise/indirect tax. But we know that this violates the definition of an excise tax in *Flint v. Stone Tracy* (220 U.S. 107) and the other definitions of excise tax stated earlier. Interestingly, they didn't label the tax on the gift as an excise tax, but that is the *only* way it can be classified, based on our discussion in section 5.1, where we talked about the legal types of federal taxes. Why didn't the court label the tax an excise? Because then they would have to talk about *Flint v. Stone Tracy* and relate the event being taxed to a business transaction involving sale and manufacture of commodities. Since this case didn't involve the sale or manufacture of commodities, then the court couldn't uphold the tax! The case also ignores the following other issues and considerations, which are very relevant to the issue of taxation:

1. Whether the income received was a result of interstate commerce or foreign commerce, as per Article I, Sections 8, Clauses 1 and 3 of the Constitution, which constrain Congress' power to taxing foreign and interstate commerce. These are the only taxable "sources" allowed by the Constitution. It would appear that the income in question in this case here didn't cross state boundaries, and yet the issue was never addressed, because if it was, the government's ability to impose the tax would be eliminated.
2. Whether the tax was on a Citizen of the 50 union states from income earned within the state. If it was, then 26 U.S.C. §862 and the source become relevant to whether the income received was taxable. If the court had addressed this issue, then once again the court would not have been able to uphold the tax.
3. What "privilege" was being taxed that related to the indirect or excise tax upheld by the court. (see *Flint v. Stone Tracy Co.*, 220 U.S. 107 (1911)). According to *Flint*, *"...it is the privilege which is the subject of the tax and not the mere buying, selling or handling of goods"*. Once again, if this issue was considered, the court would not have been able to uphold the tax.
4. Whether income beneficially received by Simmons was related to "the manufacture, sale, or consumption of commodities within the country" as per *Flint v. Stone Tracy Co.*, 220 U.S. 107 (1911)). This issue is clearly very relevant to the imposition of an alleged excise tax, and yet is was ignored by the court. If the court had addressed this issue, it also would not be able to sustain the indirect/excise tax being imposed.

Next, we look at the case of *United States v. Collins*, 920 F.2d. 619, (10th Cir. 11/27/1990):

> *Dickstein's motion to dismiss advanced the hackneyed tax protester refrain that federal criminal jurisdiction only extends to the District of Columbia, United States territorial possessions and ceded territories. Dickstein's memorandum blithely ignored 18 U.S.C. § 3231 which explicitly vests federal district courts with jurisdiction over "all offenses against the laws of the United States." Dickstein also conveniently ignored article I, section 8 of the United States Constitution which empowers Congress to create, define and punish crimes, irrespective of where they are committed. See United States v. Worrall, 2 U.S. (2 Dall.) 384, 393, 1 L.Ed. 426, 28 F.Cas. 774 (1798) (Chase, J.). Article I, section 8 and the sixteenth amendment also empower Congress to create and provide for the administration of an income tax; the statute under which defendant was charged and convicted, 28 U.S.C. § 7201, plainly falls within that authority. Efforts to argue that federal jurisdiction does not encompass prosecutions for federal tax evasion have been rejected as either "silly" or "frivolous" by a myriad of courts throughout the nation. See, e.g., United States v. Dawes, 874 F.2d. 746, 750 (10th Cir.), cert. denied, 493 U.S. 920, 107 L.Ed.2d. 264, 110 S.Ct. 284 (1989), overruled on other grounds, 895 F.2d. 1581 (10th Cir. 1990); United States v. Tedder, 787 F.2d. 540, 542 (10th Cir. 1986); United States v. Amon, 669 F.2d. 1351, 1355 (10th Cir.*

---

[94] Rutkin v. United States, 343 U.S. 130, 137, 72 S.Ct. 571, 96 L.Ed. 833 (1952), quoted in James v. United States, 366 U.S. 213, 219, 81 S.Ct. 1052, 6 L.Ed.2d. 246 (1961).

Chapter 7: Resources for Tax Fraud Fighters

> *1981); United States v. Brown, 600 F.2d. 248, 259 (10th Cir.), cert. denied, 444 U.S. 917, 100 S.Ct. 233, 62 L.Ed.2d. 172 (1979); Cheek, 882 F.2d. at 1270; United States v. Ward, 833 F.2d. 1538, 1539 (11th Cir. 1987), cert. denied, 485 U.S. 1022, 108 S.Ct. 1576, 99 L.Ed.2d. 891 (1988); United States v. Koliboski, 732 F.2d. 1328, 1329-30 (7th Cir. 1984); United States v. Evans, 717 F.2d. 1334, 1334 (11th Cir. 1983); United States v. Drefke, 707 F.2d. 978, 981 (8th Cir.), cert. denied, 464 U.S. 942, 78 L.Ed.2d. 321, 104 S.Ct. 359 (1983); United States v. Spurgeon, 671 F.2d. 1198, 1199 (8th Cir. 1982); O'Brien v. United States, 51 F.2d. 193, 196, 10 A.F.T.R. (P-H) 223 (7th Cir.), cert. denied, 284 U.S. 673, 52 S.Ct. 129, 76 L.Ed. 569 (1931). In the face of this uniform authority, it defies credulity to argue that the district court lacked jurisdiction to adjudicate the government's case against defendant.*
>
> *Dickstein's argument that the sixteenth amendment does not authorize a direct, non-apportioned tax on United States citizens similarly is devoid of any arguable basis in law. Indeed, the Ninth Circuit recently noted "the patent absurdity and frivolity of such a proposition." In re **Becraft**, 885 F.2d. 547, 548 (9th Cir. 1989). **For seventy-five years, the Supreme Court has recognized that the sixteenth amendment authorizes a direct non-apportioned tax upon United States citizens throughout the nation, not just in federal enclaves**, see Brushaber v. Union Pac. R.R., 240 U.S. 1, 12-19, 60 L.Ed. 493, 36 S.Ct. 236 (1916); efforts to argue otherwise have been sanctioned as frivolous, see, e.g., Becraft, 885 F.2d. at 549 (Fed. R. App. P. 38 sanctions for raising frivolous sixteenth amendment argument in petition for rehearing); Lovell v. United States, 755 F.2d. 517, 519-20 (7th Cir. 1984) (Fed. R. App. P. 38 sanctions imposed on pro se litigants raising frivolous sixteenth amendment contentions). Dickstein's contention that defendant was not an "individual" under the Internal Revenue Code also is frivolous. See Dawes, 874 F.2d. at 750-51; United States v. Studley, 783 F.2d. 934, 937 (9th Cir. 1986); United States v. Rice, 659 F.2d. 524, 528 (5th Cir. Unit A 1981). His disregard of governing legal precedent is further portrayed by his reference to the "alleged ratification" of the sixteenth amendment in the face of uniform contrary authority. See, e.g., Miller v. United States, 868 F.2d. 236, 241 (7th Cir. 1989); United States v. Sitka, 845 F.2d. 43, 46-47 (2d Cir.), cert. denied, 488 U.S. 827, 102 L.Ed.2d. 54, 109 S.Ct. 77 (1988); United States v. Stahl, 792 F.2d. 1438, 1440-41 (9th Cir. 1986), cert. denied, 479 U.S. 1036, 93 L.Ed.2d. 840, 107 S.Ct. 888 (1987); Sisk v. Commissioner, 791 F.2d. 58, 60-61 (6th Cir. 1986); see generally United States v. Stillhammer, 706 F.2d. 1072, 1077-78 (10th Cir. 1983). Argument reflecting such contemptuous disregard for established legal authority has no place within this circuit.*
> [United States v. Collins, 920 F.2d. 619, (10th Cir. 11/27/1990)]

This case is quoted by the IRS as a reference in our Tax Protester Rebuttal on our website at http://famguardian.org/. This ruling has the following MAJOR and BLATANT defects:

1. It ignores the ruling of *Stanton v. Baltic Mining*, in referring to the *Brushaber v. Union Pacific R.R.*, case, that *income taxes are only constitutional as excise taxes, and not direct taxes*:

    > *"that **the provisions of the Sixteenth Amendment conferred no new power of taxation** but simply prohibited the previous complete and plenary power of income taxation possessed by Congress from the beginning from being taken out of the category of indirect taxation to which it inherently belonged and being placed in the category of direct taxation"*

    Instead, the *U.S. v. Collins* ruling says that:

    > *"...the Supreme Court has recognized that the sixteenth amendment authorizes a direct non-apportioned tax upon United States citizens throughout the nation, not just in federal enclaves"*

    and yet only cites ONE Supreme Court case, *Brushaber*, which clearly *doesn't* sustain their position. This is a *very bad* precedent and *bad law* indeed! Brushaber claims that income taxes are constitutional as "excise taxes" only, not "direct taxes". Where did the court get such nonsense? I contend that in this case they were just mad at the attorney, Dickstein, and were behaving irrationally. That was why they sanctioned him and dismissed him from the court.

2. Completely ignores the fact that in the Brushaber case, the appellant was acting as an agent for a *nonresident alien, and NOT a citizen*! But in the case of *U.S. v. Collins*, the appellant was a citizen, not a nonresident alien. This is a completely different situation.

3. In addition, it ignores *all* the issues, errors, and omissions we raised in the above case of *Simmons v. United States*, 308 F.2d. 160, 8/28/1962.

The last case we want to look at is *U.S. v. Melton*, 86 F.3d. 1153, ruling on May 22, 1996. This case dealt with brothers who owned a painting business and who evaded payment of income taxes by various highly creative means, including use of cash and avoiding banks, using gold coins, and setting up foreign corporations. It's a fascinating case that has just about every major tax evasion and protester element in it. We'd highly recommend reading it. Below is an excerpt from the court's ruling:

> "While courts may have offered differing views of the income tax over time, the United States Supreme Court has consistently interpreted the federal income tax for 80 years. Since 1916, the Court has construed the tax as an indirect tax authorized under Article I, Section 8, Clause 1 of the U.S. Constitution, as amended by the Sixteenth Amendment. See Brushaber v. Union Pacific R.R. Co., 240 U.S. 1, 11, 16-19, 60 L.Ed. 493, 36 S.Ct. 236 (1916). Federal courts have all agreed that wages or compensation for services constitute income and that individuals receiving income are subject to the federal income tax--regardless of its nature. See, e.g., Brushaber, 240 U.S. at 17; United States v. Sloan, 939 F.2d. 499, 500-01 (7th Cir. 1991), cert. denied, 502 U.S. 1060, 117 L.Ed.2d. 110, 112 S.Ct. 940 (1992); Simmons v. United States, 308 F.2d. 160, 167-68 (4th Cir. 1962). In short, the debate over whether the income tax is an excise tax or a direct tax is irrelevant to the obligation of citizens to pay taxes and file returns. Simmons, 308 F.2d. at 166 n.21 (stating that "it has been clearly established that the labels used do not determine the extent of the taxing power").
>
> Furthermore, the duty to file returns and pay income taxes is clear. Section 1 of the Internal Revenue Code imposes a federal tax on the taxable income of every individual. 26 U.S.C. §1. Section 63 defines "taxable income" as gross income minus allowable deductions. 26 U.S.C. §63. Section 61 states that "gross income means all income from whatever source derived," including compensation for services. 26 U.S.C. §61. Sections 6001 and 6011 provide that a person must keep records and file a tax return for any tax for which he is liable. 26 U.S.C. §§ 6001 & 6011. Finally, section 6012 provides that every individual having gross income that equals or exceeds the exemption amount in a taxable year shall file an income tax return. 26 U.S.C. §6012. The duty to pay federal income taxes therefore is "manifest on the face of the statutes, without any resort to IRS rules, forms or regulations." United States v. Bowers, 920 F.2d. 220, 222 (4th Cir. 1990). The rarely recognized proposition that, "where the law is vague or highly debatable, a defendant--actually or imputedly--lacks the requisite intent to violate it," Mallas , 762 F.2d. at 363 (quoting United States v. Critzer, 498 F.2d. 1160, 1162 (4th Cir. 1974)), simply does not apply here.

Once again, this Appellate court ruling ignores all the same issues referenced earlier in **Simmons v. United States**. It ignores constitutional issues such as Article I, Section 8, Clauses 1 and 3, which constrain the Congress' taxing power to foreign and interstate commerce, and their relation to 26 U.S.C. §861 and the 26 C.F.R. §1.861-1 through 26 C.F.R. §1.861-14. It does not attempt to identify whether the income derives from a taxable "source". It doesn't relate the income to an occasion that is appropriate to an excise, such as the sale or manufacture of commodities involving interstate or foreign commerce. ***This is clearly a glaring error in logic and legal analysis, and yet it is allowed to stand because of a federal judicial conspiracy to uphold the income tax!***

There are many, many other cases we could discuss, but they all follow the same pattern of the two indicated above. In the interest of conserving space, we won't show any others here.

Following the expansion of the definition of "excise taxes" by the circuit courts documented above, a number of cases were heard by the federal appellate courts dealing directly with the constitutionality of the income taxes and the nature of being a "direct tax". In each case, the court unfavorably "rubber stamped" the result without dealing with the constitutional issues of direct vs. indirect taxes. They also failed to address the nature of the parties allegedly subject to the tax, such as whether they were citizens domiciled in the 50 union states, nonresident aliens, or citizens living overseas. This simply clouded the application of the income taxes even further for the average Citizen, which we believe was clearly their intent. Here are two examples of such abuse by the federal appellate courts:

1. *Ficalora v. Commissioner of Internal Revenue*, 751 F.2d. 85 (12/13/1984).
2. *Charczuk v. Commissioner of Internal Revenue*, 771 F.2d. 471 (8/29/1985).

We'll first provide the ruling in the case of *Charczuk v. Commissioner of Internal Revenue* (771 F.2d. 471), because the arguments of the "taxpayer" not only were rejected by the court, but the court also sanction of attorney fees against the appellant. Below is an excerpt from that case:

> Paul E. Charczuk *and Victoria* Charczuk *jointly filed a Form 1040 for the taxable year 1977 reflecting income of $4,763.00. This amount was entered on the line for "business income" rather than on the line for "wages, salaries, tips and other employee compensation." Attached to the taxpayers' return were seven Form W-2 Wage and Tax Statements showing that the taxpayers received wages during 1977 totaling $12,276.00. Also attached was a Schedule C for each taxpayer claiming a "net profit" of $2,668.00 for Paul* Charczuk *and $2,095.00 for Victoria* Charczuk.[95] *On June 9, 1980, the Commissioner sent taxpayers a notice of deficiency informing them that they owed $1,148.00 in taxes for 1977 based on disallowance of all expenses claimed on Schedule C for lack of verification. Subsequently, the taxpayers petitioned the Tax Court for a redetermination of the deficiency. In those*

---

[95] Each Schedule C (entitled Profit or (Loss) from Business or Profession (Sole Proprietorship)) gave the taxpayers' name, address, social security number and the amount claimed as "net profit." To the right of the area for deductions on both schedules was the instruction "See Form-21." A "Form-21" was attached for Paul ***Charczuk*** which detailed various "subtractions" for taxes, rent, subsistence, interest, auto, telephone, utilities, supplies, dues and subscriptions from "receipts" of $6,676.00. No "Form-21" or similar explanation of calculations was attached for Victoria ***Charczuk***.

proceedings the taxpayers did not attempt to challenge the Commissioner's determination by presenting evidence in support of their claimed deductions, but rather argued that the income tax itself was invalid as a matter of law. The Tax Court granted summary judgment in favor of the Commissioner. T.C. Memo. 1983-433. Taxpayers appeal from this judgment claiming the Tax Court misconstrued their arguments against the income tax and that its decision was contrary to law and "illogical." We affirm.

[...]

It takes little consideration to determine that the arguments presented by taxpayers with respect to these issues are meritless and unreasonable. However, to forestall taxpayers' patently false claim that "the issues in this case have never been addressed and answered by any Federal Article III Court" we will quote at length from the opinion of the United States Court of Appeals for the Second Circuit in Ficalora v. Commissioner of Internal Revenue, 751 F.2d. 85 (1984), cert. denied 471 U.S. 1005, 105 S.Ct. 1869, 85 L.Ed.2d. 162 (1985), which involved taxpayers who were represented by the same Thomas J. Carley who represents the taxpayers in the instant appeal. The quoted text which follows reveals that the Second Circuit in Ficalora was responding to arguments substantially identical to those taxpayers advance in this case.

I. Constitutional Authority to Impose An Income Tax on Individuals

We first address ourselves to the appellant's contention that neither the United States Congress nor the United States Tax Court possess the constitutional authority to impose on him an income tax for the taxable year 1980. Appellant argues that an income tax is a "direct" tax and that Congress does not possess the constitutional authority to impose a "direct" tax on him, since such a tax has not been apportioned among the several States of the Union. In support of his argument, appellant cites Article 1, Section 9, clause 4 of the United States Constitution which provides that:

"No Capitation, or other direct, Tax shall be laid, unless in Proportion to the Census or Enumeration herein before directed to be taken."

He also relies on the case of Pollock v. Farmers' Loan and Trust Co., 157 U.S. 429, 15 S.Ct. 673, 39 L.Ed. 759 (initial decision), 158 U.S. 601, 15 S.Ct. 912, 39 L.Ed. 1108 (decision on rehearing) (1895), wherein the United States Supreme Court held that a tax upon income from real and personal property is invalid in the absence of apportionment.

In making his argument that Congress lacks constitutional authority to impose a tax on wages without apportionment among the States, the appellant has chosen to ignore the precise holding of the Court in Pollock, as well as the development of constitutional law in this area over the last ninety years. While ruling that a tax upon income from real and personal property is invalid in the absence of apportionment, the Supreme Court explicitly stated that taxes on income from one's employment are not direct taxes and are not subject to the necessity of apportionment. Pollock v. Farmers' Loan and Trust Co., 158 U.S. at 635, 15 S.Ct. at 919. Furthermore, the Sixteenth Amendment to the United States Constitution, enacted in 1913, provides that:

"The Congress shall have the power to lay and collect taxes on income, from whatever source derived, without apportionment among the several States, and without regard to any census or enumeration."

Finally, in the case of New York, ex rel. Cohn v. Graves, 300 U.S. 308, 57 S.Ct. 466, 81 L.Ed. 666 (1937), the Supreme Court in effect overruled Pollock, and in so doing rendered the Sixteenth Amendment unnecessary, when it sustained New York's income tax on income derived from real property :n New Jersey. Id. at 314-15, 57 S.Ct. at 468-69. Hence, there is no question but that Congress has the constitutional authority to impose an income tax upon the appellant.

II. Statutory Authority to Impose an Income Tax on Individuals and Definition of Taxable Income

The appellant contends that "[n]owhere in any of the Statutes of the United States is there any section of law making any individual liable to pay a tax or excise on 'taxable income.'" . . . The essence of the appellant's argument is that 26 U.S.C. §1 does not impose a tax on any individual for any stated period of time; rather, it imposes a tax on an undefined: "taxable income".

Section 1 of the Internal Revenue Code of 1954 (26 U.S.C.) (hereinafter the Code) provides in plain, clear and precise language that "there is hereby imposed on the taxable income or every individual . . . a tax determined in accordance with" tables set-out later in the statute. In equally clear language, Section 63 of the Code defines taxable income as "gross income, minus the deductions allowed by this chapter . . .", gross income, in turn, is defined in Section 61 of the Code as "all income from whatever source derived, including (but not limited to) . . . : (1) Compensation for services . . .". Despite the appellant's attempted contorted construction of the statutory scheme, we find that it coherently and forthrightly imposes upon the appellant a tax upon his income for the year 1980.

[...]

> *This appeal is frivolous. Pursuant to Rule 38 of the Federal Rules of Appellate Procedure, we impose on the appellants double the costs of the Commissioner.*
>
> *[...]*
>
> *When the costs incurred by this Court and respondent are taken into consideration, the maximum damages authorized by the statute ($500) do not begin to indemnify the United States for the expenses which petitioner's frivolous action has occasioned. Considering the waste of limited judicial and administrative resources caused by petitioner's action, even the maximum damages authorized by Congress are wholly inadequate to compensate the United States and its other taxpayers. These costs must eventually be borne by all of the citizens who honestly and fairly participate in our tax collection system. * * * (Sydnes v. Commissioner, [74 T.C. 864, 872-873 (1980), affd. 647 F.2d. 813 (8th Cir. 1981)].)*
>
> *[...]*
>
> *Courts are in no way obligated to tolerate arguments that thoroughly defy common sense. Such conduct is permissible in our society for the very young, those attempting to make a joke or, occasionally, philosophers, but it cannot be allowed of one engaged in the serious work of a practicing attorney appearing before a court of law. Mr. Carley's conduct in this suit has been a paradigm of unreasonable behavior, and it has been exceedingly vexatious as that term is understood by the Supreme Court. See Christiansburg Garment Co. v. EEOC, 434 U.S. 412, 421, 54 L.Ed.2d. 648, 98 S.Ct. 694 (1978). (In a case arising under Title VII of the Civil Rights Act of 1964, the Court stipulated that "the term 'vexatious' in no way implies that the plaintiff's subjective bad faith is a necessary prerequisite to a fee award against him."). Given the continued character of Mr. Carley's intransigence, justice requires that he and his clients bear the full weight of the sanctions allowed by law so that the government, and ultimately all law abiding taxpayers, will not be taxed with the expense of opposing meritless contentions such as his.*
>
> *Accordingly, the decision of the Tax Court is affirmed and Paul E. Charczuk and Victoria Charczuk are ordered to pay the government double its costs on appeal. In addition, the government is ordered to submit within twenty (20) days to the court clerk, and to Thomas J. Carley, an appropriate accounting of all expenses (other than costs of the appeal) and attorneys' fees it has reasonably incurred as a result of this appeal. Thomas J. Carley may file with the court clerk a challenge to the government's accounting within ten (10) days of the government's filing only with regard to whether the expenses and fees were in fact incurred on this appeal. Upon approval of the government's accounting or any part of it by the court, Thomas J. Carley will be ordered to personally pay to the government the entire amount approved.*[96]

You will note that the court ignored all of the same issues we raised with the cases of *Simmons v. United States*, 308 F.2d. 160, and *U.S. v. Melton*, 86 F.3d. 1153. They readily identified the receipt of income as other than a "direct tax", which means that it must be an "indirect tax". The only legitimate and constitutional type of indirect tax that it could be, as authorized by the 16th Amendment, is an "excise tax". But guess what, the court didn't mention a word about excise taxes or their applicability only to businesses. The subject of this case, however, was not a business, but an natural person. We refer you again to section **Error! Reference source not found.** and following entitled "Introduction to Federal Taxation".

We hope that this section has served to emphasize the basic problem with the Internal Revenue Code that Congress is not willing to address:

1. The laws are unnecessarily complex, mainly because they have to be so carefully crafted to conceal the real truth that most citizens domiciled in the 50 union states with only domestic income DON'T owe tax.
2. Even most judges don't really understand the Internal Revenue Code and don't agree with each other on their interpretation. See section 3.20.1 "Uncertainty of the Federal Tax Laws" for more interesting reading on this subject.
3. The complexity and uncertainty of the Internal Revenue Code contributes significantly to a violation of "due process" discussed in this and section 3.20.1 "Uncertainty of the Federal Tax Laws". *The first principle of due process is that the laws are written to be clear and unambiguous enough that they can consistently be interpreted and applied by citizens and the courts. An unclear law also violates the Sixth Amendment to the Constitution.*

6.12.4.6 State Court Rulings

The State courts have held that the income tax is a direct property tax. This is revealed by the following cases:

---

[96] Courts imposing sanctions on an attorney under § 1927 must "afford the attorney all appropriate protections of due process available under the law." House Conf. Rep. No. 96-1234, 96th Cong., 2d Sess. 8, reprinted in 1980 U.S. Code Cong. & Ad. News 2781, 2783. At oral argument :n this case, Mr. Carley was offered an opportunity to explain why sanctions should not be imposed against him personally. This satisfies any right he may have had to a hearing on the matter. Cf. McConnell v. Critchlow, 661 F.2d. 116, 119 (9th Cir. 1981).

See Eliasberg Bros. Mercantile Co. v. Grimes, *204 Ala. 492, 86 So. 56, 58 (1920);* State v. Pinder, *108 A. 43, 45 (Del. 1919);* Bachrach v. Nelson, *349 Ill. 579, 182 N.E. 909 (1932);* Opinion of the Justices, *220 Mass. 613, 108 N.E. 570 (1915);* Trefry v. Putnam, *227 Mass. 522, 116 N.E. 904 (1917);* Maguire v. Tax Comm. of Commonwealth, *230 Mass. 503, 120 N.E. 162, 166 (1918);* Hart v. Tax Comm., *240 Mass. 37, 132 N.E. 621 (1921);* In re Ponzi, *6 F.2d. 324 (D.Mass. 1925);* Kennedy v. Comm. of Corps. & Taxation, *256 Mass. 426, 152 N.E. 747 (1926);* In re Opinion of the Justices, *266 Mass. 583, 165 N.E. 900, 902 (1929);* Hutchins v. Comm. of Corps. & Taxation, *272 Mass. 422, 172 N.E. 605, 608 (1930);* Bryant v. Comm. of Corps. & Tax'n., *291 Mass. 498, 197 N.E. 509 (1935);* Culliton v. Chase, *174 Wash. 363, 25 P.2d. 81, 82 (1933);* Jensen v. Henneford, *185 Wash. 209, 53 P.2d. 607 (1936);* State ex rel Manitowoc Gas Co. v. Wisconsin Tax Comm., *161 Wis. 111, 152 N.W. 848, 850 (1915); and State ex rel Sallie F. Moon Co. v. Wisconsin Tax Comm., 166 Wis. 287, 163 N.W. 639, 640 (1917).*

There appears to be no dispute about the plain requirements of the Constitution that direct taxes must be apportioned and that indirect/excise taxes must be uniform. Likewise as shown above, there is a line of decisional authority regarding the generally accepted proposition that income is property.

6.12.5   2003: Federal Court Bans Irwin Schiff's Federal Mafia Tax Book

Below is an article about a ban on this country's most famous anti-tax book published by the most famous tax protester at the time, Irwin Schiff. The article was published by the We the People Foundation for Constitutional Education and distributed via email on June 30, 2003.

Judge Bans Schiff Book on Income Tax

1st Amendment Thrashed to Buy the Tax More Time
New York Times: More Deception

On Monday, June 16, Federal District Court Judge Lloyd D. George issued a preliminary injunction banning the sale and distribution of Irwin Schiff's book about the income tax titled, *"The Federal Mafia: How The Government Illegally Imposes And Unlawfully Collects Income Taxes And How Americans Can Fight Back."*

Schiff's book, which is a personal and legal examination of the income tax fraud, and includes extensive, and specific quotations and analyses of Internal Revenue Code and Supreme Court rulings on the tax, was banned even though the Department of Justice (which bears the burden of proof) presented no evidence and no witnesses at the April 11th preliminary injunction hearing. Click Here to read the first portion of the censored book (.pdf).

In short, Judge George banned Schiff's book as "false commercial speech" without any specific analysis or any in-court evidentiary examination establishing the "falsity" of Schiff's actual speech and by blithely ignoring the substantial body of established Supreme Court constitutional law protecting free expression and publication.

With only an unsubstantiated claim of criminal speech asserted by a government witness (via a written declaration), Judge George summarily dismissed the content of Schiff's book as "largely autobiographical, containing in large part Schiff's anti-tax and anti-government diatribes and theories." Of course, it appears to be lost on the court that this is the exact type of speech protected by the First Amendment and -- even when intertwined with "commercial" speech -- requires the highest level of examination and legal justification to censor.

Allen Lichtenstein, general counsel of the American Civil Liberties Union in Nevada, said he looked forward to arguing the case before the Ninth Circuit Court of Appeals. Schiff said he had done nothing wrong and would appeal. "We argued that the book is not commercial speech, cannot be banned as false commercial speech and does not meet any other criteria for censorship," Lichtenstein said.

On Tuesday June 17, The New York Times ran an article authored by David Cay Johnston about the Schiff injunction. According to Schiff, Johnston makes two knowingly false statements distorting the perceived nature of the proceedings. Schiff has demanded a formal retraction from the New York Times.

Johnston wrote," At the court hearing, Mr. Schiff fired his lawyer after she said that she could not argue his tax claims because they lacked merit." In his demand letter to the Times, Schiff points out that the transcript from the hearing makes it explicitly clear that Schiff's attorney was not characterizing Schiff's legal assertions as false or lacking in any way, but instead that she was effectively prohibited by the court from even raising the issues in defense of Schiff under fear and threat of court sanction.

Analysis of the Order

To reach his contorted legal conclusions and to issue the preliminary injunction in favor of the IRS, Judge George ruled, without any evidentiary examination or cross-examination, to conclude that Schiff's speech is false.

With this in mind, please note on page 4 of the Order there are five distinct, separate legal elements listed for the government to successfully assert a claim for an injunction related to an "abusive tax shelter."

In his order however, the judge conveniently "combines" his analysis of the critical second and third statutory elements, (i.e., relating to making actual "false and fraudulent statements" and the defendant's "reason to know" about their falsity) together within section "B" of the Order, thereby clouding the court's grossly inadequate treatment in establishing the truth or falsity of Schiff's actual speech.

While Section "B" contains much ado concerning Irwin's past criminal tax convictions, his failed federal appeals and Schiff's extensive knowledge and expertise in Internal revenue Code, precious few words are wasted establishing the actual falsity of Schiff's speech. In fact, most of the relevant language concerning the court's finding of falsity merely lists District Court decisions of other victims of the IRS's nationwide attack on speech. The Court is in effect stating, "All these other people had false speech concerning abusive tax shelters so Schiff's speech is too."

In short, to enable the government's full and unfettered dismissal of the very significant First Amendment issues raised subsequently by the ACLU, Judge George quickly reaches the judicial conclusion of the "falsity" of Schiff's speech (relative to abusive tax shelters) by grossly mischaracterizing Schiff's legal assertions within the context of several Supreme Court cases cited that are only tangentially related to the core legal issues raised in Schiff's actual speech.

Example: The Court cites the 1916 Brushaber case which addressed the "right of Congress to impose income tax" *[sic]*. In fact, Brushaber was acting as a withholding agent for a foreign corporate entity operating inside the US and was in fact, under US law, liable *in that capacity*. **This issue is not the issue raised by Schiff in the *Federal Mafia*.**

According to Schiff's *Federal Mafia* material - if Brushaber *was* a natural citizen of living and working in the 50 sates, his personal wages would in fact be non-taxable because they don't meet the constitutional definition of "income" as defined by the Supreme Court (i.e., a corporate profit or gain). It is Supreme Court decisions such as these cited in Schiff's *Mafia* (and therefore, his alleged tax "scheme") that the Court has blindly ignored in its legal analysis.

The bottom line: **Nowhere is there a direct rebuttal or examination of the specific legal assertions advanced by Schiff in either his speech or his book.** Every subsequent aspect contained in the Court's injunction is rationalized, and squarely erected, upon this defective judicial premise.

In reality, Schiff's "abusive tax scam" is merely a detailed discussion and analysis of Internal Revenue Code, the Constitution, and US Supreme Court decisions, coupled with detailed instructions on how average Americans can implement the logical conclusions and reasonable inferences of those legal facts to protect their property and their rights.

The IRS, DOJ and now the US District Court, have failed to provide ANY specific, substantive rebuttal to ANY of the specific elements of Schiff's speech - even though these elements contain the nexus of the falsity or truth of his speech, and thereby are at the heart of determining the legality or criminality of the alleged "abusive tax scheme". **To fail to directly address the content and alleged falsity of the speech is a clear violation of due process.**

Armed with this defective and patently self-serving judicial conclusion, the Court then begins to rebut the 1st Amendment free speech issues raised in the ACLU's amicus briefs.

(Note: The 1st Amendment discussion begins on page 13 of the order)

Commercial Speech

Judge George summarily concludes not only that *The Federal Mafia* is non-protected "false" commercial speech because the book is sold for money and it contains false information that might be of "selfish" economic benefit to the audience (or Schiff) -- but that it should be banned because it *advertises* other Schiff products that naturally lead to the same alleged tax "scam." I.e., as false commercial advertising, the book should be banned.

The judge, citing the 9th Circuit Estate Preservation case, makes the implicit point that Schiff, outside this injunction, is free to continue to give tax planning advice as long as it is "legitimate" as (quote) "every honest and qualified tax consultant knows."

Judge George, having concluded that the book constitutes "core commercial speech," (i.e. "advertising, plain and simple") dismisses the tightly interwoven political content and far reaching political implications of Schiff's work and instead focuses on establishing that Schiff's book is simply a contrived "soup" of false advertising and an embedded "abusive tax scheme," which, of course, enjoy no protection.

Incitement of Imminent Lawless Acts

At the beginning of the section dealing with the "Incitement of Imminent Lawless Acts" (page 26) Judge George cites the Brandenburg v. Ohio Supreme Court case where the court upheld that even speech advocating the violation of law was protected, as long as the speech did not "incite imminent unlawful acts".

The Brandenburg case is the modern day constitutional litmus test for the legal banning of speech. Below is the definition of the word "imminent".

> **Imminent** \Im"mi*nent\, Imminent: it is the strongest -- it denotes that something is ready to fall or happen on the instant; as, in imminent danger of one's life.
>
> 1. Threatening to occur immediately; near at hand; impending; -- said especially of misfortune or peril. ``In danger imminent.'' (Source: *Webster's Revised Unabridged Dictionary*, © 1996, 1998 MICRA, Inc.)

Having already sidestepped the issue of whether filing a "zero return" constitutes an unlawful act, Judge George haphazardly, and improperly, dismisses the crucial Brandenburg "test" as inappropriate in Schiff's case because the speech in Schiff's book "incorporates the (tax) scheme" thereby implying that Schiff's speech is the actual crime and therefore that this test need not be applied.

The entire nature of the Supreme Court's Brandenburg litmus test revolves around the direct incitement of "imminent" lawless behavior - i.e., in the case of Brandenburg (and its supporting case citations) imminent *VIOLENT behavior*. (Brandenburg was a Klansman engaged in inflammatory, racist speech. His speech was upheld as constitutional because he merely *advocated* the breaking of the law.)

Judge George takes license in citing several sympathetic Court decisions, while choosing to ignore the direct guidance of the Supreme Court regarding this crucial legal test necessary to ban speech.

In short, the Court makes no attempt to establish how reading a book containing a legal analysis and instructions on how to file a tax return could result in anything resembling "imminent" activity of ANY type - whether lawful or not. The judge seems content - as the other District tax case judges seem to be - of tolerating a mere logical relationship between this "unlawful" speech and a subsequent "criminal act." With that linkage established, the "imminence" element to banning speech is cleanly dismissed out of hand.

By this court's logic, anyone who wrote a "how-to" book containing any information that was subsequently used in a crime - no matter how far removed from the alleged proximate cause -- and regardless of whether the speech was false or not - could be held liable for his/her speech or writings.

Illegal Acts

In the last section of the injunction order, the judge cements his previous conclusion of the false, (and thereby criminal), nature of Schiff's speech by citing a handful of free speech cases involving bomb makers, illegal drug manufacturers and "hit-men" that purport to, by example and association, show how speech that leads directly to and induces specific criminal conduct is not protected.

Of course unlike exploding a bomb or killing another human being -- which are reasonably understood to be plainly criminal acts - the filing of a tax return per instructions and legal advice of a court-acknowledged tax expert that specifically and plainly cites decisions of the Supreme Court and the Internal Revenue Code itself is much harder to comprehend as an overt criminal act.

Conclusion

The legal arguments and carefully selected lower level court cases cited by Judge George throughout the Order clearly appear strained in their effort to support a justifiable ban of Schiff's book and appear to set the stage for the Ninth Circuit to deny an appeal from Schiff. The clearly protected political content of the book is outright ignored. It is obvious that the government has found Schiff's speech (and many other tax "protestors") intolerable <u>simply because the speech conveys details of the income tax fraud and that they have provided methods on how to effectively contravene its effects</u>.

To be sure, the banning of speech through restraining orders and like vehicles are <u>extraordinary remedies</u> that can be implemented without a trial by jury, were designed to *temporarily* protect rights, property and the public tranquility at risk until other legal remedies could be effected. <u>They were never intended for the purposes of suppressing, or otherwise circumventing, rightful, lawful public debates and discussions about the tax codes or the abuses of government power</u>.

The extraordinary remedy of enjoining speech was never intended to replace the proper processes of due process and the enforcement of laws as executed via indictments, prosecution and the judicial appeal process. The delegated and strictly limited legal authority of our government to collect taxes DOES NOT, and CANNOT, ever trump the sovereign People's right to free speech.

That the judiciary would openly sanction the use of these extraordinary legal remedies and affirmatively deny Schiff his constitutionally protected right to speech while the government - for 13 years - has had the ability and resources to openly pursue Schiff with full, public criminal charges for his allegedly unlawful acts - AND HAS NOT -- <u>should not be tolerated</u>. That our media would ignore -- and even unquestioningly facilitate -- this carnage on our Constitution is deplorable.

In the pivotal case New York Times Co. v. Sullivan (1964), Justice Brandeis, is cited from his concurring opinion in *Whitney v. California,* 274 U.S. 357, 375-376 restating the rationale behind free speech:

> *"Those who won our independence believed . . . that public discussion is a political duty, and that this should be a fundamental principle of the American government. They recognized the risks to which all human institutions are subject. But they knew that order cannot be secured merely through fear of punishment for its infraction; that it is hazardous to discourage thought, hope and imagination; that fear breeds repression; that repression breeds hate; that hate menaces stable government; that the path of safety lies in the opportunity to discuss freely supposed grievances and proposed remedies, and that the fitting remedy for evil counsels is good ones. Believing in the power of reason as applied through public discussion,* **they eschewed silence coerced by law--the argument of force in its worst form.** *Recognizing the occasional tyrannies of governing majorities, they amended the Constitution so that free speech and assembly should be guaranteed."* [emphasis added]

Will the People silently endure these abuses? We shall see.

> *"The liberties of a people never were, nor ever will be, secure, when the transactions of their rulers may be concealed from them."*

[Patrick Henry]

"We are not afraid to entrust the American people with unpleasant facts, foreign ideas, alien philosophies, and competitive values. For a nation that is afraid to let its people judge the truth and falsehood in an open market is a nation that is afraid of its people."
[John F. Kennedy]

6.12.6 2002: Definition for "Acts of Congress" removed from Federal Rules of Criminal Procedure

The definition of the term "acts of Congress" was formerly an especially good means to demonstrate the very limited territorial jurisdiction of the United States Courts. One place to look for that definition was in Rule 54(c) of the Federal Rules of Criminal Procedure. We quoted this rule in chapters 4 and 11 of this book as a means to demonstrate the very limited jurisdiction of the federal government starting in mid 2002.

> *Rule 54(c) of the Federal Rules of Criminal Procedure (prior to Dec. 2002)*
>
> "Act of Congress" includes any act of Congress **locally applicable to and in force in the District of Columbia, in Puerto Rico, in a territory or in an insular possession.**"

Subsequently in Dec. 2002, the Federal Judiciary rewrote the Federal Rules of Criminal Procedure and took the contents of Rule 54 and moved it to Rule 1 of the Rules. They then removed the definition of "acts of Congress" from the definitions. Below is the explanation of what they did, from the notes under Rule 1:

> *NOTES OF ADVISORY COMMITTEE ON RULES - 2002 AMENDMENT*
>
> *Rule 1 is entirely revised and expanded to incorporate Rule 54, which deals with the application of the rules. Consistent with the title of the existing rule, the Committee believed that a statement of the scope of the rules should be placed at the beginning to show readers which proceedings are governed by these rules. The Committee also revised the rule to incorporate the definitions found in Rule 54(c) as a new Rule 1(b).*
>
> *. . .*
>
> *Rule 1(b) is composed of material currently located in Rule 54(c), with several exceptions. First, the reference to an "Act of Congress" has been deleted from the restyled rules; instead the rules use the self-explanatory term "federal statute." Second, the language concerning demurrers, pleas in abatement, etc., has been deleted as being anachronistic. Third, the definitions of "civil action" and "district court" have been deleted. Fourth, the term "attorney for the government" has been expanded to include reference to those attorneys who may serve as special or independent counsel under applicable federal statutes. The term "attorney for the government" contemplates an attorney of record in the case.*
>
> *[See http://www.law.cornell.edu/rules/frcrmp/NRule1.htm]*

Black's Law Dictionary doesn't define the term nor could we find any other definition that was as clear as the one above, but now, like all the other good leads that freedom fighters have discovered, the truth has once again been covered up and obscured by your deceitful public "servants" in order to perpetuate the illusion that they have more authority than the Constitution gives them. Write both your Congressman and the United States Committee on the Judiciary to complain at:

http://www.senate.gov/~judiciary/

6.12.7 1992: William Conklin v. United States

In this section, we'll discuss some of the incredible chicanery and legal trickery that was pulled by the federal courts in conspiring with the IRS in misapplying the Internal Revenue Code to extort and oppress of the rights of a specific Citizen, William Conklin. Bill is a famous tax resistance advocate who wrote a fascinating book called *Why No One is Required to File Tax Returns: Reforming Tax Laws Using Our Fifth Amendment Rights*.[97] He runs a great website found at:

http://www.anti-irs.com/

---

[97] *Why No One is Required to File Tax Returns*, by William Conklin, 1996, Davidson Press, ISBN 189183391X.

Bill used his Fifth Amendment rights exclusively to litigate not having to file federal income tax returns. On his website and in his book, he largely ignores the 861/source issue that is one of the two themes of this document. He has a lot of very good and persuasive arguments about the Fifth Amendment, and he deadlocked the federal district courts on the income tax issue for over _five years_ because of some of the very serious constitutional questions he raised that the courts refused to deal with and delayed ruling on! On his website, he states that he has won against the IRS seven times! Here are some of his cases:

1. *Church of World Peace, Inc. v IRS*, 715 F.2d. 492
2. *United States v. Church of World Peace*, 775 F.2d. 265
3. *United States v Church of World Peace*, 878 F.2d. 1281
4. *Conklin v. United States*, 812 F.2d. 1318
5. *Conklin v. C.I.R.*, 897 F.2d. 1032
6. *Tavery v. United States*, 897 F.2d. 1027
7. *Tavery v. United States, 897 F.2d. 1027, Civ. No. 87-Z-180 (1987)*, USDC Colorado

For at least the past ten years, Bill has challenged everyone by offering at least $50,000 to the first person who can show him how he can file an income tax return without violating his Fifth Amendment right to not incriminate himself! Every time he publishes a new version of his book, he ups the ante! To date, no one, including famous Hollywood criminal lawyers like Melvin Belli, has been able to satisfy his challenge! He has more than adequately made his point that direct income taxes violate the Fifth Amendment to the Constitution on this basis alone! But this wasn't enough, he took the issue all the way up to the Supreme Court. It was a hot potato for the Supreme Court so they denied his right to litigate the issue there (violation of the First Amendment right of free speech and of ability to petition the government for redress of grievances), which was another way of saying:

> *"We don't want to argue with you and we know you are right, and if people hear the truth about, we're in trouble!"*

He had to appeal to the Supreme Court because the federal district court, after a 5-year delay reaching a verdict (!), ruled against him on the surface, but proved his point indirectly!

We don't have room here to discuss all of his cases, but here is a quote from Judge Nottingham in Bill's case of *Conklin v. United States*, 812 F.2d. 1318, which he said in open court on August 27, 1992. Remember, the issue was Bill Conklin litigating to defend his right not to be compelled to incriminate himself by filing or signing an income tax return, and he filed a tax return he wouldn't sign and then litigated his right not to have to pay the $500 frivolous return penalty assessed by the IRS:

> *"And one of the fatal things that I—or things that you are overlooking—I will not say it is fatal, although it appears to me it may be fatal—is when you do not sign a return, the reason that the tax collection system is frustrated is because you are not signing under the penalty of perjury. I mean, if everybody could do what you did, the tax collection system would collapse, which you know I am sure some people would argue is not a bad result. But it is not one that I am in a position to bring about."*[98]

Are you starting to see the picture? Judge Nottingham knows it is unconstitutional but his bigger concern is that he doesn't want to undermine the tax system because his job would be threatened! According to 28 U.S.C. §134(a), federal judges must be on "good behavior" in order to hold office, and can be removed from office on bad behavior. Could it be that in this case, declaring income taxes unconstitutional might be described by the Congress, who would impeach him, as being "bad behavior"? **WE THINK SO!!!**

We'd also like to repeat some of Bill's own words from his book:

> *Notice that the judge basically told me that I could not possibly win because I would overturn the federal tax system. Of course, that was the point of my lawsuit to begin with!*
>
> *After thinking about the case for five years(!), he decided to rule against me. He took the position that the Fifth Amendment does not apply to tax returns because the Fifth Amendment applies only to "compelled testimony." In other words, the Fifth Amendment only applies to information that individuals are required to give to the government.*

---

[98] *Why No One is Required to File Tax Returns*, by William Conklin, 1996, Davidson Press, ISBN 189183391X, p 36.

> Since I had argued that the Fifth Amendment applies to tax returns because I felt that their filing was compelled by the penal provisions of the law, it is clear that Judge Nottingham took the position that individuals are not required to give information to the government on the 1040 returns (or, in other words, he was talking like the IRS talks by saying that filing is "voluntary"), and that is why the Fifth Amendment cannot be applied.
>
> ### The Court Rules in Opposition to the U.S. Supreme Court
>
> Judge Nottingham had to rule directly against the position of the Supreme Court in Garner vs. U.S., supra. Remember, the Garner Court took the position that information on tax returns is "compelled testimony" for purposes of the Fifth Amendment.
>
> Furthermore, Judge Nottingham also accused me of taking a blanket Fifth Amendment position, even though I certainly had not done that. In fact, I had completely filled out the return and provided supporting documentation and paid the tax that I voluntarily self-assessed. The Supreme Court took the position that if an individual so much as even admits to having books and records, he waives the Fifth Amendment protections of his rights because the Fifth Amendment does not apply to documents, it only applies to testimony.[99] Judge Nottingham also ruled that "Plaintiff has wholly failed to persuade me that truthful completion of the IRS Form 1040 or any related forms would tend to incriminate him."
>
> ### The Judge Answers a Question I Did Not Ask
>
> The judge answered a question that I did not as,. How could the judge know if a piece of information would incriminate me? There is no way either of us could know that! But I was not arguing that I might incriminate myself. I was arguing that I could not be required to waive my Fifth Amendment protections of my rights. As a layman, there is no way I could be presumed to know if a piece of information would be incriminating or not. His opinion duly impressed me again as to how tricky the courts can be in their "Alice in Wonderland" language.
>
> I appealed the case to the Tenth Circuit Court of Appeals. The Tenth Circuit upheld the lower Court and thus also took a position exactly opposite to the position taken by the Supreme Court in the Garner case. The circuit court judges held that information on a tax return is not compelled, and the judges also accused me of taking a blanket Fifth Amendment position even though I had answered all the questions.
>
> I could not believe it! It was as if the court had not even looked at my return! Then the Tenth Circuit Court sent the case back to the lower court for any further recommendations by Judge Nottingham. The government seized the opportunity to ask Judge Nottingham to order me to pay the amount it estimated it had cost the IRS in attorney time to respond so my complaint. I was amazed when the attorneys for the IRS submitted a $6,000 bill for their time! I was really flabbergasted when Judge Nottingham assessed me the entire amount—this for raising the "frivolous" argument of law that individuals are required to waive their Fifth Amendment rights when they file tax returns!
>
> For me, the judge's actions underscored the unfair bias of the courts against someone who is challenging the incongruities of our income tax laws. Think about the contradictions in this scenario: The judge was saying that this was an obviously frivolous issue—an issue that even I, a layman, would immediately realize could quickly be defeated. Yet when the government submitted a $6,000 bill for the time that it required for two professional attorneys to defeat my position, the judge accepted their bill and the many hours it represented without question, and considered it appropriate to pass it along to me in its entirety!
>
> ### I Appeal to the Supreme Court
>
> I guess I should have been grateful that the judge did not add his time to my bill, too. It took him five years to evaluate my "easily understood as frivolous even by the layman" argument! Of course, I appealed once again, this time on the issue of the newly-imposed $6,000 worth of sanctions. Unfortunately, the Supreme Court was too busy with other far more important issues. It decided to not even consider my objection to the $6,000 sanction.
>
> Putting aside my outrageous $6,000 fine, do you now understand why the IRS continually refers to the filing of tax returns as voluntary? The IRS knows that if it stated than an individual is required to file tax returns, a Fifth Amendment confrontation would be created, so the IRS enforces the idea that tax returns are indirectly required. The IRS requires you to volunteer, and then punishes you if you chose not to volunteer. (Did I just hear you say that you feel like Alice in Wonderland, trying to tie the Queen down to fixed definitions of words?)

His book is really fascinating and we highly recommend it! You can order it from his website. After you read his book, you will probably be as mad as I was at the IRS. Reading his book was one of many reasons I became so committed to writing this book! His book didn't tell enough of the story and I felt people needed to hear "the rest of the story", as Paul Harvey likes to say.

---

[99] See *U.S. vs. Doe*, 104 S.Ct. 1237(1984).

Among some of the many unethical, immoral, and frivolous tactics the IRS and the courts used against Bill in litigating his case were:

1. The judge hearing the case had a conflict of interest with eliminating the income tax and refused to recuse himself or address the issue of recusing himself for cause.
2. The IRS requested and the court agreed to sanction Mr. Conklin with significant legal fees for defending his rights (a violation of his First Amendment right of free speech and his right to petition the government for redress of grievances). This, in effect, amounts to penalizing someone for the exercise of a right, which we said and the Supreme Court has also said, is unconstitutional.
3. The federal court refused to publish his cases, which is to say that they wouldn't allow his cases to go into the case law databases so other people could read about them. This is another First Amendment violation.
4. The court delayed ruling on the case for *five years* without explanation!
5. They accused Mr. Conklin of litigating frivolous issues. Unbelievable!
6. They overruled the Supreme Court!
7. The Supreme Court refused to hear the appeal (denied his writ), which was a death sentence for him.

Now do you understand the "*judicial conspiracy to protect the income tax*" that we are talking about? It's pathetic and disgusting!! Judge Nottingham should have been criminally prosecuted for his conduct (and his obvious conflict of interest) in this case with all the claims listed in section 5.8 of the *Tax Fraud Prevention Manual*, Form #06.008 (entitled "Basis for Claims/Redress Against the Government Involving Wrongful Taking of Taxes")!

6.12.8 1986: 16th Amendment: U.S. v. Stahl, 792 F.2d. 1438 (1986)

> "[Defendant] Stahl's claim that ratification of the 16th Amendment was fraudulently certified constitutes a political question because we could not undertake independent resolution of this issue without expressing lack of respect due coordinate branches of government...."
> [U.S. v. Stahl, 792 F.2d. 1438 (1986)]

This case was a major scandal for the Federal appellate court. The defendant Stahl presented credible evidence that the 16th Amendment to the U.S. Constitution was fraudulently claimed to have been ratified by the Secretary of State, Philander Knox, in 1913. The court refused to deal with the issue and ignored all the evidence presented. Instead, they said it wasn't their business to deal with the issue. Congress said the same thing. This leads to the conclusion that there is a federal judicial (as well as a Congressional) conspiracy to protect the income tax.

6.12.9 1938: O'Malley v. Woodrough, 307 U.S. 277[100]

The judges' actions with regard to their own salaries provide the evidence that they cooperated with those in the legislative and executive branches of government. Their conduct is evidence of concealing the illegal kickback program. The executive and legislative branches of government must now depend on Federal judges to keep the illegal kickback programs as a source of income to the U.S. Treasury.

Had the Federal judges fought the legal issue of their basic rights as an employee the Act of 1862 would have fallen and the "individual income tax" as enforced today would not exist. There is no lawful way it can be deemed that a Federal Government employee agrees in advance to an employment agreement where the conditions of the kickback changes at the discretion of Congress or anyone else. Treaties cannot be broken. This results in the kickback being legal in part, and in part illegal. The kickback a Federal Government employee agrees to when he/she first takes a job with the Federal Government is legal, but, when changes unilaterally made by Congress create a higher kickback the portion which constitutes the change is illegal. The illegal portion is a debt obligation which the Federal Government employee is forced to discharge. Being forced to pay a debt obligation constitutes involuntary servitude. You cannot agree in advance to involuntarily serve the Federal Government (or anyone else). To force someone to do so is to ignore the laws under the First, Fifth, and Thirteenth Amendments to the U.S. Constitution.

To show that the Federal Supreme Court Justices actually cooperated with the legislative and executive branches of government in bringing the President and judges taking office after June 6, 1932, under the Federal kickback program, even though they avoided impairment of their own employment contracts, let's look at what they said in 1938 when they used

---

[100] Adapted from *IRS Humbug: Weapons of Enslavement, Frank Kowalik, ISBN 0-9626552-0-1, 1991*, pp. 27-33.

Supreme Court Chief Justice Taney's 1863 letter to the Secretary of the Treasury. Following are several excerpts from the Taney letter as used in O'Malley v. Woodrough, 307 U.S. 277 (1939):

> At page 288. The Act in question, as you interpret it, diminishes the compensation of every judge three percent, and if it can be diminished to that extent by the name of a tax, it may in the same way be reduced from time to time at the pleasure of the legislature.

The justices know the law requires equal treatment. They know the U.S. Constitution prohibits the diminishment of everyone's compensation for services by any means other than an agreement entered into on a voluntary basis prior to employment. They also know Art. III, Sec. 1, which prohibits the diminishment of compensation of Federal judges, was placed into the Constitution of the United States to keep the employment agreements of Federal judges separate from other Federal Government employment agreements so that all Federal judges could answer any legal question regarding labor contracts other than their own with objectivity in mind. They are no longer capable of reviewing violations of Federal employment agreements or any issue with regard to the Federal kickback program as a disinterested third party, making their participation divisive and their opinions, extended as case law, oppressive upon persons who are not Federal Government employees.

Though those who constructed the U.S. Constitution probably did not anticipate a Federal kickback program, the Supreme Court Justices in 1862 understood section 86 for what it was and chose to act only to prevent their own employment agreement from being impaired. They could have made their contracts "from time to time at the pleasure of the legislation." BY the statement of Justice Taney in 1863, it also can be assumed justifiably that the Justices knew of the plan of Congress to force it on the balance of society by belief. For this belief to be established and sustained, the cooperation of Federal judges was required and gained. This is documented by their conduct and recorded opinions.

The "income" kickback program changes at the pleasure of Congress. And, as we now know, all persons (whether working in the private sector or for a government entity) have been forced into the Federal Government's illegal kickback program.

O'Mally opinion at pg. 288:

> The Judiciary is one of the three great departments of the government created and established by the Constitution. Its duties and powers are specifically set forth, and are of a character that requires it to be perfectly independent of the two other departments, and in order to place it beyond the reach and above even the suspicion of any such influence, the power to reduce their compensation is expressly withheld from Congress, and excepted from their powers of legislation.

Note that they avoided using the term "powers of taxation." The justices knew the legislation they were discussing was not a "tax" (direct or indirect).

The Judiciary's independence would have been secured had they objected to the law on the legal issue of civil rights that apply to all in society, namely the violation of the Fifth Amendment by illegal, unilateral impairment of existing employment contracts through a forced debt obligation which results in the deprivation of property without due process of law. Also, the Fifth Amendment to the U.S. Constitution is violated when no choice is provided--when a person is deprived of freedom of expression as to the changes in his employment agreement.

Congressmen, most being lawyers, knew they had no lawful right to use the power of their elected position to arrange for the deprivation of property under the pretense of law; and the IRS and all other Federal Government employees are on notice as to what is includible and what is not includible in "gross income" by the I.R. Code and Regulations. To control the property of natural persons not includible in "gross income" through the force of undue influence not only violates the Constitution and laws of the United States but those of the states as well. The enforcement of the debt obligation created in this fashion is prohibited by civil rights laws and brings up questions of conspiracy with intent to defraud (subjects that will be discussed later). For now, back to Justice Taney's letter discussed in the O'Malley opinion.

> At pg. 288. "Language could not be more plain than that used in the Constitution. It is moreover one of its most important and essential provisions. For the articles which limit the powers of the legislative and executive branches of the government, and those which provide safeguards for the protection of the citizen in his person and property would be of little value without a judiciary to uphold and maintain them, which was free from every influence, direct or indirect, that might be possibility in times of political excitement warp their judgments."

Here the Chief Justice Taney admitted, and subsequent Justices concur, that they knew their duty was to protect the citizen in his person and property. Still, they chose to ignore that duty and protect only their own person and property. By choice, they indirectly stated that they person and property of all other Federal Government employees was not entitled to protection from such deprivation.

When the Justices did not fight the 1862 law on the primary civil rights legal issue, they permitted illegal impairment of all other Federal Government employment contracts and permitted debt obligations to be forced upon all Federal Government employees but themselves. These Supreme Court Justices proved their judgment could be influenced and controlled by people in the other branches of government, and they paved the way for the cooperation between all Federal judges and employees of the IRS, the Justice Department, and members of Congress. By the continued conduct of cooperation in concealing the illegal nature of the kickback program, U.S. judges provide evidence that they chose NOT to uphold their duty as the branch of government created as a check and balance on the executive and legislative branches of government. Their duty is to assume that government under the law exists.

Getting back to the O'Malley opinion, pages 288-289, we see Justice Taney's letter said:

> *Having been honored with the highest judicial station under the Constitution,* **I feel it to be more especially my duty to uphold and maintain the constitutional rights of that department of the government,** *and not by any act or word of mine, leave it to be supposed that I acquiesce in a measure that displaces it from the independent position assigned it by the statesmen who framed the Constitution; and in order to guard against any such inference, I present to you this respectful but firm and decided remonstrance against the authority you have exercised under this act of Congress, and requires you to place this protest upon the public files of your office as the* **evidence that I have done everything in my power to preserve and maintain the Judicial Department in the position and rank in the government which the Constitution has assigned to it.** *[emphasis added]*

Here the Federal Judges state they are concerned with upholding the Constitutional "rights" of the Judicial Department. A government entity does not have rights--it has duties. Hence, to protect such rights is a subjective position which violates the judges' duty to be objective.

Those who accept jobs with the government have the duty to uphold the rights of all under the laws of the Constitution of the United States. Federal judges would have complied with their duty if they had fought for their contractual rights on the general civil rights that all persons have, rather than claim a special privilege status, they would have upheld their personal rights and secured the rights of all others at the same time. Hence, they did not do everything in their power to maintain the independence of the Judicial branch of government. Indeed, they did everything in their power to ultimately make the other branches of government dependent on them.

These Justices set the standard for all Federal judges. To this day Federal judges compromise their independence when they permit the use of U.S. courtrooms for the illegal enforcement of the IRS service (the imposition of illegal kickback programs upon persons in society).

Continuing with what the O'Malley Court said at pg. 289:

> *The letter of the Chief Justice was not answered and, at his request, the Court, May 10, 1863, ordered the letter entered on its records. In 1869, the Secretary of the Treasury requested the opinion of Attorney General Ebenezer Rockwood Hoar as to the constitutionality of the Act construed to extend to judges' salaries. He rendered an opinion in substantial accord with the views expressed in Chief Justice Taney's protest. 13 Op.A.G. 161. Accordingly, the tax on the compensation of the President and or judges was discontinued and the amounts therefore collected from them were refunded--some through administrative channels; others through action of the court of claims and ensuing appropriations of Congress. See* Wayne v. U.S.*, 26 C.Cls. 274, 290; 27 Stat. 306.*

The U.S. judges' compensation for the performance of personal services, just like all other employees, is not subject to a law which impairs the obligation of the agreement of employment. However, as a result of Justice Taney's letter, you can see that the U.S. judges were placed in a class, among citizens, above all others. Their right not to be forced to accept an obligation that does not exist in law, or by employment agreement, was observed. Violation of the civil rights of all other Federal Government employees was permitted to stand, and the U.S. judges actively participated in these violations by concealment.

By claiming and receiving special status, Federal judges provided power that was implied and used by the IRS that does not exist under law. The limit of IRS power is to administer to the return of income disbursed to Federal Government employees as a result of their employment agreement.

Only through false belief can IRS employees continue to force their will upon all natural persons (Federal Government employees as well as persons working in the private sector and for other governmental entitles) by imposing conditions based upon vague laws passed by Congress. Vague laws are enacted because lawyers in our society permit their use by not challenging them.

At pages 289, 290 the O'Malley court went on to say:

> *In 1889, Mr. Justice Miller, a member of the Court since 1862 said:*
>
> *"The constitution of the United States has placed several limitations upon the general power [of taxation], and...some of them are implied. One of its provisions is that neither the President of the United States (Art. II, Sec. 1), nor a judge of the Supreme or inferior courts (Art. III, Sec. 1), shall have his salary diminished during the period for which he shall have been elected, or during his continuance in office. It is very clear that when Congress, during the late [Civil]* **war, levied an income tax, and placed it as well upon the salaries of the President and the judges of the courts as those of other people, that it was a diminution of them to just that extent."** *[emphasis added]*

These judges had a duty to declare the law unconstitutional instead of arranging for special privileges. Constitutional restrictions made it equally unlawful for the compensation of all Federal Government employees to be diminished under the pretense of law when it was in fact a unilateral employment agreement change. The conduct of the Federal judges was taken by Congress and the IRS to imply they had power to pave the way for the illegal Federal kickback programs manifested through the filing of a "U.S. Individual Income Tax Returns." The O'Malley case was decided by the Supreme Court in 1938, four years before the enactment of the Victory Tax which was used to infer that an "income tax" had been imposed upon the compensation everyone receives in exchange for their labor.

The intent of the Federal judges to cooperate with the legislative and executive branches of government in 1862 to start the Federal kickback programs was just as clear by their conduct as is the conduct of Federal judges today. Today, the intent of the Federal judges is to cooperate in perpetuating the false belief that the IRS has uninhibited power over a person's liberty and property. Though maliciously unlawful, the results of that power is real. The evidence is in the fear of the IRS which exists among the U.S. public.

The I.R. Code provides the full extent of the IRS power. It is notice to IRS employees and judges of just what is and what is not includible in "gross income" under Subtitle A of the I.R. Code, and will be revealed to you. While most IRS employees hold jobs so limited in scope they would not be cognizant of their illegal activities, Federal judges and lawyers have no excuse. U.S. judges have placed themselves in a "Catch 22" situation. If they allow a Federal Court to be misused in order to force an illegal kickback on property not includible in "gross income" or aid in depriving persons of their liberty by misuse of laws, they are acting illegally. If they claim ignorance of who is subject to the I.R. Code laws and what property is includible in "gross income," they are admitting they do not know the law. Either way they confess they are not competent to retain their jobs.

6.12.10 1924: Miles v. Graham, 268 U.S. 501[101]

When Congress passed section 213 of the Revenue Act of 1918, Federal judges were not willing to be made a party to the Federal Government's kickback schemes and avoided impairment of their employment contracts by using their judicial power [see Evans v. Gore, 253 U.S. 245 (1920) and Miles v. Graham, 268 U.S. 501 (1924)], expressed in opinions. In the Miles v. Graham, at page 509, the Justices said of the 1918 Act:

> *...No judge is required to pay a definite percentage of his salary, but* **all are commanded to return,** *as* **a part of "gross income", the compensation received as such"** *from the United States. From the "gross income" various deductions and credits are allowed, as for interest paid, contributions or gifts made, personal exemptions varying with family relations, etc., and upon the net result assessment is made.* **The plain purpose was to require all judges to return their compensation as an item of "gross income," and to tax this as other salaries. This is forbidden by the Constitution.**

In this opinion, the Justices were describing the return of income, or kickback, and its enforcement with regard to existing employment agreements. The statement made that this is forbidden by the Constitution was certainly correct, the Justices just neglected to say in positive, direct and clear language that it actually applied to all Federal government employees. Treating all salaries in this manner, including that of the judges, is "forbidden by the Constitution."

---

[101] Adapted from *IRS Humbug: Weapons of Enslavement, Frank Kowalik, ISBN 0-9626552-0-1, 1991*, pp. 23-24.

The Justices again claimed only the exemption of their salaries from this statute because of special status during their term of office. In stating the kickback is not a fixed amount, but **an amount that depends upon the deductions and credits allowed,** they confirmed the prediction of Justice Taney in his letter of 1863 that the compensation agreed to "may in the same way" [under the pretence of law] "be reduced from time to time at the pleasure of the legislature..."

6.12.11 1915: Brushaber v. Union Pacific Railroad, 240 U.S. 1[102]

The power of the IRS is restricted to the U.S. Government's income that is from within the employment agreement between the Federal Government and its employee. People NOT employed by the Federal Government are not required to include the gross income they earn for personal services in "gross income" under the I.R. Code. Doing so on a "U.S. Individual Income Tax Return" does not make income not includible in gross income under subtitle A of the I.R. Code includible in the legal kickback program. The U.S. Government is powerless to lawfully lay and collect a kickback on such income in the name of "tax." You have the right to surrender control of your personal income, but no IRS scheme can lawfully collect it without your cooperation.

By section 7701(a)(31), Congress placed the burden upon the IRS, the Justice Department, and the U.S. judges not to include income that is not includible in gross income under subtitle "A". All Federal Government employees are on notice that property which is foreign to the U.S. Government is not includible in "gross income" under the I.R. Code. This notice places a duty on the Federal Government employees to be certain only income belonging to the U.S. Government is returned.

> *Sec. 7701(a)(31). Foreign estate or trust. The terms "foreign estate" and "foreign trust" mean an estate or trust, as the case may be, the income of which from sources* **without the United States** *which is not effectively connected with the conduct of a trade or business* **within the United States,** *is not includible in gross income under subtitle A."* [emphasis added]

One's conduct produces income when employed with a source of income. The material element is the identity of the employer. In the U.S. Codes the term, "***without*** the United States" means without the U.S. Government, and "***within*** the United States" means within the U.S. Government. One's conduct cannot be effectively connected with the performance of personal services with a place, only a source of income can pay one. The place or geography is immaterial. The U.S. Codes identify geographical boundaries with the term "outside" or "inside" the United States. Congress shows intent to control us by use of vagueness when such similar phrases are used to express entirely different meanings.

By virtue of the definition of "foreign estate or trust," the burden, the duty, is upon Federal Government employees not to include income that is not includible. However, the conduct of the Federal Government employees causes the burden to be switched to each person to defend life, liberty, and property (including labor). Only with knowledge can one place the burden where it belongs--on the Federal Government employees.

The point being made now is that only when one has entered into an employment agreement within the U.S. Government is remuneration for personal services "effectively connected with the conduct of a trade or business within the United States."

Any income not effectively connected with a trade or business within the U.S. Government contains no kickback due to the U.S. Government because it is not includible in "gross income" under subtitle A of the I.R. Code. To force a kickback on income that is not includible in "gross income" is to tax such income directly, making it mandatory for the U.S. Government to observe the constitutional restrictions on direct taxation.

In 1915 the Supreme Court recognized the effect enforcement would have in converting what is called "income tax" into a direct tax when they said:

> Brushaber v. Union Pacific Railroad Co., *240 U.S. 1*, 16, 17 (1915)
>
> *Moreover, in addition, the conclusion reached in the Pollock Case did not in any degree involve holding that income taxes generically and necessarily came within the class of direct taxes on property, but, on the contrary, recognized the fact that taxation on income was in its nature an excise entitled to be enforced as such* **unless and until it was concluded that to enforce it would amount to accomplishing the result which the requirement as to apportionment of direct taxation was adopted to prevent, in which case the duty would arise to disregard form and consider substance alone,..."** *[emphasis added]*

---

[102] Adapted from *IRS Humbug: Weapons of Enslavement, Frank Kowalik, ISBN 0-9626552-0-1, 1991*, pp. 53-55.

The justices in the *Brushaber* case basically agreed with the justices in the 1895 Pollock case that generically the "taxation on income was in its nature an excise," meaning all excise taxes are in their nature a tax on income. This is exactly what i was getting at earlier when describing the power of everyone to tax income and that a tax is only direct when there is no choice with regard to becoming effected by it. The justices of both the Pollock and Brushaber cases knew taxation was not the true issue of the "income tax" enacted by Congress. The true issue being the effect on a person's labor when to enforce income tax on property "would amount to accomplishing the result which the requirement as to apportionment of direct taxation was adopted to prevent, in which case the duty would arise to disregard the form and consider substance." This statement indicates that if the issue were properly presented, the U.S. Courts would have to acknowledge that the kickback in the name of Federal "income tax" is legally enforceable only on income received as a result of an employment agreement within the U.S. Government as the U.S. Government has the right to enforce the return of its own income. All other income is NOT INCLUDIBLE IN GROSS INCOME UNDER SUBTITLE A OF THE I.R. CODE and the IRS has no jurisdiction over such property. With the IRS jurisdiction restricted to U.S. Government property it is legally impossible for them to sustain any action in court (civil or criminal) with regard to any other property.

6.12.12 Conclusions

For all the above reasons and using the examples cited in this section, it is clear that there has been a significant contribution of the judiciary to protecting and expanding the operation of the income tax and make it apply to subjects it was never intended, in violation of the U.S. Constitution and of the several rights of citizens. That makes federal judges who participate candidates for prosecution under the following criminal laws, all of which carry *heavy* penalties:

1. They are part of a "continuing financial crimes enterprise" (18 U.S.C. §225)
2. Extortionists who "entice citizens into peonage" to the IRS (see 18 U.S.C. §1581;Thirteenth Amendment;197 U.S. 207, 215 (slavery for indebtedness).
3. Are the subject of a massive conflict of interest (see 28 U.S.C. §455).
4. Are perpetrators of fraud (see 18 U.S.C. §1018).
5. Are committing blackmail by threatening prison time and fines (see 18 U.S.C. §873).
6. Are criminally encouraging the IRS to mail threatening communications (see 18 U.S.C. §876).
7. Are involved in extortion (see 18 U.S.C. §872)
8. Are encroaching on federally and constitutionally protected rights to property and liberty and the pursuit of happiness (see 18 U.S.C. §245)
9. Are involved in "a conspiracy against rights" (see 18 U.S.C. §241)
10. Are "Engaging in monetary transactions in property derived from specified unlawful activity" (see 18 U.S.C. §1957)

6.13 Legal Profession Scandals

> *"[T]he tax code is the single greatest source of lobbying activity in Washington." -- Rep. Richard K. Armey, R-Texas*

> *"An old preacher was dying. He sent a message for his IRS agent and his Lawyer (both church members), to come to his home. When they arrived, they were ushered up to his bedroom. As they entered the room, the preacher held out his hands and motioned for them to sit on each side of the bed. The preacher grasped their hands, sighed contentedly, smiled and stared at the ceiling. For a time, no one said anything. Both the IRS agent and Lawyer were touched and flattered that the old preacher would ask them to be with him during his final moment. They were also puzzled because the preacher had never given any indication that he particularly liked either one of them.*
>
> *Finally, the Lawyer asked, "Preacher, why did you ask the two of us to come?"*
>
> *The old preacher mustered up some strength, then said weakly, "Jesus died between two thieves, and that's how I want to go, too."*

6.13.1 Legal Dictionary Definitions for "United States"

We looked at five different legal dictionaries and a Collegiate dictionary for the term "United States". Here is a list of the legal dictionaries we examined:

1. *Bouvier's Law Dictionary*, Revised Sixth Edition, 1856.
2. *Law Dictionary*, Barron's, Copyright 1996, ISBN 0-8120-3096-6.
3. *Merriam-Webster's Dictionary of Law,* Copyright 1996. (http://dictionary.lp.findlaw.com/)
4. *Black's Law Dictionary, Seventh Edition*, Copyright 1999, ISBN 0-314-24130-2.
5. *Black's Law Dictionary, Sixth Edition,* Copyright 1990, ISBN 0-314-76271-X.

Interestingly, only **ONE** of these dictionaries identified the definition of the legal term "United States", and this edition was out of print after 1999! Recall that we said in section 3.12.1.23 that the definition of "United States" is a *very important* key to understanding the trick that Congress has played on the American people with the income tax. Even more interesting is that the Sixth Edition of Black's Law Dictionary was the *only* one of the above which properly and completely defined the term "United States", and *even that definition was removed from the Seventh Edition of the same dictionary by the publisher, in an apparent effort to further conceal the truth about the limited jurisdiction of our federal government*. If the average American understood that there are actually THREE independent definitions for the term "United States" as ruled by the united states supreme Court in *Hooven & Allison Co. v. Evatt, 324 U.S. 652* (1945), then a lot more people we believe would better understand the very limited application of the federal and state income tax statutes. If they understood that the term used in the Internal Revenue Code for "United States" actually means the District of Columbia, then they would understand that they are NOT residents of the [federal] United States**, but instead are residents of the United States *of America*. This is the foundation of the idea that the IRC is "special law". As we pointed out in section 1.11.3 entitled "How Come my Accountant or Tax Attorney Doesn't Know This", it seems quite clear to us that there are very good reasons why your attorney would claim he didn't know this. Here is a summary of just a few of those reasons:

1. Lawyers make money by litigating rather than settling.
2. The way to encourage litigation is to put the most assets and property possible at legal risk, or at least to fool people into thinking they are at risk.
3. There are two main ways to get the average person to put their assets at legal risk:
    3.1. Getting a marriage license from the state. Notice we didn't say getting married, because you can get married without a marriage license from the state, and instead have a prenuptial agreement and a private wedding where the priest doesn't sign any kind of marriage license.
    3.2. Owing taxes to the government, who incidentally own the courts and love to use their own home turf to steal and extort tax money out of the average citizen.
4. Lawyers therefore have a financial interest to make you believe that your assets are at risk by making you think that you owe income taxes.
5. If no one owed income taxes, we would need probably 1/2 as many lawyers (and accountants) as we have now and the few that remained would charge less for their services because they would be in far less demand. The following fields of law would see *drastic* cuts:
    5.1. Probate attorneys.
    5.2. Tax attorneys.
    5.3. Legislators and legislative analysts.
6. Can you see why the American Bar Association and most lawyers wouldn't want to put the definition of "United States" in any of the legal dictionaries?

We would venture to say that probably 70% of attorneys, after you tell them the correct definition of "United States", would claim that they didn't know the proper legal definition or even what the supreme Court said was the definition. Lawyers are just as fallible as the rest of us. We would also venture to say that even the ones who do know the correct definition and who are familiar with the supreme Court's definition of the term would *never* admit to it because it would undermine their profession! Furthermore, about the same percentage of attorneys don't know that most Americans actually have dual citizenship (federal and state), and what the rights are of each type of citizen.

After we examined four contemporary legal dictionaries in vain for a definition of the term "United States", then we went to Webster's Ninth New Collegiate Dictionary, 1983, Merriam-Webster, p. 1291 and found the following definition:

> "United States (1617) a federation of states esp. when forming a nation in a usu. specified territory (advocating a United States of Europe)."

Even the non-legal college dictionary doesn't properly define the term "United States"! Is it any wonder that most Americans don't even know what it means and are deceived into paying income taxes because of their ignorance(?) …they couldn't look up the definition of the term even if they really wanted to know, which most of them don't anyway! The *only* way to eliminate

Chapter 7: Resources for Tax Fraud Fighters

this kind of ignorance is to either read this book or to look up the definition on the Internet by reading 26 U.S.C. §7701(a)(9). We encourage you to do both, or you will be victimized because of your own ignorance.

6.13.2 The Taxability of Wages and Income Derived from "Labor" Rather than "Profit" as Described in CLE Materials

We looked through ten different student manuals and reference books addressing Federal Taxation at several law bookstores and a law university bookstore for clarification and explanation of the taxability of the following:

1. Wages.
2. Labor.
3. Compensation for "personal services."
4. Salaries.

Interestingly, NONE of the over ten federal taxation books and dictionaries and other Continuing Legal Education (CLE) materials addressed ANY of the following:

1. Wages as "property".
2. Income taxes only applying to "profit" and the nature of profit in the context of exchanging labor for wages.
3. The right to labor as a "common right" that cannot be infringed, regulated, or penalized by the government.
4. The relationship between graduated taxes on wages and slavery, or how such taxes might infringe on rights.

Several of the books had examples of how to apply the Internal Revenue Code to specific situations, but NONE of the examples used receipt of wages as a *taxable event*. We can only conclude that this omission was a deliberate decision by educators in the legal profession to conceal the dastardly truth about income taxes. We also have to assume that the most popular way to conceal the truth is to NOT mention what is NOT taxable, and only to mention what IS taxable. Is it any surprise then that we have a whole generation of tax attorneys out there who haven't heard the truth because the very curricula they rely on for their legal education excludes the *whole* truth? In such an environment, does the oath a lawyer would take if he went on the witness stand mean anything?:

> "I promise to tell the truth, the *whole* truth, and nothing but the truth, so help me God."

If you researched the background of most lawyers, you'd find that they, like most doctors, overwhelmingly got into the profession because of greed and that disproportionately few of them believe in "God". They are too egotistical and self-sufficient to believe in God or to have to depend on Him for anything. *How can a lawyer tell the "whole truth" and not lie taking the oath if he was never taught the "whole truth" to begin with and doesn't believe in God anyway?* Let's face it, like Satan, a majority of the members of the legal profession have misused the gifts that a Creator they don't believe in has given them, and never bothered to question the laws beyond what they were taught because it was so profitable to *not* question authority. Perhaps this explains why early law schools in the late 17th Century in this country required a strong theological background as a *prerequisite* to studying law. Very few, if any, universities have the same requirements for the study of law these days.

6.14 Social Security Chronology[103]

When the Social Security Administration first began assigning social security numbers in 1935, SSN cards included the statement "NOT FOR IDENTIFICATION" printed upon their face.

The card issued in 1964 contained that very statement while all cards issued today no longer do. Over the years a multitude of new, unintended uses for SSNs have evolved. The result is that SSNs are now widely and routinely demanded for purposes of routine identification. As a result, the SSN has now become a de facto National Identification Number.

The following will give you some idea of what the free Citizen who never applied for and therefore never received a social security number is up against when dealing with state and federal bureaucrats.

---

[103] Courtesy http://www.informamerica.com/SSN Chronology.html.

It is obtained from a table prepared on January 13, 1998 by Sandy Cerato of the Social Security Administration's Office of Legislation And Congressional Affairs and chronicles the implementation of the social security number for identification purposes, although it was never originally intended as such.

Nowhere within the report does it breathe mention of the fact that an SSN is not required by law of a Citizen because nowhere does any law require the Citizen to apply.

> Table prepared (1/13/98) by Sandy Cerato of SSA's Office of Legislation & Congressional Affairs
>
> 1935 The Social Security Act (P.L. 74-271) is enacted. It did not expressly mention the use of SSNs, but it authorized the creation of some type of record keeping scheme. Treasury Decision 4704, a Treasury regulation in 1936 which required the issuance of an account number to each employee covered by the Social Security program. The Social Security Board considered various numbering systems and ways (such as metal tags, etc.) by which employees could indicate they had been issued a number
>
> 1936-1937 Approximately 30 million applications for SSNs were processed between November 1936 and June 30, 1937.
>
> 1943 Executive Order 9397 (3 C.F.R. (1943-1948 Comp.) 283-284) required: All Federal components to use the SSN "exclusively" whenever the component found it advisable to set up a new identification system for individuals. The Social Security Board to cooperate with Federal uses of the number by issuing and verifying numbers for other Federal agencies
>
> 1961 The Civil Service Commission adopted the SSN as an official Federal employee identifier. Internal Revenue Code Amendments (P.L. 87-397) required each taxpayer to furnish identifying number for tax reporting.
>
> 1962 The Internal Revenue Service adopted the SSN as its official taxpayer identification number.
>
> 1964 Treasury Department, via internal policy, required buyers of Series H savings bonds to provide their SSNs.
>
> 1965 Internal Revenue Amendments (P.L. 89-384) enacted Medicare. It became necessary for most individuals age 65 and older to have an SSN.
>
> 1966 The Veterans Administration began to use the SSN as the hospital admissions number and for patient record keeping.
>
> 1967 The Department of Defense adopted the SSN in lieu of the military service number for identifying Armed Forces personnel.
>
> 1970 Bank Records and Foreign Transactions Act (P.L. 91-508) required all banks, savings and loan associations, credit unions and brokers/dealers in securities to obtain the SSNs of all of their customers. Also, financial institutions were required to file a report with the IRS, including the SSN of the customer, for any transaction involving more than $10,000.
>
> 1971 SSA task force report published which proposed that SSA take a "cautious and conservative" position toward SSN use and do nothing to promote the use of the SSN as an identifier. The report recommended that SSA use mass SSN enumeration in schools as a long-range, cost-effective approach to tightening up the SSN system, and consider cooperating with specific health, education and welfare uses of the SSN by State, local, and other nonprofit organizations.

1972 Social Security Amendments of 1972 (P.L. 92-603): Required SSA to issue SSNs to all legally admitted aliens at entry and of anyone receiving or applying for any benefit paid for by Federal funds; Required SSA to obtain evidence to establish age, citizenship, or alien status and identity. Authorized SSA to enumerate children at the time they first entered school.

1973 Buyers of series E savings bonds are required by the Treasury Department to provide their SSNs. Report of the HEW Secretary's Advisory Committee on Automated Personal Data System concluded that the adoption of a universal identifier by this country was not desirable; also found that the SSN was not suitable for such a purpose as it does not meet the criteria of a universal identifier that distinguishes a person from all others.

1974 Privacy Act (P.L. 93-579) enacted effective September 27, 1975 to limit governmental use of the SSN: Provided that no State or local government agency may withhold a benefit from a person simply because the individual refuses to furnish his or her SSN. Required that Federal, State and local agencies which request an individual to disclose his/her SSN inform the individual if disclosure was mandatory or voluntary. (This was the first mention of SSN use by local governments.)

1975 Social Services Amendments of 1974 (P.L. 93-647) provided that: disclosure of an individual's SSN is a condition of eligibility for AFDC benefits; and Office of Child Support enforcement Parent Locator Service may require disclosure of limited information (including SSN and whereabouts) contained in SSA records.

1976 Tax Reform Act of 1976 (P.L. 94-455) included the following amendments to the Social Security Act: To allow use by the States of the SSN in the administration of any tax, general public assistance, driver's license or motor vehicle registration law within their jurisdiction and to authorize the States to require individuals affected by such laws to furnish their SSNs to the States; To make misuse of the SSN for any purpose a violation of the Social Security Act; To make disclosure or compelling disclosure of the SSN of any person a violation of the Social Security Act. To amend section 6109 of the Internal Revenue Code to provide that the SSN be used as the tax identification number (TIN) for all tax purposes. While the Treasury Department had been using the SSN as the TIN by regulation since 1962, this law codified that requirement. Federal Advisory Committee on False Identification recommended that penalties for misuse should be increased and evidence requirements tightened; rejected the idea of national identifier and did not even consider the SSN for such a purpose.

1977 Food Stamp Act of 1977 (P.L. 96-58) required disclosure of SSNs of all household members as a condition of eligibility for participation in the food stamp program. Privacy Protection Study Commission recommended that: No steps be taken towards developing standard, universal label for individuals until safeguards and policies regarding permissible uses and disclosures were proven effective; and Executive Order 9397 be amended so that Federal agencies could no longer use it as legal authority to require disclosure of an individual's SSN. (No action taken.) The Carter Administration proposed that the Social Security card be one of the authorized documents by which an employer could be assured that a job applicant could work in this country but also stated that the SSN card should not become a national identity document.

1978 SSA required evidence of age, citizenship, and identity of all SSN applicants.

1981 Reagan Administration stated that it "is explicitly opposed to the creation of a national identity card" but recognized the need for a means for employers to comply with the employer sanctions provisions of its immigration reform legislation. Omnibus Budget Reconciliation Act of 1981 (P.L. 97-35) required the disclosure of the SSNs of all adult members in the household of children applying to the school lunch program. Social Security Benefits Act (P.L. 97-123) Section 4 added alteration and forgery of a Social

Security card to the list of prohibited acts and increased the penalties for such acts. Section 6 required any Federal, State or local government agency to furnish the name and SSN of prisoners convicted of a felony to the Secretary of HHS, to enforce suspension of disability benefits to certain imprisoned felons. Department of Defense Authorization Act (P.L. 97-86) required disclosure of the SSNs to the Selective Service System of all individuals required to register for the draft.

1982 Debt Collection Act (P.L. 97-365) required that all applicants for loans under any Federal loan program furnish their SSNs to the agency supplying the loan. All Social Security cards issued to legal aliens not authorized to work within the United States were annotated "NOT VALID FOR EMPLOYMENT" beginning in May.

1983 The Social Security Amendments of 1983 (P.L. 98-21) required that new and replacement Social Security cards issued after October 30 be made of banknote paper and (to the maximum extent practicable) not be subject to counterfeiting. The Interest and Dividend Tax Compliance Act (P.L. 98-67) requires SSNs for all interest-bearing accounts and provides a penalty of $50 for all individuals who fail to furnish a correct TIN (usually the SSN).

1984 Deficit Reduction Act of 1984 (P.L. 98-369) Amended the Social Security Act to establish an income and eligibility verification system involving State agencies administering the AFDC, Medicaid, unemployment compensation, the food stamp programs, and State programs under a plan approved under title I, X, XIV, or XVI of the Act. States were permitted to require the SSN as a condition of eligibility for benefits under any of these programs. Amended Section 6050I of the IRC to require that persons engaged in a trade or business file a report (including SSNs) with the IRS for cash transactions over $10,000. Amended Section 215 of the IRC to authorize the Secretary of HHS to publish regulations that require a spouse paying alimony to furnish IRS with the taxpayer identification number (i.e., the SSN) of the spouse receiving alimony payments.

1986 The Immigration Reform and Control Act of 1986 (P.L. 99-603): Required the Comptroller General to investigate technological changes that could reduce the potential for counterfeiting Social Security cards; Provides that the Social Security card may be used to establish the eligibility of a prospective employee for employment; and Required the Secretary of HHS to undertake a study of the feasibility and costs of establishing an SSN verification system Tax Reform Act of 1986 (P.L. 99-514) requires individuals filing a tax return due after December 31, 1987, to include the taxpayer identification number--usually the SSN--of each dependent age 5 or older. Commercial Motor Vehicle Safety Act of 1986 (P.L. 99-750) authorized the Secretary of Transportation to require the use of the SSN on commercial motor vehicle operators' licenses. Higher Education Amendments of 1986 (P.L. 99-498) required that student loan applicants submit their SSN as a condition of eligibility.

1987 SSA initiated a demonstration project on August 17 in the state of New Mexico enabling parents to obtain Social Security numbers for their newborn infants automatically when the infant's birth is registered by the State. The program was expanded nationwide in 1989. Currently, all 50 union states participate in the program, as well as New York City, Washington, D.C., and Puerto Rico.

1988 Housing and Community Development Act of 1987 (P.L. 100-242) authorized the Secretary of HUD to require disclosure of a person's SSN as a condition of eligibility for any HUD program. The Family Support Act of 1988 (P.L. 100-485): Section 125 required, beginning November 1, 1990, a State to obtain the SSNs of the parents when issuing a birth certificate. Section 704(a) required individuals filing a tax return due after December 31, 1989, to include the taxpayer identification number--usually the SSN--of each dependent age 2 or older. The Technical and Miscellaneous Revenue Act of 1988 (P.L. 100-647): Authorized a State and/or any blood donation facility to use SSNs to identify blood donors

(205(c)(2)(F)). Required that all title II beneficiaries either have or have applied for an SSN in order to receive benefits. This provision became effective with dates of initial entitlement of June 1989 or later. Beneficiaries who refused enumeration were entitled but placed in suspense. Anti-Drug Abuse Act of 1988 (P.L. 100-690) deleted the $5,000 and $25,000 upper limits on fines that can be imposed for violations of section 208 of the Social Security Act. The general limit of $250,000 for felonies in the U.S. Code now applied to SSN violations under section 208 of the Social Security Act. Also, penalties for misuse of SSNs apply as well in cases where the number is referred to by any other name (e.g., taxpayer identification number (TIN)).

1989 Omnibus Budget Reconciliation Act of 1989 (P.L. 101-239) required that the National Student Loan Data System include, among other things, the names and SSNs of borrowers. Child Nutrition and WIC Reauthorization Act of 1989 (P.L. 101-147) requires the member of the household who applies for the school lunch program to provide the SSN of the parent of the child for whom the application is made.

1990 Omnibus Budget Reconciliation Act of 1990 (P.L. 101-508): Section 7201 (Computer Matching and Privacy Protection Amendments of 1990) provided that no adverse action may be taken against an individual receiving benefits as a result of a matching program without verification of the information or notification of the individual regarding the findings with time to contest. Section 8053, required an SSN for eligibility for benefits from the Department of Veterans Affairs (DVA). Section 11112, required that individuals filing a tax return due after December 31, 1991, include the taxpayer identification number--usually the SSN--of each dependent age 1 or older. Food and Agricultural Resources Act of 1990 (P.L. 101-624), Section 1735: Required an SSN for the officers of food and retail stores that redeem Food Stamps. Provided that SSNs maintained as a result of any law enacted on or after October 1, 1990, will be confidential and may not be disclosed.

1994 Social Security Independence and Program Improvements Act of 1994 (P.L. 103-296): Section 304, authorized the use of the SSN for jury selection. Section 314, authorized cross-matching of SSNs and Employer Identification Numbers maintained by the Department of Agriculture with other Federal agencies for the purpose of investigating both food stamp fraud and violations of other Federal laws. Section 318, authorized the use of the SSN by the Department of Labor in administration of Federal workers' compensation laws.

1996 Personal Responsibility and Work Opportunity Reconciliation Act of 1996 (P.L. 104-193) (Welfare Reform): Section 111 required the Commissioner of Social Security to develop and submit to Congress a prototype of a counterfeit-resistant Social Security card that: is made of durable, tamper-resistant material (e.g., plastic); employs technologies that provide security features (e.g., magnetic stripe); and provides individuals with reliable proof of citizenship or legal resident alien status. Section 111 also required the Commissioner of Social Security to study and report to Congress on different methods of improving the Social Security card application process, including evaluation of the cost and workload implications of issuing a counterfeit-resistant Social Security card for all individuals and evaluation of the feasibility and cost implications of imposing a user fee for replacement cards. Section 316 required HHS to transmit to SSA, for verification purposes, certain information about individuals and employers maintained under the Federal Parent Locator Service in an automated directory. SSA is required to verify the accuracy of, correct, or supply to the extent possible, and report to HHS the name, SSN, and birth date of individuals and the employer identification number of employers. SSA is to be reimbursed by HHS for the cost of this verification service. This section also required all Federal agencies (including SSA) to report quarterly the name and SSN of each employee and the wages paid to the employee during the previous quarter. Section 317 provides that State child support enforcement procedures require the SSN of any applicant for a professional license, commercial driver's license, occupational license, or marriage license be recorded on the application. The SSN of any person subject to a divorce decree, support order, or paternity determination or acknowledgement would have to be placed in the pertinent records. SSNs are required on death certificates. Section 451 provides that, in order to be eligible for the Earned Income Tax Credit, an individual must include on his or her tax return an SSN which was not assigned solely for non-work purposes. Department of Defense Appropriations Act, 1997 (P.L. 104-208) (Division C (Illegal Immigration Reform and Immigrant Responsibility Act of 1996) (Immigration Reform): Sections 401-404 provide for 3 specific employment verification pilot programs in which employers would voluntarily participate. In general, the pilot programs would allow an employer to confirm the identity and employment eligibility of the individual. SSA and the Immigration and Naturalization Service (INS) would provide a secondary verification process to confirm the validity of the information provided. SSA would compare the name and SSN provided and advise whether the name and number match SSA records and whether the SSN is valid for employment. Section 414 requires the Commissioner to report to Congress every year, the aggregate number of SSNs issued to non-citizens not authorized to work, but under which earnings were reported. Also requires the Commissioner to transmit to the Attorney General a report on the extent to which SSNs and Social Security cards are used by non-citizens for fraudulent purposes. Section 415 authorizes the Attorney General to require any non-citizen to provide his or her SSN for purposes of inclusion in any record maintained by the Attorney General or INS. Section 656 provide for improvements in identification-related documents; i.e., birth certificates and driver's licenses. These sections require publication of regulations which set standards, including security features and, in the case of driver's licenses, require that an SSN appear on the license. Federal agencies are precluded from accepting as proof of identity, documents which do not meet the regulatory standards. Section 657 provides for the development of a prototype Social Security card. The requirements are the same as in Section 111 of the Welfare reform legislation (described above) with the exception that the Comptroller General is also to study and report to Congress on different methods of improving the Social Security card application process.

1997 Department of Defense Appropriations Act, 1997 (P.L. 104-208) (Division C--Illegal Immigration Reform and Immigrant Responsibility Act of 1996) (Immigration Reform): Sections 401-404 provide for 3 specific employment verification pilot programs in which employers would voluntarily participate. In general, the pilot programs would allow an employer to confirm the identity and employment eligibility of the individual. SSA and INS would provide a secondary verification process to confirm the validity of the information provided. SSA would compare the name and SSN provided and advise whether the name and number match SSA records and whether the SSN is valid for employment. Section 414 required the Commissioner of Social Security to report to Congress every year the aggregate number of SSNs issued to non-citizens not authorized to work, but under which earnings were reported. Also required the Commissioner of Social Security to transmit to the Attorney General a report on the extent to which SSNs and Social Security cards are used by non-citizens for fraudulent purposes. Section 415 authorized the Attorney General to require any non-citizen to provide his or her SSN for purposes of inclusion in any record maintained by the Attorney General or INS. Section 656 provided for improvements in identification-related documents; i.e., birth certificates and drivers licenses. These sections require publication of regulations which set uniform standards, including security features, and, in the case of drivers licenses, require that an SSN appear on the license. Federal agencies are precluded from accepting as proof of identity documents which do not meet the regulatory standards. Section 657 provided for the development of a prototype Social Security card. The requirements are the same as in Section 111 of the Welfare reform legislation (described above) with the exception that the Comptroller General is also to study and report to Congress on different methods of improving the Social Security card application process. 1997 Taxpayer Relief Act of 1997 (P.L. 105-34) Section 1090 requires an applicant for an SSN under age 18 to provide evidence of his or her parents' names and SSNs in addition to required evidence of age, identity, and citizenship. Report to Congress on "Options for Enhancing the Social Security Card" released on September 22, 1997.

Keep in mind that there is no authority under the Constitution for the government to require that a free Citizen number himself or withhold services if he does not. Certainly the Citizen who chooses not to obtain and use a number or who later revokes the application for the number as some have done faces a future of self-reliance and individual responsibility, with no help from Uncle Sam.

6.15   Conclusion: The Duck Test

What can one make of this pattern of alterations that disguise the truth behind the law and this pattern of behavior throughout the U.S. Government, including the Congress, the courts, the Treasury, and the IRS to misrepresent it? Is the income tax operating as a hoax? Let's apply the "duck test":

> "If it looks like a duck, waddles like a duck, and quacks like a duck, it must **BE** a duck!"

Thomas Jefferson said it better:

> "Single acts of tyranny may be ascribed to the accidental opinion of a day; but a series of oppressions, begun at a distinguished period, and pursued unalterably through every change in ministers [administrations], too plainly proves a deliberate systematic plan of reducing us to slavery."

We assert that the evidence presented in this document is more than adequate proof that the income tax does not apply not only to most Americans, but it doesn't apply to most "U.S. citizens" either! Has our detailed exposition raised doubt in your mind about what the law says? Here is what the Supreme Court has said about doubt.

> "In the interpretation of statutes levying taxes it is the established rule not to...enlarge their operations so as to embrace matters not specifically pointed out. In case of doubt they are construed most strongly against the government, and in favor of the citizen."
> [Gould v. Gould, 245 U.S. 151 (1917)]

> "Keeping in mind the well-settled rule that **the citizen is exempt from taxation unless the same is imposed by clear and unequivocal language, and that where the construction of a tax law is doubtful, the doubt is to be resolved in favor of those upon whom the tax is sought to be laid**."
> [Spreckels Sugar Refining Co. v. McClain, 192 U.S. 397 (1904)]

Shouldn't these court rulings be applied to the income tax?

Because of Article 1, Section 8 of the Constitution, Congress could not impose a tax on all income earned in the United States *of America*. What Congress did instead was to impose a municipal tax within only the District of Columbia on matters which they could tax (international and foreign commerce), and write the law in such a way that it would give the *impression* that it also applied to the income of most Americans outside that jurisdiction and in the 50 union states. The Secretary of the Treasury wrote corresponding regulations with a similar goal: to tell a truth while implying a lie. Despite a longstanding and ongoing effort by some in government to confuse and obfuscate, the literal truth has remained in the law. Though it is a complex process, the current statutes and regulations by themselves do reveal the limited application of the Internal Revenue Code. The older statutes and regulations then add extensive reinforcement and clarity to the conclusions reached by deciphering the current law. The historical documents also give ample evidence to justify an accusation, against the legislators in Congress and the authors of the regulations at the Department of the Treasury, of ***intent to defraud*** the American people of money not legally owed.

Aside from arguments about specific details, there is one giant hurdle for those who would still insist that most Americans receive taxable income: what is the alternate conclusion that accounts for *every* citation in this document? There is extensive documentation, not only in the current statutes and regulations, but throughout 87 years of statutory and regulatory history, which supports the conclusions of this document. It would be absurd to claim that a tax was imposed on the income of most Americans, and that by mistake or coincidence Congress and the Secretary put into the statutes and regulations such an enormous amount of information, spanning nearly a century, which indicates that the tax applies only to those engaged in international or foreign commerce. Quite simply, there is no conclusion other than the conclusion of this document which explains all of the evidence.

QUESTION FOR DOUBTERS: Is there some other "interpretation" of the statutes and regulations which would show domestic income of United States citizens as taxable, and also explain the meaning of all of the citations in this document?

SOURCES FOR TAX FRAUD FIGHTERS

	Page
SOURCES FOR TAX FRAUD FIGHTERS	7-1
Websites	7-2
Books and Publications	7-4
Legal Resources	7-6

Chapter 7: Resources for Tax Fraud Fighters

NOTE: Private products, companies, services appearing in this section are for *information and educational purposes only*. In the interests of maintaining our objectivity, integrity, and honesty, in no way do we intend to endorse, promote, or otherwise encourage the use of any particular company, product, or service that might be listed below.

7.1 Websites

Table 7-1: Websites

Title	Address	Description
Americans for Tax Reform	http://www.atr.org/	Tax reform website.
Asset Protection Corporation	http://www.assetprotectioncorp.com/	Asset protection.
Constitution Society	http://www.constitution.org/	VERY thorough treatment and reference on every aspect of the U.S. Constitution. VERY HIGH RECOMMENDED.
Cornell Law School, Legal Information Institute (LII)	http://www.law.cornell.edu/	Excellent reference for all major areas of law. They have most U.S. laws on the web free to everyone. This includes the U.S. Codes, the Code of Federal Regulations, the Uniform Commercial Code (UCC) and the Administrative Code. Their interface is also MUCH better than the U.S. Government printing Office's website. The search engine is many time faster as well. VERY VALUABLE.
Creative Asset Protection Strategies	http://www.capstrategies.com/	Asset protection
Devvy Kidd	http://www.devvy.com/	Legal activism and advocacy or tax freedom and constitutional rights.
Electronic Privacy Institute	http://www.epic.org	Electronic secrecy and privacy information. Encrypt your communications to protect it once you get on the net!
Family Guardian	http://famguardian.org/	Website on which the original and updated versions of this document are published and maintained. Family Guardian Fellowship, the author of this document, maintains that website.
Federal Judiciary Homepage	http://www.uscourts.gov/	Main website for all Federal Courts. Excellent reference
FindLaw	http://www.findlaw.com/	THE ultimate reference on legal matters. Has all U.S. supreme court transcripts, U.S. Codes, Code of Federal Regulations, etc. YOUR BEST LEGAL RESOURCE by far!
Freedom Above Fortune	http://www.freedomabovefortune.com/	A defected IRS agent formerly from the IRS' Criminal Investigative Division (CID) tells his story and his experiences and how he came to believe the income tax is a fraud.
Forfeiture Endangers American Rights (FEAR)	http://www.fear.org/	Forfeiture Endangers American Rights is a national nonprofit organization

http://famguardian.org/

Chapter 7: Resources for Tax Fraud Fighters

Title	Address	Description
		dedicated to reform of federal and state asset forfeiture laws to restore due process and protect property rights in the forfeiture process.
Intellectual Capital.com	http://www.intellectualcapital.com	Copyright, patent, and other protection for your writings, software, and inventions.
Legal Bluebook	http://www.legalbluebook.com	Place to purchase "The Uniform System of Citation" published by the Harvard Law Review. This book provides the standard used throughout the legal field in citing the results of other cases, laws, etc.
National Archives and Records Administration	https://www.archives.gov/	Code of Federal Regulations online, U.S. Constitution, Public Laws, Public Papers of U.S. Presidents, Federal Register, U.S. Code, U.S. Government Manual.
National Commission on Economic Growth and Tax Reform	http://zeus.townhall.com/taxcom/	Good tax reform website.
National Organization to Stop Socialism Now!	http://www.nossn.com/	They have a wealth of information about the voluntary nature of social security and how to avoid participating and being forced to use your SSN.
Office of the Undersecretary of Defense, Comptroller	http://www.dtic.mil/comptroller/	Good place to get DOD regulations on Pay and benefits.
Offshore Financial Freedom	http://www.offshoreinfo.com	Asset protection.
Otto Skinner's Website	http://www.ottoskinner.com/	Background on some of the tax protester schemes that don't work.
Pay No Income Tax	http://www.paynoincometax.com/	Publish several good books on how to pay no income tax. The host, Irwin Schiff, also hosts a radio talk show.
Prime Global	http://www.offshorepro.com	Asset protection
Save-A-Patriot Organization	http://www.save-a-patriot.org	Active federal tax resistance group. They have an "IRS insurance" program to protect you should you feel insecure when you decide to follow their advice, but some people report that they may not reliably pay up (see section 9.1). We don't know about the history of this.
Sovereignty Education and Defense Ministry (SEDM)	http://sedm.org	Resources for those who want to be free, sovereign, and totally separated from a corrupted government.
Supreme Law	http://www.supremelaw.org	This is a fabulous website that has many useful resources. Check out their Supreme Law Library, and read their publication "The Federal Zone". Its a fascinating study into taxation. (HOT!)
Tax Freedom.Com	http://www.tax-freedom.com	The most complete background on taxes we have seen. Talks about many of the issues we have seen here. They

http://famguardian.org/

Chapter 7: Resources for Tax Fraud Fighters

Title	Address	Description
		also sell a very good CD-ROM with just about everything you need to get started if freeing yourself from income taxes. They also offer you paralegal services in preparing any tax document you like. HIGHLY RECOMMENDED.
Tax Foundation	http://www.taxfoundation.org/	Our mission is to educate the public about taxes, and to that end, we • Answer the general public's questions on tax policy, tax rates, tax collections, and the economics of taxation • Answer the media's questions on these subjects, giving interviews and fact-checking stories and ads • Publish reports that boil down our complex tax system to something an informed layman can understand
Tax Reform Now (The Heritage Foundation)	http://www.taxation.org/	Tax reform strategies. Attacks things from a political level rather than a grass-roots, "praise the lord and pass the ammunition approach."
The Money Changer	http://www.the-moneychanger.com/	Gold and silver (asset protection).
US Tax Court	http://www.ustaxcourt.gov	All tax court rulings posted here. Excellent source for research into tax statutes and opinion.
US Treasury	http://www.ustreas.gov/	The people who print our money and oversee the Federal Reserve

7.2 Books and Publications

Table 7-2: Books and Publications

Title	WWW address and/or mailing address	ISBN	Author	Notes
1998 IRS Restructuring and Reform Act	http://famguardian.org/Publications/IRSRRA98/IRSRRA98.htm		Internal Revenue Service	Online version is free.
Congressional Staff Directory		ISSN 0589-3178	CQ Staff Directories, Inc.; Alexandria, VA; 703-739-0900 voice; 703-739-0234 Fax.	Containing, in convenient arrangement, useful information concerning the current congress, with emphasis on the staffs of the members and of the

The Great IRS Hoax: Why We Don't Owe Income Tax, version 4.54   Copyright *Family Guardian Fellowship*
TOP SECRET: *For Official Treasury/IRS Use Only (FOUO)*   http://famguardian.org/

Chapter 7: Resources for Tax Fraud Fighters

Title	WWW address and/or mailing address	ISBN	Author	Notes
				committees and subcommittees, together with 3200 Staff Biographies.
Constitutional Income, Second Edition	http://www.constitutionalincome.com	ISBN 0-9711880-0-9	Phil Hart	Excellent and very thorough research on the legislative intent of the Sixteenth Amendment proving without question that the amendment was never intended to tax the labor of individuals and that the income tax as it is administered by the IRS today is illegal and unconstitutional. Very good reading.
Federal Yellow Book		ISSN 014506202	Leadership Directories, Inc. Suite 923, 1301 Pennsylvania Avenue, N.W.;Washington, D.C. 200004; 212-627-4140.	The most complete source of information about every branch of the federal government. Annual subscription costs $265. You can find this in most libraries. Also available on CD-ROM and online through WESTLAW.
Handbook for Special Agents, Criminal Investigative Division, Internal Revenue Service			Department of the Treasury, Internal Revenue Service	The complete guide used by the Criminal Investigative Division (CID) of the Internal Revenue Service. Freedom Books ;544 East Sahara ;Las Vegas, Nevada 89104 ; 1- 800 TAX NO MORE
Internal Revenue Manual (IRM)	https://www.irs.gov/irm		U.S. Government printing office	Online version is free.
In Their Own Words, Third Edition	Distress Publishing C/o 1040 S. Mt Vernon Ave, G-118 Colton, CA 92324 DistressPub@juno.com		Gerald Alan Brown, Ed.D. & Charles V. Darnell, D.H.Sc.	YOU MUST GET A COPY OF THIS BOOK! EXCELLENT! A resource Book containing extracts from federal and state authorities establishing the judicial authority of the federal and state governments with special attention to sovereignty, citizenship, federal taxation, and remedies for the innocent. This book is the most valuable book we

Chapter 7: Resources for Tax Fraud Fighters

Title	WWW address and/or mailing address	ISBN	Author	Notes
				own, because it is so thoroughly researched and indexed and complete.
IRS Forms and Publications	https://www.irs.gov/forms-instructions		Internal Revenue Service	Free for downloading
IRS Humbug	http://www.mediabypass.com/cart/books.asp	ISBN 0-9626552-0-1	Frank Kowalik	The most complete and authoritative tax book we have yet seen, next to ours, of course. You HAVE to buy this book. It's great!
Law Dictionary		0-8120-3096.6	Steven H. Gifis	Publisher is Barron's Legal Guides. $11.95.
Nontaxpayer's Audit Defense Manual	http://sedm.org/ItemInfo/Ebooks/NTAuditDefenseManual/NTAuditDefenseManual.htm		SEDM	Techniques useful to nontaxpayers who are going through a tax audit.
Original Intent	http://www.wallbuilders.com	ISBN 0-925279-57-9	David Barton	Published by Wallbuilder Press, 2000.
Tax Fraud Prevention Manual	http://sedm.org/ItemInfo/Ebooks/TaxFraudPrevMan/TaxFraudPrevMan.htm		SEDM	Provide information useful in directly fighting fraud in the government, revenue agencies, and the legal profession.
The Uniform System of Citation "Bluebook"	http://www.legalbluebook.com		Harvard Law Review	THE source on how to cite and quote various legal sources in legal documents. This document can also be purchased from most legal bookstores.
US Treasury Communications with Congress	http://www.ustreas.gov/cc/		Treasury Department	Responses to questions and inquiries into the US Treasury by the U.S. Congress.
Whatever Happened to Justice		ISBN 0-942617-10-X	Richard Maybury	Published by Bluestocking Press; P.O. Box 1014, Dept. J; Placerville, CA 95667-1014.
Why You Can't Stay Silent	http://www.family.org	ISBN 1-56179-925-4	Tom Minnery	Published by Tyndale House Publishers, Wheaton, Illinois

7.3 Legal Resources

Disclaimer: We have not worked directly with these people but have met them and have heard good reports about them. We list them in alphabetical order and not necessarily in order of value or precedence.

Rivera, Ed, Attorney At Law; Ed represents many clients in tax cases, and is a rare attorney who is also a freedom fighter.   http://famguardian.org/

Chapter 7: Resources for Tax Fraud Fighters

Wellington, Dave; learn@bwn.net; Phone: 505-880-0560. Specializes in paralegal and litigation support for tax freedom fighters. Very familiar with the 861/source issue. Was a Presenter at the 2001 Freedom Rally, sponsored by Freedom Law School

8. DEFINITIONS

alien: A person born in a foreign country, who owes his allegiance to that country; one not a citizen or national of the country in which he is living. A RESIDENT ALIEN is a person admitted to permanent resident status in the country by the immigration authorities but who has not been granted citizenship.

An alien is a "person" within the meaning of the due process clause of the Fourteenth Amendment. 347 U.S. 522, 530. And alienage is treated as a "suspect" classification for purposes of equal protection analysis. For example, the Supreme Court has invalidated statuses that prevent aliens from entering a state's civil service and from receiving educational benefits. But where a job is "bound up with the operation of the State as a governmental entity"—policemen and public school teachers, for example—states may exclude aliens. 441 U.S. 68, 73.[104]

burden of proof: A rule of evidence that makes a person prove a certain thing or the contrary will be assumed by the court. For example, in criminal trials, the prosecution has the burden of proving the accused guilt because innocence is presumed.

citizen of the United States: — defined in 8 U.S.C. §1401. In the context of federal statutes: Means a person born or naturalized in the federal United States (federal zone) and a subject citizen of Congress. Typically, the U.S. government allows "nationals", who are persons born outside the federal zone and inside the 50 states to declare that they are "U.S. citizens" so that they can volunteer to become completely subject to the jurisdiction of the federal courts and become the proper subjects of the Internal Revenue Code, but technically, they are not "U.S. citizens" in the context of federal statutes as legally defined. "U.S. citizens" are possessors of statutory 'civil' rights and privileges granted by Congress and stipulated by statute, code or regulation, found mostly in 48 U.S.C. §1421b. In the context of the Constitution and the rulings of the U.S. Supreme Court: A "national of the United States" born in any one of the states of the Union and not on federal territory and defined under 8 U.S.C. §1408.

claim: the assertion of a right to money or property; the aggregate of operative facts giving rise to a right enforceable in the courts. A claim must show the existence of a right, an injury, and a prayer for damages. In tax cases, this means that the petitioner who is litigating against wrongful taking of taxes must show a law or Constitutional right that has been violated in the process of illegally taking taxes, a harm or injury that is quantifiable because of that taking, such that the court can award damages against the IRS. Otherwise, the tax case will be dismissed without prejudice because it lacks merit. Naïve and inexperienced tax freedom advocates who represent themselves in court as pro se litigants quite commonly do not specify a claim upon which they can base their case and usually end up being assessed attorney fees and having their case dismissed by the courts.

coercion: "Compulsion; constraint; compelling by force or arms or threat. General Motors v. Belvins, D.C.Colo., 144 F.Supp. 381, 384. It may be actual, direct, or positive, as where physical force is used to compel act against one's will, or implied, legal or constructive, as where one party is constrained by subjugation to another to do what his free will would refuse. As used in testamentary law, any pressure by which testator's action is restrained against his free will in the execution of his testament. "Coercion" that vitiates confession can be mental as well as physical, and question is whether accused was deprived of his free choice to admit, deny, or refuse to answer. Garrity v. State of N.J., U.S.N.J., 385 U.S. 493, 87 S.Ct. 616, 618, 17 L.Ed.2d. 562.

A person is guilty of criminal coercion if, with purpose to unlawfully restrict another's freedom of action to his detriment, he threatens to: (a) commit any criminal offense; or (b) accuse anyone of a criminal offense; or (c) expose any secret tending to subject any person to hatred, contempt or ridicule, or to impair his credit or business repute; or (d) take or withhold action as an official, or cause an official to take or withhold action. Model Penal Code, §212.5.

See also Duress; Extortion; Threat; Undue influence." [Black's Law Dictionary, Sixth Edition, p. 258]

color: "Pretense of official right to do an act made by one who has no such right. An act under color of office is an act of any officer who claims authority to do the act by reason of his own office when the office does not confer on him any such authority." [Black's Law Dictionary, Sixth Edition]

---

[104] Law Dictionary, Barron's, Copyright 1996, ISBN 0-8120-3096-6, p. 20.

color of office: "A claim or assumption of right to do an act by virtue of an office, made by a person who is **legally destitute of such right.**" *Feller v. Gates*, 40 Or. 543, 67 P. 416, 56 L.R.S. 630, 91 Am.St.Rep. 492. [Black's Law Dictionary, 4th Edition]

common right: Right derivative from common law. *Strother v. Lucas*, 37 U.S. (12 Pet.) 410, 437, 9 L.Ed. 1137. Right peculiar to certain people is not a common right. *Perdue v. Zoning Bd. Of Appeals of the City of Norwalk*, 118 Conn. 174, 171 A. 26, 28. [Black's Law Dictionary, Sixth Edition]

compel: The following definitions are offered for the word compel. These definitions bear directly on any arguments having to do with the exercise of 5th Amendment rights as it pertains to the filing of income tax returns :

Black's Law Dictionary defines the word "compel" as follows:

"To urge forcefully, under extreme pressure. The word 'compel' as used in constitutional right to be free from being compelled in a criminal case to be a witness against one's self means to be subjected to some coercion, fear, terror, inducement, trickery or threat—either physically or psychologically, blatantly or subtly; the hallmark of compulsion is the presence of some operative force producing an involuntary response. U.S. v. Escandar, C.A. Fla., 465 F.2d. 438, 442"

The Random House Dictionary of the English Language defines "compel" as follows:

"1. To force, drive, esp. to a course of action. 2. To secure or bring about by force. 3. To force to submit; subdue. 4. To overpower."

definition: A description of a thing by its properties; an explanation of the meaning of a word or term. The process of stating the exact meaning of a word by means of other words. Such a description of the thing defined, including all essential elements and excluding all nonessential, as to distinguish it from all other things and classes." [Black's Law Dictionary, Sixth Edition, page 423]

discovery: The term used to describe various methods for obtaining evidence in advance of trial, including such things as interrogatories, depositions and various motions to permit the inspection of documents etc.

distraint: the act or process of distraint, whereby a person (the DISTRAINOR), without prior court approval, seizes the personal property of another located upon the distrainor's land in satisfaction of a claim, as a pledge for the performance of a duty, or in reparation of an injury. Where goods are seized in satisfaction of a claim, the distrainor can hold the goods until the claim is paid and, failing payment, may sell them in satisfaction. Originally, distress was a landlord's remedy (see lien [LANDORD'S LIEN], 324 A.2d. 102, 104) and was distinguishable from attachment, which is a court-ordered seizure of goods or property. The persons whose goods are distrained upon has recourse against the wrongful distrainor in replevin.

Distraint has been superseded in most states of the United States by statutory provisions for debt collection, the enforcement of security interests, and landlord-tenant relations.

donation: A gift. A transfer of the title of property to one who receives it without paying for it. The act by which the owner of a thing voluntarily transfers the title and possession of the same from himself to another person, without any consideration. [Black's Law Dictionary, Sixth Edition, page 487]

due process: administering of law through courts of justice in accordance with established and sanctioned legal principles and procedures, and with safeguards for the protection of individual rights. As determined by custom and law, due process has become a guarantee of civil as well as criminal rights. In the United States, the phrase *due process* first appears in the Fifth Amendment to the Constitution of the United States, ratified in 1791. Because the amendment refers specifically to federal and not state actions, another amendment was necessary to include the states. This was accomplished by the 14th Amendment, ratified in 1868. Thus was established at both federal and state levels that no person "shall be deprived of life, liberty, or property without due process of law." The guarantee of due process requires that no person be deprived of life, liberty, or property without a fair and adequate process. In criminal proceedings this guarantee includes the fundamental aspects of a fair trial, including the right to adequate notice in advance of the trial, the right to counsel, the right to confront and cross-examine witnesses, the right to refuse self-incriminating testimony, and the right to have all elements of the crime proven beyond a reasonable doubt.

duress: "Any unlawful threat or coercion used by a person to induce another to act (or to refrain from acting) in a manner he or she otherwise would not (or would). Subjecting person to improper pressure which overcomes his will and coerces him to comply with demand to which he would not yield if acting as free agent. Head v. Gadsden Civil Service Bd., Ala.Civ.App., 389 So.2d. 516, 519. Application of such pressure or constraint as compels man to go against his will, and takes away his free agency, destroying power of refusing to comply with unjust demands of another. Haumont v. Security State Bank, 220 Neb. 809, 374 N.W.2d. 2,6.
…
A contract entered into under duress by physical compulsion is void. Also, if a party's manifestation of assent to a contract is induced by an improper threat by the other party that leaves the victim no reasonable alternative, the contract is voidable by the victim. Restatement, Second, Contracts §§174, 175.

As a defense to a civil action, it must be pleaded affirmatively. Federal Rule of Civil Procedure 8(c).

As an affirmative defense in criminal law, one who, under the pressure of an unlawful threat from another human being to harm him (or to harm a third person), commits what would otherwise be a crime may, under some circumstances, be justified in doing what he did and thus not be guilty of the crime in question. See Model Penal Code §2.09. See also Coercion; Economic duress; Extortion; Undue influence."
[Black's Law Dictionary, Sixth Edition, p. 504]

employee: (see 26 U.S.C. §3401(c)) For purposes of this chapter, the term "employee" includes an officer, employee, or elected official of the United States, a State, or any political subdivision thereof, or the District of Columbia, or any agency or instrumentality of any one or more of the foregoing. The term "employee" also includes an officer of a corporation. Refer to section 3.6.1.1 for further explanation.

employer: (see 26 U.S.C. §3401(d)). For purposes of this chapter, the term "employer" means the person for whom an individual performs or performed any service, of whatever nature, as the employee of such person, except that -

> *(1) if the person for whom the individual performs or performed the services does not have control of the payment of the wages for such services, the term "employer" (except for purposes of subsection (a)) means the person having control of the payment of such wages, and*
>
> *(2) in the case of a person paying wages on behalf of a nonresident alien individual, foreign partnership, or foreign corporation, not engaged in trade or business within the United States, the term "employer" (except for purposes of subsection (a)) means such person.*

extortion under the color of office:

> "…Unlawful taking by any officer by *color of his office*, of any money or thing of value, that **is not due to him**, or more than is due or before it is due." 4 Bla.Comm. 141; Com. v. Saulsbury, 152 Pa. 554, 25 A. 610; U.S. v. Denver, D.C.N.C. 14 F. 595; Bush v. State, 19 Ariz. 195, 168 P. 508, 509…"Obtaining property from another, induced by wrongful use of force or fear, OR under color of official right." See State v. Logan, 104 La. 760, 29 So. 336; In re Rempfer, 51 S.D. 393, 216 N.W. 355, 359, 55 A.L.R. 1346; Lee v. State, 16 Ariz. 291, 145 P. 244, 246, Ann.Cas. 1917B, 131.
> [Black's Law Dictionary, Revised 4th Edition]

FOIA: The Freedom Of Information Act. FOIA is the secret key to unlock a vast amount of information, especially information about you. Thanks to this act, everyday citizens have access to records, files, and other information just for the asking. Of course you are required to use the proper format in your request, but extremely valuable information can be obtained by using this simple procedure that very few use. The IRS, for instance, keeps literally countless secret files on citizens (law-abiding or not) of the United States. Most folks would be interested in knowing what kind of information is being kept on them by the government. By using FOIA, you can find out what they know what they don't..... in addition to protecting yourself and building your case against them.

foreign country: IRS Publication 54 (2000), p. 12, defines this term as follows:

> *"A foreign country usually is any territory (including the air space and territorial waters) under the sovereignty of a government other than that of the United States…. The term 'foreign country' does not include Puerto Rico,*

> *Guam, the Commonwealth of the Northern Mariana Islands, the Virgin Islands, or U.S. possessions such as American Samoa."*

You will note that this definition is consistent with 26 U.S.C. §7701, which defines "United States" as the District of Columbia and the States" and "State" as the District of Columbia. Another way of stating this is that the "U.S." includes only the "federal zone" as used in the tax code and as described in section 4.7. With this definition in mind, the 50 states of the United States <u>of America</u> are considered as foreign countries while any federal possession or territory is considered part of the "federal zone".

<u>Foreign government:</u> "The government of the United States of America, as distinguished from the government of the several states." (Black's Law Dictionary, 5th Edition; *removed from the Sixth and Seventh Editions by a legal profession that wants to hide the truth and sell you into slavery to the U.S. government by unlawfully extending the jurisdiction for personal income taxes outside the federal zone*.)

<u>Foreign Laws:</u> "The laws of a foreign country or sister state." (Black's Law Dictionary, Sixth Edition)

<u>Foreign States:</u> "Nations outside of the United States…Term may also refer to another state; i.e. a sister state. The term 'foreign nations', …should be construed to mean all nations and states other than that in which the action is brought; and hence, one state of the Union is foreign to another, in that sense." (Black's Law Dictionary, Sixth Edition)

<u>forum:</u> Lat. A court of justice, or judicial tribunal; a place of jurisdiction; a place of litigation; an administrative body. Particular place where judicial or administrative remedy is pursued. *See also* Venue. (Black's Law Dictionary, Sixth Edition). The federal district, circuit, and Supreme courts and the "federal zone" constitute the ***forum*** within which the government of the United States operates and exercises exclusive jurisdiction. In more limited cases, it also has jurisdiction in criminal matters that involve multiple states.

<u>income:</u> Below is the definition, taken from the Supreme Court case of *Eisner v. Macomber*, 252 U.S. 189 (1920) and the definition found in Bouvier's Law Dictionary:

> *'Income may be defined as the gain derived from capital, from labor, or from both combined,' provided it be understood to include profit gained through a sale or conversion of capital assets, to which it was applied in the Doyle Case, <u>247 U.S. 183, 185</u>, 38 S.Sup.Ct. 467, 469 (62 L.Ed. 1054).*

<u>Internal Revenue Service:</u> The current name of the "Bureau of Internal Revenue" (BIR) of Puerto Rico. The "Federal Alcohol Administration" created on 8-29-1935, 49 Stat. 977; 27 U.S.C. §201, was abolished and absorbed in the BIR on 4-2-1940 by Reorganization Plan No. III of 1940, 5 F.R. (Federal Register) 2107, 54 Stat. 1232, set out in the Appendix to Title 5, Government Organization and Employees. Department of the Treasury Order (TDO) 221 of July 1, 1972, established the BATF and transferred to it the alcohol and functions of the Internal Revenue Service. Public law 97-258 §5(b), Sept 13, 1982, 96 Stat. 1068, 1085 repealed §2 of the 1940 Reorganization Plan No III and the first section of which enacted Title 31, Money and Finance. Reference: US Statues at Large and 27 U.S.C. §201

<u>levy</u>, n: A seizure. The obtaining of money by legal process through seizure and sale of property; the raising of the money for which an execution has been issued.

The process whereby a sheriff or other state official empowered by writ or other judicial directive actually seizes, or otherwise brings within her control, a judgment debtor's property which is taken to secure or satisfy the judgment.

In reference to taxation, the word may mean the legislative function and declaration of the subject and rate or amount of taxation. People v. Mahoney, 13 Cal.2d. 729, 91 P.2d. 1029; or the rate of taxation rather than the physical act of applying the rate to the property, Lowden v. Texas County Excise Board, 187 Okl. 365 103 P.2d. 98, 100; or the formal order, by proper authority declaring property subject to taxation at fixed rate at its assessed valuation, State v. Davis, 335 Mo. 159, 73 S.W.2d. 406, 407; or the ministerial function of assessing, listing and extending taxes, City of Plankinton v. Kieffer, 70 S.D. 329, 17 N.W.2d. 494, 495, 496; or the extension of the tax, Day v. Inland Steel Co., 185 Minn. 53, 239 N.W. 776, 777; or the doing of whatever is necessary in order to authorize the collector to collect the tax, Syracuse Trust Co. v. Board of Sup'rs of Oneida County, 13 N.Y.S.2d. 390, 394. When used in connection with authority to tax, denotes exercise of legislative function, whether state or local, determining that a tax shall be imposed and fixing amount, purpose and subject of the exaction. Carkonen v. Williams, 76 Wash.2d. 617, 458 P.2d. 280, 286. The qualified electors "levy" a tax when they vote to impose it.

See also Assess; Assessment; Tax.
[Black's Law Dictionary, Sixth Edition, p. 907]

lien: A claim, encumbrance, or charge on property for payment of some debt, obligation or duty. Sullins v. Sullins, 6 Wash.2d. 283, 396 P.2d. 886, 888. Qualified right of property which a creditor has in or over specific property of his debtor, as security for the debt or charge or for performance of some act. Right or claim against some interest in property created by law as an incident of contract. Right to enforce charge upon property of another for payment or satisfaction of debt or claim. Vaughan v. John Hancock Mut. Life Ins. Co., Tex.Civ.App., 61 S.W.2d. 189, 190. Right to retain property for payment of debt or demand. Bell v. Dennis, 43 N.M. 350, 93 P.2d. 1003, 1006. Security for a debt, duty or other obligation. Hurley v. Boston R. Holding Co., 315 Mass. 591, 54 N.E.2d. 183, 193. Tie that binds property to a debt or claim for its satisfaction. United States v. 1364.76875 Wine Gallons, More or Less, of Spirituous Liquors, D.C.Mo., 60 F.Supp. 389, 392. Liens are "property rights". In re Pennsylvania Central Brewing Co., C.C.A.Pa., 114 F.2d. 1010, 1013. The word "lien" is a generic term and, standing alone, includes liens acquired by contract or by operation of law. Egyptian Supply Co. v. Boyd, C.C.A.Ky., 117 F.2d. 608, 612.

A charge against or interest in property to secure payment of a debt or performance of an obligation. Bankruptcy Code §101.

Lien by operation of law. Where the law itself, without the stipulation of the parties, raises a lien, as an implication or legal consequence from the relation of the parties or the circumstances of their dealings. Liens of this species may arise either under the rules of common law or of equity or under a statute. In the first case they are called "common –law liens;" in the second, "equitable liens;" in the third, "statutory liens."
[Black's Law Dictionary, Sixth Edition, p. 922]

national: means a person born or naturalized outside the *federal* United States (federal zone) but inside the country United States and who is subject to the *political* but not *legislative* jurisdiction of the federal government at the time of birth as the Fourteenth Amendment (illegally ratified) requires. Synonymous with "American Citizen", "American National", "Natural Born Sovereign Citizen", or "nonresident alien". Typically, the U.S. government allows and even encourages "nationals" to incorrectly declare that they are "U.S. citizens" so that they can volunteer to become completely subject to the exclusive jurisdiction of the federal courts and become the proper subjects of the Internal Revenue Code, but technically, they are *not* "U.S. citizens" as legally defined. 8 U.S.C. §1452, and 8 U.S.C. §1101(a)(22)(B) define who are "nationals". The following code section from 8 U.S.C. §1101(a)(22)(B) defines the type of "national" that most Americans born in the 50 union states outside of the federal zone qualify as. It is highlighted to bring attention to it:

> TITLE 8 > CHAPTER 12 > SUBCHAPTER I > Sec. 1101.
> Sec. 1101. - Definitions
>
> *(a) As used in this chapter -*
>
> *(22) The term "national of the United States" means*
>
> *(A) a citizen of the United States, or*
>
> ***(B) a person who, though not a citizen of the United States, owes permanent allegiance to the United States.***

Note that the "United States" term as used in the above section refers to the *federal* United States, also called the "federal zone". 8 U.S.C. §1401 indicates that all "citizens and nationals of the United States" are also "nationals of the United States". 8 U.S.C. §1101(a)(22) indicates that not all "nationals" are also "U.S. citizens". Throughout this book, when we use the term "national", we mean either a "citizen, but not a national, of the United States" as described in 8 U.S.C. §1452 and 8 U.S.C. §1101(a)(22)(B).

occupations of "common right": Any profession you can choose to do or undertake in private industry in any field or trade (even if its for the government) and which do not depend on the authority granted you as part of a political office, being either elected or appointed. Occupations that are *not* of common right are things you can only do as an officer or politician working for a government agency by virtue of the rights and privileges granted to you as a consequence of your election or appointment to that political office and the authority delegated to you by the law itself. See the case of *Simms. v. Ahrens*, 271 S.W. 720 for further details.

prima facie: On its face; not requiring further support to establish existence, validity, credibility, etc. An example of this would be an allegation or assertion made by the IRS against a citizen that is never refuted. Therefore, when any kind of assertion or allegation is made that is incorrect, it is important to deny the assertion or it will often be accepted as undisputed fact by the court.

illegal tax protester: A person who resists illegally the paying of appropriate taxes. *As of January 1, 1999, the U.S. Congress has eliminated the ability of the IRS to designate a taxpayer as an "illegal tax protester"*. Here is a part of the IRS Restructuring and Reform Act of 1998 that talks about this (form the website at http://www.irs.gov/):

Background: The IRS designates individuals who meet certain criteria as "illegal tax protestors" in the IRS Master File. Congress was concerned that taxpayers may be unfairly stigmatized by a designation as an illegal tax protester.
C. Change(s):

1. The IRS shall not designate any more taxpayers as "illegal tax protesters." Removal of existing "illegal tax protester" designations from the individual master file is not required to begin before January 1, 1999.
2. IRS personnel must disregard any designation in a taxpayer's file (i.e., revenue agents report or other paper records) as of the date of enactment.
3. As of the date of enactment, IRS personnel should not describe taxpayers in written documents as "illegal tax protesters."
4. The IRS may designate appropriate taxpayers as nonfilers. The IRS must remove the nonfiler designation once the taxpayer has filed valid tax returns for two consecutive years and paid all taxes shown on these returns.

D. Impact: The provision requires reprogramming master file databases.

Law: that which is laid down, ordained, or established. A rule or method according to which phenomenon or actions co-exist or follow each other. Law, in its generic sense, is a body of rules of action or conduct prescribed by the sovereign within a jurisdiction, and having binding legal force. United States Fidelity and Guaranty Co. v. Guenther, 281 U.S. 34, 50 S.Ct. 165, 74 L.Ed. 683. That which must be obeyed and followed by citizens subject to sanctions or legal consequences is a law. Law is a solemn expression of the will of the supreme power, which is the ultimate "sovereign", of the State. California Civil Code, §22. The "law" of a state is to be found in its statutory and constitutional enactments, as interpreted by its courts, and, in absence of statute law, in rulings of its courts. Dauer's Estate v. Zabel, 9 Mich.App. 176, 156 N.W.2d. 34, 37.

In the United States of America, the People, both collectively and individually are the "sovereigns", according to the Supreme Court:

- *Chisholm, Ex'r. v. Georgia, 2 Dall. (U.S.) 419, 1 L.Ed. 454, 457, 471, 472) (1794)*: "From the differences existing between feudal sovereignties and Government founded on compacts, it necessarily follows that their respective prerogatives must differ. **Sovereignty is the right to govern; a nation or State-sovereign is the person or persons in whom that resides. In Europe the sovereignty is generally ascribed to the Prince; here it rests with the people; there, the sovereign actually administers the Government; here, never in a single instance; our Governors are the agents of the people, and at most stand in the same relation to their sovereign, in which regents in Europe stand to their sovereigns.** Their Princes have personal powers, dignities, and pre-eminences, **our rulers have none but official; nor do they partake in the sovereignty otherwise, or in any other capacity, than as private citizens.**"
- *Juilliard v. Greenman, 110 U.S. 421 (1884)*: "There is no such thing as a power of inherent sovereignty in the government of the United States…In this country *sovereignty resides in the people, and Congress can exercise no power which they have not, by their Constitution entrusted [delegated] to it. All else is withheld.*"
- *Perry v. U.S., 294 U.S. 330 (1935)*: "In the United States, sovereignty resides in the people…the Congress cannot invoke sovereign power of the People to override their will as thus declared."

- ***Yick Wo v. Hopkins, 118 U.S. 356 (1886)***: "Sovereignty itself is, of course, not subject to law, for it is the author and source of law…While sovereign powers are delegated to…the government, sovereignty itself remains with the people."

Therefore, the People are the authors of the law as the "sovereign" or supreme power of the state. The law constitutes essentially a binding written legal agreement or contract among the sovereigns to conduct their affairs according to some standard of conduct. The sovereign is never the proper subject or object of most laws, unless he violates the contract and thereby injures the equal rights of other fellow sovereigns. Instead, the servants of the sovereign People working in government are the main object and subject of most civil laws, and laws are enacted mainly with the purpose to delegate and confine the authority of public servants so that they do not injure or undermine the rights of the true sovereigns, the People. Furthermore, only statutes which have been enacted into "positive law" are considered binding upon all persons within the jurisdiction of the law. The legislative notes under 1 U.S.C. §204 indicate that the Internal Revenue Code is not "positive law", and therefore it can only be described as "special law" or "private international law" (contractual law) applying to specific persons. Subtitle A of the I.R.C., in fact, is limited mainly to those engaged in a "trade or business" and who work for the U.S. government as Trustees. The Internal Revenue Code cannot be described either as "law" or "positive law" unless and until:

1. The IRC is first enacted into "positive law" by a majority of the representatives of the sovereign People. This provides evidence that they voluntarily consented to enforcement actions required to implement the law. Without such consent, no enforcement actions may be attempted, because according to the Declaration of Independence, all just powers of government derive from the consent of the governed.
2. Regulations must be written by the Treasury for the enforcement provisions of the enacted positive law, and these regulations must be published in the Federal Register. This puts the public on notice of the enforcement actions that will be attempted against them in enforcing the law, as required by the Fifth Amendment due process clauses.
3. The enforcement regulations are then incorporated into the Code of Federal Regulations, Title 26.
4. Delegation of authority orders are written for all the enforcement agents within the Internal Revenue Service authorizing them to conduct enforcement actions.
5. The enforcement agents must be designated as enforcement agents by receiving a black enforcement Pocket Commission and being specially trained and commissioned as "public trust" employees.

Unless and until all of the above have occurred, the Internal Revenue Code, according to 1 U.S.C. §204 cannot be described as "law" and can only be described as "prima facie evidence of law", which is simply "presumptive" evidence of law. That means that it may be rebutted. Since "presumption" causes prejudice and prejudice is anathema to any legal proceeding and violates due process of law, then the Internal Revenue Code is not admissible as evidence of "law", which means that it does not furnish any evidence that the people ever consented to its enforcement against them. Consequently, it is unenforceable. Until it becomes "positive law", it can only be described as a "code", or a "statute", but not as "law".

pseudotaxes — a term identifying revenues to the U.S. government derived from Subtitles A and C of the Internal Revenue Code and collected from nonresident aliens who are *not* in fact and indeed: 1. Engaged in the excise taxable activity called a "trade or business", which is defined in 26 U.S.C. §7701(a)(26) as "the functions of a public office"; 2. Have no income from the District of Columbia; 3. Do not have a domicile in the District of Columbia. For everyone meeting this criteria, the revenues collected under the authority of I.R.C. Subtitles A and C are not "taxes" as legally defined, but an unconstitutional abuse of federal taxing power. Public servants in the government love to call such revenues "taxes" in order to deceive the people and lend undeserved dignity to the THEFT that enforcing such as system against improper parties amounts to. This is covered in *Great IRS Hoax* sections 5.1.2 earlier.

resident: under the Internal Revenue Code, an "*alien*" who is domiciled within either the District of Columbia or the territories of the United States. This "individual" has a "res" that is "identified" within federal jurisdiction, which is limited under the Internal Revenue Code to the District of Columbia and territories or possessions of the United States identified in Title 48 of the U.S. Code. Federal territories are generally identified with the term "State" in the U.S. Code, while states of the Union are identified with a lower case "state" in the U.S. Code and are treated as "foreign states". "Residents" live exclusively in federal "States" but not in "states" of the Union and therefore are not protected by the Bill of Rights within the Constitution as per *Downes v. Bidwell*, 182 U.S. 244 (1901). Pursuant to 26 C.F.R. §1.1441(c)(3)(i), an alien can be neither a "citizen" nor a "national" of the United States. The terms "alien", "resident", and "resident alien" are all synonymous in the Internal Revenue Code, as confirmed by 26

C.F.R. §1.1-1(a)(2)(ii) and 26 C.F.R. §1.1441-1(c)(3). "citizens of the United States" under 8 U.S.C. §1401 *cannot* legally be classified as "residents" under the Internal Revenue Code and are not authorized by the code to "elect" to be treated as one either. The reason is because the purpose of law is to protect, and a person *cannot* elect to lose their constitutional rights and protection, even if they want to! However, by filing an IRS form 1040 or 1040A, they in effect make this illegal election anyway, and the IRS looks the other way and does not prosecute such unintentional fraud because they benefit financially from it. The only way to avoid this election is to instead either file nothing or to file a 1040NR form instead of a 1040 or 1040A form. The rules for electing to be treated as a resident are found in IRS Publication 54: Tax Guide for U.S. Citizens and Resident Aliens Abroad. See *Great IRS Hoax*, Form #11.302, Section 4.10 for further definition of this term and the following sections for amplification: 5.5.3, 5.5.4, and 5.4.8.

special law: "One relating to particular persons or things; one made for individual cases or for particular places or districts; one operating upon a selected class, rather than upon the public generally. A private law. A law is "special" when it is different from others of the same general kind or designed for a particular purpose, or limited in range or confined to a prescribed field of action or operation. A "special law" relates to either particular persons, places, or things or to persons, places, or things which, though not particularized, are separated by any method of selection from the whole class to which the law might, but not such legislation, be applied. Utah Farm Bureau Ins. Co. v. Utah Ins. Guaranty Ass'n, Utah, 564 P.2d. 751, 754. A special law applies only to an individual or a number of individuals out of a single class similarly situated and affected, or to a special locality. Board of County Comm'rs of Lemhi County v. Swensen, Idaho, 80 Idaho 198, 327 P.2d. 361, 362. See also Private bill; Private law. Compare General law; Public Law."
[Black's Law Dictionary, Sixth Edition, p. 1398]

<u>The Internal Revenue Code, 26 U.S.C., Subtitle A, Income Taxes, for instance, is special law that applies ONLY to the District of Columbia and federal territories over which the United States government exercises exclusive legislative jurisdiction, but not including nonfederal areas within the borders of the several states.</u> The U.S. Government, however, has done a fine job making the tax code LOOK like it is general law. Most Congressmen know this, of course, and if you write them to ask if the I.R.C. is special law, they have been known to try to avoid answering or have given weasel-worded answers. See http://www.supremelaw.org and the case of People v. Boxer for more details on an example of this.

source of income: "Place where, or circumstances from which, income at issue is produced. Union Electric Co. v. Coale, 347 Mo. 175, 146 S.W.2d. 631, 635." [Black's Law Dictionary, Sixth Edition, page 1395]

State: in the context of <u>federal</u> statutes, <u>federal</u> court rulings, and this book means a <u>federal</u> State of the United States, the District of Columbia, Guam, Puerto Rico, Virgin Islands, Northern Marina Islands, and includes areas within the external boundaries of a state owned by or ceded to the United States of America. Federal "States" are defined in 4 U.S.C. §110(d) and 26 U.S.C. §7701(a)(10). In the context of the U.S. Constitution only, "State" means a sovereign "state" as indicated below. The reason the constitution is different is because of who wrote it. The states wrote it so they are capitalized. Federal statutes are not written by the sovereign states so they use the lower case "state" to describe the sovereign 50 states, which are foreign and outside the territorial jurisdiction of the U.S. government.

> "It is to be noted that the statute differentiates between States of the United States and foreign states by the use of a capital S for the word when applied to a State of the United States"
> [Eisenberg v. Commercial Union Assurance Company, 189 F.Supp. 500 (1960)]

state: in the context of <u>federal</u> statutes, <u>federal</u> court rulings, and this book means a <u>sovereign state</u> of the Union of America under the Constitution for the United States of America 1789-1791. In the context of the U.S. Constitution only, "State" means a sovereign "state" as defined here. Below is a further clarification of the meaning of "states" as defined by the U.S. Supreme Court in the case of *O'Donoghue v. United States*, 289 U.S. 516 (1933), where they define what is *not* a "state":

> *After an exhaustive review of the prior decisions of this court relating to the matter, the following propositions, among others, were stated as being established:*
>
> *'1. That the District of Columbia and the territories are **not states** within the judicial clause of the Constitution giving jurisdiction in cases between citizens of different states;*

*'2. That territories are **not states** within the meaning of Rev. St. 709, permitting writs of error from this court in cases where the validity of a state statute is drawn in question;*

*'3. That **the District of Columbia and the territories are states as that word is used in treaties with foreign powers, with respect to the ownership, disposition, and inheritance of property**;*

'4. That the territories are not within the clause of the Constitution providing for the creation of a supreme court and such inferior courts as Congress may see fit to establish.'

Below is a summary of the meanings of "state" and "State" in the context of both federal and state laws:

Table 8-1: Summary of meaning of "state" and "State"

Law	Federal constitution	Federal statutes	Federal regulations	State constitutions	State statutes	State regulations
Author	Union States/ "We The People"	Federal Government			"We The People"	State Government	
"state"	Foreign country	Union state	Union state	Other Union state or federal government	Other Union state or federal government	Other Union state or federal government
"State"	Union state	Federal state	Federal state	Union state	Union state	Union state
"in this State" or "in the State"[105]	NA	NA	NA	NA	Federal enclave within state	Federal enclave within state
"State"[106] (State Revenue and taxation code only)	NA	NA	NA	NA	Federal enclave within state	Federal enclave within state

So what the above table clearly shows is that the word "State" in the context of federal statutes and regulations means (not includes!) federal States only under Title 48 of the U.S. Code[107], and these areas do not include any of the 50 Union States. The word "state" in the context of federal statutes and regulations means one of the 50 union states, which are "foreign sovereigns", "foreign states", and "foreign countries" with respect to the federal government as clearly explained later in section 5.2.11 of this book. In the context of the above, a "Union State" means one of the 50 states of the United States* (the country, not the federal United States**).

State Citizen/National: A biological person who was born in the country United States and who is treated as a citizen of every state of the Union under Article IV, Section 2, Clause 1 of the United States Constitution. This person owes allegiance to his state and obedience to its laws. In exchange for this allegiance, he is entitled to demand protection from the government and the laws and that state. A person need not

State national: A biological person who was born in *any state of the Union* and who is treated as a citizen of every state of the Union under Article IV, Section 2, Clause 1 of the United States Constitution. This person owes allegiance to his state and obedience to its laws. In exchange for this allegiance, he is entitled to demand protection from the government and the laws and that state. He is also treated as a "national of the United States" or a "non-citizen U.S. national". "State nationals" are defined in 8 U.S.C. §1101(a)(21), 8 U.S.C. §1101(a)(22)(B), 8 U.S.C. §1452, 8 U.S.C. §1408(2), and are indirectly referenced under *The Law of Nations, Book I, Section 215*.

Tax: A charge by the government on the income of an individual, corporation, or trust, as well as the value of an estate or gift. The objective in assessing the tax is to generate revenue to be used for the needs of the public.

---

[105] See California Revenue and Taxation Code, section 6017

[106] See California Revenue and Taxation Code, section 17018

[107] See https://www.law.cornell.edu/uscode/text/48/

> *A pecuniary [relating to money] burden laid upon individuals or property to support the government, and is a payment exacted by legislative authority. In re Mytinger, D.C.Tex., 31 F.Supp. 977,978, 979.* **_Essential characteristics of a tax are that it is not a voluntary payment or donation, but an enforced contribution, exacted pursuant to legislative authority._** *Michigan Employment Sec. Commission v. Patt, 4 Mich.App. 228, 144 N.W.2d. 663, 665. Annual compensation paid to government for annual protection and for current support of government. Alabama Power Co. v. Federal Power Commission, C.C.A.5, 134 F.2d. 602, 608. A ratable portion of the produce of the property and labor of the individual citizens, taken by the nation, in the exercise of its sovereign rights, for the support of government, for the administration of the laws, and as the means of continuing in operation the various legitimate functions of the state. An enforced contribution of money or other property, assessed in accordance with some reasonable rule or apportionment by authority of a sovereign state on persons or property within its jurisdiction for the purposes of defraying the public expenses.*
>
> *In a general sense, any contribution imposed by government upon individuals, for the use and service of the state, whether under the name of toll, tribute, tallage, gabel, impost, duty, custom, excise, subsidy, aid, supply, or other name. And in its essential characteristics is not a debt. City of Neward v. Jos. Hollander, Inc., 136 N.J.Eq. 539, 42 A.2d. 872, 875.*
> [Black's Law Dictionary, Sixth Edition, p. 1457]

"taxes", as legally defined, are a mandatory payment to the government exacted by operation of law which is <u>not</u> voluntary and which support <u>only</u> the government. If the monies paid can be used for wealth transfer or supporting private persons or organizations, then they do not qualify as "taxes", according to the U.S. Supreme Court

> *To lay, with one hand, the power of the government on the property of the citizen, and with the other to bestow it upon favored individuals to aid private enterprises and build up private fortunes, is none the less a robbery because it is done under the forms of law and is called taxation. This is not legislation. It is a decree under legislative forms.*
>
> *Nor is it taxation. 'A tax,' says Webster's Dictionary, 'is a rate or sum of money assessed on the person or property of a citizen by government for the use of the nation or State.' 'Taxes are burdens or charges imposed by the Legislature upon persons or property to raise money for public purposes.' Cooley, Const. Lim., 479.*
>
> *Coulter, J., in Northern Liberties v. St. John's Church, 13 Pa.St., 104 says, very forcibly, 'I think the common mind has everywhere taken in the understanding that taxes are a public imposition, levied by authority of the government for the purposes of carrying on the government in all its machinery and operations—that they are imposed for a public purpose.' See, also Pray v. Northern Liberties, 31 Pa.St., 69; Matter of Mayor of N.Y., 11 Johns., 77; Camden v. Allen, 2 Dutch., 398; Sharpless v. Mayor, supra; Hanson v. Vernon, 27 Ia., 47; Whiting v. Fond du Lac, supra."*
> [Loan Association v. Topeka, 20 Wall. 655 (1874)]

"Taxes" which are paid voluntarily and/or which are spent on wealth transfer or to support private purposes are referred to as "donations", and when their payment is enforced, they are called "extortion".

Tax Class: A one digit number indicating the type of tax that a tax falls under. This number appears in the Individual Master File (IMF) maintained by the taxpayer. This number or digit is the third digit of the DLN, or Document Locator Number, assigned to each document that is entered in an Individual Master File. The Tax Class codes are as follows:

> 0 = IRAF
> 1 = Withholding and Social Security
> 2 = Individual Income Tax
> 3 = Corporate Income Tax
> 4 = Excise Tax
> 5 = Estate and Gift Tax
> 7 = CT-1
> 8 = FUTA

This number appears throughout the IRS' IMF file maintained on each individual, and it is also associated with specific forms of the Internal Revenue Service. Use of this code within the individual's IMF is described in IRS Publication 6209. Section 2 of Publication 6209 describes the association of specific IRS forms with Tax Class codes. You can order a copy of IRS Pub. 6209 from Freedom Law School at http://www.livefreenow.com/.

Interestingly, NOWHERE in Publication 6209 are the simple Tax Class codes defined, even though they are used extensively in that document, and furthermore, at the bottom of every page, it says "FOR OFFICIAL USE ONLY". This is double speak that really says the IRS doesn't want this book getting into the hands of tax freedom fighters, which is why they keep the "secret decoder ring" (the Tax Class Codes) separated from the code listing and in other innocuous publications no one seems to be able to get ahold of!

Below is a summary of the Tax Class codes for specific forms, derived directly from Section 2 of IRS Publication 6209. It ought to be clear examining the codes below that your employment tax authorized by the W-4 form is actually a gift or estate tax, and NOT an income tax, because it uses Tax Class 5!

Form	Title	Tax Class
W-2	Wage and Tax Statement	5
W-4	Employee's Withholding Certificate	5
W-4E	Exemption from Withholding Allowance Certificate	5
W-4V	Voluntary Withholding Request	5
706	United States Estate Tax Return	5, *6
1040	U.S. Individual Income Tax Return	2, *6
1041	U.S. Fiduciary Income Tax Return (for Estates and Trusts)	2, *6
1099-INT	Statement for Receipts of Interest Income	5
1099-MISC	Statement for Receipts of Miscellaneous Income	5
1120	U.S. Corporation Income Tax Return	3, *6

Taxpayer: The term "taxpayer" means any person who is either liable to pay an any internal revenue tax or who isn't liable but "volunteers" to pay anyway. Read section 3.6.1.15 for further explanation.

United States:

"This term has several meanings. It may be merely the name of a sovereign occupying the position analogous to that of other sovereigns in family of nations, it may designate territory over which sovereignty of the United States extends, or it may be collective name of the states which are united by and under the Constitution. Hooven & Allison Co. v. Evatt, U.S. v. Ohio, 324 U.S. 652, 65 S.Ct. 870, 880, 89 L.Ed. 1252."
[Black's Law Dictionary, Sixth Edition, p. 1533]

The term was conveniently _removed from Black's Law Dictionary Seventh Edition by a legal profession that wants to hide the truth and sell you into slavery to the U.S. government by unlawfully extending the jurisdiction for personal income taxes outside the federal zone._ Look on the IRS website for this definition...you won't find it because they don't want you to know.)

United States: A term which has many meanings in the context of law. Below are a few examples quoted from the Internal Revenue Code (26 U.S.C.):

> *§168. Accelerated cost recovery system*
> *(g) Alternative depreciation system for certain property*
> *(6) Imported property*
> *(B) Imported property*
> *For purposes of this subsection, the term "imported property" means any property if -*
> *(i) such property was completed outside the United States, or*
> *(ii) less than 50 percent of the basis of such property is attributable to value added within the United States.*
> *For purposes of this subparagraph, the term "United States" includes the Commonwealth of Puerto Rico and the possessions of the United States.*
> *§ 217. Moving expenses*
> *(d) Rules for application of subsection (c)(2)*
> *(3) If -*
> *(B) the condition of subsection (c)(2) cannot be satisfied at the close of a subsequent taxable year,*
> *In the case of a member of the Armed Forces of the United States on active duty who moves pursuant to a military order and incident to a permanent change of station -*
> *(3) United States defined ...*

> *For purposes of this subsection and subsection (i), the term "United States" includes the possessions of the United States.*

§ 638. Continental shelf areas
For purposes of applying the provisions of this chapter (including sections 861(a)(3) and 862(a)(3) in the case of the
performance of personal services) with respect to mines, oil and gas wells, and other natural deposits -
(1) the term "United States" when used in a geographical sense includes the seabed and subsoil of those submarine areas which are adjacent to the territorial waters of the United States and over which the United States has exclusive rights, in accordance with international law, with respect to the exploration and exploitation of natural resources; and
(2) the terms "foreign country" and "possession of the United States" when used in a geographical sense include the seabed and subsoil of those submarine areas which are adjacent to the territorial waters of the foreign country or such possession and over which the foreign country (or the United States in case of such possession) has exclusive rights, in accordance with international law, with respect to the exploration and exploitation of natural resources, but this paragraph shall apply in the case of a foreign country only if it exercises, directly or indirectly, taxing jurisdiction with respect to such exploration or exploitation. No foreign country shall, by reason of the application of this section, be treated as a country contiguous to the United States.

§ 927. Other definitions and special rules
(d) Other definitions
(3) United States defined
The term "United States" includes the Commonwealth of Puerto Rico.

§ 993. Definitions
(g) United States defined
For purposes of this part, the term "United States" includes the Commonwealth of Puerto Rico and the possessions of
the United States.

§ 3121. Definitions
(e) State, United States, and citizen
For purposes of this chapter -
(1) State
The term "State" includes the District of Columbia, the Commonwealth of Puerto Rico, the Virgin Islands, Guam, and American Samoa.
(2) United States
The term "United States" when used in a geographical sense includes the Commonwealth of Puerto Rico, the Virgin
Islands, Guam, and American Samoa. An individual who is a citizen of the Commonwealth of Puerto Rico (but not
otherwise a citizen of the United States) shall be considered, for purposes of this section, as a citizen of the United States.

§ 3306. Definitions
(j) State, United States, and American employer
For purposes of this chapter -
(1) State
The term "State" includes the District of Columbia, the Commonwealth of Puerto Rico, and the Virgin Islands.
(2) United States
The term "United States" when used in a geographical sense includes the States, the District of Columbia, the Commonwealth of Puerto Rico, and the Virgin Islands.

§ 4121. Imposition of tax
(d) Definitions
(3) United States
The term "United States" has the meaning given to it by paragraph (1) of section 638.

§ 4132. Definitions and special rules
Definitions relating to taxable vaccines
(7) United States
The term "United States" has the meaning given such term by section 4612(a)(4).

§ 4612. Definitions and special rules
(a) Definitions
(4) United States
(A) In general
The term "United States" means the 50 States, the District of Columbia, the Commonwealth of Puerto Rico, any possession of the United States, the Commonwealth of the Northern Mariana Islands, and the Trust Territory of the Pacific Islands.
(B) United States includes continental shelf areas
The principles of section 638 shall apply for purposes of the term "United States".
(C) United States includes foreign trade zones
The term "United States" includes any foreign trade zone of the United States.

§ 4662. Definitions and special rules
Definitions
(2) United States
The term "United States" has the meaning given such term by section 4612(a)(4).

§ 4672. Definitions and special rules
(b) Other definitions
(2) Taxable chemicals; United States
The terms "taxable chemical" and "United States" have the respective meanings given such terms by section 4662(a).

§ 7651. Administration and collection of taxes in possessions
(2) Tax imposed in possession
(B) Applicable laws
All provisions of the laws of the United States applicable to the administration, collection, and enforcement of such tax (including penalties) shall, in respect of such tax, extend to and be applicable in such possession of the United States in the same manner and to the same extent as if such possession were a State, and as if the term "United States" when used in a geographical sense included such possession.

§ 7701. Definitions
When used in this title, where not otherwise distinctly expressed or manifestly incompatible with the intent thereof -
(9) United States
The term "United States" when used in a geographical sense includes only the States and the District of Columbia.
(10) State
The term "State" shall be construed to include the District of Columbia, where such construction is necessary to carry out provisions of this title.
[Code of Federal Regulations]

TITLE 26--INTERNAL REVENUE
CHAPTER I--INTERNAL REVENUE SERVICE, DEPARTMENT OF THE TREASURY
Sec. 1.911-2 Qualified individuals.
(g) United States. The term ``United States'' when used in a geographical sense includes any territory under the sovereignty of the United States. It includes the states, the District of Columbia, the possessions and territories of the United States, the territorial waters of the United States, the air space over the United States, and the seabed and subsoil of those submarine areas which are adjacent to the territorial waters of the United States and over which the United States has exclusive rights, in accordance with international law, with respect to the exploration and exploitation of natural resources.

U.S. citizen: defined in 26 C.F.R. §1.1-1, 8 U.S.C. §1101(a)(22)(A), and 8 U.S.C. §1401. In the context of federal statutes: Means a person born or naturalized in the federal United States (federal zone) and a subject citizen of Congress. Typically, the U.S. government allows "U.S. nationals", who are persons born outside the federal zone and inside the 50 states to declare that they are "U.S. citizens" so that they can volunteer to become completely subject to the jurisdiction of the federal courts and become the proper subjects of the Internal Revenue Code, but technically, they are not "U.S. citizens" as legally defined within nearly all federal legislation and statutes. "U.S. citizens" are possessors of statutory 'civil' rights and privileges granted by Congress and stipulated by statute, code or regulation, found mostly in 48 U.S.C. §1421b.

U.S. person: this term is defined in 26 U.S.C. §7701(a)(30) as follows:

TITLE 26 > Subtitle F > CHAPTER 79 > Sec. 7701.
Sec. 7701. - Definitions

(a)(30) United States person

The term "United States person" means -
(A) a citizen or resident of the United States,
(B) a domestic partnership,
(C) a domestic corporation,
(D) any estate (other than a foreign estate, within the meaning of paragraph (31)), and
(E) any trust if -
   (i) a court within the United States is able to exercise primary supervision over the administration of the trust, and
   (ii) one or more United States persons have the authority to control all substantial decisions of the trust.

voluntary:

> "Unconstrained by interference; unimpelled by another's influence; spontaneous; acting of oneself. Coker v. State, 199 Ga. 20, 33 S.E.2d. 171, 174. Done by design or intention. Proceeding from the free and unrestrained will of the person. Produced in or by an act of choice. Resulting from free choice, without compulsion or solicitation. The word, especially in statutes, often implies knowledge of essential facts. Without valuable consideration; gratuitous, as a voluntary conveyance. Also, having a merely nominal consideration; as, a voluntary deed."
> [Black's Law Dictionary, Sixth Edition, p. 1575]

voluntary compliance: An oxymoron meant to confuse taxpayers. Voluntary implies that it is not compelled and that there is no punishment for _not_ doing it. They add the word compliance as a way to confuse the citizens into thinking that they have to do it and will be punished for not doing it. However, when used in the context of income taxes, what it means is that you don't have to comply and don't have to volunteer to pay income taxes.

Made in the USA
Columbia, SC
19 November 2023